# UNDERCOVER REPORTING

# Medill School of Journalism
VISIONS *of the* AMERICAN PRESS

GENERAL EDITOR
David Abrahamson

*Selected titles in this series*

HERBERT J. GANS
*Deciding What's News: A Study of "CBS Evening News," "NBC Nightly
News," "Newsweek," and "Time"*

MAURINE H. BEASLEY
*First Ladies and the Press: The Unfinished Partnership of the Media Age*

PATRICIA BRADLEY
*Women and the Press: The Struggle for Equality*

DAVID A. COPELAND
*The Idea of a Free Press: The Enlightenment and Its Unruly Legacy*

MICHAEL S. SWEENEY
*The Military and the Press: An Uneasy Truce*

PATRICK S. WASHBURN
*The African American Newspaper: Voice of Freedom*

KARLA K. GOWER
*Public Relations and the Press: The Troubled Embrace*

TOM GOLDSTEIN
*Journalism and Truth: Strange Bedfellows*

NORMAN SIMS
*True Stories: A Century of Literary Journalism*

MARK NEUZIL
*The Environment and the Press: From Adventure Writing to Advocacy*

# UNDERCOVER REPORTING

## THE TRUTH
## ABOUT DECEPTION

Brooke Kroeger

*Foreword by Pete Hamill*

MEDILL SCHOOL OF JOURNALISM

Northwestern University Press
Evanston, Illinois

Northwestern University Press
www.nupress.northwestern.edu

Printed in the United States of America

10   9   8   7   6   5   4   3   2   1

**Library of Congress Cataloging-in-Publication Data**

Kroeger, Brooke, 1949–

    Undercover reporting : the truth about deception / Brooke Kroeger ; foreword by
Pete Hamill.

      p. cm.—(Medill School of Journalism Visions of the American press)

    Includes bibliographical references and index.

    ISBN 978-0-8101-2619-0 (pbk. : alk. paper)

    1. Investigative reporting—United States—History. 2. Reporters and reporting—
United States—History. 3. Journalism—Social aspects—United States—History.
4. Journalistic ethics—United States—History. I. Title. II. Series: Visions of the
American press.

PN4888.I56K76 2012

070.430973—dc23

                                        2011048189

*To my students*

# CONTENTS

# FOREWORD

*Pete Hamill*

Long ago, during the first year of my apprenticeship as a news-paperman, someone told me that a reporter is the person chosen by the tribe to enter the cave and tell them what lies within. If a furious storm is raging, the tribe might find safety and warmth. But if the reporter does not go deep enough, a dragon might await them, and all could perish.

That was, of course, a hopelessly romantic version of the re-porter's role, but I was young enough to embrace it. As a street reporter, I discovered that the dragon could have many forms, all of them human. There were caves all over the big bad city. And a reporter could see the dragons and their acts in the cold dead eyes of the hoodlum; the corpse of the mutilated girl; the ashes of lives left by arson; the killer's smirk as he performed his perp walk. Making notes about the who of it, the what of it, the where and how and why. And what the weather was. Then rushing back to the newspaper to write it for the next day's paper, passing the report to all the tribes of New York.

On some nights, I felt as if I were a bit player in some extraor-dinary film noir. There in the shadows of Brooklyn or the Bronx lay various dangers, bad guys and cops, too many guns, and too much heroin. My press card would protect me. Or so I thought. At the same time, I was adding to my sense of the reporter as witness, living a life in which no day was like any other day (or night), and absorbing the lore and legends of my craft. I listened to the tales of old reporters and photographers. I watched movies about foreign correspondents, and read many memoirs, biographies, novels by men and women who had worked in dangerous foreign places. In my imagination, I covered wars long before I was in one.

Then one day in the Strand bookshop in Manhattan I found a copy of a book by a man named John Roy Carlson. It was called *Undercover*. I began to read it and found myself in the world of prewar right-wing organizations, pro-Nazi bundists, stone racists, and gun nuts—guided there by this fellow Carlson. He had spent several years infiltrating these groups, posing as an acolyte, listening to their paranoid visions. I checked the clips in the newspaper's morgue and discovered that his real name was Avedis Boghos Der-ounian, born in Greece of Armenian parents, an immigrant who had grown up in Mineola, New York. *Undercover* was a huge best seller, at one point topping the *New York Times* nonfiction lists. More important to a young reporter, it was a chronicle of time spent in the company of dragons.

I began to imagine myself changing my identity, donning a disguise, truly living in a melodrama that was about pursuing the truth. That is, I wanted to go undercover, too, and live for a while as a spy in the caves of America. While serving in the U.S. Navy in 1953 in Pensacola, I had seen what the Ku Klux Klan could do in the Southern nights. Could I pass myself off as a recruit in the country's most enduring terrorist organization? Could I master a Southern accent? What if I was drinking with some of the hard-core white guys? Would I suddenly lapse into the accents of Brooklyn? And then, of course, reality asserted itself. I worked for a newspaper that was seventh in circulation in a town with seven newspapers. The editors could not afford to send a reporter into the undercover life for months. Or even a few days.

But I remained fascinated by the way Carlson had played his dangerous role, wondering whether the technique could still be used. And whether there were others in the history of journalism who had gone undercover. This was a long time before the computer, the Internet, Google, Wikipedia. The discovery of certain books depended on chance and luck, wandering through the dusty aisles of used bookstores. I did find my way to the muckrakers, to Lincoln Steffens, Ida Tarbell, Upton Sinclair. But the urgencies of the newspaper present often shoved the past off stage.

One major problem I had at the time was that there was no book that even vaguely resembled this superb account by Brooke Kroeger. Here we have the full story, with its roots in the nineteenth century. Brooke Kroeger (herself an experienced reporter) takes us from reporters posing as purchasers of other humans at pre–Civil War slave auctions all the way to the *Washington Post* reporters who gained access to the filthy halls of Walter Reed Hospital in 2007. She brings to the story an academic exactitude that is mercifully free of academic jargon. She understands the risks taken by most undercover reporters, both women and men.

John Roy Carlson appears in her book, of course, but his role in the larger story is a lot smaller than it once was in my youthful imagination. It is possible that even he was not aware of some of his predecessors. Good reporters named James Redpath, Albert Deane Richardson, and Henry S. Olcott took turns for Horace Greeley's *New York Tribune* in covering the ongoing story of slavery. At the time, of course, there were no recording devices; the reporters often scribbled notes with pencils in the pages of slave catalogs.

Women, too, are part of the cast in this book. The most famous of the early group was Nellie Bly, but she was not the only female reporter (and falls into Brooke Kroeger's category of "stunt girls"). One of the first was a long forgotten woman named Helen Stuart Campbell. Beginning in 1880, she wrote about the urban poor using what she learned as a volunteer at a mission, then revealing the miseries of women employed in the needle trades and department stores. Others were to follow, freed from the banalities of writing domestic pieces about fashion and food. Women were reporting from dangerous places in the United States before they were allowed to vote. They are doing it now.

I suspect that this book will inspire young apprentice journalists who still believe in the importance of uncovering the truth, in spite of the risks. The risks may or may not be obvious. And there are other hazards to negotiate. The ethical problems of assuming another identity, of posing as someone you are not, of performing a falsehood—all are very ably covered by Brooke Kroeger. The full story has much to teach us all, both reporters and readers. I wish I'd had something like it when I was young, staring at the mouths of urban caves.

# PREFACE

This book unabashedly celebrates the great American journalistic tradition of undercover reporting and offers an argument, built on the volume of evidence, for the restoration of its once-honored place in the array of effective journalistic techniques. Even the most cursory analysis of a century and a half of significant undercover investigations by journalists makes clear how effective the practice can be. Repeatedly, they have proved their worth as producers of high-impact public awareness or as hasteners of change. Like almost no other journalistic approach, undercover reporting has a built-in ability to expose wrongs and wrongdoers or perform other meaningful public service. It can illuminate the unknown, it can capture and sustain attention, it can shock or amaze. The criticism that has bedeviled the practice in more recent years comes from the ethical compromises it inevitably requires, its reliance on some of journalism's most questionable means, and the unacceptable excesses of the few. Deception not only happens in the course of reporting undercover, it is intrinsic to the form. For would-be truth tellers, this is a shaky ground.

Yet at its best, undercover reporting achieves most of the things great journalism means to achieve. At its worst, but no worse than bad journalism in any form, it is not only an embarrassment but can be downright destructive. This book suggests that the capacity of undercover reporting to bring important social issues to public attention and thus to motivate reformers to act far outweighs the objections against it, legitimate though they may be. Its benefits, when used selectively, far outweigh the lapses, which, it turns out, are more of a preoccupation in only some quarters of the profession than they are with the public.

The stories I have chosen to highlight in the following pages have been culled from an idiosyncratic collection of sources: prize and award lists; oblique and direct references found with key word searches in various databases, often incomplete, and in books that cite or allude to recent and archival newspaper, magazine, and journal articles and essays; citations in lawsuits and in law reviews and academic journals; and some old-style reeling of the microfilm. Others emerged from cursory mentions in works of media criticism, commentary, history, ethics, or other, often out-of-print journalism texts. To the numerous authors and journalists who informed my thinking and to those on whom I relied the most, I offer special thanks. You'll find their names in the text, sometimes repeatedly, and in the endnotes and bibliography. Special thanks to those who took the time to speak and message with me at length, including Soma Golden Behr, Barney Calame, Ted Conover, John Davidson, Tim Findley, Tom Goldstein, Chester Goolrick, William Hart, Tony Horwitz, Woody Klein, Paul Lieberman, Lee May, Dick Reavis, William Recktenwald, Ray Ring, Emily Sachar, John Seigenthaler, Paul Shapiro, Jeff Sharlet, Ken Silverstein, Patsy Sims, Paul Steiger, Vivian Toy, Craig Unger, Bill Wasik, Edward Wasserman, Steve Weinberg, Michael Winerip, and Merle Linda Wolin. Warm gratitude also to academic colleagues at New York University and beyond. Some pointed me to or allowed me to use little-known material; others read and critiqued sections of the manuscsript in draft. Those include Rob Boynton, Ted Conover (also my colleague), Pete Hamill, Richard R. John, Richard G. Jones, Perri Klass, Joe Lockard, Jean Marie Lutes, Mike McIntyre, Robert Miraldi, Doug Munro, Patricia O'Toole, Jay Rosen, William Serrin, Clay

Smith, Stephen Solomon, and Steve Wasserman. Alex Goren and Gail Gregg were even willing to listen when I needed to read aloud. Superb research assistants helped greatly at various points: Joanna Bednarz, Nicholas DeRenzo, Hilary Howes, Ryann Liebenthal, William Marshall, Michael Mindel, and Miranda Stanton. Indispensable to the retrieval process were those at the other end of interlibrary loan and in the archives of Investigative Reporters and Editors, Inc., since so much of this ephemeral record has not been well or fully indexed, let alone digitized. Throughout the project, the support and encouragement of the book's editor, David Abrahamson, has been exceptional. Thank you, also, to the team at Northwestern University Press, including Rudy Faust, Marianne Jankowski, and Gianna Mosser.

Here, too, is a salute to the long memory of veteran journalists and news librarians, which figured prominently in the unearthing and amassing of the material, as did the published recollections of the individual editors and reporters mentioned above. Many examples found their way into the book because they are among the best remembered or most controversial undercover projects. Others made the cut because of the investigation's inventiveness, enterprise, or uniqueness, or the peer or public impact it had in its day. Still others became important because I stumbled on them by chance and could not resist the impulse to share them. Others helped to illustrate larger points.

Yet despite nearly four years devoted to the pursuit of the most worthy examples in American history, comprehensive retrieval remains an elusive goal. The long list of undercover projects I have compiled is surely still incomplete. New investigations hit the news as I type. I hope the database created as an extension of this project, found on the web at http://undercoverreporting .org or through the website of the Elmer Holmes Bobst Library at New York University, will continue to grow with the help of more sources from the crowd, both across the United States and from abroad. For this unique digital repository, special thanks go to the Bobst team—Brian Hoffman, Monica McCormick, and Alexa Pearce, and, in the early stages, Jessica Alverson—and to Jane Tylus and her committee at the Humanities Initiative of the Faculty of Arts and Science at NYU, and to my deans during the past six years, Richard Foley and Jess Benhabib, George Downs, and Dalton Conley. All lent vital support to this undertaking, and to me personally. Brian Hoffman designed the site and William Marshall helped give it shape as he loaded the initial material. Both thought carefully about its functionality. In the latter stage of production, Abby Ohlheiser made it even smarter.

Literally hundreds of pieces dating from the 1820s have been considered for inclusion, with more surfacing all the time. For research purposes, organization of the material has been sorted by year, by reporter, by method, by subject, by medium, by outlet, by honors, and by whatever documentable impact the work can claim. Chapters are organized roughly by reporting theme. They focus on those few examples that most clearly illustrate the nature of undercover reporting about the subject at hand, or that help support the central argument about the genre and why it matters. Most of the pieces or series noted had important impact or received outsized attention in their day. (Chapter 13 is more of a kitchen sink of noteworthy themes that did not warrant a chapter all their own.) *Impact* and *outsized attention* mean everything from prizes and awards to best seller lists to heavy coverage in the press to a place in the cultural conversation to legal or ethical challenges to direct spurs to legislation, reform moves, or other forms of response or action. Please note that in the interest of length, much of the long-lost material exhumed for this project has been reburied in the endnotes, where it is still worth a visit. Browsing the headlines and succession of dates for, say, a *Chicago Tribune* or *Sun-Times* series from the 1970s, from initial disclosures through to stunning public impact—arrests, trials, firings, institutional shutdowns—provides a parallel narrative along with loud testimony to the method's reformative power. Turn to the database for the opportunity to find and read the full texts of the stories themselves.

The criterion for inclusion in the book and the database is a very wide tent, intermingling all types of media in a twenty-first-century way. The main focus is journalism for significant purpose that required (mostly) physical acts of deception by reporters or their surrogates—anything from shadowing, artful dodges, and blending in with the crowd to radically altered identities. Excluded for the most part are works designated as fiction or works that are at least partly fictionalized, although it is impossible to leave out Upton Sinclair's *The Jungle,* which, the author assures us, is a full-fledged work of unvarnished reportage. George Orwell's *Down and Out in Paris and London* receives attention, even though he is not American and his book includes otherwise forbidden composite characters. Why include them? Because both Sinclair and Orwell invariably figure in even the spottiest recounting of high points in undercover reporting's history. They inspire too many imitators to ignore. Speaking of Orwell, a few seminal works by journalists from other countries also were deemed too important or too illustrative to exclude, even though this book primarily focuses on undercover's American exponents.

This project started with no hypothesis but with a keen interest in undercover reporting going back two decades ago to the start of my work on Nellie Bly. Its central argument emerged from assembling and analyzing the patterns of these hundreds of projects and their back stories and then plotting them on a virtual timeline against relevant contemporaneous currents in the field.

Also, in the interest of restricting length, in addition to the numerous newspaper series fully cited in the endnotes, I have included references to a good deal of rich ancillary material both in the endnotes and in the database. The pieces I could not locate in time for the book's publication I am hopeful will eventually appear in the database.

The following pages crisscross three American centuries to relive some familiar favorites from the annals of undercover reporting and to revive some remarkably executed projects that were new at least to me. All of these efforts have attracted significant attention of one kind or another—locally, nationally, publicly, or professionally—and all of them provide the opportunity for a wonder-filled ride along the highways and byways of significant, carefully planned, high-risk, high-reward journalism that has sought and often managed to make a difference.

Brooke Kroeger

UNDERCOVER REPORTING

ONE

INTRODUCTION

Two reporters witnessed the mistreatment of Iraq war veterans at the nation's premier military hospital and documented it in articles[1] that brought swift and sure results. Within a day after the series began, Walter Reed Army Medical Center had work crews on site upgrading its mold- and rodent-infested outpatient facilities.[2] Within weeks, the hospital's commander, the secretary of the army, and the army's surgeon general had lost their jobs.[3] Congress scheduled special field subcommittee hearings on-site at the hospital, inviting testimony from some of the reporters' named sources. Three blue-ribbon panels began investigating how wounded U.S. soldiers who had served their country so valiantly could be treated so badly under the army's own watch.

Praise was nearly universal[4] for the work of Dana Priest and Anne Hull of the *Washington Post,* and it was no surprise to anyone the following year when they and photographer Michel duCille won the 2008 Pulitzer Prize for Public Service. Leonard Downie Jr., the newspaper's executive editor at the time, captured best the underlying meaning of their triumph at a time when economic and technological convulsions in the traditional delivery of news had put at risk the very survival of serious, intensively reported journalism, the kind that requires unique skill and training undergirded by large commitments of time and money. To the Pulitzer judges, Downie wrote, "At its core, truly great journalism is about righting wrongs and changing systems that are unfair or do not work."[5] His reporters had done exactly that. The newspaper, indeed the whole profession, proudly—deservedly—celebrated the achievement. Priest and Hull had spent more than four months doing journalism in the public interest at its shining, steam-blasted best.

In the rush to extol what was clearly the major achievement of U.S. journalism in winter 2007, no one gave more than glancing notice to how the two reporters had managed to gain and maintain such unfettered access to a U.S. military institution, let alone a military hospital, over so many months. Only the sparest details of how they got that story trickled out in those early weeks, the period when interest in the project was keenest. To readers, Hull and Priest reported on method in a single sentence, as Downie, who opposes misrepresentation and undercover reporting, similarly explained to the Pulitzer judges in his letter of nomination.[6] He said their more than four months at Walter Reed were spent without official knowledge or permission.[7] They declined to discuss method with the *Post*'s own media columnist,[8] or with a reporter for the *American Journalism Review*.[9] At the gentle urging of a public radio interviewer, they gave up just a bit more. "I mean we didn't go through the army for permission, nor did we go through Walter Reed," Hull said. "We went to the soldiers, removing that middle filter, because we wanted to hear what their lives were like, and we wanted to witness these problems firsthand, and that required lots of time with these people as they went through their days."[10]

At about the same time, the *Post*'s ombudsman reported that "the two set out, mostly separately and never undercover, and did the kind of plain old gumshoe on-the-record reporting that often goes unrecognized in this high-tech age." She quoted Priest saying of army officials that "no one was really paying attention," which allowed the two reporters to stay "below the radar for as long as we did."[11]

The ombudsman's framing of the enterprise as "never undercover" provoked no known counter at the time or thereafter. But was that really the case? A few bloggers, apparently indifferent to the *u*-word's burdensome implications, praised the *Post* with compound offhanded references to its "undercover reporting," "undercover investigation," or "undercover reporters,"[12] but that was about it.

Thirteen months after the series was published, Hull and Priest provided a fuller explanation[13] of how they had so deliberately and effectively avoided detection until they were ready to reveal themselves to officials at Walter Reed six days before the first story ran.[14] It meant identifying themselves at the guard gates with their driver's licenses like every ordinary visitor to the hospital does. It meant not announcing their *Post* affiliations or declaring their real intentions to anyone who might then be obliged to thwart their actual purpose. It meant avoiding unwelcome questions by playing on the common assumptions and expectations of officials who encountered them in the hospital environment. It meant constant vigilance and a series of stealth moves designed to help them blend in unremarkably with the surroundings, making themselves scarce whenever those who might question their presence or worse, kick them out, appeared on the scene. It meant separating, so that one could continue reporting in case the other got caught. It meant avoiding encounters with anyone who might be obliged to report them. It meant intentionally shedding such tools of the trade as cameras and reporters' notebooks so they would not raise unwelcome questions during routine bag searches. It meant imploring the trusted sources they developed during those four-plus months not to reveal what they had learned of the reporters' purpose or even to acknowledge the reporters personally should they meet up by chance on the hospital grounds. It meant helping their sources understand how to avoid inadvertently giving the reporters away, including careful coaching in *phraseology*—Hull's term—for themselves and for the soldiers, families, and hospital personnel whom they took into their confidence.

Key for Hull and Priest and for their sources was to steer authorities away from asking the awkward questions to which truthful answers would be required under ethical and policy guidelines common to journalists, the military, and hospital personnel alike,[15] and to afford themselves the freedom to "roam around the 110-acre facility at various hours of the day or night and talk to soldiers and Marines without the interference of Army public affairs."[16] Undercover assignments often require this approach. Also key was the end goal: to be in a position to create the kind of impact in print that would force Walter Reed to respond to the urgent, repeated complaints from patients and their families that it had ignored for far too long.

The extraordinary impact of the series eliminated the need to further justify why the clandestine behavior had been necessary, but it came nonetheless a month after their first stories appeared—in the form of a cautionary tale from Philadelphia. A local television crew, attempting to replicate the *Post*'s successful work at a Veterans Administration hospital in Philadelphia, fell into the trap of exposure-too-soon that Hull and Priest had so carefully finessed: that crew was detained and fined and had its cameras and film confiscated. On top of that, no story resulted except for an embarrassing one about the crew's arrest for staging what local media reports described as "an unknown undercover investigation."[17] More to the point, there were no meaningful results to show for the botched effort.

It is a fact that Priest and Hull met the minimum requirement and common understanding of most reporters, as contained implicitly or explicitly in every journalistic code of ethics.[18] That is, the obligation to be up front when confronted and never to tell an outright lie. And clearly, Priest and Hull at all times were prepared to identify themselves as reporters should the direct question ever be put to them. To their great relief, it was not. They entered a public place they had every right to enter. They identified themselves with a driver's license like everyone else. Open to debate, however, and one of the issues this book will explore, is whether there is really a difference for a journalist between not ever telling a lie—emphasis on the word *telling,* because lies, to qualify as lies, are verbalized—and the deliberate projection of a false impression with the clear intention to mislead, to deceive.[19] It is at least fair to say that in attempts to obscure their identities to authorities at Walter Reed,[20] the human targets of their inquiry, those with the most to lose, Hull and Priest went as far from wearing a press badge as it is possible to get, short of posing as a patient or a hospital staffer, which the *Post*'s guidelines expressly forbid. Those points at the far end of the ethical continuum generally bear the label "undercover." Was their approach perfectly legitimate, even unavoidable, given the circumstances and the stakes? Especially in light of the results, most, I think, would argue yes. Did the use of these tactics undermine the value of the enterprise or call it into question? It did not.

So why the apparent effort to avoid the obvious term of art? Why distance the enterprise from the label, as if bringing attention to the undercover aspects of their efforts would sully the achievement? Sadly and unfairly, it is because the label "undercover" *would* have sullied the achievement, at least in the eyes of some important players. Not historically, but more recently, this is largely due to a movement against undercover reporting in some quarters since the late 1970s, a movement the *Post*—once a daring, open, and exemplary proponent of the practice—helped to instigate.

This book argues for a restoration of honor and legitimacy to the discomfiting techniques of undercover reporting because of their value to so much of the journalism that has mattered in the past century and a half and because so much of the journalism that matters relies on these methods anyway, at least in part. To make this case, the book draws heavily on a long, continuous, rich, and proud historical record to give a cumulative sense of how many great exposés of myriad types have benefitted from the use of subterfuge and deception for a number of legitimate purposes. These include helping to expose wrong or to extract significant information or to create indelible descriptions of hard-to-penetrate institutions or social situations that deserve public attention.

What also emerges from the record is that over and over again, "going undercover" has proved to be an indispensable tool in the high-value, high-impact journalism of changing systems and righting wrongs. It also has aggrandized journalistic legends at the institutional level, advanced the reputations of great editors, and catapulted individual reporters to enviable careers. It has provided an enduring, magnetic, if sometimes tricky narrative form that never ceases to fascinate, even when the execution fails to scale the high journalistic or literary walls. Colossal lapses and misfires aside (these, too, will be addressed), undercover reporting has also been at the forefront of important published and broadcast efforts to create awareness, correct widespread misconceptions, provoke outrage, and give a human face—whether that face inspires horror or compassion or a little of both—to any number of institutions and social worlds that otherwise would be ignored, misunderstood, or misrepresented for lack of open access.

Even the most cursory review of the reporting that has proudly worn the undercover banner bears witness to this fact, as the following pages endeavor to show. Prizes for undercover journalism are plentiful, and not just in the distant past. Like almost no other reportorial approach, setting out deliberately to fool some of the people at least some of the time has repeatedly produced important, compelling, and—this might be the key to the method's enduring popularity—often riveting results.

Undercover reporting is also on the side of the angels. At its best, the method speaks directly to eight if not all ten essential journalistic tenets pinpointed by Bill Kovach and Tom Rosenstiel in their book, *The Elements of Journalism: What Newspeople Should Know and the Public Should Expect*: pursuing truth, being loyal to citizens, being obliged to verify, independently monitoring power, providing a forum for public outcry, maintaining independence from those journalists report about, exercising personal conscience, and, perhaps most pertinently, making the significant interesting and relevant.[21]

Several observations quickly emerge from even the most cursory browsing of the online database at http://undercoverreporting.org, created to complement this project. Taken in the aggregate, the body of work contradicts some commonly held perceptions. It shows that scores of significant undercover sensations date back much further than Nellie Bly's asylum exposé in 1887, and that no move to banish or degrade the practice has had even the slightest effect on the slow, selective, but steady rate of production or publication. Slow and selective because going undercover is meant to be the journalism of last resort. But steady, well into the twenty-first century. This is despite the waves of peer opposition and the many and repeated assertions to the contrary.

Sorting the known projects by date and by category also reveals how often over the centuries the subjects and reportorial strategies repeat and repeat—perhaps with a decade or two between outings—and yet the potential for impact remains surprisingly fresh.

Undercover enterprises have started as books that also became newspaper or magazine serials. They have started as newspaper or magazine series that later developed into books of a very different sort, sometimes books of policy or advocacy that barely refer to the more sensational original project. Some have been collaborations between newspapers and television programs and some represent collaborations between publications or television programs and law enforcement agencies, and groups that foster better government or other advocacy groups. Some start in one format and stay in that format. Since at least the early 1960s, as technology began to allow, scores of television series and segments have relied on the hidden camera, which, combined with reporter-producer moxie, has created its own undercover subspecies. Newspaper reporters also have used miniature cameras even well before the advent of television. There have also been undercover radio investigations. More recently, publications that originate online have begun to add a new shelf to this bulging old closet. As a medium, the web is a particularly promising format for undercover journalism, especially in its ability to meld audio and video documentation to word stories and add still photographs and a written-word account to recorded segments. As importantly, the web also brings the ability to add backup citations, interview transcripts, and other extensive primary documentation via links, hypertext, and topics pages.

What unites the projects reviewed for this book is the need they created for the reporters or their surrogates to engage in a deceptive ruse or some sort of identity acrobatics great or small to do the work. They have posed as; lived as or among; worked as; interned as; volunteered as; signed on or trained as; become paying customers or patients or clients of; blended in as if; functioned as; fellow-traveled as; become; endured; petitioned; cold-called; avoided correcting the mistaken impression of; projected the false impression of or given off the impression of being; gained access with incomplete or misleading information to; presented as; gathered information unannounced; finessed an application form to; took advantage of employer ignorance; contrived to; got confidential permission to; cross-dressed as; turned personal experience into; shadowed without telling everyone involved; infiltrated; snuck into; slipped in or encountered by chance; used privileged access to; entered for the purpose of testing; staked out or stalked unseen; secretly filmed or recorded; exercised—or caused someone else to exercise—his or her rights as ordinary citizens, visitors, or customers without revealing the actual intent; or encountered something firsthand by chance or through unconnected personal experience and then revealed it in publication as if that had been the intention all along.

Though a few of the most astounding subjects and themes are one-offs, others recur with surprising regularity and often without diminishing return. Some are repeated simultaneously or within weeks of the original as collaborations across a state or as examples of the flattery that is imitation. Some represent the rebirths of good ideas across the centuries.

Some stories exemplify the importance of the reporters involved, who must have the skill, physicality, daring, and relish for undercover work, but also, often, a distinct literary flair. This has contributed heavily over the years to what has set the work apart. Some, of course, are far more interestingly reported than they are written, and to date, not one of the best of them has ever made a good movie. Novelists slumming as journalists are among the strong contenders for greatness in the genre. Other equally superb entries gained their place in workmanlike prose, simply on the quality of the idea, the concept, or the investigative success. Some emanate from crack newspaper and television "I-Teams" expressly in the role of public watchdog, assigned to investigate wrongs and expose wrongdoing in the performance of high public service, driving reader- and viewership in the process. Sometimes just having been able to obtain the pictures, the film, or the documentary evidence mattered more than the words or the voice-overs. There is no single pattern to the impetus to undertake the projects except, perhaps, the prospect of serving the reader and the recognition that can result for the reporters and their organizations, as well as the hope to do some good.

The collection also highlights the importance of the reporter persona in many, but by no means all, of these projects, especially in the "I-am-you" experiential narratives—Orwell's *Down and Out* comes to mind—anointed by time.

It says a lot about a story with an expected shelf life of a day, a week, or a month when it ascends into legend, when almost anyone can summon it routinely to make a point in casual conversation, even more than a hundred years after the tom-toms first beat news of it across the time zones. Nellie Bly's incarceration in a madhouse for the *New York World* was such a story[22] and the best known in what would become a very long line of exposés of public and private health-care institutions. John Howard Griffin's skin-dyed transformation from white journalist to black man in segregated 1959 for a long-defunct magazine called *Sepia* was another.[23] As a book, still in print, *Black Like Me* has sold more than 10 million copies. It also has spawned a not-always-flattering body of literary criticism, a classic Eddie Murphy parody, and any number of imitators, one as recently as 1994 for the *Washington Post,* dyed black skin and all. Pamela Zekman's Mirage Tavern ruse of 1978 for the *Chicago Sun-Times* may well turn out to have Bly-like staying power—even nonjournalists will mention it when asked to recall examples of great undercover exposés.

The research confirms that well before and long after Bly, Griffin, or Zekman shot into the journalistic firmament, and for the periods before, after, and in between, significant stories that required elaborate or simple ruses have been a journalistic staple. Contrary to one often-summoned thought stream, the practice has never gone out of vogue. Recognition for even the most stunning of these investigations has usually been fleeting. This is about news after all. Many resurface in these pages for the first time in decades, deserving of a place in the collective portrait of great journalism. They tighten our grasp on what undercover reporting can do and mean.

And so to begin, with the earliest-known examples of reporters who went undercover to expose, underscore, and deepen understanding of the most perplexing of American social systems and the gravest of social wrongs.

# TWO

# REPORTING SLAVERY

From the mid- to the late 1850s, no U.S. newspaper was more aggressive or influential than Horace Greeley's *New York Tribune* in the use of its pages to hasten the downfall of slavery. Whenever and however possible, the newspaper featured detailed on-site reporting on the evil of the age. In the South, this won no friends for Greeley or his envoys. By the 1850s, *Tribune* reporters who ventured into the region on short or extended journalistic forays never failed to remind readers of the dangers they had faced down to do so. To be discovered, they and their editors knew, could provoke anything from their being run out of town in a tar-slathered "costume of feathers"[1] to the hangman's noose.

Reporters such as James Redpath, Mortimer Thomson, Henry S. Olcott, and Albert Deane Richardson had no name for the elaborate strategies and tactics they devised to keep themselves safe when reporting from the South, but what they did gave undercover reporting a distinct shape and definition.

By way of casual travelers and the established newspaper exchanges, Northern newspapers circulated freely and relatively quickly in the cities of the South. Editors in New York understood well the need to protect the identities of those who corresponded for them from the region, going to whatever lengths necessary to provide camouflage in print. This was no doubt one of the reasons that the *Tribune*'s exclusive Southern datelines in this period were likely to be signed by "our special correspondent," or with a pseudonymous surname such as "Hopper," or a single initial such as *V* or *W*,[2] or no signature at all. Pen names and datelines without bylines were already a well-established journalistic convention long before the 1850s.[3] But in the pair of decades before the Civil War, both for safety's sake and to ease access to meaningful information, Northern journalists reporting from locations in the South put on additional layers of protective covering. The risks were clearly real, however journalistic calling and the chance for glory overcame fear; necessity birthed the means.

James Redpath was only nineteen in 1852 when Horace Greeley snapped him up for the *Tribune* from the *Detroit Advertiser.* Two years later, he became the newspaper's exchange editor, the one who "reads and mutilates newspapers from nine in the morning until six in the evening."[4] In that role, he compiled a column called "The Facts of Slavery," culled from matter-of-factly reported Southern newspaper items with sale prices and other details that were republished for their Northern shock appeal.[5]

For Redpath personally, this piqued a fascination with slavery that beckoned him south "thrice on an anti-slavery errand"[6] to Charleston, South Carolina; Richmond, Virginia; Montgomery, Alabama; and later on to Savannah, Georgia. The journey from Richmond to Montgomery, all seven hundred and fifty miles, he did on foot. His third tour, wholly in Virginia, focused more on slavery's influence on "agriculture, education, and material prosperity"[7] than on his talks with slaves, although they are also included. The long periods in the region deepened his familiarity with the story and thus the quality of his understanding and by extension, his reporting. "Costume of feathers"[8] was a figure of speech he used in a preface to explain why his Southern datelines kept shifting from city to city. His method—yet another species of the emerging genus undercover—turned him into a kind of journalistic North–South double agent. To support himself and gain local trust, he took jobs in his own name for short stints at a couple of Southern newspapers. But from each locale, he surreptitiously sent pseudonymous reports back to abolition journals in the North using a self-styled correspondence relay system. Dispatches got tucked inside letters to relatives in Michigan who forwarded them to editors in New York.[9]

Six years later, in the last months before the war broke out, Albert Deane Richardson went south for the *Tribune*. The newspaper's managing editor predicted he would only last two weeks, but he kept on reporting as "Our Special Correspondent" long enough to become the last *Tribune* correspondent to leave the South.[10] (His subsequent reporting of the conflict included his eventual capture and escape.) He avoided detection with "systematic duplicity," and "a padlock upon one's tongue."[11] From the time he stepped onto the train at Louisville in February 1861, he began presenting himself to fellow travelers and to those he encountered in the cities as a resident of the territory of New Mexico, which he knew well from previous reporting experiences as the *Tribune*'s lead correspondent in the West. He claimed to be traveling to New Orleans en route to Vera Cruz and the city of Mexico. This allowed him to appear to unionists and secessionists "as a stranger with no particular sympathies," with whom they could converse freely. "While I talked New Mexico and the Rocky Mountains," he explained, "my companions talked Secession, and told me more, every day, of its secret working than as a mere stranger, I could have learned in a month."[12]

Richardson also elaborated inventively on Redpath's postal relay system, adding preparation, nuance, and flourishes worthy of a spy thriller. For instance, Richardson got the *Tribune* to publish two New Orleans–dated letters written by a friend who had recently been there. This made it harder to identify Richardson because of the impression it created that the newspaper had a correspondent in the city weeks before Richardson actually arrived.[13]

He sent his dispatches by mail or by express, addressing them to one of six New York banking and commercial firms, which in turn forwarded them to the *Tribune*. He wrote them like ordinary business letters. He developed a cipher system "by which all phrases between certain private marks were to be exactly reversed in printing." That is, if the words *patriot* and *an honest man* appeared in brackets, it meant *demagogue* and *a scoundrel*. Other marks indicated *delete these words*. A paragraph that started at the edge of a sheet was to be printed precisely, but one begun halfway across the page meant it contained something to be translated by the cipher. Richardson said that even if discovered, the letters would have been incomprehensible. "Whether tampered with or not, they always reached the office," he said. "I never kept any papers on my person, or in my room, which could excite suspicion if read."[14]

Richardson extended his cloaking to the style and tone of the writing itself, assuming the pose of "an old citizen, sometimes remarking that during a residence of fourteen years in New Orleans, I had never before seen such a whirlwind of passion, etc." He later confessed—rather oxymoronically—that he had changed names, places, and dates while remaining "always faithful to the fact," *fact* being a term thoughtful readers might challenge. Near the end of his stay, knowing that he would be safely back North before the articles appeared in print, he became bolder about disclosing even the most specific details from his reporting.

Given the journalistic admonition to "do no harm," changing identifiable personal or geographical details remains, in some instances, a reluctantly accepted journalistic practice. Editors allow it to protect the identity or location of people whose privacy, position, or personal safety such disclosure could jeopardize. Responsible publications will then serve their readers by taking further pains to indicate when such alterations have been made, adding the explanation in a preface or sidebar or in the text itself, sometimes signaled with an asterisk. Explanations are offered with varying degrees of specificity. Sometimes, but not always, they also provide the reasons why. The same is true for medical and social science journals as they attempt to ensure the privacy of human subjects in the clinical case reports they publish, constricted further by HIPAA, the Health Insurance Portability and Accountability Act, violations of which can carry penalties of up to $50,000.[15] In all these instances, disclosure allows the writer to remain faithful to the reader if not to the fact. To serve both masters would mean the more forthright approach of omitting all potentially harmful specifics and explaining the reasons for doing so. It is by far my personal preference, even given its higher narrative cost. As for Richardson, even if such disclosures to readers had been customary, he could not have revealed his fabrications until well after he left New Orleans. The identity he sought to protect was his own.

In 1859, two years before the start of the war, at least two exceptional surgical reporting strikes took place undercover. The first involved an epic slave auction in Savannah, Georgia, on March 2 and 3 of that year. Not only was this yet another opportunity to chronicle for Northern readers the callous spectacle of cruelty that was slavery but it signaled the breaking up of a great old Southern plantation, heralding the era's coming demise. The auction involved literally hundreds of slaves and a very well-known Northerner as its central figure, Pierce Butler, of the wealthy and socially prominent Philadelphia Butlers,[16] former husband of the celebrated English actress Fanny Kemble, his fortune dissipated and debt mounting fast. The sale involved most of the slaves Butler personally inherited in the 1830s, virtually half of the nine hundred slaves on the two absentee Butler properties, a rice plantation near Darien, and a cotton plantation just off the Atlantic coast at the extreme northern point of St. Simmon's Island.[17] The *Tribune* would find a way to send a star reporter to Savannah.

In the Southern press, slave sale stories provided local and regional readers with matter-of-fact market information and listings of prices fetched. For the *Tribune,* however, they presented rare opportunities to acquaint Northern readers with slavery's quieter horrors. They evoked empathy and provided a vicarious encounter with the unapologetic, legal exhibitions in human commerce that were regularly being staged in the land of the free. Digital archives of the *Tribune* contain a neat short stack of exclusively reported slave sale clippings from the 1840s and 1850s. Although the writers avoid stock imagery in these reports, themes recur from piece to piece with only the dateline shifting from St. Louis to New Orleans[18] to Petersburg or Richmond in Virginia.[19] They include the disturbing examination of slaves as livestock, prospective buyers making lurid comments to slave women and touching them suggestively, the wrenching stories of loved ones coldly separated from one another, the perverse pride a slave would sometimes take in commanding a high personal price.[20]

And yet from the standpoint of editorial judgment, nothing in those years could match the immediacy of a slave auction for a white Northern correspondent who wanted to provide a graphic, if only impressionistic sense of the slave system's wicked ways. For the clever reporter posed as buyer, the events provided rare, unimpeded access and the most efficient setting possible for encounters with the closed quadrangle of plantation owners, buyers, sellers, and chattel. The setting provided the opportunity for casual if fleeting conversation with another man's slaves. Taking notes could happen unremarkably; prospective buyers routinely scribbled in their catalogs. The correspondent who did not identify himself as a reporter could play on the presumptions of unsuspecting others as to his real intent. He could observe and question undetected, as Hull and Priest would do a century and a half later, helping to develop the now time-honored reporter's ploy of just blending in, of playing on an impression—or, more precisely, not correcting impressions formed at a glance, that the reporter has no purpose beyond that of ordinary spectator, client, customer, patient, guest, or visitor.[21]

Not incidentally, the 1850s were the postpublication glory days of *Uncle Tom's Cabin,* which was soon to become not only the second best-selling book of the 1850s but of the entire nineteenth century, just behind the Bible. Harriet Beecher Stowe's intention was clear from the start, as she explained to the editor of the *National Era,* which first published the work as serial fiction from June 1851 to April 1852.[22] Stowe likened her purpose not to that of the journalist but to the painter, to present slavery as clearly as possible. "There is no arguing with *pictures,*" she said, "and everybody is impressed by them, whether they mean to be or not."[23]

The novel's lack of realism[24] and the racial stereotypes it embedded in the collective imagination emerged from the many sources Mrs. Stowe relied on, and later went to the trouble of documenting in a companion volume.[25] She confidently reimagined harrowing newspaper accounts of slave escapes and troubles; slave memoirs and lectures; conversations in her family parlors with reformers, clergy, and scholars; her personal encounters along the Underground Railroad in Cincinnati and elsewhere; and the shared recollections of long-time family retainers. And yet the sum total of her on-the-ground experience in the South was said to be one visit to Kentucky of a few days' duration some seventeen years before she wrote the novel.[26]

There is no known direct link from Stowe's literary sensation in fiction to the urge of young journalists in the years immediately following its publication to report the slave plight in eyewitnessed fact. Indeed, they were doing so long before Stowe's serial appeared.[27] They did this despite the mounting risks and the respect and admiration their own writing expressed for Stowe's depictions of character and place. ("God Bless Thee, Mrs. Stowe!"[28]) Without reference to *Uncle Tom's Cabin,* Redpath, for example, declared as his objective to report on slavery in the slaves' own words. This was two years after Stowe's book appeared and greatly helped by the stenographic skill Redpath had acquired as a teenaged reporter back in his native Berwick, Scotland.[29] His intention, he said, was to produce work in which "the bondsman might define his position on the all-engrossing question of the day. Almost everybody has done it. Why then not he?"[30]

The *Tribune* did not enlist the high-minded Redpath to cover the great Savannah auction. Redpath, in any event, had spent three months working for the *Savannah Daily Morning News* during his first southern sojourn five years earlier, in 1854.[31] He might easily have been recognized—a sure disqualifier, even if he had been available to go. The *Tribune* sent a contemporary of Redpath's, a popular humor columnist named Mortimer Thomson, who had been busy perfecting his undercover technique in a series of far less risky forays around New York City.

By 1859, Thomson, known on the page as Q. K. Philander Doesticks, P. B. ("Q. K." stood for "queer kritter"; "P. B." for "perfect brick"), had amassed a significant national following. He had joined the newspaper's staff the year after Redpath left to go South. This followed Thomson's expulsion from college and stints both in a traveling theatrical troupe and selling jewelry. By 1858, three short years after his work began appearing in the newspaper, five collections of his articles had been republished as popular books. Latter-day scholars not only compared Thomson to Ring Lardner[32] (Mark Twain, however, scoffed at Doesticks's writing as no match for his own)[33] but have credited him with coining such terms as *brass knuckles, dumbbell, gutter-snipe, patent leather, free love, good and ready, grin and bear it,* and *hot stuff.*[34] Peers considered him "one of the *Tribune*'s best descriptive writers."[35] He also did police reporting and theatrical reviews during his *Tribune* years, but it was for his humor sketches, especially his popular "Doesticks Letters," that he was best known. Much of the work involved undercover or situational poses as a narrative device—Doesticks as a fireman, Doesticks as free lover—in prose that repeatedly drew on racial slurs to achieve its effect.[36] Thomson had heart, but an abolition activist like Redpath, he was not.

The last of Thomson's collections, *The Witches of New York,* came out shortly before the trip to Savannah. It repurposed a sixteen-part series of sketches the *Tribune* published between January and May 1857.[37] The stories, under the same title as the book, described Thomson's encounters with New York's astrologers and fortunetellers, women around town "engaged in every imaginable crime from prostitution to infanticide," as one scholar put it.[38] He tied the pieces together loosely by using the same strategy for every sketch: Doesticks undercover, presenting himself to his targets not as a reporter but as an ordinary paying client, and telling his readers how conscientiously the work had been done, with every fortuneteller visited individually to record her exact words in answer to the same questions "so that the absurd differences in their statements and predictions result from the unmitigated humbug of their pretended art and from no misinformation or misrepresentation on the part of the seeker."[39]

By October 1858, the *Tribune* reported, with thanks to Thomson's efforts, that police had amassed enough evidence to arrest more than a dozen "professors of the black art."[40] In the coming years, for reporters to present themselves as paying clients or patients in efforts to expose quacks, fakirs, mesmerists, and all manner of charlatan would become a common undercover ruse, still in use, despite the court challenges such antics have invited, such as the medical quackery case against *Life* magazine in 1963, *Dietemann v. Time, Inc.,* which set an important precedent for hidden camera cases.[41]

At the time of the Savannah assignment, Thomson was a man deep in grief, mourning the loss of his wife in childbirth only three months earlier.[42] He was well aware of the considerable danger in which he placed himself and took precautions—as a guest of the area who would have been entitled to courtesies—not to "placard his mission and claim his honors." But he also put himself in the thick of the action, "armed with pencil and catalogue, doing his little utmost to keep up all the appearance of a knowing buyer . . . conducting himself like a rich planter, with forty thousand dollars where he could put his finger on it."[43]

This inspired match of reporter to assignment resulted in one of the most significant antislavery narratives in the run-up period to the Civil War. The newspaper first published Thomson's account within a week of the end of the sale, on Wednesday, March 9, 1859, devoting a full page to it—all six narrow columns, no illustrations. Considering the infinitesimal size of the newspaper typeface, the piece was the length of a pamphlet or even, with appendices and other padding, enough for a short book. The headline, like the piece itself, dripped irony and contempt: AMERICAN CIVILIZATION ILLUSTRATED; . . . HUMAN FEELINGS OF NO ACCOUNT . . . MR. BUTLER GIVES EACH CHATTEL A DOLLAR.[44]

From memory and from notes, Thomson fashioned his report in haste during a train trip back to New York from Savannah—at least a day and a half of travel time.[45] Over the next several weeks, newspapers across the country reprinted the article. Demand was such that the *Tribune* republished it in its entirety two days after it ran the first time.[46] Poems about the sale appeared. Abolition groups circulated the report widely in pamphlet form. The *London Times* carried a four-column condensed version of it on April 12, 1859, and commented on it the next day[47]—there was that Fannie Kemble connection—and it appeared as a pamphlet in Edinburgh, Glasgow, and Belfast.[48] The *Times* said Thomson had, to use the phrase of the day, "photographed" the slave system perfectly.[49]

Within the year, the London publishing house of Ward and Lock produced the piece in book form but under Greeley's name, not Thomson's, and with grossly racist cover art and a title to match: *Aunt Sally, Come Up! Or, the Nigger Sale.*[50]

The *Atlantic Monthly* heralded Thomson's reportage as a major achievement that furnished—"with caution, and the aid of Masonic influences"—"the best and most minute description of an auction-sale of slaves that has ever been published." The *Atlantic* writer marveled at how the story "admirably illustrates the enterprise and prompt energy which often distinguish the journalism of America above that of any other country."[51]

Predictably, newspaper editorialists from across the South poured ire on the achievement. William Tappen Thompson, a humor writer himself and Redpath's former editor at the *Savannah Daily Morning News,* accused his namesake-without-the-*p*-no-relation of "misrepresentation and falsehood," adding that he clearly intended "to impose on the willing credulity and excite the mawkish sentimentality of the abolition fanatics of the North" and could induce from Southerners "only feelings of scorn and contempt."[52]

The *Savannah Republican* also had some choice words for Doesticks, calling him "a somewhat notorious individual" who "was hired as a spy by Horace Greeley of the *The New York Tribune.*"[53] The *Atlantic* countered that the Southern reaction to the Doesticks piece was "ludicrous to witness" and that its vociferousness only "proved how keenly the blow was felt."[54]

All the same, the staying power of Doesticks's story was such that abolition groups reprinted it as a pamphlet four years later, in 1863, identifying it this time as a companion "sequel," although it was a prequel to the other significant white eyewitness account of slavery in this period, Fanny Kemble's *Journal of a Residence on a Georgia Plantation in 1838–39.*[55] The *Tribune* seized on the moment to republish the Doesticks piece then as well.[56]

Thomson's work also suggests a warning to any would-be reporter attempting such a ruse at any time: keen on-site observation and a premeditated, near stenographic recording of events can only go so far in and of itself. Thomson's work, in fact, was far from flawless. His grasp of the background of the Butler slaves was wanting; his view of life on the old plantation far too idealized and he incorrectly asserted that no Butler slaves had been sold before the Savannah auction.[57]

Thomson's reporting also suffered from the shortcomings that beset so much of the era's "slave tourism."[58] It emanates from the unwitting preconceptions white Northern reporters almost invariably brought to such an assignment, even when what they witnessed antagonized them. They could not escape their own historical framework, their position as white Northern observers. In a more general way, it is a cautionary criticism for all experiential reporting, no matter how well-briefed the authors or how earnest their motivation.

And yet journalism is in the business of haste. The work is meant to be fleeting, a snapshot of contemporary events as they unfold. Nothing to journalists or their publications is more satisfying than work that endures across the decades or centuries, but that is never the primary purpose of the work. The journalist's job is to record, report, and process information responsibly, with as much awareness and context as it is possible to provide in the very limited timeframe allotted—emphasis on those last five words. The reader turns to the work of the journalist because the essential value is the speed and style of delivery, and for that, the reader is called upon to make the necessary mental accommodations to accept what is offered for what it is. It stands to reason that the stronger the ability of the reporter to deliver nuance as well as historical, political, and theoretical insight and context—not to mention accuracy and literary elegance—and deliver it speedily—the better the reporter and the more valuable the work. And at its most perfect, journalism achieves a level of sophistication that can rival the most exacting scholarship. It is a happy event for reporter, publication, and reader when all those pieces come together. But to expect or even want journalism to be produced with a scholar's rigor in a scholar's style at a scholar's pace is to defeat its essential purpose. Journalism needs a similar intent, but it appears as ephemera for good reason.[59]

The sting to the South of the Doesticks escapade no doubt intensified Southern fury against Northern journalists and made more dangerous their already vulnerable position as stealth correspondents in the region. This was brought powerfully home nine months later in Charles Town, Virginia, in December 1859, during the lead-up to the execution of John Brown.[60] The *Tribune*'s correspondent in that city, whose name never appeared as a byline,[61] had been filing heavily detailed reports—jailhouse quotes from Brown, his wife, local preparations—that in turn "vexed the peace of the whole South" and had newspapers in the Gulf states calling on Virginians "to clean out the reptile!"[62]

Threat to the life of the Charles Town correspondent became too great, and at the most inopportune moment—just days before Brown's hanging—he fled town. The *Tribune* seemed destined to have no reporter on the scene until Henry S. Olcott, the newspaper's New York–based junior agricultural editor, heard the call and volunteered. He asked but one consideration: that his friend Greeley "would allow me to do it in my own way. With some remonstrance about the risks I would run, he at last consented, and gave me carte blanche to go and come and do as I chose."[63]

What Olcott did was join a party of recruits to the Petersburg Grays, one of the Virginia regiments being sent to Charles Town to guard Brown's body. En route to Charles Town, Olcott twice managed to elude the direct gaze of men whom he had previously met, men who easily could have identified him and his despised newspaper affiliation. He also took pains to explain how in joining the militia, "his editorial plowshare, so to speak, turned into a sword, and his pruning-hook into a spear." He fully intended to honor the commitment he had made and do his soldierly duty if and when called upon. Seamlessly, he managed to fit in with his fellow recruits and felt perfectly safe among them. He made no secret of his "surprise and something stronger, at the farcially great preparation they had made to hang one poor wounded old man" and didn't think they would be surprised to learn "the terrible secret" that he was also going to write about it.[64]

For Olcott, the most terrifying incident of the whole affair was when he realized that his trunk was sitting at the Charles Town station, with his own initials emblazoned on it, alongside those locally hated words, *New York*. He knew it was "sheer impossibility" to leave it unclaimed or go to claim it himself "without imminent danger of discovery and the defeat of my mission . . . for as it came up with the Grays' reinforcements, its owner would be certainly hunted up. I considered it a matter of life and death." Olcott, like Thomson, drew on his Masonic connections, confiding in a "fine, brave young fellow of the Staff, a perfect gentleman" who went to the courthouse for him to claim the trunk.[65]

After the hanging, it was out of the question for Olcott to run the risk of filing his report from the city. Two seemingly eyewitness accounts appear in the *Tribune* of December 5, one datelined Baltimore and the other Harper's Ferry. Subsequent scholarship indicates at least one of them was cobbled together in the New York office.[66] Neither report alludes in any way to how the correspondent or correspondents managed to get so choice a vantage point.

Of the dispatches these four men wrote, only Thomson's explained in detail as part of his reportage not only why he had resorted to subterfuge to get the story but precisely what his subterfuge was. Thomson also was the only one among them to be safely back in New York before his story ran. The others all waited for their postwar memoirs to reveal the methods they had used and their reasons for them. Olcott, in fact, waited a full fourteen years after the John Brown hanging to tell his story for publication.

In the explanations, none of these reporters seemed particularly concerned with the moral ambiguity of his actions, or how his deception might reflect on his personal truthfulness, the integrity of his publication, or the larger question of the standing in the democratic process of the fourth estate. Only the sour-grapes attacks from the South made any note at all of these larger questions. To these Northern reporters writing from the South, the urgent, undisputed given was the need to report on what was happening as it was happening. They also were unapologetic about what it took to preserve their personal safety and have access to as much reliable information as possible—"unvarnished" in this era seems always to have been the preferred adjective—in a situation where the information mattered absolutely to their readers and could not have been gotten by other means. They provide no further self-justification or reflection on the matter, even in the extended memoirs three of them wrote long after the immediate dangers had passed. What comes through in the omission is a presumption that the work's intrinsic value trumped any and all other considerations. Perhaps as importantly, for their personal legacies, for the journalist as actor on a national stage, for the value of the journalism they were able to produce, and for the journalistic form they pioneered, their skillful masquerades and the dangers they so cleverly avoided gave sinew and staying power to the riveting true tales they told. A full century and a half later, these stories retain their narrative punch.

# THREE

# VIRTUAL ENSLAVEMENT

The worldwide shortage of raw cotton provoked by the Civil War meant opportunity for planters in other tropical and subtropical regions, who began hiring foreign laborers on contracts of indenture to help meet rising production demands. As copra and sugar replaced cotton and the plantations' economies expanded even more, the search for workers moved further afield. Before World War I, nearly a million Pacific Islanders and half a million Asians had been hired under these arrangements to work on plantations in the Pacific; another 4,500 Pacific Islanders had signed contracts for other destinations, including 1,100 islanders in the early 1890s who were bound for Mexico and Guatemala.[1]

In a practice derisively known as "blackbirding," a flotilla of vessels scoured the Melanesian islands in search of recruits. Disturbing tales abounded of ocean-borne high jinks, kidnappings, and shootings. Despite the criticism of resident missionaries and the investigations of naval captains, verifiable information about the practice was difficult to obtain. Blackbirding functioned within three nearly impenetrable universes: ships out on the high seas, the islands their captains plied, and privately owned plantations from Queensland to Tahiti to Latin America. True or false, and the trade winds of historical theory have blown all directions, in the popular imagination, indenture became and remained slavery's just-as-evil twin.[2]

Still, fresh recruits kept signing on. Decade after decade there was outrage over the inhumanity the practice appeared to condone. *Did* the islanders have agency, as scholars would ask a century later, meaning did the workers subject themselves willingly and with full understanding to the punishing contracts they signed? Did they leave home to escape ruinous drought and famine, as was sometimes reported? Were the blackbird captains and their local enablers simply marrying the needs of islanders for work and income to the needs of planters, providing a necessary connection, as they claimed? Or did they connive to coax, dupe, inveigle, coerce, or snatch "the natives" into indentured arrangements? Periodic British inspection reports did little to convince a wary public, ever suspecting the worst. Ferreting out how the system of black-birding really functioned and explaining it to readers was work for reporters. With the right access, they could best provide an "unvarnished" insider's look at a recruitment voyage from start to finish. Obtaining that access without allowing their presence to change the usual dynamics was key. At least three reporters did it: two aboard ships sailing out of Queensland, Australia, and one out of San Francisco.

George Morrison was a twenty-year-old Australian medical student looking for an adventurous diversion after failing his intermediate exam (for "recommending an excessive dose of medicament as a cure for syphilis"[3]). He used the found time to self-style an assignment to see how the labor trade of Queensland worked. This was in 1882, a good six years before Nellie Bly's detective antics launched the era of stunt journalism in the United

States. Morrison signed on to sail as an ordinary seaman aboard the *Lavinia*. The ship's captain quickly deputized him to help the ship's doctor, too, giving him yet another lens for his clandestine investigations.

The brigantine left north Queensland the last day of May, carting eighty-eight laborers[4] back to their island homes in the New Hebrides and Banks. Three months later, the first week of September, the ship returned to Queensland with a new batch of recruits. By the end of October, Morrison's eight-part travelogue began appearing in the *Leader,* the weekly magazine-style companion publication to the newspaper, the *Age.*

Despite the blunt header, THE CONTRIBUTOR: A CRUISE IN A QUEENSLAND SLAVER. BY A MEDICAL STUDENT, Morrison's articles expressed only the mildest criticism of all that he had witnessed. Wide-eyed wonder was the tone of the piece.[5] Yet half a year later, as Queensland began taking steps to annex New Guinea, Morrison took up the subject of blackbirding once again. He was back from other daring adventures, and his reputation as a journalist— medical school was on hold—had built steadily in the intervening months.[6] With no explanation for his about-face, Morrison revised his original assessment, this time sharply denouncing "the Queensland slave trade" in a letter to the *Age.* ("I do not use this word in any claptrap sense. It is the way we always speak of the trade on board the schooners engaged in the trade itself."[7])

In plainspoken, credible detail, he described the trickery involved in getting islanders to sign contracts, the air of intimidation created by the brandishing of rifles, and the shooting at islanders who jumped ship to escape. He detailed the complicity of government officials in some of the most questionable aspects of the trade, including certification of good health before voyage. Morrison said the *Lavinia*'s health inspector, for example, was also one of its owners. He described "the fearful death rate" once islanders got to the plantations, and the mercilessly degrading treatment of women, even those with the putative protection of their own husbands on board. The ships he called veritable brothels. "Not even a depraved sailor, and there are more than one or two in this trade, will have anything to do with a woman returning from Queensland," Morrison wrote. He also provided the editors privately with information that "may lead to the disproof or verification of every statement contained in this letter."[8]

The *Age* followed up with a long and forceful editorial the next day, describing Morrison as a "practical man, inclined to take the world as he finds it, and only interposing with his exhaustive knowledge when he finds facts unwholesomely misstated." It ended with a blistering, more sweeping admonition: for Australia to condone blackbirding, "the curse of forced labor," would be to imperil the country's very future.[9] The editors published more editorials and letters, both supportive and dubious of Morrison's account.[10] In days, the government initiated a full-scale inquiry. By February 1884, Queensland's premier, Sir Samuel Griffith, released the results of his investigation, not only dismissing Morrison's assertions but impugning his ability to make them. Griffith called him "a very young man who does not bear a high reputation and whose narratives need to be received with much caution."[11] Morrison lashed back, threatening to take his findings to Britain. Were Griffith not protected by parliamentary privilege, he wrote, he would sue the premier for libel.[12] But then Queensland's governor, Sir Anthony Musgrave, reviewed the case and threw his support squarely to young Morrison's account.[13]

By March 1884, Britain's Western Pacific Commission issued its report on the Pacific labor trade, condemning the system. Published accounts said the report called for an increase in the naval force and number of deputy commissioners assigned to oversee the activity. It also recommended an end to the connection between the high commissioner of the Pacific and the governor of Fiji, where islanders were working, and called for the commissioner's relocation to New Guinea.[14]

With his slave trade exposé, and the *Age*'s follow-up, Morrison had provided an insider view of blackbirding that engaged the public and led to a powerful government response. It also propelled him toward an illustrious career in journalism. His work over the next thirty-five years took him across the world, most notably as the Peking correspondent of the *Times* of London from 1897 to 1912 and then as an adviser to the president of the new Republic of China until his death in 1920.[15]

Nearly a decade after Morrison's adventure on the *Lavinia,* blackbirding, still darkly under cloud, came inauspiciously to American shores. The American brig, the *Tahiti,* left for the South Seas from San Francisco harbor in summer 1891 in search of sugarcane workers for the western coast of Mexico. Some four hundred Gilbert Islanders signed contracts and boarded the vessel, bound for San Benito. But in early September, severe storm damage forced an unscheduled repair stop some fifty miles north of San Francisco at Drake's Bay.[16] Blackbirding's dreadful reputation and the *Tahiti*'s hold full of black human cargo generated a spate of local and national newspaper coverage. The ship's arrival raised disturbing questions about the reimportation to American shores of practices a major civil war had been fought so bitterly to stop.

The first stories described the islanders aboard as "thought to be slaves,"[17] "contract slaves,"[18] or "practically slaves."[19] From Drake's Bay, the ship's captain, W. H. Ferguson, insisted to reporters that absolutely nothing questionable was afoot. In Brookyln,

Edward Leavitt, the brother of the rig's majority owner, the New York attorney Humphrey Leavitt, repeated the same assurance to a reporter for the *New York Tribune*. Captain Ferguson, speaking to reporters at Drake's Bay, further reported that "the natives behaved well, except on one occasion, when several women quarreled over love affairs and slashed each other badly with knives."[20] Both he and Leavitt's brother confirmed that the islanders aboard had signed legitimate contracts and that the Mexican government had assured their passage home at contract's end.

But the *Tribune*'s San Francisco–datelined story included further information gleaned from other, unnamed sources, doubting how willingly the islanders had come aboard ship.[21] IS IT A CARGO OF SLAVES? That was the front-page headline on September 8 over a story about the *Tahiti*'s docking. There was no way to know authoritatively. On September 9, in a second-day headline on page seven, came a row-back: THE *TAHITI*'S PASSENGERS NOT SLAVES. The story went on to say that three hundred of them had sailed on the *Tahiti* with three-year contracts at eight dollars a month and a guarantee of return. "As they were nearly starving at home owing to the protracted drouth [*sic*]," the story said, "they thought the contract was a good one."[22]

Three months passed between the repair stop at Drake's Bay—when "all of the horrors of the slave traffic on the African Coast were recreated"—and the tragic discovery of the *Tahiti* "bottom up, with her rudder gone and her ballast shifted,"[23] eleven miles southwest of Lizard Point. The ship capsized on October 10 but lay undiscovered until the end of November 1891. At the time, all the islanders were believed to have perished, along with Leavitt and the captain—not Ferguson, though; he had turned the ship over to Captain C. Erickson at Drake's Bay, giving as the reason for not completing the voyage an illness in his family. From San

Francisco, the *Tribune* correspondent reported on November 30 that no one was believed to have survived. The report went on to say that because the vessel's papers were in order, all efforts to stop the human shipment at San Francisco had failed.

Eight months later, reports reaching San Francisco told of two survivors, a "Russian Finn" and a Gilbert Islander; both had been among a small group of passengers who managed to escape the capsized ship in a tiny boat. The Mexican traveler who told the story, identified in newspaper articles as Leon Nartel, said he actually had met the two survivors four months earlier and heard their jaw-dropping story firsthand: one woman aboard the little craft had died of hunger and thirst, he recounted, and the others subsisted on her body for a time to stay alive; two others went mad from drinking sea water and jumped to their deaths before the boat drifted toward the Mexican coast to a fisherman's rescue.[24]

Memory of the tragedy aboard the *Tahiti* was still fresh when two reporters half a world apart went undercover once again to investigate blackbirding by stunt. Within two months of each other, W. H. Brommage undertook the perilous assignment as a young man's adventure, an account of which William Randolph Hearst's gutsy young *San Francisco Examiner* published on his return. J. D. Melvin set out with a secret mandate from the editors of Australia's conservative newspaper, the *Argus.*

Brommage was an Englishman with a seafaring background who had been working as a telephone company clerk in San Francisco before the voyage of the *Montserrat,*[25] which left San Francisco Harbor April 23 bound first for the British Columbian port of Nanaimo, where it picked up a huge shipment of coal both for its own use and for sale at sea. The detour was a means of camouflaging the journey's real purpose, at least according to Brommage's account. The ship then headed out to the Gilbert Islands to recruit sugarcane workers for the plantations of Guatemala. Brommage was soon promoted from common sailor to quartermaster, giving him an even more intimate view of all that happened during the nearly six months at sea, which he surreptitiously recorded in a little notebook.

Melvin, a Scot living in Australia, shipped out as supercargo two months later for the *Helena*'s voyage from Queensland to the Solomon Islands and back again.[26] The ship left Bundaberg on the Burnett River July 30, carrying with it sixty workers back to the Solomons after completion of their contracts. It returned three and a half months later with ninety fresh recruits for Queensland on November 18, 1892. The *Montserrat* left San Francisco April 23 with just the crew and a few passengers, including an island king and his circle of aides. It returned to San Francisco on October 14 after leaving the nearly four hundred Gilbert Islanders it had recruited on plantations in Guatemala.[27]

Both newspapers published lengthy promotional prologues to the first reports, taking pains to explain how the stories had been reported and the reasons for perpetrating the ruses and assuming the risks. As the *Argus* explained, issues of far-reaching consequence were at stake. The Queensland labor question mattered to the whole of Australasia and perhaps beyond "since the subject has been discussed by Imperial statesmen, and will continue to be a topic on which the Imperial Parliament will have a deep interest."[28]

The *Argus,* especially, went to lengths to attest to the significance of the undertaking and the honorable standing of its reporter. It ran Melvin's account in fourteen installments over two and a half weeks, describing the writer as "a capable, experienced, and trusted journalist, who has been very successful in many important ventures requiring tact, discrimination, and perseverance."[29] In fact, Melvin had worked for the paper since the late 1870s. He was known for his scoop during a hotel siege and for finding a way to board the *Iberia* (exactly how was not clear—by bribery or by posing as a crewman) to accompany colonial troops to Sudan in 1885. He was instructed specifically to watch the recruiting process closely, to pay attention to whether or what questionable tactics were used to induce the laborers into accepting service, to see how the recruits were treated aboard ship, and, "above all, he was to be fearless and impartial in his reports," so that he could provide "an irreproachable record."[30] He assumed the guise of a man down on his luck who wanted shipboard work for a few months as he waited for money to arrive from friends in Scotland. "His incognito was complete," the newspaper reported, "and not one person on board the *Helena* knew that he was a journalist engaged on a secret mission."[31]

In his last installment, Melvin offered this conclusion: that all the safeguards the government had put in place since Morrison's day—at least on the *Helena* in summer and fall 1892—were working just fine, and that the islanders "all embraced the opportunity of going to service in Queensland as something highly desirable. No kidnapping, force, fraud, misrepresentation, or cajoling was resorted to."[32]

Brommage in the *Examiner* offered up a far less boring read. His account appeared over two days, October 15 and 16, 1892, emblazoned across the front and second page of the newspaper with numerous illustrations, engraved from his "kodaks." A sensational, cascading twenty-six-line headline blared A SALE OF SOULS and captured much of what was to come in the fourteen thousand words that followed.[33]

An italicized prologue provided context. It explained how the tramp steamer *Montserrat* had sailed for the South Seas from San Francisco on April 23 on an ostensible trading voyage "but in reality, as was suspected at the time, to go on a slave-trading expedition ... to make laboring contracts with the simple people of the islands to work on the plantations of the fever-stricken west coast of Guatemala for five years." Although the contracts were legitimate, they obliged the islanders to work for little or no pay under a burning tropical sun, to "live like dogs and die like sheep in the cane-covered marshes" of a strange country whose language they did not speak. Ships engaged in blackbirding, the *Chronicle* said, "are no less slavers than those swift barks that in other days sailed from the west coast of Africa to the southern shores of America."[34]

The opening paragraph was a simple, declarative sentence: "The steamer *Montserrat* is a slave ship." The account did not miss a trope. There was an evil ship captain (Ferguson of the *Tahiti,* no less), a lecherous pirate, complicit island kings, missionaries and traders, women in terrifying distress, and children manipulated into service. The British who staged surprise inspection visits, buying coal for their own brig's voyage, found everything in good order. Islanders were allowed only a subsistence amount of freshwater during the long voyage, which they sucked from a skinny tube inserted into a water barrel. For enough water to wash, they had to transfer mouthfuls one after the other from the barrel to a bucket, only to see the bucket kicked over before they could use the water. There was "Black Tom," a heroic figure in Brommage's story, a former American slave who moved from island to island in the Gilberts, carrying warning tales of the drownings aboard the *Tahiti*. Brommage's long and up-close observation of the Gilbert Islanders as they lived aboard ship even gave rise to a plausible theory he ventured about how their carelessness might have caused the

*Tahiti* to sink.[35] The report concluded with Brommage's detailed account of a torturous seventy-mile trek overland to one of the Guatemalan plantations.[36]

The *Examiner,* to its credit, also ran as a sidebar a lengthy rejoinder from Ferguson, who answered much of the criticism implicit in the Brommage report. Ferguson reminded the reporter that British officials from the *Royalist* boarded the ship four different times for inspection, brought with them their own interpreter, and "questioned the islanders closely, and in all cases were informed that they were leaving home of their own free will."[37] Ferguson also disputed an account in the main story about his threats to kill Black Tom, saying that the reporter had romanticized the former slave and that he was "not the big, desperate fellow he is described to be, but a sickly harmless creature with one of his hands cut off."[38]

Ferguson argued that conditions on his ship were among the best in the sea, that no children under the age of twelve were on the voyage, and that all of those under fifteen had parental consent. He said the facsimile of a labor contract that the *Examiner* published as an illustration actually was a child's three-dollar contract and that adult male laborers received seven dollars a month and females, six. "They get this money without a deduction of any kind being made for food, clothing, medicine or education for their children," he added, "and at the end of three years, they are returned to the place they came from, better off than they ever were."[39]

Ferguson did not comment on Brommage's eyewitnessed account of how the captain and his agent, Peter Garrick, had responded to the king of Marakei's questions about the fate of the *Tahiti* passengers. The king took Ferguson at his word when he denied Black Tom's tragic version. Ferguson told the king that the ship indeed capsized, but that a passing vessel brought news of the accident to San Francisco, from where a man-of-war had been sent to rescue all the islanders.

"Are you telling me the truth?" Brommage quoted the king as having asked.

"Why, yes," Ferguson replied, "Why should I lie to you? Why should I be here if everyone was drowned? I cannot swim, while your people can live in the water."[40]

The king gave Ferguson permission to recruit among his people once again.[41]

What seems clear from the distinctly different reports of Morrison, Melvin, and Brommage is how much circumstances appear to have varied from ship to ship, captain to captain, crew to crew, island to island, plantation to plantation, and—by no means least—from publication to publication. Clearly, the more eyes engaged in getting "unvarnished" firsthand information, the more stories that appeared, the more accurate the cumulative portrait of the trade. Whatever the biases of the publications, all three reporters were careful not to generalize about the state of blackbirding beyond their own experiences with specific captains aboard specific ships. They stuck to what they said they witnessed. All three newspapers also took pains to publish alternative points of view—not only from those who came off badly in the original reports, such as Ferguson, but also from government officials and knowledgeable readers who responded to the articles in letters to the editors.

In each case, this was the journalism of sustained participatory observation during which the real intent of the reporters was not revealed while they were shipboard. Their editors in each case took special pains to tout the personal reliability of these envoys and explain the subterfuge in detail. The firsthand reporting gave the stories powerful credence. What the reader needed was to be able to trust equally that neither the reporter nor the publication had distorted the account. The newspapers went to lengths to provide those assurances, too.

Surprise British man-of-war inspection visits of a few days duration, conducted by a captain sympathetic to the islanders' plight, certainly served a purpose. But they could never provide anything similar to what the reporters were able to learn undercover, by staying aboard ship from port to port, observing day in and day out under conditions of such confinement over so many months. The possibility of such inspection visits did, in and of themselves, create some controls and deterrents to blackbirding misdeeds, and they were reported at least in brief summary form in the press. But how much more effective would be the prospect, the ever-present, candid camera-like possibility of a sleuthing journalist whose work could be splashed over many pages for many days and who just might be on shipboard unannounced.

For these journalists, as it was for the Civil War–era writers of a generation earlier, deception allowed a level of exploration into hidden worlds that simply could not have happened otherwise. The stories they then could tell, in narrative form with anecdotes and examples, clearly engaged the general public on all sides of the issue, as evident from the published outpouring in the days that followed, and, at least in Morrison's case, they brought a government response.

The reporters and their publications were unapologetic about having assumed a pose to do their real work and also emphasized that they engaged fully in their cover jobs as sailors, duties they also contracted to perform. Undercover reporters invariably share how faithful they were to the tasks they take on as part of their real assignments. Yet they also manage to maintain observational distance. As detached but deeply engaged observers, they take care never to lose sight of their animating purpose.

The adopted personas in all these cases allowed the journalists to maintain their reportorial posture, even as they immersed themselves in gathering information and cultivating sources. Proximity and vantage point meant everything. Their various poses got them as close to the action as it was possible for white men to get. Behind their respective guises, they observed at extremely close range and reported what they witnessed. What they could not do was "live" the life of those whose plight they sought to describe. Developing those techniques would fall to their undercover successors in the exploration of other subjects in the years ahead.

# FOUR

## PREDATORS

Some of the most daring and effective of the known undercover investigations into the murky world of human trafficking have been the work of journalists abroad, starting with the textbook-perfect execution and impact of W.T. Stead's child prostitution exposé for London's *Pall Mall Gazette*. Stead's 1885 series about preying on the young[1] had everything, right down to the affirmation by government panel of the newspaper's salacious and horrifying findings. He even had the help of the Salvation Army's reformed prostitutes and procurers who returned to their former haunts to help gather and verify the information. Later, he would go to enormous lengths publicly to exonerate the charity. Docilely, he accepted a three-month jail term on an abduction conviction. As part of the investigative process, to verify how the system worked, Stead had been complicit in buying a child from her mother at the going rate of five pounds sterling. The newspaper then arranged to have the child whisked to safety abroad instead of to the brothel to which her mother agreed to send her.[2]

For weeks, newspapers the world over followed and reprinted the *Gazette*'s revelations of entrapment and abduction, and the outright sale of children. The newspaper tracked the defilement of virgins, and the violence against the helpless young women who fell into these clutches. Stead was careful to position the exposé not as a moral outrage, but solely as the exposure of a crime. Waves of international embarrassment followed swiftly for Britain, inducing Parliament to implement the Criminal Law Amendment Act and thus raise the age of sexual consent from thirteen to sixteen.

Stead's approach was utterly thorough.[3] He consulted evidence collected by a committee of the House of Lords three years earlier with the resolve to update it, and he spent four weeks, helped by two aides "alternately in brothels and hospitals, in the streets and in refuges, in the company of procuresses and of bishops."[4]

He gave no names or addresses, emphasizing that his purpose was "not to secure the punishment of criminals but to lay bare the working of a great organization of crime."[5] To ratify the integrity of the operation, he gave that information in all its particulars ahead of time to two archbishops, members of parliament, charitable organizations, earls, and a public criminal investigator. He brought "the most experienced officers" into his confidence and interviewed them all for background and a deeper understanding before setting out. Throughout the operation, his team steered clear of the police, who might have tipped off the brothel keepers. He interviewed victims and near victims. The reporting was unassailable and the impact just as large.[6]

As for the girls, Stead pointedly positioned his prostitutes as "innocent victims" forced into a life of sin and described what they endured in sensational enough detail to be considered obscene, triggering legal action.[7]

A July 16, 1885 editorial in the *Independent* is perfectly on point as to the motive, impact, profit, and the significance of Stead's investigation: that "vice and crime cannot be effectively dealt with in secret," and in cases such as this one where needed legislation was likely to fail, "something is required to arouse the public and secure such an expression of sentiment as law-makers and law-breakers must regard." "However distasteful and distressing it may be," it went on, "the pure" must be confronted with "human misery and wretchedness."[8]

Stead's work has been credited not only with generating major reform movements in England and the United States, the eventual repeal of the Contagious Disease Act, and reform in the age of consent laws, but also "the articulation of late-nineteenth century feminism."[9]

No doubt the newspaper benefitted financially from the series. Circulation was up again, but more significantly, the *Independent* asserted, "no journal is more quoted or more sought after in London than *The Pall Mall Gazette*."[10] The result, it concluded, "is quite consistent with a good motive."[11]

Sexual slavery since then has endured as a topic for undercover reporting, yet even for U.S.-based reporters, the settings also tend to be foreign.[12] Such projects often involve the collaboration of recognized human rights organizations, law enforcement agencies, or both.[13] In 2005, Peter Van Sant and a CBS crew from the network newsmagazine *48 Hours* went undercover in Bucharest to infiltrate a sex trafficking ring. The crew purchased a girl they identified as Nicoleta and then transported her to a shelter for trafficking victims. In the second half of the report, Van Sant returned to the United States to illuminate the prevalence of the human sex trade across the Mexican border into California. In this case, the reporting focused on the mother of a young girl sold into slavery in Mexico by a "well-known family of slave traders"[14] and then brought to work in the New York City borough of Queens, where she eventually escaped and then helped in the criminal investigation of her abductors.[15]

Van Sant's reporting was unusual in that it attempted to establish a link between international sex trafficking and the United States. His undercover techniques mirrored not only Stead's from the late nineteenth century but also those of contemporaries who have covered similar ground.

Of those involving partnerships with human rights organizations, ABC News, in March 1998, broadcast a report of its undercover investigation into sex trafficking in Israel, helped by Global Survival Network, which produced undercover videos that documented the sale of Russian women to Israeli pimps in Tel Aviv. ABC paired the footage with reporter Cynthia McFadden's interviews with an official from the Israeli Ministry of the Interior and an Israeli trafficker, who described the details of the girls' captivity. After the official expressed shock that this was happening, the human rights lawyer from Global Survival Network who obtained the footage cut in to explain that government complicity is essential to the operation of such prostitution networks. To bring off the ruse, the lawyer and her colleagues feigned interest in buying women through a dummy corporation they had formed for this purpose.

At the end of the broadcast, Diane Sawyer announced that Jacob Golan, the trafficker, had for the first time been arrested for running a brothel, but spent only a day in jail before the charges against him were dropped.[16]

Ric Esther Bienstock led the most dramatic of the more recent investigations of this kind. She and a documentary film crew infiltrated the sex trafficking trade between the Ukraine and Turkey. "Sex Slaves," their harrowing documentary for PBS's *Frontline,* aired in 2006.[17]

Bienstock's reportorial approach, again, like Stead's, was to infiltrate the trafficking source to uncover its mechanisms. Because Bienstock was a woman who did not speak Russian, her role in this process was mostly vicarious but still possible, thanks to the technological assist of the hidden camera. In addition to standard documentary fare, including personal testimonials from girls traded into prostitution who have since escaped, the cameras allowed Bienstock and her crew to track traffickers as they procured and sold women.

In one segment, Felix Golubev, Bienstock's Russian-speaking producer, posed as a buyer with a camera hidden in his shirt and managed to get an inside look at how the system functioned. He encountered a trafficker called Nina who told him she received up to six hundred dollars per girl. She encouraged Golubev to hold the passports of the girls he bought to keep them from running off once they arrived in Turkey and grasped the extent of their peril. Later, a man named Vlad, the trafficker who sold his friend's pregnant wife to a Turkish pimp, explained the system of "debt bondage" to which the women would be subjected—forced to pay off an initial fine that would be inflated continuously with "fees" that made their indentured servitude almost endless. If she ever managed to clear her debt, her pimp could "then simply sell her to someone else."

In another segment, the crew's hidden camera followed a trafficker identified as Olga as she made her way through Turkish customs and into Istanbul's Russian district, where, in the apparent presence of Turkish police officers, she brazenly traded the women she had led into the country. Meanwhile, Katerina and Anya, two of Olga's previous victims, narrated how Olga had tricked them in the same way, promising the women work in a shop and then trading them to a couple of men she said were the owners of a café and who would take them to their new apartment in Turkey. "We guessed that she was selling us," Katerina said, "but we hoped we were wrong. We hoped that we had misunderstood things."

At the end of the program, the narrator explained that Tania, a girl from the Chernobyl area who had been traded into a prostitution ring in Turkey, had decided to go back to Turkey. Noting that she supported her family members financially, the program mentioned a brother with chronic abdominal problems who died a month after the filming.[18]

In a discussion section of *Frontline*'s online development of the story, a viewer angrily chastised the producers for not helping the boy, "whom if I remembered correctly, could have been treated and perhaps saved with a six hundred dollar procedure." The producers responded by explaining that they did in fact pay for Tania's brother's procedure, though it was unsuccessful, but that Tania's return to prostitution was motivated by other factors as well.[19]

Undercover reporting also figured prominently in the first sports program ever to win a coveted duPont–Columbia Award in 2006,[20] after receiving a sports Emmy in 2005. It was a production of the HBO series *Real Sports with Bryant Gumbel* about camel racing in the United Arab Emirates, reported by Bernard Goldberg. "The Sport of Sheikhs"[21] first aired in October 2004.

This was a case where the field producer, David Higgs, resorted to equipping himself with hidden cameras after police and local authorities resisted his efforts to report the story openly. What Higgs was able to document on camera backed up Goldberg's interview with Ansar Burney, a human rights worker who told him that a United Arab Emirates (UAE) ban on the use of jockeys under fifteen years of age or under one hundred pounds remained largely ineffectual. Burney charged that most of the young camel jockeys had been forced into a form of enslavement to their trainers, having been bought or kidnapped from their homes in Bangladesh, Pakistan, and elsewhere. Some of these boys were barely old enough to speak, and most seemed unable to remember their families or where they had come from. The report showed that they had been starved to keep their weight down and that they trained under grueling conditions, forced to serve physically and often sexually abusive masters. Higgs's hidden camera footage showed tiny boys who lifted their shirts to display bodies covered in bruises. They spoke of rape and abuse at the hands of violent masters. The living conditions were shockingly poor. Some slept outdoors on bare sand. Goldberg then implicated the UAE's prime minister for involvement in the illegal trade. On camera, he also confronted a U.S. State Department official, John Miller, asking why the United States had declared the UAE a "model for the region in excellent protection of children from camel jockey work" in 2004, given the footage the HBO team had collected. Miller's unsatisfying explanation was a lack of State Department manpower to uncover all the world's offenses, at which point Goldberg suggested, and Miller denied, that the more likely reason was the critically important relationship of the UAE as a U.S. ally in the Middle East.[22]

This is as good a point as any to note the remarkable undercover work on other topics of journalists based in countries other than the United States. In the English-language media, Britain tops the list of proponents. Prominent are the names of Donal MacIntyre (admired but also sometimes accused of being the "master of the bleedin' obvious"[23]); Roger Cook of ITV's *The Cook Report;* and Mark Daly (who famously went undercover as a Manchester policeman to expose racism in the ranks). Australia, New Zealand, India, Canada, and South Africa all have produced exemplars as well as media critics, who, like those in the United States, never hesitate to call out lapses and excesses when they happen. What is offered in the following few paragraphs is at best short shrift.

A few undercover reporters are known to U.S. readers via translation of their articles and books, starting first and foremost with Germany's Günter Wallraff,[24] who sees the journalism of disguise and role-playing as "a powerful instrument of agitation."[25] He has spent a career exposing not only Germany's social and political ills but also those of such countries as Greece and Portugal. Best remembered of his exploits are his pose as Ali, the Turkish guest worker, "the lowest of the low" who is "hired and fired, sat upon and spat upon, used and abused, vilified, reified and thrown on a heap (in Turkey, preferably) when he is done with,"[26] and as an editor at *Bild-Zeitung,* his investigation of "gutter-press journalism."[27] As one scholar put it, Wallraff's forte is to use deception to uncover deception in making the case for open government, and by revealing the condition of the lowliest worker, to reveal the state of the nation.[28]

Abbie Hoffman called Wallraff's work "journalism as guerrilla theater," and Wallraff himself "the reporter as life-actor," someone who puts things "in a different focus"[29] whenever he gets on stage. Hoffman's profile in *Mother Jones* in 1979 also recounted Wallraff's most stunning escapades to date, as well as his imbroglios, the accusations against him, the censorship attempts (later there would be plagiarism charges to defend against, too), and the various court challenges he has faced from government and industry.[30]

Fabrizio Gatti and Roberto Saviano are two Italian standouts. Gatti has repeatedly gone undercover to reveal shocking situations, including a wrenching account of rampant de facto slave labor on a number of tomato farms in Puglia, which won the 2006 Journalist Award of the European Union.[31] Saviano, who investigated Naples-based organized crime for his book *Gomorrah,* won the 2006 Viareggio Literary Prize, among other honors.[32] From Spain, Antonio Salas, a pseudonym, spent five years infiltrating "the shadowy, interconnected world of international terrorism"[33] as Muhammad Abdallah, a Spanish-Venezuelan with Palestinian grandparents who, in efforts to remain convincing in a hammam bathhouse, went so far as to have himself circumcised.

One of Ghana's boldest journalists, Anas Aremeyaw Anas, has also risen to the international fore. He has gone undercover in a mental hospital, a brothel, and a hotel, where, "on the trail of Chinese sex traffickers, he donned a tuxedo and delivered room service at a swanky hotel that the pimp frequented with his prostitutes."[34] In June 2008, the U.S. State Department acknowledged his positive role in its report on human trafficking,[35] and the Ghana Journalists Association named him Journalist of the Year for 2006.[36] He has also received the Kurt Schork Award from the Institute for War and Peace Reporting[37] and the Every Human Has Rights Media Award.[38] His reporting has resulted in arrests and convictions and earned him a shout-out from U.S. President Barack Obama on his visit to Ghana in July 2009.[39]

Bringing him to international attention was his January 2008 undercover investigation for Ghana's *Crusading Guide* (now the *New Crusading Guide*) to expose the sexual exploitation of twelve to sixteen-year-old girls at a brothel in suburban Accra known as the "Soldier Bar." By taking a job as a janitor at the brothel, Anas managed to collect undercover video evidence of the sexual exploitation of little girls by paying adults.[40] The newspaper submitted Anas's video evidence to the police, who then raided the bar, arresting 239 sex workers. Among them were 60 minors. Anas reported that the ministry in charge of women's and children's affairs sent the arrested girls to safety and that during the raid, police, who did not believe he was a reporter, slapped him and then jailed him briefly along with some 200 sex clients.[41]

Anas has explained his unorthodox methods like this: "Sometimes you need the illegality in order to obtain the information. I think that it boils down to the public interest." Without elaborating, he said he thought there were "levels of illegality." Of his own response to the corruption in Ghana's political system, he said, "It's a reaction: I watched my society carefully and decided that this is how I have to work and I think it's paid off very well. I have chosen to belong to the remedy."[42]

In the United States, perhaps the most popular and notorious example of undercover reporting on the broader category of sexual predators was *Dateline* NBC's "To Catch a Predator" series. Hosted by Chris Hansen, it launched in 2004. Hansen worked with the online watchdog group Perverted Justice to lure potential online sexual predators to houses where they believed they would find underage teens they had met during online chats. Then, via hidden camera, Hansen exposed and confronted the men while police officers waited to arrest them in a coordinated sting operation. The show was a ratings hit for NBC; its first two episodes drew an average of 8.5 million viewers. Fifteen thousand people emailed *Dateline* after the third episode, which drew 11 million viewers.[43] Although the program led to a number of arrests and convictions,[44] it also raised questions and criticism, especially after an incident in November 2006. One of the show's targets, a Texas county prosecutor named Louis Conradt Jr. shot himself to death in front of police officers who had forced their way into his home as a *Dateline* camera crew waited outside.[45] In 2007, Marsha Bartel, an NBC producer for more than twenty years, sued the network for breach of contract, charging that she was laid off from the show "because she complained to her supervisors that the 'Predator' series repeatedly violated the standards of ethical journalism."[46]

Some critics questioned NBC's payments to Perverted Justice after one of its agents joined the group in the fourth episode;[47] others took issue with the program's air of entrapment[48]—what Hansen described as "enticement."[49] The show's cooperation with law enforcement also raised questions—in one instance, a police officer deputized a Perverted Justice operator.[50] There also was concern that the program exaggerated a relatively minor problem. (A National Center for Missing & Exploited Children study indicates that "more than seventy percent of sexual abuse of children is perpetrated by family members or family friends," not unknown online predators.[51]) Rival news organizations and other journalists wondered in print whether *Predator* meant to be reporting news or creating it.[52]

A local station's entry into the world of cybersex in 2003, the year before the start of the "Predator" series, already had raised similar issues. Jennifer Hersey was a twenty-six-year-old television news producer at station WFTV in Orlando, Florida, when she presented herself as a thirteen-year-old girl in an online chat room and exchanged instant messages with a man who exposed himself on a webcam and encouraged her to do the same. He turned out to be a former sheriff's deputy and a prosecutor. Media ethicists at the time took issue with Hersey's encounter as the basis for the man's arrest, the positioning of a journalist as "an active arm of law enforcement," in the words of Gary Hill, then chairman of the Society of Professional Journalists Ethics Committee and director of investigations for KSTP-Channel 3. Bob Steele, of the Poynter Institute, added, "We should not in any routine way be collaborative and cooperative with law enforcement agencies. If we are, it erodes our watchdog roles." Other ethicists consulted at the time contended—as the *Washington Post* reporters similarly contended about their handling of officials at Walter Reed—that journalists should first publish their work and then let authorities do their own investigating afterward—"unless a crime is about to be committed or someone's life is in danger."[53]

Back in 1885, the *Independent* asked its readers if Stead and his *Pall Mall Gazette* should be commended or condemned for its actions in the child prostitution exposé. It offered three tests in the form of questions, all of which are good measures, then or now. "Are the statements true? What are the organization's motives in making them? In what manner are they made?" Facts, the editorial went on, "may be so used as to do great moral injury, as when the manner of reporting crime tends to make the revolting elements attractive, and represents the criminal as hero. This is the vice—we had almost said the crime—of the daily press."[54]

# FIVE

# HARD LABOR, HARD LUCK, PART ONE

Chronology suggests a direct link from Helen Stuart Campbell's mostly forgotten reporting on the plight of the poor in the 1870s to the undercover journalism of her more celebrated successors in the decades ahead. She is an important but largely overlooked figure in the development of undercover reporting, an early model whose work more closely resembles that of the twenty-first-century reporter than the stunt girls who followed her in the 1880s and 1890s. A full decade before Nellie Bly personified newspaper stunt girl derring-do in the cause of social reform, Campbell, an economist, was buttressing with research and hard facts the affecting narratives she fashioned from firsthand encounters with slum dwellers and women at the low end of the work force.

The record is too scant to know if Campbell's volunteerism in New York's poorest neighborhoods was, from the outset, a guise she assumed for the sake of her reporting, good Christian works performed as a charitable impulse, or a salve for her own soul. We know only that her writing life began in the early 1870s with successful magazine serial fiction for children and columns on diet, cooking, and home economics. We know also that her experience at the Water Street Mission caused her to abandon the lighter subject matter. Of her efforts at the mission, we learn only that over a period of three years, she returned "again and again" to the facility in notorious Five Points to take her place "among 'the regulars.'" We do not know at what point, or even if, she let the mission director or any of her subjects know that they would become the grist for her tales of transformation. "With my own eyes," she reported, "I saw men who had come into the mission sodden with drink, turn into quiet, steady workers," even though now and then one "fell." She saw "foul homes, where dirty bundles of straw had been the only bed, gradually become clean and respectable; hard faces grow patient and gentle; oaths and foul words give place to quiet speech."[1]

We know, too, that Campbell, who was born in 1839, was of newspaper reading age when journalists started using undercover tactics to report from the South before the Civil War. And in 1871, when she was thirty-two and writing children's stories as Helen C. Weeks,[2] her married name before her divorce, Augustus St. Clair ran a sensational reportorial sting for the *New York Times* against the city's abortionists.

Whatever inspired Campbell, she capitalized on her role at the mission to enhance her reporting in an innovative way. The magazine *Sunday Afternoon* ran a series of six of her prose sketches between January and July 1879. That December, *Lippincott's* published her appeal to revamp the institutional treatment of the insane on the model of "The city of the Simple," the Belgian village of Gheel,[3] in a piece she based not on reporting undercover but on an interview with an unnamed physician who was deeply involved in asylum work.[4] *Lippincott's* then picked up the rest of her mission series and featured it from May to October 1880 under the common header "Studies in the slums."

A good sign of the attention the slum series received was its compilation in 1882 into a widely reviewed book under the title *The Problem of the Poor.* For its preface, Campbell wrote that urgings "from many quarters" convinced her to turn the magazine pieces into a book. "Our poor are fast becoming our criminal class," she wrote, "and more and more it is apparent that something beyond preaching is required to bring order out of the chaos which threatens us."[5]

From these intimate encounters with the private miseries of the derelict and disadvantaged, she then fashioned a novel[6] that seemed not to venture all that far from fact.[7]

The one-two punch of *The Problem of the Poor* and *Mrs. Herndon's Income* established Campbell's authority as a go-to periodical writer on poverty and launched her eventual career as an economist.[8] In keeping with the times, she helped energize a focus on firsthand reporting for newspapers and magazine on issues of social reform. The *New York Tribune,* in fact, then commissioned Campbell to turn her attention to the appalling situation of women working in the needle trades and department stores. Those twenty-one stories, titled PRISONERS OF POVERTY, ran with great fanfare—editorials, impassioned letters to the editor, national exposure through the newspaper exchanges—throughout fall 1886 into spring 1887. The reporting also got major attention from reviewers when it came out in book form,[9] although the *Tribune* publicly dismissed many of her proposals as impractical.[10] Campbell did a similar exercise focused on women wage workers in London and Paris, which appeared in 1889. *Prisoners of Poverty Abroad* moved William Dean Howells to remark in *Harper's:*[11]

> When one reads of the Lancashire factories and little children laboring for sixteen hours a day, inhaling at every breath a quantity

of cotton fuzz, falling asleep over their wheels, and roused again by the lash of thongs over their backs or the slap of "billy-rollers" over their little crowns; and then again of Irish Whitefeet, driven out of their potato patches and mud-hovels, and obliged to take the hill side as broken men—one pauses, with a kind of amazed horror, to ask if this be earth, the place of hope, or Tophet, where hope never comes.[12]

The *Tribune*'s prologue to the series emphasized Campbell's exceptional reporting and her willingness to present the facts she gathered without embellishment, stressing how she had familiarized herself not only with the poor and their suffering but also with the many charitable organizations working on their behalf. The newspaper estimated that there were some two hundred thousand women working at jobs in New York alone, with seven dollars a week their highest average earnings. Campbell said her intention was to tell the whole truth, even if it meant discrediting "heartless and dishonest and brutal employers of female labor, who grind the last copper out of their helpless workers and even in some cases plot and plan to cheat them out of a few cents."[13]

When the book came out, Campbell added a note of her own, explaining that her sketches were "a photograph from life; and the various characters, whether employers or employed, were all registered in case corroboration were needed." Her only purpose, she said, was not to offer solutions but to "render definition more possible, the questions that perplex even the most conservative can have no solution for this generation or for any generation to come."[14]

The response to both the series and the book was enormous. Ida Tarbell noted presciently in the *Chautauquan* in 1887 that Campbell's "thrilling pictures of the life of the poor of New York City is a type of work which sooner or later the press must espouse."[15] "It is the duty of one-half of the world to find out how the other half is living," Tarbell went on, "and no means can be more effective and far-reaching than that which Mrs. Campbell is using."[16]

Tarbell may have admired the undercover approach but did not use it in her own very straightforward investigation of Standard Oil.[17] Dozens of other women did go undercover, however, adding their own variations and embellishments to the way they executed these assignments. Men did, too. In fact, consciously or not, Campbell channeled the male pre– and post–Civil War reporters who had so skillfully forged undercover techniques to find answers. Their approach was to assume the most convincing poses they could bring off for the situations they were attempting to investigate—as tourist, slave auction buyer, Southern newspaperman, casual traveler, regiment guardsman, sailor. All of them no doubt got closer to their subjects than they likely could have had they announced their real intentions, pencil and notebook in hand. Indeed, sometimes they got perilously close, giving their stories the elements of danger, bravery, excitement, and intrigue. The lady mission worker among the down-and-out in the city's worst slum suggests the same. It is no accident that the word *photograph* so often characterizes reporting done undercover for its capture of the skillful minuet these reporters performed as clandestine observers locked in step with the unknowingly observed.

Their example from the late 1850s onward legitimated the practice. Published explanations of undercover reporting in that earlier period never fixate on the ethics of the method; its efficacy was presumed. Over and over again, we see that what mattered at the point of publication, if it mattered at all—and in Campbell's case it did not—was to explain the reporter's actions for the sake of heightening interest in the work, but without any apparent need to justify the approach on ethical grounds. The point of the explanation was to establish and vouch for the integrity of the reporter, the veracity of the publication, and the truth of the words.[18]

It fell to those who followed in the late 1880s and 1890s to help the method evolve. It was the Age of Reform, after all, an ideal setting for undercover reporting to flourish. Sensation already was a byword. Onto the dance floor came growing numbers of ambitious, daring young reporters who choreographed jaw-dropping new moves. They sought to understand their subject by becoming them, at least for a time, assuming roles as the downtrodden, the exploited, the oppressed, and underserved. The observer endeavored to become the observed, and then to report from the standpoint of contrived but still actual personal experience. Future generations of undercover reporters refined this approach even more.

Using guises of various sorts, reporters had the same multipronged objective: to gain access to closed-off worlds more quickly, more easily, and more effectively than they could by announcing their intent—just as their undercover predecessors had done—and then to ingratiate themselves with the people about whom they were reporting and to insinuate themselves into the lives of these individuals or to find novel ways of circulating unobtrusively among them. The reporters' further purpose was to experience the conditions, the cruelty, and the difficulties in as much the way their subjects experienced them as possible, and to fill in what was by then an already tried-and-true narrative framework with details amassed from actual experiences.

Sometimes, when the publications did not provide an explanatory prologue or when the writers have not disclosed the details of how they got that story, it is hard to tell from the articles and books alone how they collected the information. In other cases, the writers anchor the text with their personal experiences and reflections.

Either way, their point was to invite a vicarious, deeply empathetic reaction from readers, whose outrage and cries for reform the publications then could galvanize with editorials, follow-up stories, published letters to the editor, and other efforts aimed at inviting response. The point, as with the effective exposés of previous years, was to focus public attention on important social issues, to invite a wide public conversation, and to have impact. In the most successful cases reforms followed, as did more notoriety and boosts in circulation for the publications. For the writers, it meant career-building personal notice. This perfect circle of positive outcomes reinsured the place of undercover reporting in the evolution of journalistic practice. The pitfalls, then as now, were overexposure and a tendency to veer off into the ridiculous or purely sensationalistic. The key to repeated success was to limit the themes to the pressing matters of the day and to produce these types of stories sparingly enough to avoid wearing out the terrific impact they could have at their best.

It was not Campbell or her Civil War era predecessors, but Bly who emerged as the nineteenth century's top celebrity exponent of the undercover technique. Someone who should have been no more than a cursor blip on the screen of history retains almost mystical staying power. The prominence she gained in her early twenties as the star Sunday feature writer for the *New York World* stayed with her for the remaining thirty-five years of her short life. She died at age fifty-seven in 1922.[19] In the years in between, she reengaged public interest in herself with two guest reappearances at the *World* during the 1890s, including a groundbreaking jailhouse interview with Emma Goldman and exceptional coverage of the Pullman Strike from the workers' standpoint.[20] In those years, she shocked her fans by marrying on the fly a man forty years her senior; embroiling herself in highly dubious business dealings as head of her husband's company; and filing or defending herself against messy, debilitating family and business lawsuits. She escaped prosecution in the business case by going to Austria, where she reported from the eastern front in World War I for the *New York Evening Journal* and then returned to the United States in 1919 to write regular op-ed columns in the last years of her life under the editorship of her old friend, Arthur Brisbane.

None of what followed would have mattered to the public had it not been for those brief two and a half years as a stunt girl at Joseph Pulitzer's newspaper. That performance—and it was a performance—fixed her place in legend without any of the usual props for literary legacies that endure: an exceptional body of work; devoted descendants with an asset to protect; a foundation; or even an archive of personal papers preserved for scholars at a manuscript library. The sole sustainers of Bly's legacy have been timing, charisma, and her pioneering role in making stunt and undercover reporting matter. What tops a ten-day incarceration as an inmate of the women's lunatic asylum on Blackwell's (now Roosevelt) Island, her very first *New York World* assignment, published over two Sundays in October 1887? What outpaces a triumphant race across the globe in a record-shattering seventy-two days for a finale in winter 1889–1890?[21] In the one-hundred-plus weeks in between, Bly regularly led the front page of the *World*'s Sunday feature section. Although she sometimes wrote political campaign interviews, frivolous features, and even failed at a personal column in those early years,[22] it was the stunt work—all told, about a score of exposés—that gave her high wattage.

As to her timing, poor and immigrant groups teemed into the city in this period, crowding the metropolis with new social problems that cried out for empathy, explanation, and understanding.

The mass circulation newspaper had arrived. The well-fixed half of the population became increasingly curious about the lives of these newcomers who, as they assimilated, became newspaper readers, too. Also, the times brought a new place for women in the world of work in general and in "The New Journalism" in particular. All of this contributed to Bly's instant rise.

The writing persona Bly created also was exceptional. Particular to her style was her choice of attention-getting issues and the inventive, widely imitated techniques she developed to bring these issues alive. Among her many exploits, she exposed a corrupt Albany lobbyist by pretending to be a prospective client,[23] caught a trafficker in infants by posing as an unwed mother who had a child to give away,[24] checked out the city's matrimonial agencies by posing as an applicant,[25] did a variation on the old Doesticks black arts ruse by pretending to be a patient with an ailment, and then visited a number of doctors to compare what they variously diagnosed and prescribed.[26] She hired a mesmerist for an evening's entertainment and then explained the sham to her readers,[27] sought employment as a maid through the offices of an unscrupulous employment agency,[28] labored in a paper box factory,[29] and danced in the chorus to explain why girls who weren't harlots or gold diggers would choose a life on the stage.[30] She investigated private investigators by posing as a suspicious wife,[31] gained admittance to a home for women in unfortunate circumstances,[32] slept in a Lower East Side tenement during the hottest nights of August,[33] and engineered her own arrest so that she could find out what happened to women who wound up in jail.[34]

There was, and still is, the novelty she so perfectly depicted of an oh-so-genteel lady scribbler among those coarse, tobacco-spitting male reporters of the city room and out amid the evildoers in the big bad world. Danger! Daring! But more key to Bly's celebrated success were her clandestine approaches, her bravery, her moxie, and how this self-described "New American Girl" displayed these abilities on the printed page. What the public got was a well-dressed, wily, ladylike darling who liked to feature her wasp waist and a million-dollar smile in her stories. She was not only fearless, she got results. In her earliest efforts for the *World,* her insane asylum exposé brought an appropriation to improve the asylum, and she ran that lobbyist out of the state capital. Her trip around the world was a global sensation. Her inspiring combination of attributes incited worldwide attention, not to mention deep professional jealousy. All of it made her gossip fodder in the local magazines and journalism trade publications, aggrandizing her celebrity status even more. She had a knack for making the attention stick.

One strong aspect of the Bly persona was its air of authenticity, an absolute necessity for the undercover reporter in any age. The persona she cultivated was a clean mirror image of her private self, at least as glimpsed through her legal actions, testimony, documented business dealings, and what little personal correspondence survives. The persona both pervaded and magnetized the work. But just as significant was the *World*'s willingness to position Bly for stardom. Editors emblazoned her name on the page in big headlines, commissioned handsome illustrations, and offered full-page story display for her every published piece. The importance of this institutional support cannot be overestimated, and it was no doubt fed by the interest from readers that both Bly, as celebrity exponent, and the undercover method itself repeatedly demonstrated.

There is often, still, a clear correlation between the merit and the attention, prominence, prize nominations, and publicity lavished on undercover stories and their writers within the publication's editorial structure—largely to acknowledge the time and resources this kind of work commands—and the impact the individuals and their stories are able to generate once the work appears. Then as now, the relatively large number of newspaper and magazine undercover investigations deemed worthy of publication at book length is a telling indicator.

In Bly's short stint as a stunt girl, she addressed almost every major social issue of the day and foreshadowed many future undercover themes, including safety in public transportation, if you count an ancillary benefit of her trip around the world as a Victorian girl out on her own. In the process, she generated meaningful attention for herself and her newspaper and energized and animated a fledgling journalistic form. Imitation was inevitable, in cities across the country, in Canada, and overseas. By the turn of the nineteenth century into the twentieth, men increasingly were going undercover once again, too. More and more, the role of the journalist expanded beyond that of recorder, explainer, and reflector on the news to that of explorer and hard-hitting investigator. More sophisticated "detective" techniques soon emerged, harkening back to Campbell to produce stories that reflected far greater investigative skill, with or without a personal narrative dimension. Tarbell's Standard Oil exposé would be an obvious case in point. University-trained sociologists and ersatz ethnographers tried their hand. As for the undercover method, the sheer excitement it created, its bravura, its ability to get results and public attention—and for women just entering the field, the way it opened locked doors—assured its permanence as an effective reporting approach.

For late nineteenth-century reporters and writers, female or male, no investigative fields were more fertile to till than the world of work and the lack of it. In the 1880s and 1890s, male writers would produce their share of undercover work, largely among the unemployed, but in that period, women predominated in stealth reporting on workplace hardship and abuse.

As it happened, work was not a major theme of Bly's stunt reporting, although she did do the couple of brief turns noted above. In her well-shaped shadow, the clones came swiftly. Eva McDonald, another twenty-two-year-old, was among the very first. Early in 1888, the Minnesotan outfitted herself from a rag-bag on assignment from the *St. Paul Globe* and went undercover for very brief periods in dozens of local mattress, bag, shirt, and blanket factories. McDonald wrote as Eva Gay but later went on to distinguish herself as a labor organizer under her married name of Eva Valesh. So effective was her reporting that the competing *Minneapolis Tribune* sniped in print that her tales of "poor working women employed at starving wages who were compelled to work in mere hovels"[35] had practically been the direct cause of a labor strike by local women.

Not long after, Charles Chapin, editor of the *Chicago Times,* hired Nell Cusak to investigate conditions for women in the factories of Chicago.[36] Under the byline Nell Nelson, her twenty-one part WHITE SLAVE GIRLS series[37] was provocative enough to warrant a book contract. Her explanatory prologue emphasized the same "just-the-facts" virtues that other undercover writers highlight to justify their subterfuge. She told of her "earnest endeavor" to "give all absolute facts with all their bearings to portray with exceptional fidelity and guardedness the state of things as existing."[38]

Nelson got gratifying attention from the Chicago Trades and Labor Assembly, which endorsed her series at its August 19, 1888 meeting. One speaker told the assemblage that the Nelson articles about women workers had done more to open the eyes of the "skeptical class" than a report about a laboring man ever could.[39] Over the coming days, her Chicago newspaper gave prime front-page display to the responses of readers, proudly touting praise. One letter, from a Dr. Charles Gilman Smith, said the series was better than anything the newspaper had produced in the previous ten years. Another, a poignant one from a seamstress who signed herself Mary McGray, provided a perfect opportunity to send Cusak back out for new fodder to keep the story going. The letter writer thanked Cusak for her efforts on behalf of her "poor sisters, the shop-girls of Chicago" who can't stand up for themselves. "Oh, you have not told half; you do not know half we have to bear," she wrote. "We are indeed slaves, worse slaves than those my brothers died to free. I wish you could see my book for the last month; you would wonder how I have lived."[40]

Nelson traced the woman by match light down a dark hallway to a sorry little flat. The woman's face brightened when the reporter introduced herself, and as they settled in to talk, the woman gave as wise a critique of undercover reporting as any seasoned professional observer could. She got how effective the method was at attracting interest to a social problem across social classes. ("Your articles have helped the girls more than you'd think. Every hand read them and so did every boss and manager.") She understood its power to champion the weak ("I cannot fight for my rights and this is the case with many of us.") But gently, she chastised the writer for superficiality, for spending too little time reporting on each of the factories she visited. ("That is the employers' defense and the employees' complaint. If you only had staid [*sic*] for a payday now I am sure you could have moved the public to pity.") She even assessed the use of deceit in Nelson's approach, first questioning it, but then, in the same thought, apprehending astutely from her own experience how impossible it would have been for Nelson to get meaningful information without sneaking around. The seamstress told of what she witnessed when her manager had foreknowledge of another reporter's arrival, and how he had managed the visit to hide the flaws and show off the factory to its best advantage.[41]

The seamstress went on to elaborate on her own experience in doing the work and redoing the work, never knowing what she would earn until payday and then inevitably being disappointed by the little that ended up in the envelope. A neighbor came by the apartment to say hello, carting a sack of groceries that she never mentioned but that she discreetly, and with obvious intent, left behind. The seamstress brought her brother out of his room to meet the reporter. Moved by his merry temperament and his troubles—"left arm shriveled to the bone"—Cusak gave him all the coins in her purse to buy tobacco. She put that in her story, too.[42]

Indeed the story of Nell Nelson's encounter with the seamstress symbolizes the value, virtue, and vice of undercover reporting. It underscores its ability to make the significant interesting to wide swaths of the population and its incredibly rich means of providing graphic, real-life examples and illustrations of pressing societal issues. It provides the opportunity for an unadorned insider view that otherwise would not be possible. It can be a powerful means of telling truth to power, and of speaking for those who cannot. It promotes more detailed, if not necessarily deeper understanding and enables the collecting of knowledgeable sources of information both before and after publication.

On the down side is the contradiction of truth-seeker as deceiver, the awkward ethical conundrums invited by the intimacy of these encounters (the tobacco money), and the inherent superficiality of a drive-by encounter with distress, whether the time involved is a day, a week, a month or two or three, or even a year.

As the wise seamstress said, the brevity of the Nell Nelson experience in each factory left her open to criticism and gave "employers' defense and the employees' complaint."[43]

There were other issues caused by the superficiality or at least the incompleteness of the reporting, too. One of the manufacturers who Nelson named filed a $50,000 lawsuit for misrepresentation against the *Chicago Times*.[44] From Cedar Rapids, Iowa, the *Evening Gazette* challenged her for slipshod analysis, specifically for ascribing the deplorable conditions she encountered to employer avarice when other factors bore greater responsibility for the situation, including cutthroat competition and a mania for selling.[45]

Whatever the inadequacies, the series and its aftermath achieved and surpassed its major objectives: it brought serious attention to the issues, it brought readers of all societal strata to the newspaper, and it worked out well for Cusak personally. Not only did she land a book deal; the editors of the *New York World* ran the series soon after, in fall 1888, in typical Pulitzer fashion, right under Bly's retroussé nose.[46]

As the 1880s turned over to the 1890s, the girl/reporter/working girl ruse continued to engage editors, reporters, and readers. In 1893, Elizabeth Banks, who worked briefly for the *St. Paul Globe,* could not find steady work in the United States, so she took herself across the ocean where readers of the *Weekly Sun* got to know her as the self-proclaimed "American Girl in London." Her undercover investigation of domestic servants[47] led to a series of seven undercover pieces that a British publisher compiled into a well-received book the following year under the title *Campaigns & Curiosity.* Interestingly, Banks's recounting of her escapades in a 1902 autobiography[48] provoked an attack on her journalistic ethics. This was not so much for disguising herself as a maid, but for the very un-British indiscretion she had shown in telling tales on the families in whose homes she found work and shelter. In a "London Letter" column to the *New York Times Sunday Review of Books,* William L. Alden presaged some of the criticism that eventually would stalk the practice of undercover reporting. Banks's articles were "certainly not in accordance with the ethics of decent London journalism," he wrote, and "were generally thought to be in extremely bad taste."[49]

Chapin moved on from Chicago to become editor of the *St. Louis Post-Dispatch* in 1896 and hired Lucy Hosmer to make the rounds of the city's shoe factories as "another helpless girl cast upon the world to battle for her daily bread."[50] At least three Canadian women took up the form. Ella S. Atkinson as Madge Merton was one; she disguised herself as an elderly housekeeper for a story on working conditions for domestics. Kathleen "Kit" Black Coleman attracted flattering attention in 1892 for venturing overseas and cross-dressing as a male worker in London to spend a few days reporting for the *Toronto Daily Mail* on life in London's East End.[51] Escorted by a male detective, she wandered into "all sorts of queer places"[52] in the hamlets along the Thames as part of the male writer tramp-fest that had been under way since as early as 1782.[53] And Alice Freeman taught school in Toronto by day and then transformed herself by night into Faith Fenton, undercover reporter for the *Empire.*[54]

In summer 1898, Chapin, by then in New York and editor of the *New York Evening World,* paired reporters Catherine King and Charles Garrett to pose as young people in search of work. LIVED THREE MONTHS ON FIVE CENTS A DAY was the headline on Garrett's series, which the newspaper promoted in a front-page introduction as "the remarkable disclosure of the inner life of this great metropolis."[55] King's story ran several pages deeper into the paper under the headline GIRL TOILERS OF THE CITY.[56]

From the timeline of girl-reporter exploits in this period, the pattern of prominence, publicity, and profit becomes obvious, as does how crucial were the vision, the backing, and often the instigation of editors and publishers to the success of these undertakings. Also clear is how prevalent were women in the doing, uniquely positioned as they were to investigate subjects where women were newly and deeply involved. A graph by date could easily show how Campbell begat Bly begat Valesh begat Nelson begat Banks begat Atkinson, Freeman, Coleman, Hosmer, and no doubt others. The twentieth century, and then the twenty-first, would bring along even more.

The tramps: Carl Philipp Moritz tramped through England in 1782 with only four guineas in his pocket; Bayard Taylor tramped through Europe and wrote a book about his experiences in "the college of the world" in 1846; Lee Meriwether dropped out of Harvard and passed as a worker to tour Europe on fifty cents a day in 1885.[57] All retain their place in the long tramping procession, but only Josiah (Frank) Flynt Willard qualified as an expert social investigator. Although mostly forgotten now, he was the tramp's tramp, revered in his day as *the* "tramp authority,"[58] which was Jack London's phrase. His "Josiah Flynt" adventures on two continents in the 1890s appeared in some of the most prestigious publications of the period, including *Contemporary Review,* the *Atlantic Monthly,* the *Century,* and *Forum.*[59] By mid-decade, Flynt's name-recognition was pervasive enough to inspire a poem by Philip Morse.[60]

Flynt claimed a scientific methodology for his work, an approximation based on field observation, he later said, of how his fellow students at university in Berlin performed science lab experiments "to discover the minutest parasitic forms of life, and later publishing their discoveries in book form as valuable contributions to knowledge."[61] His purpose, he said, was "to give a picture of the tramp world, with incidental references to causes and occasional suggestions of remedies."[62] Contemporaries, such as the English poet Arthur Symons, described as unmatched his ability to transform himself into his tramp identity, "Cigarette."[63]

Flynt compiled his stories into a book, *Tramping with the Tramps,*[64] which was published to appreciative reviews in all the major venues in 1899 and widely read. In a class of five hundred books the next year, librarians contacted for an annual *New York Times* survey voted it number twenty-two of the top fifty books.[65]

The *New York Times* reviewer recalled that as Flynt's articles began appearing, starting in 1891, readers reacted to his stories with incredulity, a "suspicion bred from the 'literary' treatment given of late to a great deal of reputed science,"[66] but then came to understand that they were true, which "seemed incredible only because it was so novel."[67]

As the new century arrived, Flynt switched his focus to gambling and pool rooms and also produced short stories and a memoir, titled *My Life,* that a *Times* reviewer admired for its lack of artifice: "There are no insufferable reminiscences; he did not assume a pose and write a book about himself. The attitude is always that of the boyish investigator."[68] Flynt died the year before its publication in 1908. He was thirty-eight.

So much poseur journalism had been produced by the last years of the nineteenth century that by the start of the twentieth, reporter derring-do already had the feel of reporter derring-did. This did not, however, stop writers or the newspapers and magazine editors who published them from presenting stories conceived in this form. In February 1894, Stephen Crane, in the year before publication of *Red Badge of Courage,* performed two quick-hit acts of "class transvestitism" for the *New York Press.* The first piece, "An Experiment in Misery," is an etching the poet John Berryman considered one of Crane's finest.[69] It brought Crane "a measure of the popularity"[70] he sought. A week later, its flipside appeared, "An Experiment in Luxury."[71]

Given how common such stories were at the time, it is likely, as scholars suggest, that Crane was helped to publication both by the pairing of misery with luxury—though that, too, was a worn device—and his news sense: Coxey's Army of the impoverished was just then on its march to Washington. Michael Robertson also notes Crane's unusual skill at freeing his prose from the all-too-common ploys of "moralizing, sentimentality, and proposals for reform" and how the "catalysts of poverty and wealth" transformed his reporter's consciousness as he immersed himself in each experience, however briefly.[72]

At least two sociologists got into the undercover game as writers in the late 1890s. Alvan Francis Sanborn masqueraded as a tramp in a variety of lodging houses so that he could provide "transcripts from life. I have written true things simply about poor people"[73] for a book he called *Moody's Lodging House, and Other Tenement Sketches,* published in 1896. Walter Wyckoff, a lecturer in sociology at Princeton University, left home without a penny and spent two years trying to understand the life of the itinerant day laborer. Scribner serialized his book in its magazine and then published it in hardcover in 1897. In his introduction, Wyckoff explained what inspired him to move out of the library and set off incognito to do his research as a day laborer at West Point, as a hotel porter, as a hired man at an asylum, as a farm hand, and as a logger. He titled his book *The Workers: A Study in Reality,* and said it was inspired by a chance encounter with a well-traveled adventurer whose "catholic sympathy with human nature, made him a man wholly new and interesting to me,"[74] especially when it came to the large social questions. He said, "I could but feel increasingly the difference between my slender, book-learned lore and his vital knowledge of men and the principles by which they live and work."[75] He reported without preconceptions, he said, and produced an account that was "strictly accurate even to details; apart from confessed changes in the names of the persons introduced."[76]

As for Sanborn, the *Bookman* compared him favorably to Flynt in the way he "exploited the *vie intime* of the lodging-house tramp."[77] The reviewer also admired "the matter-of-fact brevity" in his descriptions of "disgusting and debasing details" and the way he struck a "blow to sentimentalism which is at the root of most of our mistaken dealings with the poor and the social outcast, by neither being shocked by facts nor seeing them for better or worse than they are."[78]

Another reviewer, this one writing for the *Critic,* compared Sanborn's work somewhat less favorably to a book by Julian Ralph of the *New York Sun,* published at about the same time. *People We Pass* was a collection of short stories, sketches of life on the Bowery, derived from Ralph's close encounters with the poor, amassed not by stealth or in disguise but "in the regular way of his business during a twenty years' service as a reporter for a New York newspaper."[79] Though admiring of Sanborn's work, the reviewer far preferred Ralph's, even though it "lack[s] the romance attaching to Mr. Sanborn's experiences in a disguise" and "is not so scrupulous in unpleasant details."[80]

# SIX

# OF JACK LONDON AND
# UPTON SINCLAIR

The books of two of undercover reporting's most iconic male role models appeared in the very first years of the twentieth century. Jack London's *People of the Abyss* was a purported sociological investigation and Upton Sinclair's *The Jungle* was a novel of social reform. At the time of publication, both writers were men in their twenties deeply in the thrall of socialism and yearning for literary recognition. They took on the era's two great themes of social justice—exploited workers and the down-and-out—and in the process, established literary legacies that have inspired a hundred years worth of emulation.

Sinclair's decision in fall 1904 to set his novel in the meat-packing district of Chicago followed by just over a year the bonanza of attention London received in 1903, with his account of seven weeks the previous summer—the same amount of time Sinclair spent in Packingtown—among the wretched of London's East End.

To gain close access, London approached the project much as the tramping Josiah Flynt and so many others had done in the previous decade.[1] London costumed. He even altered his speech pattern ("'Hello, mate,' I greeted him, sparring for a beginning. 'Can you tell me the way to Wapping?'"[2]), if not his manner of speech ("'Worked yer way over on a cattle boat?' he countered, fixing my nationality on the instant"[3]). This out-of-work American sailor routine made his American accent plausible. He got help with contacts from the Social Democratic Federation as well as lengthy official reports on social conditions in the area, which he mined for authoritative information to include in the book.[4]

Once on the East End, London moved easily among the locals, as Sinclair would later do in Packingtown, interviewing a variety of people at length. But London took the additional step of immersing himself as a participant in the everydayness of local life. Sinclair checked into a hotel but London took a sad little room in the district and left it empty on more than one occasion to sleep on a rain-soaked street or in one of the city's homeless shelters, known as spikes. He ventured out to Kent on a hop-picking expedition to experience firsthand what the unemployed were willing to endure to earn a few extra pence. In Kent, by dint of his get-up, he also gave off the impression of being an out-of-work seaman, "without a ship, a man on the beach, and very like a craft at low water."[5]

In almost all of his encounters, London was cagey about his actual purpose. The exceptions were in his meetings with a travel agent he met at the start, whose help he sought to get his bearings; the U.S. consul general, whom he informed of his intentions, just in case he ran into difficulty (to cover herself legally, Nellie Bly in 1887 quietly informed the office of the district attorney before her commitment to the women's lunatic asylum);[6] and a detective who lived on one of the East End's better streets and became London's local guide to safe rooming quarters.

To readers, London likened himself not to a detective, investigator, or an ethnographer like Flynt, but to an explorer, "open to be convinced by the evidence of my eyes, rather than by the teachings of those who had not seen, or by the words for those who had seen and gone before."[7]

London found ways to intensify the drama of his undertaking, the sense of danger and hardship, as reports of such escapades often will. He titled his first chapter "The Descent," suggesting the plunge into a forbidding netherworld. He signaled the dangerous position in which he had placed himself in a description of the travel agent's response—so "cold-blooded" that it gave London visions of his "own mutilated cadaver stretched upon a slab."[8] A reluctant cabbie took him first to a shop that sold old clothes so he could dress for the part. He bargained relentlessly with the owner and then purchased his new uniform: "a pair of stout though well-worn trousers, a frayed jacket with one remaining button, a pair of brogans which had plainly seen service where coal was shoveled, a thin leather belt, and a very dirty cloth cap." He opted for new underwear and socks, "but of the sort that any American waif, down in his luck, could acquire in the ordinary course of events."[9] He sewed a gold sovereign into the armpit of his scratchy undershirt, or singlet, just in case.

As he made his way around the district, he found to his complete surprise that his costume enriched his reporting in surprising ways. Appearance allowed him to become one with the people he met. Someone even dropped a penny in his palm. Unexpectedly, the disguise also quelled London's own uneasiness, making him feel a part of, not apart from, the crowd. "The vast and malodorous sea had welled up and over me, or I had slipped gently into it," he wrote, "and there was nothing fearsome about it—with the one exception of the stoker's singlet."[10]

Throughout his stay, he mostly allowed the people he met to

think what they would of his self-presentation, drawing their own conclusions from the way he looked and his folksy congeniality. He made friends and collected stories. He avoided revealing his actual purpose to newfound companions, except when caught out. For instance, in the queue for permission to spend a night in a shelter, London befriended two older men, a carter and a carpenter, both down on their luck. The spike, as it happened, turned all three hungry men away. London, to entice his new companions into spending the rest of the evening in conversation with him, let them watch him as he cut the hidden gold sovereign out of his singlet and then offered them both a coffee house meal, which they accepted. Knowing that the mere possession of such a valuable coin had given him away, he also confessed his actual purpose, that he was a mere investigator, a student of the social sciences, trying to figure out how the other half lived. But both men were "superbly class conscious," which caused them to "shut up like clams." Then, "in degraded humility," even though one had eaten only a roll that day and the other, nothing at all, they each ordered only two slices of bread and tea. London added eggs, bacon, and more tea and bread to their orders, with them "denying wistfully all the while that they cared for anything more, and devouring it ravenously as fast as it arrived." The food, he said, had a remarkable effect. "At first, they were melancholy, and talked of the divers times they had contemplated suicide," he wrote. "They grew more cheerful as the hot 'tea' soaked in, and talked more about themselves."[11]

London also was full of preachy commentary, meant to engage his readers viscerally and empathetically in the experience ("But O dear, soft people, full of meat and blood, with white beds and airy rooms waiting you each night, how can I make you know what it is to suffer"[12]). And along with the asides came forty pages of analysis and proposals for change.[13]

Day and night, London worked to get all 63,000 words of his book down on paper. He managed to do so by late September. His publisher, George Brett, accepted the manuscript, and followed up with a two-year stipend in exchange for the right to publish London's next six books. But at the same time, Brett was firm: the next books could not show the same "signs of haste" that were evident in *Abyss,* adding, "There is no real place in the world of literature for anything but the best a man can do."[14]

For readers, as it turned out, the rushed writing was less of a problem. Once in print, *People of the Abyss* sold more than twenty thousand copies in the United States. American critics were of two minds. One U.S. critic hailed the book as "the most vivid and truthful picture that has yet been drawn of the saddest side of modern civilization."[15] Another, in the *Bookman,* slammed it as "patronizing snobbishness" from yet another son of "our petted aristocracy . . . who imagines he is contributing to the literature of sociology."[16] British reviewers were equally dismissive. The *London Daily News* accused London of describing the East End in "the same tortured phrase, vehemence of denunciation, splashes of colour, and ferocity of epithet" that he developed for the Klondike, adding, "He has studied it 'earnestly and dispassionately'—in two months! It is all very pleasant, very American, and very young."[17]

London also drew sharp rebuke for treating himself to the occasional retreat to cleaner quarters for a bath and a decent meal, a choice many of his undercover successors also would make. The *Bookman* reviewer, Edward Clark Marsh, called him out for being more amusing than convincing. What can a man know of poverty,

Marsh asked, if he has ready access to money, good food, and a warm bed?[18]

There is no getting around the manufactured aspects of a reporter's undercover ruse. However long these forays last, they have no chance of matching the fates and experiences that shape the lives of others. To claim otherwise would be foolhardy. Yet how does that negate the value of the exercise, the earnest effort to illuminate a way of life at least somewhat more brightly and interpret its impact at least somewhat more cogently for readers who are unlikely ever to know its pains or joys? The experiences and encounters the author reports are no less real because time, chance, and opportunity delimit them, no less legitimate because the hardships are self-imposed and can be escaped at will. They are certainly incomplete. But why must that invalidate them any more than we would invalidate a snapshot or a sketch? What's important is not to claim for them more than is their portion, not to claim any more than they actually have the potential to represent.

London followed up the next year with his most famous and even more successful work, *The Call of the Wild*, affirming his place in American letters. But it was *Abyss* that rescued him from writing about the Klondike, not to mention crushing debt. Years later, London himself would say that of all of his books, *People of the Abyss* remained his personal favorite. "No other book of mine took so much of my young heart and tears," he later wrote, "as that study of the economic degradation of the poor."[19] The sentiment gets repeated over and over again among reporters and writers who have had meaningful undercover experiences at some point in long, successful careers.

The success of *Abyss* was not lost on London's aspiring young literary peers, either. A passage in Sinclair's 1911 novel captures the yearning London's achievement inspired in him for those "far-off heights of popularity and power."[20] Of course, by 1911, Sinclair could well afford to offer up such a generous memory. Five years had passed since *The Jungle* had taken Sinclair to that same welcome place.

Over the coming century, the undercover label stuck to *The Jungle*. Reporters planning undercover missions have never ceased to summon this reportorial tour de force for inspiration. This is in large part a tribute to Sinclair's "accurate touch," as Morris Dickstein described it, and his "enormous dossier of irrefutable detail, straightforwardly presented and linked to an affecting human drama."[21]

Yet Sinclair presented the work in the form of a novel that met the emerging standard for investigative heft, set by the work of muckraking paragons of the day like Ida Tarbell and Lincoln Steffens, who did not go undercover. Time nonetheless has fused the earlier stunt work of the 1880s and 1890s with these more sophisticated but slightly later efforts. Sinclair, like his colleagues at *McClure's* and the forgotten Helen Campbell before them, went to greater lengths to verify and analyze their findings.

In Sinclair's own mind, *The Jungle* signaled a "new proletarian literature in America,"[22] a melding of "the content of Shelley into the form of Zola."[23] He considered his novel a departure from the work of those "skilled," "middle-class," "expert psychologists" of the French school who never "share in the emotions of their characters."[24] He, by contrast, approached his subject from the inside out and then crafted his story about the lives of the immigrant "wage slaves" of Chicago's meatpacking district to support his own fervent political agenda. Sinclair's fanatical embrace of socialism had come only a couple of years earlier.

Like Campbell, Sinclair had long been a writer of magazine serial fiction, in his case, since he was a teenager. During his nonstop weeks in Packingtown during October and November 1904, the access he engineered with his socialist connections and his training as a reporter enabled him to produce almost unbearably graphic accounts of what he witnessed and heard. These he supplemented with meticulous corroboration. His aim, he said, was to give voice to the voiceless "with a knowledge that no man could impeach" and to illuminate "the cause and the meaning of all the evils that are raging in modern society—of neurasthenia, melancholia, and hysteria; of drunkenness, insanity, and suicide; of prostitution, war, and crime."[25]

Sinclair allowed the reporting to take him where it would go. The complete surprise was where that effort led. He intended to provide a searing examination of Big Beef, its power and corruption, and the grisly working conditions of the immigrant poor. But his story soon began to turn on his stark depictions of how contaminated meat was making its way from the packinghouses of Chicago to the dinner tables of the world. Bad meat won. "In other words," he is forever quoted as saying, "I aimed at the public's heart and by accident I hit it in the stomach."[26]

The serial he produced was shocking—repulsive—in the hastily written version that appeared starting in February 1905 in the socialist magazine *Appeal to Reason,* which commissioned the work for $500.[27] The details were no less appalling in the heavily sanitized version Doubleday and Page released as a novel exactly a year later, a project the publishing house took on after a competitor, MacMillan, squeamishly reneged. First, however, Doubleday sent its attorneys to Chicago to make sure the powerful processors of the Beef Trust would have no grounds to sue.[28]

The poetry of Percy Bysshe Shelley and the passionate political writing of Émile Zola may have been Sinclair's literary muses, but his real inspiration was Mrs. Stowe.[29] Sinclair's aim was a book with the political and social impact of *Uncle Tom's Cabin*. Sinclair deeply wanted his book to be that popular. He wanted it to be literature—art—that would "shake the country out of its slumber."[30] Stowe's success led him to believe that a novel was more likely to achieve all of this than a work of nonfiction, and so a novel his book became.

His subject matter, like Stowe's, was hardly new. In the months and years before he headed to Chicago, there had been any number of newspaper exposés of packinghouse conditions. Editorial attacks on the excesses of Big Beef were common.[31] In fact, a failed strike in Chicago that summer of 1904 had given him the idea for the book's setting.[32]

Sinclair knew his challenge would be greater than Stowe's, that the grim world of the wage worker could never provide so rich a tableau as the life of the chattel slave of a half century earlier. To begin with, wage slaves had no appreciable monetary value, nor, despite their appalling circumstances, were they actually subject to shackle. Packingtown's real masters were machines that offered few opportunities for dialogue or character development.

And then as a setting, Packingtown was no verdant plantation. In a dank and joyless place without natural beauty, where the only recreational release was alcoholic stupor, his challenge was to bring the story alive. Sinclair wanted to "frighten the country by a picture of what its industrial masters were doing to their victims."[33] To do that, he knew that the story would have to be utterly convincing. The book would have to ring true.

Did *The Jungle* ring true? Was it true? Sinclair did not seek to quiet his critics with a companion volume of sources as Stowe had done, but he did take pains to reply to his many doubters, both directly and in the newspaper and magazine articles he wrote or that quoted him during the long publicity blitz that followed the book's publication. In the *Independent,* he declared that the book was "an exact and faithful picture" of conditions in Packingtown, true "not merely in substance but in detail, and in the smallest detail." Students, he said, could go to it as they would a sociological study or reference work.[34]

He said he intentionally avoided taking the fiction writer's usual liberties. "I have imagined nothing," he wrote, "I have embellished nothing; I have simply dramatized and interpreted." Where he dealt with conditions in Packingtown, he said, he did not concoct any episodes or depictions. None of the incidents he did invent— when his protagonist, Jurgis, loses a hundred dollar bill, for example, or when he gets inside a rich man's palace—had any bearing whatsoever on the lives of the people of Packingtown. Everything he described "to my own positive knowledge" happened to someone in Packingtown, he said, and every one of his facts and figures "is absolutely accurate and exact, the result of patient inquiry and investigation."[35]

During the weeks he spent reporting from Chicago, he said he insinuated himself into the lives of hundreds of working men but also spoke with bosses, superintendents, doctors, lawyers, merchants, saloonkeepers, real estate agents, policemen, clergymen, settlement house workers, undertakers, and criminals, "testing the statements of one by those of another and verifying every minutest detail."[36] On his return, he kept up a correspondence with many of his sources, sometimes writing the same source repeatedly to verify a single statement.[37]

He said his medical facts came from local physicians; political musings and assessments from local politicians; conditions in the slaughterhouse, by department, from those who did the jobs. He learned about how criminals were treated from a young physician who was jailed for practicing without a license, a license the doctor said was denied him when he refused to pay graft. "As a writer of fiction," he would later say, "I could be required to be true only in the way of art, and not in the way of a newspaper; but as it happened, I was able to be true in both ways and the book might as well have the credit for it."[38]

Most valuable of all is what stays indelibly with the reader and with those who learn of the book at second hand, that is, what Sinclair saw for himself: condemned hogs rendered into lard, spoiled hams doctored with chemicals; rats scurrying in the sausage rooms, and worse.

Sinclair provided scant explanation of how he went about his reporting. With time and distance, the assumption lingers that Sinclair amassed all that revolting detail by pretending to be a worker and taking a job at one or more of the plants.[39] As a result, he has inspired any number of undercover ruses of all description that involved reporters getting hired as workers to be able to report as graphically and as accurately as he had.

We know from Sinclair's own accounts soon after the book was published that during his time in Packingtown, he went "among the packing houses, and into every corner of them, from the roof to the cellar,"[40] a statement he repeats more than once. We also know that during his weeks in Chicago, he was open about his purpose. Recounted often is an anecdote about Sinclair's booming announcement in the lobby of the Transit House Hotel on arriving at the stockyards on Chicago's South Side: "Hello! I am Upton Sinclair, and I have come to write the *Uncle Tom's Cabin* of the labor movement."[41] Everyone up and down the cattle-to-meatpacking food chain, reporters included, met and mixed at the Transit House.[42] We also know that he had the indispensible help of several expert local guides. He expressed gratitude to the local workers and their families who knew him long before he ever got to Chicago by way of his byline in *Appeal to Reason*. In his piece for the *Independent,* Sinclair explained how they had taken him under their wing and showed him everything he wanted to see. He told of a man who had lived and worked in the district all his life, someone who knew "all the watchmen and spotters by their first names, he would introduce me, and start up a conversation about family affairs, while he piloted me into places where strangers had seldom come before."[43]

Five months later in *Cosmopolitan,* Sinclair volunteered a little more information, explaining how he used his socialist connections to ingratiate himself, sitting with the workers in their homes by night and then following them around by day at work or to whatever or whomever they took him to see. "I studied every detail of their lives, and took notes enough to fill a volume," he said. "I spared no pains to get every detail exact, and I know that in this respect *The Jungle* will stand the severest test—it is as authoritative as if it were a statistical compilation."[44]

But not until the publication of a paragraph in his 1932 book of reminiscences (one he repurposed for his autobiography thirty years later) did he provide a few more specific and more telling details of his time in Packingtown. He dressed himself pretty much as the locals did and "found that with the simple device of carrying a dinner-pail I could go anywhere." Once inside the packinghouses, he "just kept moving" and if he needed to look more carefully at something, he would "pass again and again through the same room."[45]

*The Jungle* has inspired a century's worth of stunning "posed as" investigations in the food processing industry and beyond, many involving grueling stints by reporters who got jobs and worked the line for a number of weeks. Yet Sinclair's "worked as" was really no more than a "blended in." He enacted his own undercover operation by enlisting the help of his worker sources to obscure his purpose and avoid getting thrown out of the plants. He deflected suspicion by looking the part of a meatpacker in a disguise no more elaborate than a dinner pail in his grip. But he never became a meatpacker, not even for a day.

Within weeks of the book's publication, *The Jungle* became an international best seller. Within months of its U.S. debut, it would be translated into seventeen other languages. Within a quarter of a century, it would go through sixty-seven reprints in England alone.[46] "Just now," Sinclair wrote eight months after the book's publication, "*The Jungle* is the sensation of the hour."[47] By the end of that first year, with one hundred thousand copies of the book in print, Sinclair had been paid royalties of the then considerable sum of thirty thousand dollars.[48] Still, his achievement was no rival for Stowe's. He did not become the best-read author of the twentieth century after God, nor did a sitting president credit his book with touching off a movement, let alone a civil war.[49] But President Theodore Roosevelt did read *The Jungle,* after which he sent to Sinclair a three-page critique and an invitation to the White House to discuss his findings. Roosevelt also sent a team of two investigators to Chicago and invited Sinclair to go along.[50] Sinclair declined to make the trip, but asked his new friends in Packingtown to keep tabs on the delegation and its preannounced visit.

Sinclair considered the report they produced to be disappointingly mild, and although Roosevelt alluded to its findings several times, the president never released it publicly.[51] Nonetheless, by June 1906—not even four months after *The Jungle*'s publication—two important pieces of national legislation passed into law. For the Federal Meat Inspection and Pure Food and Drug acts of 1906, at least in memory, the book was widely acknowledged to have played a role.[52] To a number of labor reforms the United States adopted by the time of Sinclair's death at age eighty-nine in 1968, he also could lay some claim.[53]

Sinclair's great gift was not as an originator of ideas but as a changer of attitudes.[54] That derivative but critical function comes not from Sinclair the novelist or Sinclair the polemicist but from Sinclair the reporter, practicing the journalism of verification with graphic precision. He also was able to capitalize on the interest in exposé at the turn of the last century and outpaced other estimable investigative works of the period—those by Tarbell and Steffens—by choosing a subject that crossed all ideological lines. In Ronald Gottesman's words, he made "the stomach rebel in everyone,"[55] as he inadvertently happened on an important principle of modern-day reform: "Involve the public in the pain caused by the deficiency in need of remedy."[56] And yet as a work of literature, the book has left successive generations of critics shaking their heads in dismay.[57]

So why does *The Jungle* endure so insistently when so many finer works have not? Jane Jacobs said Sinclair, with his offstage presence as all-knowing narrator, probably unintentionally "hijacked his own novel by upstaging his own characters."[58] Indeed, the characters Sinclair created have found no lasting place in the collective imagination. What *The Jungle* does have in full measure, however, is Sinclair's prodigious reporting. What has been worth keeping all these years is the remarkable way he found to involve the public in the pain.

Between London and Sinclair, there was plenty of inspiration, both for future undercover and immersion reporters and for the novelists who like to be their own best material or at least to collect their own material in the raw. On the strength of these efforts, both London and Sinclair managed to jumpstart flailing careers and in the process, established themselves as writers who counted. As role models, Sinclair epitomized the obsessively assiduous investigator with a cause. (Even George Orwell, who was quick to dismiss Sinclair as a "dull empty windbag," deeply respected his reporting. "And you can be sure they are authentic facts, for no one has ever got away with a libel action against Upton Sinclair," he once wrote of *The Jungle*.[59]) London added the elements of personal charisma, an adventurous makes-you-stick-with-it storytelling ability, and rugged theatrical panache. With their successes, they demonstrated that with gumption, social conscience, political passion, reporting skill, talent, and eye-popping flair applied to an imaginative subject with a clear point of view, other enterprising young writers could leverage this immersion/undercover format, at least for the income they always seemed to need so desperately, and perhaps, for meaningful public service and professional acclaim as well.

═══════════◇═══════════

# SEVEN

# HARD LABOR, HARD LUCK, PART TWO

Shortly before the exposés of Jack London and Upton Sinclair exploded the possibilities of the undercover narrative, women writers remodeled the newspaper stunt girl for the magazine and book readers of the new century. The sisters-in-law Van Vorst, Marie and Bessie (aka Mrs. John), were among the most successful. They made the circuit from the pickle factories of Pittsburgh to the shoe factories of Lynn, Massachusetts, to the cotton mills of North Carolina and published their experiences as a five-part series in *Everybody's* in 1902. As a book, their collection of stories became a best seller in the "Miscellaneous" category when published by Doubleday and Page the following year. Titled *The Woman Who Toils,*[1] the book held its own for a full half a year against such formidable competitors as Helen Keller's *The Story of My Life* and Booker T. Washington's *Up from Slavery.*[2]

What most distinguished the Van Vorst ladies from their stunt girl predecessors was the more polished narrative and the pronounced angling of their experiences to emphasize their own class-consciousness. The book's subtitle positioned it as "The Experience of a Literary Woman as a Working Girl." Repeatedly in the text, written half by one and half by the other, both women were more pointed in emphasizing their own privileged and cultured upbringing over their status as well-known literary figures. Their starting point was an unapologetic sense of superiority over the wage earners they had spent months impersonating, living, and working among.[3] Reviewers were quick to point to this approach as both a plus and a minus.[4] As for revelations, they reported on the surprising number of young women whose only reason for working in the factories was near folly—to earn pocket money for clothes and leisure—and how that had depressed wages and opportunity for women who needed the jobs to support themselves or their families.

*Everybody's* followed up the Van Vorst investigation with a four-article series on domestic servitude. Lillian Pettengill's pose recalled the earlier work of Elizabeth Banks from England and Madge Merton in Canada, but with a Seven Sisters college twist.[5] Pettengill had spent the year after her 1898 graduation from Mount Holyoke as "Eliza," the household maid. Both she and Banks acknowledged that they initially turned to housekeeping to support themselves when other avenues wouldn't open. But with that, they both fell on the idea of turning hard luck into stories and income. Pettengill characterized what she had done as setting out to see "this particular dog-life from the dog's end of the chain."[6] In the end, she argued in favor of domestic service over factory life. She also railed against the prevailing stigma on working in someone else's home, a point Banks also had made from across the Atlantic Ocean. Doubleday published Pettengill's magazine series as a book, which reviewers quickly likened to the Van Vorsts' far more successful effort.[7]

As the Pettengill book was making its rounds, Bessie Van Vorst rebutted in *Harper's* the younger writer's affirmation of the servant's life. Van Vorst based her observations on her time as a scullery maid in one of the factories, where the disgusting, daily backbreaking cleanup inevitably fell to the female employees. Experiencing the work herself allowed her to observe that even with the shorter workday of the cleanup crews, the free hot dinner, and the greater freedom of movement these tasks afforded, she still would choose the factory floor over having to be "occupied with humanity's *debris*" as one of those who "have abandoned or ignore an ideal, who prefer relative material ease to relative moral freedom."[8]

Over the next hundred years, and the record is surely incomplete, women writers undertook at least another score of undercover assignments to showcase the problems of the worker and the unemployed. In the aftermath of Sinclair's immense success with *The Jungle,* Rheta Childe Dorr spent the better part of a year in 1906 and 1907 under contract to *Everybody*'s to witness and experience the feminization of the trades. She went undercover to work in the accounts division of a department store and as a commercial laundress and then in a number of factories across the country, including manufacturers of shirts, cakes and biscuits, and spun yarn.[9] But she struggled with writing for publication.

"I had the stuff, reams of it, but I couldn't write it," she recalled in her memoir. "I could write paragraphs, pages of description, paint vivid pictures of factory life and character, but separate articles I could not write at all." The reporting, she determined, had taken her thinking in an altogether different direction. It wasn't really about "the women's invasion" at all. "It's the Man's Invasion and it's got to be stopped," she recalled telling her editors. She explained that men owned all the women's jobs. Hers is a cautionary tale about reporting that does not produce the story that editors have envisioned.[10]

The magazine assigned her a collaborator, a "brilliant writer," she called him, named William Hard. Soon, she felt that he began treating her like a secretary, sending her on reporting errands for this or that fact. Eventually, he just cast her aside. Months passed and no pages arrived for her to proof. Then she spotted a newsstand poster for the forthcoming October 1908 issue of *Everybody's*, promoting a new series called THE WOMAN'S INVASION but under the sole byline of—William Hard.[11] Dorr threatened legal action. By the time the magazine appeared a few weeks later, not only was Dorr's byline on the series alongside Hard's but she had also managed to stop him from republishing the serial in hardcover under his name alone. What troubled her most, Dorr later wrote, was not how dismissively she had been treated, but that "in the truest sense, the articles were not mine." She wanted the series to be quickly forgotten and "that other articles I should write would give me a better reputation."[12]

She in fact got that opportunity. Benjamin Hampton had recently taken over *Broadway* magazine, naming it *Hampton's Broadway* magazine. After hearing about Dorr's undercover experiences, he wanted them for the magazine and set out to make her a writer. ("Your articles all begin:'Once upon a time there was a little dog and his name was Fido,' and they all end, 'Come to Jesus.'"[13]) The magazine did not survive but Dorr's subsequent efforts do, in her 1910 book, *What Eight Million Women Want*.

How little conditions had improved by 1921. Cornelia Stratton Parker cloned the working girl ruse for a series in *Harper's* that the company's publishing arm turned into a book the following year titled *Working with the Working Woman*. For Parker's reports, she followed the standard script—got jobs as a seamstress in a dress factory, as a pantry girl in a New York hotel, as a packer in a chocolate factory, as a laborer in a brass works operation, as a laundress, and as a pillowcase labeler in a bleachery. In the book's introduction, she explained the modest goals of her project, "to see the world through their eyes—for the time being to close my own altogether."[14]

A decade after Parker's effort came the Great Depression. Interest in the women who worked hard for little gave way to a focus on women with no way to earn at all. Adela Rogers St. Johns, the Hollywood screenwriter and novelist, recalls in her memoir the summons from William Randolph Hearst—the telephone was his scepter, she said—that brought her to his ranch at San Simeon to get the details of a novel assignment.[15]

For Hearst, an exposé could only be regarded a success, St. Johns explained, "if it created news that the other papers were forced to follow."[16] At the ranch, serving up generous helpings of caviar, Hearst called the situation of unemployed women a national emergency that needed detailed eyewitness reporting more than editorial comment. "We must appeal first to their hearts,"[17] she recalled him saying. He wanted her to go out and *be* an unemployed woman, to "uncover mistakes and demand new drive in this emergency" by conducting herself as if her state was truly tragic. He wanted her to take the era's theme song, "Brother Can You Spare a Dime," as her personal anthem and carry no more than a dime in her own pocket. "I want you to tell it exactly *as it is*," she recalled him saying. "We have no sacred cows, social, political, religious, nor professional. I know of not one we need consider at this time."[18]

A week later, St. Johns, in rimmed glasses and a dress purloined from the Metro-Goldwyn-Mayer wardrobe, put on a raggedy old coat and started her brief out-of-work life as May Harrison, following Ernie Pyle's advice to "unpack your heart." She produced a sixteen-part series that appeared from mid-December until just past Christmas. The "sob sister" moniker never bothered St. Johns. She wore it proudly. "Why not?" she asked. "Who are we that we should not weep for our brothers?"[19]

St. Johns walked "right into the experience" and described what she had accomplished as an altogether new technique, a new journalistic form. "To reach hearts," she said, "you have to do more than report facts. Get under the skin, become part of another life, let your heart beat with another's heart. *Be* it. Become it."[20]

Of course it was not a new technique at all. The ephemeral nature of newspapers and magazines may have kept recollection of that legacy deeply submerged, but by 1931, women reporters had been assuming guises to get their stories for nearly half a century and men for a generation or three before that. Not even her subject matter was new. Twenty-six years earlier, under Chapin's editorship of the *New York Evening World,* Emmeline Pendennis had performed a variation on the same theme. Presenting herself as Helen King, a woman who had lost her bags and purse, she produced a series that explored over two weeks where a young woman without means in New York could go for help. The *Evening World* followed up with a crowd-sourcing exercise, although no one called it that at the time, inviting readers to share their similar experiences.[21]

Although many others, male and female, attempted this type of ruse, no other works of this kind particularly stand out[22] until the start of the next decade when Whiting Williams, the former assistant to a college president and a personal director for a Cleveland Steel Company, produced *What's on the Worker's Mind: By One Who Put on Overalls to Find Out* in 1920. Over seven months,

Williams worked as a common laborer in the steel mills and in a rolling mill, as a coal miner in two towns, as a shipbuilder, as an oil man in a refinery, and as a worker in the iron mines. He "adopted no half-measures in the manner of disguise," equipping himself with "a different name, a slim pocketbook, rough clothes, an unshaven face and a grammarless lingo." He made a point of announcing that he had "cheated no employer,"[23] working hard in his effort to better understand the ruptured relations between "Labor, Management, and the Public—the investors of brawn, brains, and bullion, and the 'bourgeoisie.'"[24]

Williams also told his readers up front that he had changed or obscured all identifying details of individuals, companies, and geographic locations "because neither commendation nor criticism of communities or companies is intended or desired." He was just as unwilling to offer conclusions or prescriptions, but did pinpoint what he had heard again and again as the foremost worker complaint: terrible foremen. His goal, he said, was to observe closely but undetected so that he could get inside the feelings of the workers he got to know, something he did not believe a conventional journalistic interview could elicit. He believed that actions spring from feelings, not from thoughts, and that "people cannot be interviewed for their feelings. The interviewer can only listen, and then try to understand because he is not only hearing but experiencing and sympathizing."[25]

A reviewer for the *New York Tribune* said that Williams had "succeeded to a far greater degree than many men who have launched similar projects and merely posed as workingmen," but in the end, considered his observations "perhaps, more interesting than important." The reviewer also pointed out a key flaw in Williams's method, which critics of such immersion efforts still find objectionable: that two weeks of tossing bricks from pile to pile was time too short to "get the exact point of view of a man who has spent thirty years doing the same job."[26]

By 1927, when the aspiring young writer Eric Blair began his "underworld" explorations among the down-and-out of Paris and London, the circumstances that led him to do so could not have been more cliché. He badly needed money. He badly wanted eyewitness material that would help him to be the writer he yearned to become. His experiences as a colonial official in Burma had left him with such a burning discomfort with his upbringing that he began tramping from time to time—"sometimes from choice, sometimes from necessity,"[27] as his personal antidote to privilege,[28] his way of "getting out of the respectable world altogether."[29] The most searing of his recollections of life on the road were those from his earliest experiences. He recalled how strange he found it to be "on terms of utter equality with working class people."[30]

A faint but distinguishable trail leads directly from Jack London to Blair, who had read *People of the Abyss* in his student days at Eton and credited it with enlightening him—"at a distance and through the medium of books"[31]—and helping him to grasp the humanity of members of the working classes. In later years, too, he wrote introductions to collections of London's stories and did broadcasts about the older author's later works.[32]

Literary scholars have been quick to point out how much of young Blair's roadmap to the East End seems to have been drawn by London twenty-five years earlier. Like London, Blair traded in his own clothes for secondhand rags and made the rounds of all of the same East End haunts, from the doss houses to the spikes to the casual wards.[33] The book that resulted, Blair's first, also gave rise to the pseudonym he insisted upon to mask his embarrassment over the work—George Orwell.[34]

There was no call for embarrassment. True, *Down and Out in Paris and London* sold modestly in Europe in 1933 and just as poorly in the United States, where it was published six months later.[35] By 1936, it was so thoroughly out of print that Orwell wrote in letters, only half in jest, that the last two known people still to have copies of it in their possession were himself and his mother. Reviewers, nonetheless, saw the book's merits from the start, and presaged its status as a minor classic long before Orwell was Orwell. The effusive but unsigned reviewer for the *Washington Post* called it a story of such "absolute destitution, brightened all through by hope and determination" that no reader, whether sympathetic or unsympathetic to the conditions Orwell described, could believe the work was fiction.[36]

The *New York Times* reviewer also approved, even though he found the narrative to be "not wholly unvarnished."[37] Indeed, Orwell himself acknowledged enough refashioning of his characters into composites to cost the work its journalistic purity. As the author himself explained in his personal introduction to the book's 1934 French edition:

> As for the truth of my story, I think I can say that I have exaggerated nothing except in so far as all writers exaggerate by selecting. I did not feel I had to describe events in the exact order in which they happened, but everything I have described did take place at one time or another. At the same time I have refrained, as far as possible, from drawing individual portraits of particular people. All the characters I have described in both parts of the book are intended more as representative types of the Parisian or Londoner of the class to which they belong as individuals.[38]

The *Post* reviewer was taken with "the simple force" of Orwell's writing, its courage and lack of self-pity, adding, "No man but one who himself had experienced some of the pangs of destitution could show such an absolute understanding or tell his tale so well."[39] As Orwell became Orwell, the book got the whoosh of a second wind, engaging successive generations of readers and inspiring undercover reporters ever since, including Pete Jordan, who, in homage, washed dishes as a *plongeur* in all fifty U.S. states so that he could write about it.[40]

# EIGHT

## THE COLOR FACTOR

Sometimes an undercover assignment requires more than costuming and cunning. Clothes, wigs, mustaches, and suggestive accessories have often provided adequate disguises, but a totally convincing performance of racial or ethnic identity requires more. Over and over again, the unfortunate national habit of reflexive racial, ethnic, sexual, and national stereotyping has been the undercover reporter's best ally.

Walter White was a master of the undercover interview and used the technique repeatedly in his investigations of racial strife for the National Association for the Advancement of Colored People. From 1918 to 1928, his postmortem[1] reports appeared in the NAACP's magazine, the *Crisis,* as well as in a number of mainstream newspapers and magazines. White's work met, even exceeded, the accepted professional journalistic standard. On location, he never appears to have misrepresented himself, but then he never gave away his actual purpose, either. As reporters often do, he simply didn't say, and let those he casually questioned act off their own erroneous assumptions and think what they might.

White, who was black, reclaimed the southern accent of his

youth and used the natural disguise of his blue-eyed, white-looking self to fit in among the "bucolic wise men" of the small, southern towns in which he so often found himself, to gain the trust of "the morons who lounge about the village store."[2] In all but three instances, no one even suspected that the congenial, straight-haired, light-skinned stranger was not the white man he appeared to be, nor did they grasp his ulterior purpose until he was long gone and his reports appeared in print.

His method was to chat informally with local white people— some of whom had witnessed[3] the forty-one lynchings and eight race riots he investigated in towns such as Estill Springs, Tennessee, where he traveled within a week of the lynching and burning of Jim McIlherron, or in his native Georgia, where he investigated a brutal attack on ten men and a woman in her last trimester of pregnancy. From casual interviews and documentation, he fashioned in deadpan delivery the searing crux of his reports. Only years later did he reveal his disarmingly simple technique. "Nothing," he told the largely white readership of the *American Mercury* in 1929, "contributes so much to the continued life of an investigator of lynchings and his tranquil possession of all his limbs as the obtuseness of the lynchers themselves." Yet on those occasions when his appearance did raise suspicion, he "found it desirable to disappear slightly in advance of reception committees imbued with the desire to make an addition to the lynching record."[4]

At mid-century, the subject of race rejoined destitution and the low-wage worker as a fervent social topic. Again, exploiting the common tendency to stereotype other people could be used to excellent reportorial advantage, and was. This was especially true when the main subject centered on members of a given group— think migrant workers who happen to be black or undocumented factory workers who happen to be Latina or Asian—or when bias itself was the focus, as in a sting to expose discriminatory real estate practices.[5]

That race got the media's targeted attention in the second half of the twentieth century is as clear a sign of the times as the small but growing presence of reporters of color in major mainstream newsrooms. "We had what passes for equality when people were hired for who they were," Lee May recalled. The *Atlanta Constitution* hired him in 1973. The push for newsroom diversity in and of itself opened up these opportunities, as did the fact, or at least the presumption, that black journalists reporting on riots or protests were more effective at collecting reliable information. "Back in the day," May said, "it was how colored journalists came to *be* in many cases."[6]

May, along with Marvel Cooke, Dale Wright, and Neil Henry, were among the reporters who took on the assignments they proposed or their editors offered without considering the danger or physical hardship the effort would require. Done well, the resulting stories virtually assured front-page bylines, perhaps a nomination for major journalism awards, and, most compellingly, a chance to expose wrongs and play a part in righting them.

Cooke led this charge. In 1950, she was the only black and the only woman reporter at the *New York Compass.* Soon after her hire, she went undercover to investigate the "slave markets" that had resurfaced for the first time since the Great Depression on designated street corners of Brooklyn and the Bronx.

The realities of segregation were such that white readers of that upstart evening newspaper could be excused for assuming her investigation was a first. Actually, the ruse was a reenactment of one she herself first used in 1935 for a cosigned article she wrote with Ella Baker about exactly the same phenomenon. The

Cooke-Baker piece for the *Crisis* presented the inner workings of the "slave mart" system, to find out who engaged with it and why and, to learn, as they put it, "how far does its stench spread? [and] what forces are at work to counteract it?"[7]

Indeed, Cooke's redux for the *Compass* fifteen years later reprised many of the themes in the earlier effort. Both pieces highlighted the larger economic realities that reduced black women, once employed full time in white households, to working piecemeal for a pittance. As women reporters, Cooke and Baker were able to share the terror these women experienced from men who menacingly hounded them on the street as they awaited their employers-for-less-than-a-day. And they chronicled the way some employers cynically bargained the workers down to well below an acceptable hourly rate of pay. Both the *Compass* series and the earlier piece in the *Crisis* drew comparisons to the slave auctions of the South in the pre–Civil War era, and both concluded with the requisite if superficially handled prescriptions for what to do about it.

For Cooke, of course, the suspected evildoers of 1950 were not the women she stood among on the streets, but those who perpetrated the exploitative hire-by-the-hour system itself.[8] Her five-part *Compass* series[9] did not indicate how many days Cooke remained in the role of "Margo" the maid, except to say she stayed "long enough to experience all the viciousness and indignity of a system which forces women to the streets in search of work."[10]

The *Compass* series started in the newspaper's Sunday magazine section on January 8 and continued with installments for the next four days. Cooke was by then nearly fifty. Not only did the stories detail how the accomplished University of Minnesota graduate had taken her place among the women on the street,[11] as she had done before, but this time she also accepted at least two jobs. She then returned to the street to stand with the other black women, casually seeking their interpretation of what she experienced. All of this she shared with readers, along with the ins and outs of what the women did in efforts to avoid getting cheated further in these temporary jobs, and how she fended off the advances of men who trolled the line in that other pursuit.

In both pieces, the affecting streetwalker episodes illustrate the potency of, say, a woman journalist, operating undercover, recording her own personal terror at being mistakenly pursued as prey, rather than relating that experience secondhand through the account of some anonymous woman met on a street corner days or perhaps only hours earlier.[12] As a commenter on Bill Moyers's blog so aptly observed in another context in 2007, the reporter is a more believable, more reliable source than an informant. "The journalist is accountable to the public he/she serves," the commenter wrote. "The reader has no way to test the integrity of the informant."[13]

Cooke reported other telling personal experiences that helped generalize for readers what these women routinely encountered in the homes of strangers. Without the experience of doing domestic work in this way, the most telling specifics likely would not have surfaced. For instance, one employer falsely accused Cooke of skipping several panes of glass while washing a mullioned window. Cooke mentioned this to one of her street corner companions, who explained that such accusations were a common ploy used to renege on the agreed wage. In that instance, Cooke told the women to keep "as a Christmas present" the thirty-eight cents Cooke had earned in those first forty-five minutes on the job. With quiet ceremony, she then put on her coat and left the white woman's house.

White helped Ray Sprigle, a reporter for the *Pittsburgh Post-Gazette*, to spend four weeks in the South as a black man in late summer

1948,[14] a feat John Howard Griffin would repeat eleven years later, in 1959. Both men were white and thus required a far more elaborate physical transformation than White or Cooke. When skin staining and chemical compounds failed for Sprigle, he resorted to marathon tanning sessions in Florida to produce a reasonably convincing effect. In fact, he said, only two people challenged him during his month of travel. Griffin took even more elaborate measures for his longer sojourn on assignment for a magazine called *Sepia*.[15] Operatically, he dyed his skin black. In his case, the magazine serial catapulted into a major best-selling book called *Black Like Me*.[16]

A decade later, Grace Halsell followed Griffin's lead to write *Soul Sister*. She too dyed her skin and spent extended periods in Harlem and traveling through the South, living, experiencing, and documenting her encounters with white people. The one other known skin-dyed excursion into blackness for publication is the work of Joshua Solomon, an undergraduate student at the University of Maryland whose account of a short-lived trip to Atlanta as a black man appeared as an article in the *Washington Post* in 1994.[17]

*Black Like Me* had not been in book stores for a year when editors of the *New York World-Telegram & Sun* asked that newspaper's first black journalist to report on the migrant laborers who traveled up the Atlantic seaboard each summer to till the fields of Long Island. At least two bellwether investigations of the subject preceded Dale Wright's assignment, including Howard Van Smith's series for the *Miami News* in 1958, which won the next year's Pulitzer Prize for National Reporting, and the now classic Edward R. Murrow documentary *Harvest of Shame*,[18] which CBS aired as an after-turkey-feast reflection on Thanksgiving Day, 1960. Wright was the first known reporter to go undercover as a migrant worker himself and did so between April and October 1961.[19] Undercover was an approach the editors of the *New York World-Telegram & Sun* unhesitatingly embraced. The word *World* in its proud lineage harkened to the *New York World* of Nellie Bly, after all.

Years later, long after Wright had moved on to other pursuits, he recalled in an interview how eager he had been at the time "to get my hands on a big story."[20] He told the scholar Robert Miraldi that he had a feel for what the risks and hardships would be; they did not concern him. He devised a plan, wrote an editorial memo, read and learned as much as he could about the issue, and then set out to live the migrant life. The editors set no limitations on him except to stay as long as it took to get the story. In preparation, Miraldi writes, Wright also got a phony identification card from a Social Security office. Renamed Dave Wright, he bought work clothes and then flew to Miami with a little money hidden in his belt and a tiny notepad tucked into a pocket. He then trekked deep into Dade County to find a job picking tomatoes.[21]

Wright's stories described his murderous aches and pains, the outrageously bad housing conditions, the hopelessness all around him. To those who would argue that interviewing and research can create as powerful a result without the dreaded resort to subterfuge,[22] Wright told Miraldi, not so. Some of his most poignant encounters with workers could only have happened undercover, he said, such as the one with Red Fisher, a migrant worker with tuberculosis who took Wright to his home to meet his five children.[23]

In six months on assignment, Wright's actual time in the fields was six weeks.[24] The book his reporting inspired, published four years later, was titled *They Harvest Despair: The Migrant Farm Worker.* It was far more deeply focused on matters of policy than

Wright's personal experiences as chronicled in the newspaper, although those personal experiences certainly framed his thinking. As he recalled in the book's preface, he "lived, worked, ate, and more than once suffered with crews of transient harvesters on long journeys that ended in the rich, black vegetable fields of Eastern Long Island,"[25] and then caused a "national furor" with his "long, hard, painstaking look at the migrant farm worker along the Atlantic seaboard."[26]

Two New York congressmen, the Democrats John V. Lindsay and William Fitts Ryan, had the series entered into the *Congressional Record* and three different social service agencies distributed "tens of thousands" of copies of it in pamphlet form. The American Newspaper Guild cited the series as one of the two most distinguished pieces of reporting for 1961 in the United States or Canada, awarding Wright two Heywood Broun awards for that year. Other national journalism prizes for the series included the Society of the Silurians and the Paul Tobenkin awards for distinguished public service. The newspaper nominated the series for the 1962 Pulitzer Prize for National Reporting. In addition, Wright reported that after the series ran, both New York and New Jersey took remedial steps to reorganize their migrant farm-labor programs, including, in New York's case, pilot programs and teams of experts sent to acquaint workers with their rights and responsibilities. Wright could have been speaking for any number of immersion reporters in the way he explained his purpose, which was to provide "an amplification of the migrant's own faint cries . . . of bitterness, resentment, unhappiness, the futility of existence cut off from the rest of humanity."[27]

Typically for reporters, Wright offered "no sociological cause-and-effect studies" or "clinical analyses." In statistics, he dealt only briefly. The book, he said, "has none of the flavor of do-gooder philosophizing." There was already plenty of documentary evidence to confirm the transient harvester's plight. What qualified Wright to tell the story, he said, was that he had experienced it. He made absolutely no claim to having wholly inhabited the migrant's experience. How could he have? His choice of words was precise. His key qualification was limited to having "lived and labored alongside the migrant farm worker."[28]

Wright died nearly fifty years later, on Christmas Eve 2009, at the age of eighty-six. The Associated Press carried his obituary, which the *New York Times* also featured. It recalled his significant role as "the first reporter to integrate the newsroom at the old *New York World-Telegram & Sun*,"[29] and noted that he later served as press secretary to New York Mayor Edward Koch, the late Senator Jacob K. Javitz, and Governor Nelson Rockefeller and had been an editor at *Ebony* and *Jet*. His obituaries recalled the migrant series as among his most cherished accomplishments, a reflection of his belief in journalism as a "vehicle for social change."[30] Wright the barrier-breaker (at his death, his family recalled him telling of childish pranks played on him in the newsroom—food at his desk was spat on, he was locked out of the bathrooms)[31] demonstrated once again one of the ancillary values of bringing reporters of color into white newsrooms, as Cooke had previewed a full decade earlier.

With *Soul Sister* in 1969, Grace Halsell failed to repeat Griffin's publishing sensation with *Black Like Me*.[32] A substantial body of heavily debated academic literature has grown up around the animating premise of these two books, the decision by both reporters to attempt to experience life across the color line from the perspective of a white person presenting as black through an extreme act of skin dyeing.[33] Both books have sections on race and work. Among the stories Halsell tells are those surrounding her day work as a domestic in Southern homes. In one episode, she thwarts the aggressive, entitled sexual advance of an employer's husband and in another describes the more insidious and degrading sting of a bologna sandwich, offered by her employer at arm's length and on a paper plate, with the instructions to "open yourself a Coke."[34]

The outlines of these encounters are familiar from the writings of black women novelists of the Harlem Renaissance forty years earlier; Nella Larsen's *Passing* comes readily to mind.[35] Halsell's stories are not nearly so well told as Larsen's, but her undercover pose, her actual act of passing, whips the mind around in ways that manage to add new dimensions to the telling. If we accept Halsell as a reliable narrator, these are not invented or embellished scenes from a novelist's imagination based on secondhand reports of the encounters of others, à la Harriet Beecher Stowe. These are actual incidents in the life of an actual person. True, she concocted the circumstances with prior intent to publish, but not what happened once she was in place. The encounters were real.

For subsequent books over the coming decade, Halsell enacted two other temporary transformations. For her 1973 *Bessie Yellowhair,* she lived on a reservation in the Southwest with a Navajo family, lost "her sense of being white,"[36] as the jacket copy asserts, dyed her skin ochre, and then "took the dress and identity of the Yellowhair family, and answered an ad placed by a suburban California family for a live-in Navajo maid."[37] Five years later, Halsell, who was Texas-born and fluent in Spanish, dressed up like a Mexican peasant, swam the Rio Grande twice, and once scooted under a border fence for *The Illegals,* her book aimed at "the efforts of a poor, energetic, and ambitious people to better themselves, much like the great waves of nineteenth and early twentieth-century

European immigrants."[38] It happened to be published very soon after two other authors with a Texas connection took up the subject: John Davidson's "The Long Road North," appeared in the October 1977 issue of *Texas Monthly,* and later as a book, and Dick J. Reavis's more policy-oriented book, *Without Documents,* was published in 1978. Reavis does have a final section with case studies of illegal immigrants that includes a description of his own river crossing with an undocumented worker, though he keeps himself very much in the background.[39] Although the work on migration bears mention in a discussion of the undercover genre, the method in most of the cases is more immersive than undercover. The excursions into deception are more limited; the reporters attempt to blend in rather than to impersonate, and they make their real intentions known. Davidson used the term *shadow*[40] to describe his approach, which is more exact.

A *Los Angeles Times* reviewer compared the Reavis and Halsell books in 1978, praising Reavis for the facts and evidence he gathered. Halsell's "heart-rending vignettes about courageous, hardworking Mexicans struggling against overwhelming odds," were way overdone in a debate "already tinged with so much emotion," he wrote, but she had nonetheless humanized those caught up in it.[41]

Halsell's experiences also have another mind-flipping overlay. Like Griffin's, they are the experiences of a privileged white person presenting herself in guises that allow her both to experience encounters that otherwise would never happen and to observe those encounters at the same time, as if from both sides of a two-way mirror—her image. The pose enables her to communicate to her reader, who may recognize herself in these encounters, a sense of anger and shame at the behavior of people of her own kind; the insult, degradation, and fear she experienced as a would-be member of her briefly adopted kind; and the inconsideration and inhumanity of one human being toward another. Halsell, in the epilogue to *Soul Sister,* explains the dichotomy, the paradoxical, unresolved role she created of oppressor and oppressed. Would she do it again? No. Was she glad she did it? Yes. Why? Because it expanded her sense of the world.[42]

When *Soul Sister* came out in 1969, the *Washington Post* assigned the book to a black reviewer, Dorothy Gilliam, who presaged the criticism to come. She wrote of her revulsion at Halsell's audacity in calling herself "soul sister" after the experience of a few months when she had "never managed to escape the prison of her own generation."[43] "This is not only an affront," Gilliam wrote, "but is foolish."[44]

The paradox for Marvel Cooke's reporting was not the bifurcation of oppressor and oppressed, but her class status as a black woman doing day work for a spell, a black woman in 1950 who was also a university-educated full-time staff reporter at a mainstream New York daily. Would Cooke, could Cooke have been able to walk out on a day's wage, however inadequate, had she not been pretending to make her living at itinerant housework? Could she have walked out on even thirty-eight cents and a full day's wage if she had really needed the money?

More importantly, did the ability to enact such a prideful response, the escape hatch of being able to walk away from a humiliating or brutalizing encounter, point up the inherent lack of authenticity in many such undercover ruses? Jack London escaping to seek a comfortable room and a bath comes to mind. Does that unreality, in part, invalidate at least some of the information she gathered and what she sought to convey? Does it underscore the sheer contrivance of adopting such a pose? Or does it allow her to relate the experience more closely to the reactions the majority of her white readers would be likely to have in such a situation, thus validating her experience for them and strengthening the impact of the work for those most likely to encounter it?

The team assembled by the *Atlanta Constitution* in 1979 for its undercover investigation of wage exploitation was greatly enabled by the willingness of two of the newspaper's black journalists, Lee May and Charlene Smith-Williams, to report on location under arduous physical conditions. May, an editorial writer at the time, answered the call to head south to work in Georgia's turpentine-producing woods. Smith-Williams hired out as a motel maid. Their contributions were central to a sweeping investigation titled "THE UNDERPAID AND UNDER-PROTECTED."[45] Paul Lieberman and Chester Goolrick, as project leaders, were deeply involved in the reporting, too, but the richest details came from May, who, Lieberman recalled years later, "deserves more credit than any of us for doing the most significant field research by far. He was a genius at observation and emotional control."[46]

Thirty years after those two-plus weeks of the hardest labor he had ever done, the details remained etched on the underside of May's eyelids. He remembers using his own full given name—Eddie Lee May—and doing no more to disguise himself than dressing down, leaving his then somewhat exotic Honda back in Atlanta in favor of a local clunker, and adopting a posture more humble than his own. He recalled the experience of working long hours in a field where the water came up to his ankles and in heat so intense that the gallons of water he drank each day did not make him urinate. "I can tell you that is the truth," May said. "That is why this reporting is essential."[47]

Collecting the individual stories of the turpentine workers themselves was critical to understanding the people who did the work. May found that they did not see themselves as exploited and disaffected, nor did they harbor any smoldering anger because they owed their souls to the company store, as he and his editors back in Atlanta had been inclined to believe before he went. The company did, in fact, have a strangulation financial hold on many of them, May found, but it was not a source of conversation or apparent discontent. And the known management rationalization—that minimum hourly wages made no sense in a situation where every Monday was lost to hangovers from the weekend's binge drinking, even when the workers showed up—reflected the reality.

May also learned that despite however much there might have been to complain about (his own first week's wage, after deductions to the company store for food and the little he managed to accomplish, required him to reach into his own pocket and pay the company for the privilege of working for it), turpentiners not only refrained from complaining themselves but deliberately distanced themselves from anyone who might. Lieberman said they lived "by a different credo."[48]

May's explanation was more nuanced. "The series disabused us of the notion that we were all heroic, rushing in to save the day," he said. "It is wrong to believe that everyone who works in horrendous situations—what we think are horrendous situations—thinks the situation is all bad. Some people might call it Stockholm Syndrome. If you work in a situation long enough, it certainly becomes normal, no matter what anyone else thinks." Complainers were misfits. "I think it might have been the only thing they thought they could do to earn a living and this is what they did," he said. "And anyone in the situation who does something to rock the boat will be blamed. . . . And if you have to do something, you'd rather not have someone around reminding you of how bad it is."

In the doing, May also divined the work's special allure. "I quickly learned in those moments of taking a break and looking up at the sky that this work had a certain appeal. If you have to do labor and you have to do hard work—some thought and I came to understand—this was better than driving a truck hauling furniture some place."[49]

In short, as Lieberman explained, what May discovered by being there as one of the workers was "much more interesting than what your ideological prejudices would have inclined you to believe or write." And Lieberman pointed out another benefit of having a reporter experience the situation firsthand. To publish information that called into question the pillars of that Southern Georgia community meant you needed to be able to verify what others might tell you. "You can't make accusations on the basis of the reports of semi-literate workers," Lieberman said. "To see for yourself is being responsible in this case."[50]

Goolrick made the trip south with May to interview the turpentine bosses and get an official response to May's findings before the series went to press. He enjoyed watching the turpentine boss's reaction when the question was put in May's presence: "Do you pay your workers minimum wage?"[51]

May added, "There were no fist fights, no bursting out, which reaffirmed my belief that what I had done was the right thing to do. They didn't try to lie. They couldn't and they knew it." As for the turpentiners, May went back to see them, too, with an offering of a bottle of whiskey. There was indeed always whiskey. "They welcomed me back," he said, "as a turpentine brother."[52]

The series won the 1980 Grand Prize in that year's prestigious

Robert F. Kennedy Journalism Awards.[53] For May, who later went on to work as the *Los Angeles Times*'s bureau chief in Atlanta and then as that newspaper's White House correspondent, nothing in his fine career matched the experience of those weeks in the woods. "In some ways," he said, "it's the most lasting. It was what many of us going into journalism had in mind for the kind of work we wanted to do—work we considered important on many levels, exposing wrongs, exposing problems in society that needed fixing, helping improve conditions for people who needed something better to happen in their lives. It was work that allowed us to use the best of our skills—work that would be known and appreciated by a lot of people and institutions in our society, and, in some way, work that would help improve the lot of some segment of our society and make aware the conditions that needed working on by those who could help make those conditions better."[54] And, he added, "I'll say it. This is the only way this information could be gathered. If you believe it is worth having, you do what you have to do."

"Merlina" was a diminutive that Merle Linda Wolin already had used from time to time before she joined the staff of the *Los Angeles Herald-Examiner* in 1979, proposing that she become the city's first and only reporter assigned to cover LA's already teeming Hispanic community as a regular beat. Editors Jim Bellows and Frank Lalli liked the idea—Wolin was fluent in Spanish—and told her to go ahead and develop a story list.

In those first few weeks, as she left the newspaper's downtown offices each night, she could hear a "bzz-z-z-t, bzzz-z-z-z-t"[55] coming from a number of what appeared to be abandoned buildings. In Spanish, she asked around to find out what it was. Sewing machines, she learned. The area was rife with sweatshops. The more she asked around about it, the more people became fearful and declined to talk. It was quickly clear that doing a series up front as a reporter, interviewing bosses and workers, would have yielded little information of value.

Wolin went back to her editors and proposed a plan to go undercover in the guise of an undocumented sweatshop worker from Portuguese-speaking Brazil. This would cover for her not-American-but-not-native accent in Spanish. Bellows and Lalli were skeptical that a Jew from Wyoming who had cofounded *Mother Jones*—whose only sewing experience was as a childhood 4-H'er—could be convincing in such a performance. But Wolin reminded them that she had studied theater arts at Berkeley and was still very much an actress at heart. She convinced them she could bring off the role-play since so many Latin Americans have Spanish or German background. "But how I carried myself was most important. I walked more hunched over, more humble. Embarrassingly humble, especially in front of a man or any authority figure. *That,* I had to work on: casting my eyes downward." She created a character named Merlina de Novais, a woman who had left a difficult family situation in Brazil and had made her way north, who found a coyote to bring her across the border and who was living with distant relatives in Los Angeles. And, like millions of others, she was trying to find an entry-level job in the garment industry, then the third largest in the state, after agriculture and aerospace.[56]

The newspaper's instruction was never to lie. One can adopt an alias with impunity, it turns out. An alias is not legally a lie.

Friends at Spanish-language radio helped Wolin dress the part in cheap, brightly floral-printed polyester with a big cross at her neck. She used a pancake makeup with a warm brownish-tint and painted her nails dark red. In her wallet, she kept only bus fare, a picture of Jesus, and a little Cuban calendar that featured Che Guevara. In the space of five weeks, she managed to land three different jobs, even though her sewing skills by no means met the industrial standard. The newspaper cut her loose to pursue the story for the better part of a year, including the court proceedings over a suit she brought against one of the employers who refused to pay her. She was so convincing that every night, when she returned to the paper to compose her thoughts from the day, none of her colleagues recognized her until she spoke.

The series[57] may now be as forgotten as that defunct Hearst newspaper, but it won an appearance for Wolin before a Congressional subcommittee investigating home labor[58] and recognition as a Pulitzer Prize finalist in the Public Service category for 1982.[59] Actually, it was reported to have been the Pulitzer jury's unanimous first choice for the prize, a decision the Pulitzer board also reportedly overturned. John J. Goldman of the *Los Angeles Times* quoted some jury members saying that the board objected to her pose as an illegal alien and others saying that the board did not consider any of the jury's recommendations to be first-rate. He said the jury had anticipated the objection and submitted a supplementary confidential report in Wolin's case to defend the choice, pointing out that she had solicited responses from factory operators as well as from the workers. Goldman quoted the *Herald Examiner*'s editor, Mary Anne Dolan, expressing exasperation. "If they are going to, in essence, disqualify entries because undercover reporting was involved, they ought to say so beforehand. If that's the reason we lost, it makes a joke of the whole process."[60]

At the subcommittee hearing, Wolin reminded the congressmen of the journalist's role. "I report," she said. "I describe what I see. I am not an expert who has studied the ramifications of this type of employment, nor someone who can tell you authoritatively whether it should be legalized."[61] She went on to describe the experiences of hundreds of Latina women doing piece work from home for impossibly low wages because they had no choice.

The Wolin series was published simultaneously in the city's Spanish language newspaper *La Opinion* and was read each day over a local Spanish-language radio station and summarized on local Spanish-language television each night. Both newspapers did reprints in the hundreds of thousands of copies, and both reprints sold out. In her testimony, Wolin recalled how the radio host took sick one day and neglected to tell his substitute to read that day's installment and how jammed their switchboard was with calls from workers wanting the next installment of the series. "It was very important to them," Wolin said, "because it was the first time that they saw anyone in what they considered to be America or the traditional media take up what for them is a daily reality."[62]

Looking back, Wolin said in an interview for this book that "Sweatshop" is still the high point of her ranging career. There are stories, she said, "that you can only understand by having an inside witness to make them credible. I'm sure that covers the gamut of shady, dangerous occupations where people are making tons of money off those who are most vulnerable in our midst. I could not have gotten this story interviewing workers. There. Was. No. Way."[63]

Orwell's *Down and Out* inspired Neil Henry's assignment for the *Washington Post* to spend two months in the winter 1980 as "a homeless vagrant" in Baltimore and Washington, DC. Henry's task was to investigate and report[64] on conditions inside the flophouses, soup kitchens, and homeless shelters "as the homeless themselves experienced it."[65] The work produced a twelve-part series. Three years later, Henry transformed himself again to explore the lives of migrant workers in the tomato and tobacco fields of North Carolina "and the systemic abuses they suffered at the hands of farmers and paymasters."[66] That effort was published in six parts. Henry completed his reporting using a technique similar to the one Goolrick and Lieberman developed for the Georgia wage-exploitation series. Henry returned to North Carolina as Neil Henry, *Washington Post* reporter, to interview his former bosses. He acknowledged his subterfuge and sought their reaction to what he had learned in the fields.

As Henry recalled in his much later book, *American Carnival,* his series on homelessness for the *Post* "elicited more powerful and approving public feedback than anything I have ever published." He said his migrant series, which bore the supertitle THE BLACK DISPATCH, a moniker for the transport vans, "stirred widespread public anger over the abuses and prompted vows by the state of North Carolina to reform the system."[67]

The local newspaper guild chapter named him Journalist of the Year for 1983 for the series, and he received an honorable mention from the awards committee of the Robert F. Kennedy Foundation.[68] His work also was singled out for notice in a ten-page ominously titled cover story in *Time,* headlined "Journalism Under Fire"[69] in September 1983. Yet a few of Henry's peers, at the *Washington Post* and across the country, questioned critically the way he and his editors had conceived of and executed these projects.

Tom Goldstein called attention to Henry's migrant work in his 1985 book, *The News at Any Cost: How Journalists Compromise Their Ethics to Shape the News,* and to that of another *Post* reporter, Athelia Knight, who took prison buses in 1984 from the strip of downtown Washington, DC, at Eleventh and G streets, known as "The Avenue," to Lorton Prison in the Virginia suburbs. Her purpose was to investigate whether it was easier to get drugs at Lorton than on the street.[70] Eight times she boarded the buses with five different drivers, during which she variously saw women stuffing marijuana cigarettes into balloons that they then would partly swallow to get past inspections, or hiding them in clothing; one woman concealed a white powdery substance in a hat. Riders, she said, were mostly "black teen-agers and women in their 20s and 30s," a cohort in which Knight, a young black woman of roughly the same age, managed to blend in without attracting unusual attention. On one trip, she said, riders were smoking marijuana or PCP-laced cigarettes; on another trip, a passenger tried to sell her marijuana. On a few trips there were no incidents.[71] At the prison, she offered her driver's license for identification but no more, and submitted to pat downs and even the more intrusive body searches that the other women were sometimes ordered to endure.[72]

Writing of Henry, Goldstein noted his "scraggly" bearded pose, and how "ughsome," "foul-smelling," and "exhausted" he soon became without money to buy a change of clothes. Goldstein found the pose to be sheer "make-believe" (much in the way that critics had chided Jack London's pose for *Abyss* back in 1902), since as a reporter with a *Washington Post* income and expense account, Henry easily could have found a way to bathe and clean up. "There is a real question of just what he was observing," Goldstein wrote.[73] But he also pointed out that Henry carried a notebook, a press pass, and his own Social Security number for identification if asked. To some of his companions, Henry revealed his actual identity.

Henry saw the experience differently, looking back on it thoughtfully a quarter of a century later, by then as a professor who would later become dean of the graduate journalism school at the University of California, Berkeley. "Well-meaning"[74] as the earlier criticism may have been, Henry said it did nothing then or later to dispel the intense pride he felt in the undercover work he had done—"gut-wrenching experiences—very deep learning experiences that profoundly affected me."[75] Never before or since, he said, had the public feedback from something he had published been "more powerful and approving"[76] than it was in these two cases. Without equivocation, he said, the stories "still resonate with profound meaning for me and are among the most purposeful and valuable journalism I will ever practice. I tell this to my students."[77]

Undercover or not, authentic experience or not, in situations where certain physical characteristics help a reporter to blend in unobtrusively, the ability to look the part has always been an important journalistic tool. This is true not only in cases such as Wolin's in the Los Angeles sweatshops but also for Knight on the prison bus and for a slew of housing and employment discrimination stings. In projects variously undertaken from the 1960s to the 1990s, editors at newspapers such as the *Miami Herald*,[78] the *Dayton Journal Herald*,[79] and the *Hartford Courant*[80] assigned teams of black and white reporters to pose as prospective tenants or homebuyers and thus put reports of questionable practices in the local real estate markets to a real-time test.

Two projects are pertinent to review in this connection: one undertaken by the *Courant* and one abandoned by *Newsday,* both in 1989. In the first case, *Columbia Journalism Review* presented the *Courant* with a coveted "laurel" for its effectiveness in exposing and confirming the "widespread practice of racial discrimination by area realtors." It affirmed the way *Courant* reporters had posed as prospective homebuyers in the market for homes in the then pricey $200,000 range. The supposed black clients were "subjected to financial grilling, racial steering, and tactics that effectively barred them from even seeing the inside of a house." *CJR* also pointed out that while the Greater Hartford Association of Realtors praised the investigation as a "very valid means of getting to the bottom of the issue,"[81] the *Courant*'s own ombudsman, Henry McNulty, opposed it in his column,[82] even as he acknowledged what was good about it: its meticulous preparation, careful writing and clear presentation, and its excellent results. But he simply could not get beyond the lies it took to do the work. Reporters had altered their names and provided other false information to obscure their identity as reporters, a practice that the newspaper's guidelines actually allowed. Misrepresentation was prohibited, but with an escape clause for when a "legitimate story in the public interest" required a more elaborate finesse. McNulty also appreciated a sidebar the newspaper had provided to explain the methodology. But for him this was not enough. He was willing to draw a distinction between "actively giving a false name and passively letting someone assume a reporter is just an average consumer." That passive approach, for him, would have passed muster, but not what they had done. Even when the goals are as noble as these were or when the work produced positive results that strike "a blow for justice and equality," as this reporting had done, for him the results did not justify the subterfuge. "A news story, however important, can't be based on deception," he later wrote. "It was not an easy conclusion to reach. There's a long history of reporters' disguising themselves to root out corruption."[83]

McNulty's reflections appeared in a case study about the project that he wrote several years later, repeating the thoughts he expressed in his readers' representative column, which appeared two weeks after the initial report, citing the impact of the series: the governor had ordered a statewide investigation of racial discrimination by real estate agencies, and the state's human rights commissioner said he had plans to begin random testing of real estate agencies that month. Later, in the case study, McNulty said a few readers agreed with his position; most reporters at the newspaper did not. They argued that the deception was benign when compared to the illegal activity it disclosed. For the study, McNulty asked the newspaper's executive editor, Michael Waller, if he thought the *Courant* could have done the story without the deceptive element. Waller's conclusion was no. It would have been too hard to find actual buyers in exactly the same timeframe who met the color criteria. And Waller saw a distinction between perpetrating a ruse as reporters doing a job and asking others to perform those deceptive roles. "He's probably right," was McNulty's rejoinder. "So I say, with deep regret, that we couldn't—and so, we shouldn't—have done this investigation, despite its social importance."[84]

*Newsday* went through a similar exercise that same year as part of a monumental series based on computerized modeling to examine all aspects of racial segregation on Long Island, from housing to education to community life and to the more informal relations among the groups. For the housing portion of the series, the plans being considered over the year and a half the project was in the works were incredibly elaborate, including a "massive, scientifically designed experiment that would statistically measure the prevalence of racial steering in Long Island's huge real estate industry."[85] This was described in a *CJR* piece that detailed the chronology of the project, which was published two years after the fact. As mid-level editors inched closer to backing a plan, they began exchanging letters with a testing expert who proposed a sophisticated plan with the potential, *CJR* said, to "challenge the belief that in modern America a black family with means can buy a house anywhere." The mid-level editors sent detailed plans for the project to the newspaper's then editor, Anthony Marro, who received them just as the *Courant* story was getting attention, including the negative blast from its own McNulty. Hard questions went back and forth. During his days as a reporter at the *New York Times,* Marro had been privy to a number of Justice Department stings gone wrong. He was reported to have had reservations about the lack of probable cause and was troubled by the proposal's call to pick the agents at random, which statistical method requires. *CJR* quoted him as saying: "The question is, should there be a threshold of bad conduct before a newspaper unleashes this sort of thing on unsuspecting people?" He was not sure *Newsday* had reached that point with the island's realtors.

Marro had other concerns, too. He worried that reporters might lack the training or talent for an undercover sting and if the newspaper did not use actors, how might their behavior be tracked for consistency? Someone suggested body microphones, but that would have introduced a host of other issues that would then have to be grappled with, and then, there was the problem of keeping the project secret with so many players involved, and the agony of what one leak could mean. Email may have been in its infancy, but the fax machines buzzed in every real estate office on the island.

On Labor Day, 1989, Marro said no, more on the grounds of the "technical obstacles" than the reluctance to go undercover. As *CJR* quoted Marro saying, "I saw many downsides. If anything went bad, that could possibly compromise and complicate a worthwhile series." The article also noted that Marro dismissed at least one suggestion from someone in the newsroom that his decision to say no to the testing was influenced by the fear of losing real estate advertising, or, the *CJR* writer wondered, given the objection to undercover reporting in some circles, the newspaper feared jeopardizing the overall project's prize prospects with an undercover dimension. But every editor at the newspaper denied this ever entered into consideration in any way. As it happened, *Newsday* in fact entered the segregation project in the Pulitzer's Public Service category, but did not win or place.[86]

A race-and-class discrimination story that got considerable notice in 1992 was the pose as a busboy at a white country club of a thirty-year-old black attorney, educated at Princeton and at Harvard Law School.[87] The spate of attention the piece received in *New York* magazine landed Lawrence Otis Graham a Hollywood deal and a contract for the expansion into a book of his original undercover reporting from the Greenwich Country Club.[88]

Color, gender, and other physical attributes also worked for at least one reporter during the early years of the women's liberation movement. Not just any feminist could have succeeded as well as the young and beautiful Gloria Steinem in her application to become a Playboy Bunny for a two-part series she reported in 1963 for *Show*. The magazine is long forgotten but not that story; it lives on among the most amusing and talked about of undercover exploits. It was instrumental in stopping Hugh Hefner's clubs from giving physical examinations to applicants. It also made Steinem a celebrity, drawing some attention she did not find altogether welcome.[89] She returned an advance for a book contract to expand the idea, and at about the same time, rejected an assignment to expose high-end prostitution by posing as a call girl, an idea she found as insulting as it was frightening.[90]

For a long time, Steinem saw as a huge career blunder her eleven days as Bunny "Marie Ochs," hired under her grandmother's name and Social Security number.[91] It led to no serious new assignments and her least favored, but often-invoked characterization.[92] It was only later that she understood the usefulness of the ruse to allow her to expose Playboy's "phony glamour and exploitative employment policies."[93] In autobiographical notes included in *Outrageous Acts and Everyday Rebellions,* a book compiled from a collection of her writings, she lists it among her personal celebrations by saying, "My exposé of working in a Playboy Club has outlived all the Playboy Clubs, both here and abroad."[94]

As to her depiction of the Bunny of 1963 in general, a relook at the experience thirty-six years later presented a wholly alternative view. Katherine Leigh Scott was New York Bunny "Kay" at exactly the same time Steinem did her reporting. Scott started her story by recounting a chance exchange with Steinem at a book publisher's party thirty years after their mutual Playboy experience. Scott's own reaction surprised her. "As one of the Bunnies she had portrayed in the article," she wrote, "I still harbored after all these years a mild residue of resentment over what had seemed at the time a kind of betrayal."[95]

In Scott's latter-day view, she and her fellow Bunnies in those days were women of aspiration, a group comprised of teenagers who were seeking careers as actresses or models, college students, and single mothers, all in search of convenient hours, flexible schedules, and more money than their fathers had ever earned for what amounted to basic waitressing. The "social revolution that engulfed the 1960s had yet to trickle down to women,"[96] Scott wrote, and unlike the picture Steinem had created, Scott saw the decision to submit to the Bunny's life as a willing exploitation of sexuality, sure, but also "intelligence, wit, upper arm strength, youthful exuberance and full range of survival instincts. We saw an opportunity and grabbed it."[97]

At the time, she recalled the common reaction to Steinem's piece as "more or less, 'Good for her.'" Yet Scott wondered anew how Steinem could have worked among this group of women for eleven days, observed them, heard them share their thoughts, and then profiled them with such condescension. ("One wonders what she had expected. Erudite discussions in the dressing room? New York's intelligentsia convening in the Playmate Bar?"[98])

Scott didn't think Steinem was in a position to identify with the others, nor did she care to do so, since at that point in her life, she would not have considered working as a waitress, let alone one in bunny ears, except for the sake of a story. "Her viewpoint," Scott said, "was that of a journalist—or more to the point, a privileged professional."[99]

A little nationality-and-affiliation sleight of hand enabled the *Miami Herald* to cover the Pope's visit to Cuba in 1998. The island nation ignored all of the *Herald*'s requests for visas for the visit because, as the *New York Times* put it, Cuba's state security apparatus considered the newspaper a "Cuban exile mouthpiece."[100] Doug Clifton, the *Herald*'s executive editor at the time, explained to readers that all the Havana-datelined stories about the papal visit that had been namelessly signed "*Herald* Staff Reporter" were actually the work of three *Herald* reporters who arrived in Cuba as tourists on their own foreign passports. ("One of the virtues of an internationally diverse staff," Clifton wrote, "is greater access to writers with foreign passports.") And, he said, those photographs that the newspaper credited as "Special to the *Herald*" actually were shot by *Herald* photographers whom an unnamed newspaper "friendly to our cause" had credentialed as a professional courtesy. Clifton further explained that given past refusals, they suspected early that visas would not be granted. So contingency plans were made. "Without going into much detail, we came up with several strategies," Clifton wrote. "None of the twelve journalists on the formal list could be part of the contingency plan and no journalist

who had been ejected on a prior 'undercover' trip could be involved either." Clifton said he would have preferred to go without
"the skullduggery and deceit," but was very proud of what they
had produced.[101]

In New York of the mid-1990s, undocumented Asians, not Latin
Americans, were the more common holders of the dreaded sweatshop franchise, practically beckoning the Asian American reporter
Jane H. Lii to go undercover as a sweatshop worker in 1995 for
the Metro section of the *New York Times*.[102] Helen Zia for *Ms.*
magazine followed the next year with a similar, although more
often cited report.[103]

Sometimes the inverse happens. Sometimes the reporter tailors
the assignment to create the ethnic or racial fit, rather than the
other way around. For Barbara Ehrenreich's *Nickel and Dimed:
On (Not) Getting By in America,* she picked low-wage situations
where her whiteness would not bring undue attention to her.
For the domestic service chapter, for example, she went to Maine,
where the state's "demographic albinism," she explained, made
it "a perfect place for a blue-eyed, English-speaking Caucasian
to infiltrate the low-wage workforce, no questions asked."[104] As
in most surreptitious reportage, much of the nuance in what she
learned could only have been gleaned from firsthand experience.
What struck her especially was the centrality of pain for her coworkers and how the infirmities they suffered—"Lori and Pauline
are excused from vacuuming on account of their backs"—affected
the workload of others, "which means you dread being assigned
to a team with them."[105] What are the chances of knowing to ask
the question that would elicit the response that would reveal this
important aspect of the story? And yet through direct engagement,
but only through direct engagement, would it become immediately obvious.

Ehrenreich's infiltrations ushered undercover reporting into the twenty-first century in a big way. Her first report on low-wage work, in the January 1999 *Harper's*, centers on her experiences waitressing for a restaurant chain. This and her excursions into other jobs appear in the book.

Soon after its publication in 2001, James Fallows in the *Atlantic* engaged Ehrenreich in an extended public exchange of letters. He compared her book to Griffin's *Black Like Me* and Michael Harrington's *The Other America,* both published in the early 1960s. Both, he wrote, had made "white, affluent Americans of the Kennedy-Johnson era say to one another, 'Wait a minute! You mean everyone isn't living the Ozzie and Harriet lifestyle?'" Fallows said those books had "helped the influential part of American society imagine what the lives of those they didn't see each day could be like."[106]

Ehrenreich said she had never read *Black Like Me* and distinguished what she had done from Griffin's adventures in dyed-black skin. Her deceptions, she said, were only two: that she omitted from job applications one year of college and her "rusty old Ph.D. in biology" so that she would not "come across as some kind of downwardly tripping alcoholic washout, or worse." And she waited until the end of each foray to identify herself to her coworkers as a writer on assignment—a revelation that underwhelmed them. Unlike Griffin or Harrington, she felt no sense of exploring strange new lands. The turf was familiar. Her former husband had been a warehouse worker, truck driver, and steel worker before he became a labor organizer, and their home had often been filled with "blue- and pink-collar people."[107]

What was new in the experience would only have revealed itself in the doing: how very hard the work was, how restrictive were the working conditions—"no talking" really got to her—

and how difficult were the personal circumstances of so many of her coworkers. What also surprised her was how much she found herself caring about how she performed each day. Fallows pushed the Harrington-Griffin example further, saying the similarity he saw was not in tone or approach, but in the way that both of the earlier books "broke an intellectual and imaginative barrier. They managed to make the American reading public, including its influential upper layers, care about issues that had slipped from respectable notice."[108]

At the time, May 2001, he predicted Ehrenreich's book would have like impact "because it is readable, funny, and vivid rather than scolding or hand-wringing from a distance," as newspaper accounts of a nation divided have tended to be.[109] A decade after it first appeared, the book had sold in paperback and hardback, at last count, more than 1.5 million copies.

# NINE

# UNDERCOVER UNDER FIRE

Ted Conover was twenty when he delayed his last year of college to spend four months[1] "hopping freight" across the western half of the United States to write about the last generation of American hoboes, placing himself at the far end of a long and fruitful vine of American writers who tramp dating back to the 1800s.

Conover's adventure began in fall 1980, about five months after the *Washington Post* published Neil Henry's wrenching twelve-part series about the DC area down-and-out. What Conover had in mind was more vagabond than vagrant, not a big city newspaper's sharp local focus on a burgeoning and increasingly intractable social problem through the device of the reporter as derelict, which Henry had ably produced. This was to be Conover's own ranging chronicle of HoBodom, as he both encountered and experienced it. He channeled as literary muses Jack London and George Orwell, John Howard Griffin, Jack Kerouac, and even Hermann Hesse.[2] Conover admired Henry's recent newspaper work, too, and before setting out on his own travels, made a point of seeking out the *Post* reporter for advice and affirmation.

The genius in stories such as these but on a variety of topics—so prevalent in the late 1970s and 1980s—is the ability their writers demonstrated to insinuate themselves into the action as participant-observers, to gain the trust of chance companions and an invitation into the private-most aspects of their lives, not only to witness the dangers and hardships that beset them but to experience them, too, as they were being lived. "I self-identified as an American from the semi-urban West," Conover recalled years later, "and considered the big city rescue missions on the East Coast to likely be the scariest places on earth; that made me extra-admiring of Neil." Beyond that, he said, that Henry wrote for the *Washington Post* "and that they [the *Post* editors] endorsed his participatory approach heartened me, I would say—made me feel more confident about my own idea."[3]

On return from his travels, Conover's confidence no doubt grew greater after completing the senior thesis in anthropology[4] ("Between Freedom and Poverty: Railroad Tramps of the American West") that inspired his quest. An Amherst student magazine published an episode from his travels, "A Morning with Pops," which the college's alumni magazine republished in 1981.[5] The rest of this Conover anecdote sounds like a young writer's dream sequence, but it is factual: The excerpt attracted the attention of a local reporter for the Associated Press, whose published interview with Conover in turn caught the attention of NBC's *The Today Show.* The program featured Conover on a morning when the literary agent, Sterling Lord, happened to be watching. Lord then agreed to represent him. Viking published *Rolling Nowhere: Riding the Rails with America's Hoboes* in January 1984,[6] a book that propelled the young Conover into a career as writer-participant-observer in the kissing-cousin genres of undercover and immersion reporting.

Conover's most significant personal asset for the project was not race but youth, like so many would-be tramps before him. He was twenty-four by the time *Rolling Nowhere* was in its first printing and had already "crossed the country on my bicycle, worked in a Spanish sausage factory, done community organizing as a VISTA volunteer in inner-city Dallas and, of course, spent four months on the rails with hoboes."[7] To his dismay, the publisher positioned the book as the work of a naïf. Several major reviewers highlighted this too as the real charm of the book but also as its weakness,[8] a view he also came to accept in time. "These are a young man's adventures," he writes in the preface to an edition of the paperback published in 2001.[9]

His second book, *Coyotes,* published in 1986, detailed his experiences following undocumented Mexicans on their migratory path to the United States, men Conover later called "the new America hoboes."[10] The work grew out of some of his encounters during the reporting phase of *Rolling Nowhere* but also was inspired by a piece by John Crewdson in the *New York Times* that described a Mexican border crossing into Arizona. "The piece was written in the third person and I remember concluding that Crewdson had probably not done the actual crossing himself," Conover recalled. "But why couldn't a writer do that, I remember thinking, and why couldn't that story be told dramatically, in the first person?"[11]

This Conover outing was not to be undercover. It could not have been. Not even by dyeing his blond hair dark or by color correcting his blue eyes to brown—neither of which he attempted—could Conover have passed for a campesino. Even in the same style of dress and baseball cap—there is a photograph of Conover and his companions arranged around what appears to be a campfire—his Dutch-Nordic features mark him. And even if he could have passed physically, although his Spanish was fluent, his accent would have given him away.[12] Beyond that, as John Davidson and Dick

Reavis had found nearly a decade earlier, to be able to travel along, or shadow, required the explicit or tacit permission of everyone involved in the journey. The writers easily could have been border patrol spies; their very presence could put their companions at risk.

Sometimes trust was established in a hurry. Davidson, for instance, met Javier only hours before they both got on a bus for Mexico. But Davidson had the advantage of an introduction from a well-known activist who worked on behalf of illegal immigrants, which helped establish him as worthy. "I looked like a college grad," he said. "Glasses, Brooks Brothers shirt. I didn't look like I was in the border patrol. He could read me pretty easily. He was smart enough to know that I was all right."[13]

For encounters with other border-crossers and the coyotes, he and Javier cooked up a story about Davidson being Costa Rican to explain why he didn't look Mexican, but he doesn't recall ever having to use it. (Shades of Merle Linda Wolin's pose as "Merlina," the ostensible Brazilian sweatshop worker, for her sweatshop series in the *Los Angeles Herald-Examiner*.) "The real deception was between myself and my wanting to take myself out of the story and not have it be about me," Davidson said. "Who I was deceiving was the reader."[14]

In a prologue to Davidson's 1977 piece for *Texas Monthly*, he recounts how Javier agreed to be shadowed to Mexico and then back to San Antonio. "Then you would know what it's like to be a wetback," he told Davidson. "That way you could get the joke."[15] Conover met his companions while he already was in central Mexico. It had not been his plan to accompany them in this way, but after a Mexican farmer told him, "It is better to see once than to listen many times," he became "intoxicated with the idea of experiencing a crossing,"[16] knowing how much could go wrong.

Davidson, Reavis, and Halsell in the late 1970s and Conover in 1987 would not be the last to attempt by clandestine means to humanize cross-border migration, a subject that dings all sides of the social, political, and economic triangle. It is another sign of the nature of ephemera that these authors and their editors and agents might well have genuinely believed that each effort was utterly singular. All of these undertakings happened years before magazine and newspaper articles were widely accessible through Internet search engines. Even as late as 2010, finding the stories required some digging, especially stories published in smaller circulation newspapers and magazines of the predigital middle years of the twentieth century or those contained in books that have long been out of print and did not circulate widely when they were in print.

The issue of illegal immigration certainly has not gone away, nor has the need to tell the story again and again, each time with a more customized approach. Charlie LeDuff, for the *New York Times* in 2001, trailed along with a group of illegal immigrants from Mexico City to the meet-up with their coyote at the border and from there to the street corners of Farmingville, Long Island.[17] The following year, the *Los Angeles Times* published Sonia Nazario's "Enrique's Journey,"[18] a thirty-thousand word, six-chapter series that chronicled the eight attempts of a boy to get from Tegucigalpa, Honduras, to the United States. The series was based on exhaustive interviews with the main subjects and their families, but no undercover work, and won the 2003 Pulitzer Prize for Feature Writing.

Nazario updated her earlier work into a book published in 2006, centering the narrative on Enrique's repeated treacherous train-hopping experience. To better describe what he endured, she retraced his journey by train herself. A reviewer in her own newspaper cites as the book's great strength the way the author "complicates our notion of Latin American migrant-ness," but also notes as a deficit how short the book is on intimate details—"the color of a t-shirt or the timbre of a voice—which compromises the density of the work."[19] Witnessed, such details present themselves almost effortlessly; secondhand, not so readily.

A year later, the firsthand approach was back. In collaboration with the *New York Times,* Sandra Ochoa, a reporter for *El Tiempo,* a newspaper in Cuenca, Ecuador, investigated the first piece of a coyote pipeline by taking the dangerous eight-day voyage of 1,100 nautical miles from an Ecuadorean beach resort to the northern coast of Guatemala.[20]

All of the great undercover and dangerous near-undercover adventures of this period took place at a time of ethical angst, especially among top newspaper editors, over the state of American journalism. Polls showed a plummet in public trust of the media.[21] A *Time* cover story in 1983 titled "Journalism Under Fire," captured and chronicled the prevailing mood, and Tom Goldstein revisited all of this in his book two years later. Journalism's ethics and excesses—in a more general way—were on the firing line, followed by newly vigilant efforts to self-police the field.

In all such considerations, the journalistic use of undercover tactics inevitably surfaced in the writers' accounts, even if not in the survey results. The rise of hidden camera use and the growing popularity of the "gotcha!" exposés for television audiences were much in the collective professional consciousness, as was a surprise imbroglio that erupted during the Pulitzer Prize deliberations of

1979. This was over a major undercover *Chicago Sun-Times* investigation, during which the newspaper opened and operated a tavern called The Mirage.

SHOULD REPORTERS PLAY ROLES? was the headline over a published debate in the bulletin of the American Society of Newspaper Editors between two Pulitzer Prize board members at the time, Clayton Kirkpatrick, president of the *Chicago Tribune* Company, who argued yes, and Eugene C. Patterson, president and editor of the *St. Petersburg Times,* who argued a somewhat qualified no. Patterson acknowledged that his newspaper had indeed sponsored its own investigations involving undercover techniques: a reporter posed as a night nurse to investigate nursing home abuse and another as a home buyer to expose illegal racial "steering." But he echoed other editors in saying he would not do so in those instances again. He said both stories could have been reported straight with harder work and that he had changed his mind "about the wisdom, if not the rectitude" of stunt journalism in cases where aboveboard reporting would do. But he still reserved the right to use "fakery" as a last resort if it was the only way to serve the public interest. "This isn't a goody-two-shoes business," he said. "But posing as something we aren't does put our pursuit of truth on a tainted tangent going in and I don't think we ought to take it as a norm. A phony means to an honest end still leaves a faint disquiet in me."[22]

For journalism's high priests, there was, in the intensity of that atmosphere, not a good enough answer to the question, "How can deeply committed truth-seekers deceive to get information?" And with that, the Pulitzer Prize prospects of undercover exposés went from dim to dark for a decade and a half.

In September 1979, the *Los Angeles Times* media writer, David

Shaw, assessed this ostensible movement away from acceptance of journalistic "masquerades." He gathered a number of recent instances to mention, including a *Detroit News* reporter who posed as a congressman to show how lax security was at ceremonies on the White House lawn;[23] an *LA Times* reporter who posed as a graduate student in psychology to expose conditions at a local mental institution;[24] a *Wall Street Journal* reporter who worked an assembly line for three weeks to investigate charges the company was violating fair labor practices;[25] and a *Boston Globe* reporter who posed as a guard at a youth detention center to report on maltreatment. The *Chicago Tribune*'s slew of worthy exposés were on his list, as well as the work of reporters for the *Detroit Free Press* who used undercover tactics to expose questionable marriage counselors, to expose a surgery mill, and to investigate racially discriminatory real estate practices.[26] He also noted the more dubious effort of a *Rochester Democrat and Chronicle* reporter who took a job clerking at a secondhand bookstore to learn that book reviewers were reselling the books they got for free.[27]

Another Detroit reporter pretended to have arthritis to catch a man selling phony medication. As Neil Shine, the paper's managing editor, told Shaw at the time, "She didn't go up to him and say, 'Hi, I'm the medical writer from the *Free Press*. Are you a charlatan?'" Shaw also mentioned another common practice: for reporters on the police beat phoning from the press room at headquarters to call officers at other precincts, saying, "This is Flanagan at LAPD," intentionally giving the false impression that the reporter was a cop without exactly saying so.[28] Other papers, too, sponsored major undercover investigations in this period, including the *Seattle Times,* the *Nashville Tennessean,* the *Washington Post,* the *Boston Globe,* the *Chicago Sun-Times,* and the *Atlanta*

*Constitution.* The *Los Angeles Times* itself featured a number of other undercover investigations, many by Mike Goodman.[29]

The outright lying Reavis did as he reported undercover for *Texas Monthly* during that period did not concern him or the magazine's editors in the least. The trade-off for him was simple. It grew out of his experiences as a civil rights worker in Alabama in summer 1965, impersonating a local white man on assignment from the Southern Christian Leadership Conference. His job at the SCLC was to put his southern drawl to work ferreting out such hard-to-get information as who had been jailed, what the bonds were, whether or not whites were being admitted to the literacy test while blacks were forced to wait in line. "When I became a journalist," he emailed, "I didn't see much difference between what I'd done in Alabama and what I was doing as a writer." That meant on one occasion borrowing the identification of a man whose name happened to be Will Rogers. "Do you write?" a woman asked him. "No and I don't do rope tricks, either," he shot back, and thus avoided further prying. In one other instance, to assume a new identity for a story, he pulled the death certificate of a dead junkie and in another, to investigate security firms that hire guards with felony convictions in their background, he passed six lie detector tests with "a mixture of lies and truth." He used his real name, age, and place of birth but claimed he only had been arrested once for drunken disorderliness. "That is not true," he said. "I have a jail record some dozen arrests long—I was a civil rights and anti-war agitator during the sixties—but I've never been jailed for drunkenness. I lied about my employment record, address, personal references, and numerous other things. I posed as a West Texas welder who had recently moved to Houston to forget a divorce. The principle that guided me in filling out the application was one a convict would use: tell the truth if you can, but lie as necessary to get the job." He said the story resulted in a change in Texas, California, and Louisiana law, obliging security firms to run police checks on the guards they hired.

Reavis now teaches at North Carolina State University at Raleigh and harbors no remorse whatsoever for falsehoods he told in the line of work. He shares the common view that a journalist's job is to find out the things people need to know so that they can have good government. "If you have to lie to do it, you do it," he said by telephone. "The people need the information. So it never bothered me." In 2010, Simon and Schuster published *Catching Out: The Secret World of Day Laborers,* his account of working by the day and hour not only to write a book about the needed social and economic reforms for day workers but for its own sake: to supplement his retirement savings. He hasn't continued, though. At age sixty-four, he said, the necessary stamina loomed much larger for him than it had when he was in his thirties. Next to covering guerrilla movements in South America, he said his undercover stories, echoing so many others who have used this approach, provided the most satisfying work of his career. "Most of the writers at *Texas Monthly* had Ivy League educations and I didn't," he said. "I thought, 'What can I do that they don't or won't do?' And I enjoyed every minute of it."[30]

It is instructive that Henry got his first undercover assignment from the *Washington Post* in the winter 1980. The timing is significant. It came shortly after Shaw's summarization a few months earlier of the more ethically conscious mood among top newspaper editors. This was in the aftermath of the controversy provoked by the *Sun-Times* Mirage sting during the Pulitzer judging in the spring of 1979. Henry was singled out both in the 1983 *Time* cover story and in Goldstein's 1985 book, likely only because the timing and placement of both his series made them convenient high-end contemporary examples.[31] Likewise, Goldstein also mentioned as a Pulitzer finalist the *Wall Street Journal's* 1983 undercover exposé of temporary slave labor camps in the Southwest. George Getschow had posed as a day laborer to get inside the camps.

Henry recalls that his editors at the *Post* were not overly concerned about this criticism of undercover reporting that happened to waft his way. This was especially noteworthy for another reason: Henry's migrant assignment in 1983 was approved despite a more general sensitivity to ethical standards at the *Post* in the aftermath of returning a 1981 Pulitzer Prize when the story turned out to have been fabricated. At the *Post,* undercover assignments like Henry's had long been "something of a maverick tradition,"[32] Henry explained in *American Carnival,* mentioning Ben Bagdikian's self-engineered prison sentence on an ostensible murder conviction in 1972.[33] Also, the approval of both of Henry's undercover undertakings came well after the *Sun-Times* brouhaha, even though the newspaper's executive editor, Benjamin C. Bradlee, was one of that project's most outspoken critics. Shaw quoted Bradlee as saying, "In a day in which we are spending thousands of man hours uncovering deception, we simply cannot deceive. How can newspapers fight for honesty and integrity when they themselves are less than honest in getting a story? When cops pose as newspapermen, we get goddam sore. Quite properly so. So how can we pose as something we're not?"[34]

To Goldstein, Bradlee explained why he could split hairs between what the *Chicago Sun-Times* reporters had done during Mirage and what *Post* reporters were permitted to do, such as Henry for migrants and the homeless and Athelia Knight for her bus-to-Lorton reformatory series. "I see a really seminal distinction," he said, "between planning any kind of a deception, however much the end might seem to justify the means, and embarking on a project where your occupation as a journalist is not advertised," because in the second instance there is no pose, "no sign around the reporter's neck." Also, at no point, he said, did Henry or Knight lie.[35]

# TEN

# SINCLAIR'S LEGATEES

The 1990s were especially rich in journalism that combined the nauseating backdrop of abuses by food handlers with boundary-pushing undercover techniques. Such stories helped capture two Pulitzer Prizes for National Reporting in this period and prompted landmark lawsuits over the use of hidden cameras in television reports. In the end, both court cases resulted in salutary judgments in support of freedom of the press, but their impact on the profession could not have differed more. One, an emergency ruling from the U.S. Supreme Court, affirmed the use of these edgier journalistic tactics; the other became a costly and protracted embarrassment, not only for the network involved but for the entire profession.

As for the two Pulitzer Prize winners, Tony Horwitz for the *Wall Street Journal* in 1995 and Charlie LeDuff in a group award for a 2001 *New York Times* series titled HOW RACE IS LIVED, the similarities in their assignments and the high peer recognition the work received make them instructive examples of the undercover method—in newspaper format—at its most developed. No doubt their personal qualities, talent, background, brawn, and previous experience were essential aspects of this exceptional work. Yet no less crucial to their achievement, and to the achievements of so many great undercover projects past, was the role of bold but exacting editors. That skillful guidance deflected the knee-jerk criticism of deceptive reporting tactics that had started to become routine, the kind that had caused problems for some major projects of this nature since the late 1970s. Against the surreptitious methods deployed in these two cases, not a negative word was said.

Speaking more generally of all four stories, the food-handling motif was by no means incidental to the impact they caused well beyond their publication or broadcast dates. Each also, inevitably, summoned the specter of Upton Sinclair. Although none of the four was destined to generate anywhere near the staying power of *The Jungle,* cumulatively they played a significant role in refining best practices for journalists who resort to undercover tactics and in re-affirming the reasons for not abandoning the method when circumstances strongly suggest its use. The professional recognition accorded to the CBS, Horwitz, and LeDuff stories helped recalibrate and relegitimate the use of extraordinary reporting measures. On the cusp of a new century, they brought clarity to what and how much deception the courts and the profession would tolerate—and even celebrate—in pursuit of the journalism that counts. On the darker side of this quartet, the special assist from Food Lion etched a deep and clear new dividing line between what is acceptable for journalists to do and what is not.

THE JUNGLE REVISITED[1] was the *Journal*'s headline over the comment Horwitz offered to accompany his December 1994 series, headlined NINE TO NOWHERE, on the dullest, dead-end jobs in the United States.[2] Poultry-processing ranked first on his list and produced the most memorable piece in his three-part series. Horwitz concluded that safety consideration had vastly improved since Sinclair's day, thanks in part to *The Jungle*'s enduring legacy. But increased automation had spawned new hazards, including the risk of "cumulative trauma"[3] from rapid, repetitive, monotonous motion, and undue stress from the pressure of processing chickens at a rate of one bird every second. This was six times faster than the rate for beef and pork. Horwitz took jobs for a week each at processing plants in Morton, Mississippi, and DeQueen, Arkansas, in what he considered an essential aspect of the four months he spent reporting for the project.

Six years later, LeDuff spent some time finding the right setting for an extensive industrial workplace profile, his assignment in a major series the *New York Times* undertook to explore the everyday realities of race consciousness in fin de siècle America. He settled on a major pork-producing plant in Tar Heel, North Carolina, where he spent three weeks on the line.[4] His story portrayed what Joseph Lelyveld, the newspaper's chief editor, would later describe as "color-coded apartheid,"[5] the tense and racially stratified relations among the facility's white, black, Indian, and Mexican managers and employees.

With stories centered not on poultry or pork per se, but on broader societal issues, both reporters, like Sinclair, aimed directly at the reader's heart. And, just as Sinclair observed about reaction to his own work a century earlier, they more powerfully punched the stomach. Horwitz had us by the first paragraph:

> MORTON, Miss.—They call it "the chain," a swift steel shackle that shuttles dead chickens down a disassembly line of hangers, skinners, gut-pullers and gizzard-cutters. The chain has been rattling at

90 birds a minute for nine hours when the woman working fever-
ishly beside me crumples onto a pile of drumsticks.[6]

and LeDuff by a similarly evocative third:[7]

> It is called the picnic line: 18 workers lined up on both sides of a
> belt, carving meat from bone. Up to 16 million shoulders a year
> come down that line here at the Smithfield Packing Co., the larg-
> est pork production plant in the world. That works out to about
> 32,000 a shift, 63 a minute, one every 17 seconds for each worker
> for eight and a half hours a day. The first time you stare down at
> that belt you know your body is going to give in way before the
> machine ever will.[8]

In 1994, earlier the same year Horwitz would venture south to
pursue the chicken processors, CBS produced a program on the
*E. coli* threat then imperiling the safety of the nation's beef. To
obtain only generic footage[9] of questionable practices at slaugh-
terhouses, producers for the television newsmagazine *48 Hours* did
not find ways to take jobs themselves, as Horwitz and LeDuff
would later do. Instead, they found a willing current employee
and convinced him to film for them at a Federal Beef Processors
plant in Rapid City, South Dakota. With a tiny hidden camera that
CBS supplied, the employee caught his fellow workers in blatant,
bacteria-spreading violations of the health code. Footage showed
one man sharpening his knife on the boning room floor, and then,
without sterilizing it or even washing the blade, using it to cut into
a piece of meat. Another worker lanced an abscess on a piece of
meat and then hosed the spurted pus off the table without taking
any precautions to keep the ooze away from a pile of freshly cut
meat stacked beside it.[10]

The company immediately sought and got an injunction to stop CBS from airing the footage, charging that to make it public would divulge trade secrets and damage the local economy. CBS challenged the ruling, which the South Dakota Supreme Court upheld. CBS then appealed to U.S. Supreme Court Justice Harry Blackmun, who very swiftly overturned the lower court judgment in an emergency ruling and allowed CBS to include the footage in its broadcast without delay. Blackmun refused to exercise prior restraint and argued that to block the network would "cause irreparable harm to the news media and is intolerable under the First Amendment."[11] The segment aired on February 9, 1994. It made the firm's name public, ostensibly because of the company's legal action, and caused the firing of the whistle-blowing employee.[12]

By recruiting a current employee to film inside the slaughterhouse, CBS producers avoided the ethical quandaries that Horwitz and LeDuff created for themselves with their more direct approach. More pertinently, the CBS producers found a work-around for the protracted mess in which their counterparts at ABC ended up fifteen months earlier because of a segment aired on *Prime Time Live* about the handling of perishables at stores in the Food Lion supermarket chain.

The broad outlines of what happened are well known: To verify reports from seventy different sources of unsanitary practices at Food Lion supermarkets, producers for the ABC newsmagazine *Prime Time Live* took jobs as supermarket workers and went to work with tiny concealed cameras turned on. The resulting broadcast aired November 5, 1992, replete with gross but powerful footage of employees in such questionable acts as redating expired meats and poultry, trimming pork with spoiled edges to repackage for longer sale, marinating chicken in water and liquid that hadn't been changed for days, and slicing slimy turkey and coating it in barbecue sauce to resell as a gourmet special.

The broadcast had immediate and deleterious impact on the business prospects of what then was the nation's fastest-growing supermarket chain. The company's stock price plummeted;[13] a shareholder filed suit.[14] Unrelated adverse publicity came down from a federal Labor Department case on allegations of child labor and overtime violations at the stores.[15] By Christmas, the company had slowed expansion plans,[16] and two weeks after that announced it would be closing eighty-eight stores.[17]

Voicing over a camera shot of a pair of hands, one with pen filling out an application, the program's host, Diane Sawyer, explained the undercover method the show's producers had used. She said only that several *Prime Time* producers "posed as applicants for work at more than twenty stores," two of whom got hired to work in the meat departments of two different stores and in the deli of a third, and that none of the employees in those stores "knew who we really were or that we had hidden cameras."[18]

Also as part of the broadcast, Sawyer reported that ABC had sent ahead to Food Lion a summary of the report with a request to interview the company's chairman, Tom Smith. Food Lion responded that it would permit the interview only if ABC omitted the hidden camera footage from its segment. ABC declined and Food Lion sued, charging that the videotape had been obtained illegally. ABC also aired a news conference clip of Vincent Watkins, the company's vice president, saying there was a "high probability" the videotape had been "concocted to show the same type of allegations the union has made in the past." Sawyer said it was true some of the sources for the report had come through the union; others had joined forces with the union in seeking a government investigation of off-the-clock work—another charge against the company; and still others were suing Food Lion directly. "But we remind you," Sawyer said, "*Prime Time* went undercover so we would have independent verification of what our seventy sources told us."[19]

She also told *Prime Time* viewers that the day before the segment aired, ABC received a letter from Food Lion, attacking one of the producers, Lynne Neufer Litt, for "arranging to work late and alone, giving her the opportunity to fraudulently create a news story."[20] Sawyer countered that "*Prime Time* staged nothing, that what you saw on hidden camera is exactly as it happened. Remember none of the employees knew who we were or that they were being taped. And that night the meat was left in the grinder, our producer was not the person assigned to do the cleaning."[21]

Food Lion fought back with a vengeance, launching an elaborate public relations blitz immediately after the segment aired to counteract the damage to its reputation.[22] The company sued ABC[23]—not for libel, but for what it alleged were wrongs committed during the newsgathering process—fraud, trespass, unfair trade practices, and breach of the duty of loyalty. In depositions taken shortly after the broadcast, late in 1992, more details of how the footage had been obtained emerged: not only did producers apply to work at Food Lion supermarkets, but they did so under disguised names, supplying false background information, false addresses, false employment histories, false references, false reasons for seeking the work, and even, according to court documents, false documentation to corroborate the false information they had provided.[24] The United Food and Commercial Workers International helped them secure the ostensible references, and at the producers' request, also led them to unionized supermarkets at which they could rehearse for their job interviews with Food Lion personnel.[25] The union at the time was known to be actively agitating against the company. For balance, ABC also sought and found a number of sources to corroborate their findings, sources outside of the ranks of union activists and supporters.

The legal case waged on for seven long years. In the end, ABC lost on trespass and breach of duty of loyalty, but it won in another sense. From an initial damage award of $5.5 million[26]—with its potentially chilling effect on other media companies contemplating aggressive reporting of this nature—the amount was progressively decreased, first to $315,000 in punitive damages plus a small compensatory amount down to a symbolic penalty of a dollar on each of the two charges.[27]

In short, the case ended in a bare Pyrrhic victory for both companies, costly in time and reputation, but with one auspicious outcome for the media: the federal appeals court ruling severely limited the amount plaintiffs can recover in damages in newsgathering cases. This provided ABC—and other media outlets by extension—with First Amendment protection against large awards that are based on publication damages.[28]

Interestingly, in the early months—even the first couple of years—after the broadcast was televised, reporters, media critics, and commentators made more of the business woes the broadcast had caused for Food Lion and the "troubling"[29] growth in use of tiny hidden cameras than of the ethical and legal issues raised by what ABC's producers had said on their job applications. The organization of Investigative Reporters and Editors gave ABC a prestigious IRE Contest Award for the Food Lion program in 1992.[30] Even as late as two years after the broadcast, early in 1995, before the first legal ruling was issued, a writer found plenty to admire in the ABC report. In a brief mention in the story about Horwitz, Susan Banda described as "stunning" the impact of an unnamed investigation into supermarket practices as she noted in the same breath the "the tangled ethical problems"[31] that misrepresentation and hidden camera work can cause.

Database searches indicate that only a spare handful of stories about the case in those early days even mentioned the falsified applications. Fewer still included the details of what had given Food Lion its grounds for legal action.[32] It was only later, when the first multimillion-dollar damage award was announced at the end of January 1997,[33] that journalistic interest in the case and condemnation of the actions of the ABC producers heightened. At the Columbia University Graduate School of Journalism at the end of February 1997, panelists took both sides of the issue. While Paul Starobin of the *National Journal* condemned undercover tactics as so much "trick journalism," Floyd Abrams, the first amendment attorney who represented ABC in the case, likened the severity of what ABC's producers had done to jaywalking, not vehicular homicide, or "minor offenses we can live with." He conceded that the producers actions involved "some moral ambiguity," but, he said, "these stories are awfully important to do. It's worth the moral ambiguity."[34]

On April 2, 1998, the IRE supplied to the court an amicus curiae brief in support of undercover reporting in general. Without specific reference to the merits of ABC's case, it singled out thirteen seminal investigations over the preceding one hundred years to assert that undercover newsgathering techniques were "well within the mainstream of American journalism."[35] It concluded that popular broadcast programs were no less deserving of First Amendment protection than the work of other media, and that "the nature of press practices from the time of the Revolution onward suggests a broad based constitutional interest in protecting newsgathering activities regardless of how reporting techniques and technologies may evolve."[36]

The IRE brief notwithstanding, it was in this latter stage, well after Food Lion first sued, that criticism of ABC in legal and media circles got loud and then louder still. Even Horwitz commented on the Food Lion case in a lengthy essay by Susan Paterno for *American Journalism Review.* Her 1997 piece weighed the pros and cons of deceptive practice in journalism, citing various advocates and detractors, and rehearsing all the common arguments pro and con. Said Horwitz, "You know the subject you're writing about will review the story with a fine-tooth comb and try to attack you. If you leave yourself vulnerable to questions, if you've lied on the application, from a practical point of view, it's a dicey thing to do."[37]

In early August 1997, a round of by then scathingly negative commentary followed news of the first reduction in the damage award. More came at announcement of the final verdict in October 1999.[38] For journalists, "Food Lion" became the decade's cautionary phrase.

Horwitz was living abroad in 1992 and 1993 with no awareness whatsoever of the unfolding Food Lion drama, nor, in 1994, of the CBS case.[39] In a series of telephone and emailed interviews, he recalled how the idea for his project hatched in 1994. The *Wall Street Journal* had assigned him to be a roving national reporter, based in Virginia and attached mostly to the Pittsburgh bureau. On a visit to New York, he sat in on an editorial planning meeting led by the newspaper's then managing editor, Paul Steiger. Most of the suggestions coming out of the group involved life in affluent Manhattan, far in every way from Horwitz's usual haunts. Someone suggested a "ten best" idea, and Horwitz heard himself blurting out, "What about a story on the ten worst jobs in America?" Steiger smiled and said, "That's a great idea. Do it."[40]

As Horwitz began researching the topic, he realized the major pitfall of a "ten worst" story was that it could easily become "a not particularly worthwhile gross-out feature." From a previous assignment, he had cultivated a source at a turkey processing plant in Springfield, Missouri. That led him to poke more deeply into the poultry industry, one of the country's fastest-growing sectors. "Gradually, that became the frame," he said. "Not just lousy jobs, but ones that also reflected broader trends, such as workplace surveillance and the growing risk of repetitive strain injuries."[41]

He had enough information going in to be convinced that interviews alone would never capture the full extent of the situation for workers. He came to the conclusion that the best and most efficient way to investigate would be to take jobs in a couple of plants himself. This was not a particularly far-fetched plan. Before becoming a journalist, Horwitz had lived and worked in the South, including the two years he spent as a union organizer in rural Mississippi, "so knocking on doors and trying to get folks to talk about their work was pretty familiar to me," he said. Not every reporter is cut out for such an undertaking, but Steiger never doubted Horwitz's suitability for the assignment. It was not incidental, he said, that Tony "has this kind of open face and people just want to embrace him. It is a plus that he has physical courage and was physically strong."[42]

As for LeDuff, like Horwitz and so many of their immersion predecessors, he was known for fearlessness, physical stamina, and writing prowess and since joining the *Times* in 1996 for covering the other half. His next major story after the slaughterhouse was the four thousand mile journey from Mexico City to Farmingville, Long Island, in the shadow of two illegal immigrants making their way to an uncertain future in off-the-books jobs that paid fifteen dollars an hour in 2001.[43]

Stealth outings were nothing new for Horwitz, either. As a

young reporter for the *Fort Wayne Sentinel,* in November 1984, he investigated a local massage parlor. "My job was to play the part of client, get a massage, and go far enough to establish that other services were on offer, which of course they were," he recalled.[44] "I think the piece contributed to a number of parlors being closed down, but couldn't swear to it since I left Indiana and moved to Australia a few weeks after the story appeared."[45]

Six years later, during the first Gulf War, Horwitz tired of hanging out at a hotel in Saudi Arabia with hundreds of other reporters "waiting to be lied to by the military." He got hold of a Saudi uniform, which looked just like a U.S. uniform, and joined up with a French photographer who had done the same and who also had a jeep he had camouflaged to resemble a U.S. Army vehicle. This allowed them to travel through military checkpoints and observe preparations for war. Along with other "unilaterals," or journalists working outside the official system, they based themselves in a Saudi town at an army outpost not too far from the Iraqi border.

"One day the French guy caught wind of the impending ground invasion and he and I drove to the border and simply pulled into a convoy of allied tanks and other vehicles as they rolled into Iraq," Horwitz said, "So we had the story of the first day's battle in Iraq to ourselves." But the two reporters were soon captured and handed over to U.S. military police, who put them into a fenced holding pen with captured Iraqi soldiers before escorting them to another location, driving their own jeep between truckloads of Iraqi prisoners. "When we reached a paved highway, the mad Frenchman gunned it and sped past our escorts in their Humvees, reckoning that they wouldn't abandon hundreds of Iraqi prisoners to chase two journalists. Luckily he was right and we got our stories and photos out that night."[46]

In later situations, Horwitz said he has gone to special effort to "blend in," a common tactic, sometimes more for safety than as strategy. Horwitz does not consider this approach quite the same as a full-blown undercover effort. "For instance, I wanted to spend some time in a biker bar in Tennessee that seemed to be the source of Klan activity. After getting roughed up the first time I visited, with a notebook, I returned in bandanna, sunglasses, etc., so I could hang out incognito and take in the scene."[47]

Steiger recalls working out a protocol for the chicken-processing assignment with his deputy, Byron "Barney" Calame, the *Journal*'s main arbiter for standards and ethics, then and later. Calame is a self-described "stickler"[48] who was charged with ensuring that high ethical standards and *Journal* policy were always observed. In interviews, both Steiger and Calame immediately recalled any number of *Journal* investigations over the years that had involved these edgier techniques. Steiger mentioned authorizing one assignment for which reporters sought advice as ordinary citizens from an IRS hotline—not saying if the questions emanated from their own tax returns or from someone else's—and then, without embarrassing the IRS employees, they compared in print the often-contradictory responses they received.[49] In another instance, Alix M. Freedman, for a 1993 investigation of a rent-to-own company called Rent-A-Center, took out a rental contract herself and also attended, without announcing herself, one of the company's closed sales meetings in Las Vegas—until she was escorted out.[50] Back in 1985, Timothy K. Smith signed up in the Alabama woods with Frank Camper's Mercenary Association, a private paramilitary training camp and, Steiger said, surely, with a sense of self-preservation well in mind, Smith did not reveal why.[51] "We had what we felt was an internally consistent set of principles in multiple cases," Steiger said.[52]

Calame, too, recalled other *Journal* stories over the years that required an ethical stretch—reporters at the offices of matrimonial lawyers posing as candidates for divorce, a reporter becoming a substitute teacher in the Los Angeles public schools, a Detroit reporter who went to work in an automobile plant. These went back to his days as Los Angeles bureau chief and even earlier.[53]

Calame said the newspaper had become progressively more careful in its use of covert reporting, especially "in the late 1970s into the 1980s," the "Journalism Under Fire" period. So it was not Food Lion that turned the corner for him. In fact, he wasn't even aware of the case until 1998, when he began doing ethics training for new Dow Jones hires. For Calame, a predominant issue such considerations always must address is collateral damage, harm to civilians, caused by repercussions to those who either do not know they are being quoted for publication or don't understand the possible consequences of being quoted or described, even if they are aware.[54]

Steiger's view is that the publication always must endeavor to be careful before resorting to more extreme reporting measures, but that does not mean it should shy away from using them if the story warrants it. Reasonable people might well disagree about where to plot these various investigations on an ethical continuum—"Tony's at one end; calling the IRS is at the other," he said—"but they all fit the policy."[55]

"And one last thing," Steiger said, "is that I don't have—Barney would probably argue—a religious feeling that we would never lie for any story." Could there be stories, he asked himself, for which serving the public interest was so great a consideration that he would breach normal rules? "I've never encountered something like that and I don't know what that would be, and I would try to do it without breaching those rules," he said. "But this is not something handed down from the mount." The fundamental issue, he said, is credibility: "What should journalists do to be accepted and credible by the lights of society? A policy of not lying fits with that. But it's not a moral absolute."[56]

In the instance of Horwitz's foray into chicken processing, Steiger said that he and Calame had a clear sense of "cutting the line very finely.... We wanted him to get into the chicken factory, but not to lie to get in there."[57]

Calame recalled the planning in much the same way. The application was a big hurdle and Calame went through a number of possible scenarios with Horwitz as to what the application form might ask and how he might respond faithfully to those questions without torpedoing his plans on the one hand—that was Horwitz's main preoccupation—or violating *Journal* guidelines on the other. Calame too recalled that the edict to tell no lies was bedrock, and that Horwitz was told he should feel free to leave blanks where the truthful answer would give too much away. He could use "Dow Jones," the *Journal*'s parent company at the time, as his current employer; but he expressly could not say it was his *previous* employer, if the question were phrased that way, because that would have been a lie.[58] He could omit his education, an undergraduate degree from Brown University and a master's in journalism from Columbia University. If questioned in a way that compromised his assignment, he was either to deal with what was asked directly and truthfully or to demur and say, "'I'm sorry, this was a bad idea,' and walk away."[59]

Horwitz said his editors gave him a gratifyingly "long leash." He could not recall ever being questioned on how much time or money he spent on an assignment—though his were usually fairly low budget. "Nor did they ever second-guess my judgment," he said. "What you found on the ground was always what mattered most. Those were the days, eh?"[60]

In LeDuff's case, the lead up to the assignment was in many ways similar. Not long after the story was published, he told an interviewer that he first spent several months poking around in six or seven southern states, looking for the right setting for a story. All roads, he said, led to Tar Heel and its Smithfield plant. LeDuff was largely attracted by the local population, which appeared to be about evenly mixed racially. "At the courthouse there, there's a plaque that lists the fallen vets of World War I. Whites on top, Indian in the middle and colored on the bottom in the color red. It sort of struck me as, 'Wow, there is stuff going on here.' And that's ultimately how I ended up in that part of the country."[61]

He thought it was important to observe the plant from the inside, as a fellow worker, if he wanted "to get into the heads of people's lives." He also liked drawing on his own blue-collar background. "It reminds me, I can still do it. When this job goes away, I can cut up a pig. I'm pretty good at it. I can dig a ditch. I can lay shingles. I can drive a truck. I'm interested in who does the work. I was excited."[62]

LeDuff sought permission to take a job at the plant from Michael Winerip, the editor assigned to oversee his progress on the story. Winerip was supportive of the idea, but got blowback from the supervising editors on the series, Soma Golden Behr and the late Gerald Boyd. Their concern was misrepresentation, which *Times* policy expressly prohibits. For Winerip, the standard was simple and could be expressed in three words: "We can't lie."

The three editors went back and forth on the misrepresentation issue. Winerip reviewed a copy of the Smithfield job application to see if LeDuff would need to run afoul of newspaper policy to get hired. There was wording that went something like, "Are you currently employed? Can we speak to your employer?" Winerip felt strongly that without crossing the line, the answers to those questions could be, "Yes, I'm currently employed" and "No, you cannot speak to my employer." Behr and Boyd remained doubtful, so the three took the question up the editorial ladder to Lelyveld, who heard their arguments. He sided with Winerip in favor of the project.[63]

At that point, Winerip said, to the best of his recollection, the only specific instructions to LeDuff were not to lie, to disclose at some point before publication to those he wanted to quote by name, and to obtain their permission to do so.[64]

Both Horwitz and LeDuff make a point of describing the application process within the text of their stories, including what information they provided their temporary employers. Horwitz said the plant manager in Morton "barely glanced at an application that listed my university education and Dow Jones & Co." as his employer. He also disclosed his Columbia degree. And LeDuff similarly reported that he was hired under his own name. He acknowledged that he was currently employed, "but was not asked where and did not say." Both indicated that demand for workers was too great at these firms for managers to spend much time scrutinizing applications from the willing. As LeDuff put it, the plant would take just about any man or woman with a pulse and a sparkling urine sample, with few questions asked."[65]

In the stories, neither reporter concealed his direct participation as a worker, but Horwitz is more explicit in the personal allusions he includes in the piece, although he handles them subtly. Along with the woman who crumples beside him in his opening paragraph, there are a smattering of references to "my first shift,"[66] and "where this reporter later worked," and, the most overt, "At break times I would find fat globules and blood speckling my glasses, bits of chicken caught in my collar, water and slime soaking my feet and ankles and nicks covering my wrists."[67]

LeDuff uses the second person repeatedly to reveal his first-hand knowledge, with phrasing such as "you begin to understand." He also describes certain actions without an antecedent to give the reader a clear sense of whose experience is being described: "Standing in the damp 42-degree air causes your knees to lock, your nose to run, your teeth to throb."[68] He reveals how long he worked at the plant, too. "Slaughtering swine is repetitive, brutish work," he writes, "so grueling that three weeks on the factory floor leave no doubt in your mind about why the turnover is one hundred percent."[69]

In later interviews for this book or elsewhere, both reporters gave similar reasons for why they felt taking the jobs and experiencing the work was essential to their stories. LeDuff does not characterize his work as undercover since he has said he was open about his purpose with the local people he met. Horwitz has no discomfort with the term. He was quiet on the job but was forthright about his actual purpose in cases where he visited his fellow workers at home or had concern, the same general concern Calame expressed, that his article might inadvertently identify individuals for whom there could be negative repercussions.

LeDuff, who is part Indian, had an easier time blending in than the blond Horwitz, who was hard to miss among all the black workers in Morton and the Hispanics in DeQueen, but not so much as to raise many unwanted questions, he said. "Though I did my best not to stand out," he said, "I sensed that some people sensed I didn't really fit in."[70] Yet the fact that he had worked alongside them "and understood how tough the work was gave me entrée and inclined them to open up."

To an interviewer, LeDuff said something similar: "People respected what I did because, 'Hey man, I want to know enough. I want to stand next to you. I'm gonna be there.'"[71]

Why exactly could the story not be told without getting hired at the plants? Horwitz's recollection is that in 1994, few if any reporters had been inside these factories for anything more than a sanitized tour. Rumors were circulating widely at the time, often from union sources, about horrific conditions inside these facilities, but little if any hard information was available. And more viscerally, he said, it was essential to be able to depict "the grindingly repetitive nature of the labor, and the toll that takes on workers." It would have been hard to appreciate or communicate that without doing it himself.[72]

In LeDuff's case, the value of being inside had partly to do with experiencing the work to be able to describe it precisely, but he also found it necessary for the sake of creating relationships with the people he was profiling. He wanted to be able to observe their interactions in real time at close range, to earn their trust by working with them side by side. Also, having done the work allows the reporter to "dispense with the opening round of questions: 'Do your hands hurt, sir? What's it like in there?'" LeDuff told an interviewer. "I find that if you're coming to people, you're not a vulture like some reporters who circle around and wait for the opening to get in there. People know what you're doing. They feel you hawking them. Go straight to their space, state your intentions and do it."[73]

As to the act of going undercover in and of itself, Horwitz defended the practice, especially for stories like his poultry-processing piece.

He has no problem with the notion of it. "It gives you a real view of the place and gives you a view of what it feels like," he said. "You gain a keener understanding than you would get from watching someone else do the job."[74] He never agonized about the ethical quandary. "You have to trust your instincts," he said. "You know when you're stepping over the line, doing something that feels wrong. It's an instinct. You know in your gut. A sense of, 'I shouldn't be here. People might regret what they're telling me,' especially with ordinary people or in a police state. Those were the situations in which I agonized most. In this one, I didn't. I observed the ground rules. 'Are you a reporter?' 'Yes.' And to tell the truth if asked."[75]

LeDuff has said he did not consider his pork-plant effort undercover because he didn't deceive anyone: "I didn't go undercover. I didn't use a false name. I went there and worked. I didn't whack anybody. I am very satisfied with how I handled it."[76] To the reporter for the *IRE Journal* back in 1995, Horwitz offered this advice to anyone attempting something similar: Work out the assignment with one's editors first; work out the ethical issues of misrepresenting oneself; decide what information to share and what not to share "so that you can avoid a lot of questions without being dishonest."[77]

And, he added, be prepared for the intensified exhaustion that living a double life demands. The act of "passing" itself is an aspect of undercover reporting rarely discussed. In Horwitz's case, as in so many others already described, he took hurried notes in bathroom stalls during brief breaks, or ran out to his car to record his fleeting thoughts on tape. Some version of that furtiveness is in the retelling of almost every undercover reporting experience. Horwitz said after he left the plants, when he disclosed what he had done to one of his chicken-processing employers, he also sent back the week's pay he had received for his ruse. The boss declined to accept the returned check, telling Horwitz that he had earned it.[78] Horwitz in turn gave the returned money to charity.

Both of these stories received major media attention, in the immediate aftermath of publication and again when the Pulitzer Prizes were announced in 1995 and 2001. Horwitz's package of stories was also a finalist that year for the prestigious Loeb Award for business reporting. It set off a flurry of activity in the Occupational Safety and Health Administration and calls for Senate hearings.[79]

Yet even long before the annual journalism prize season began, Horwitz's story had been singled out for special notice. "Gripping"[80] was how a writer for the *IRE Journal* described it in a profile that gave special attention to Horwitz's undercover work among 1994's ranging investigative efforts, soon after his series appeared.

LeDuff got a similar spotlight six years later, including a coveted television interview with Charlie Rose. The *New York Times* reproduced the full HOW RACE IS LIVED series as a book by the same name that garnered attention from reviewers. Rose asked LeDuff if any good had come out of his efforts. He replied that his purpose was not to judge or offer context or prescriptions but to be a describer of situations, a relater of information. "I'm just telling you," he told Rose. "I can't explain it. I'm just telling you."[81]

More recently, there have been similar, if less ballyhooed, efforts, too, such as the anthropologist Steve Striffler's *Chicken,* published by Yale University Press in 2005.[82]

In 1995, as gratifying as the national peer recognition the story received was for Horwitz and the *Wall Street Journal,* it went entirely unnoticed as an event just as significant in the annals of undercover reporting. Horwitz's NINE TO NOWHERE represents the first time a work of newspaper journalism with a blatant undercover reporting dimension was to win outright a Pulitzer in any category since the Mirage tavern exposé of 1979. The accolade, I would submit, represents a tacit reaffirmation of the undercover approach at the Pulitzers after fifteen long years on the disgrace bench. Or at least, so it seemed.

In the IRE's laudatory piece about Horwitz, the *Journal* writer, Susan Banda, explained what she perceived to be the prevailing attitude of the day toward undercover reporting: "A technique maligned and mostly avoided by many print journalists at least since *The Chicago Sun-Times*' Mirage Bar project raised ethical questions about the practice in the late 1970s."[83] What she meant by "maligned" is clear enough. But her assessment in January 1995 of undercover reporting as "mostly avoided by many print journalists" is an understandable but incorrect impression. At the time, with so few newspapers, magazines, or television productions searchable in indexed form, a month would not have been enough time to check and enumerate them effectively. Now, with the aid of so many ways to search, it is clear that for all the apparent agita over undercover techniques in the fifteen years from the Pulitzer board's Mirage consideration in 1979 to the Horwitz win in 1995, the practice continued unabated. Many of the nation's newspapers, magazines, and television stations continued to engage in about as many undercover blockbusters as they had in the preceding decade and a half.[84] Calame pointed out that Pulitzer panels have often included a judge or two who is adamant on a given principle—like, no series that have an appended correction, even one, can win. And board members serve for several years. Perhaps the change reflected the composition of a new board to some extent. But given the history and the timing, it is significant in itself that the *Times* and *Journal* submissions went unchallenged in 1995 and 2001, given the inclusion in the series of these two pieces with their prominent undercover aspects.

As new issues with food handling have presented themselves, so have new means of reporting them. For example, among the numerous local television reports of issues with food handling at wholesale markets[85] came the work of Dave Savini, a Chicago investigative reporter, described in a summer 2009 article in *Nieman Reports,* the publication of Harvard's Nieman Foundation.[86] With a small video camera, he captured footage of an unrefrigerated truck backing into Chicago's Fulton Street meat market on a hot summer day and then being loaded with "thousands of pounds of pork, cases of yogurt, and crates filled with fruits and vegetables."[87] He then followed the truck to a restaurant more than a hundred miles away in Delavan, Wisconsin. A producer back at the television station, CBS2-Chicago, ran the license plate number that Savini telephoned in, cross-checking it with Wisconsin business licenses. Savini called Wisconsin agencies that might be able to inspect the load and located an inspector who agreed to help. The inspector placed a three-way call to a local police station. After a slow-speed chase, the driver pulled over and allowed the inspection. "We also try to maximize the impact of our stories by expanding their scope," Savini told the magazine writer, adding that the team cultivates sources, stakes out key roads "where drivers often hit viaducts, ripping off the tops of their refrigerated trailers and exposing frozen meat to sweltering heat," with wholesalers totally unaware of what they are receiving.[88]

Not only food safety but also the rights of animals destined for slaughter remains a vital theme that lends itself to undercover exposure. Sometimes, it is undertaken by animal rights advocates, such as the horrifying footage shared in the documentary *Food,*

*Inc.,* in 2008, or the footage posted by the Humane Society of the United States in December 2010 showing the pig gestation crates still widely in use at that point by Smithfield, the nation's largest pork producer. The company pledged in 2007 to dismantle the system within a decade. The *Virginian-Pilot* followed the story closely, with reaction from Smithfield, and with further dissemination by the Associated Press.[89] But the lack of wide reaction beyond Norfolk compared to the impact of a Sinclair or a Horwitz or a LeDuff gives cause to wonder if the advocacy-based origins of the footage (without the benefit of distribution as clips in a major documentary) did not mute the response.

Neither Steiger nor Calame has any recollection of heightened concern in those post-Mirage years over how the judges might receive a Pulitzer nomination for such an enterprise. What motivated the nomination of the Horwitz series was simply this, Steiger said: "It was an amazing, amazing job of reporting and writing."[90] His letter to the Pulitzer judges is unapologetic on the issue of method for what was the centerpiece story for the series. He writes only of Horwitz "[d]onning work clothes but prepared to acknowledge his *Journal* affiliation if asked."[91] Nothing more. No further explanation; no apologia or justification. He emphasizes instead Horwitz's preparation and effort: not only the four months he spent reporting the series but the two years in all he had been chronicling the lives of "Americans enmeshed in the gears of wrenching economic change."[92]

## ELEVEN

# HARD TIME

Reporters have been infiltrating prisons, hospitals, and mental institutions at least since Nellie Bly auditioned for the *New York World* in 1887 from an asylum in the middle of the East River. Then and much later, those who have dared to pose for journalism's sake as patients, inmates, guards, and aides are short on fear and long on empathy and endurance, both physical and emotional. Their excursions into radically different lives last anywhere from a day to a year—a week or two is more the standard. Their efforts often follow hard-to-verify rumblings of horrid conditions, filth, overcrowding, abuse, neglect, or administrative wrongdoing. Responding to a news imperative after slayings, riots, or during lockdowns is another reason for the effort, as is the chance to assess a new administrator's touted reforms or sometimes to provide readers with an inside look at an opaque but public institution that deliberately walls the public out.

In almost all cases, such stories want most of all to elicit reader empathy, to open a window into an unseen world, providing a stark but tacit warning. Undercover investigations of asylums, hospitals, and nursing homes often have an implicit it-could-happen-to-you dimension, as did a series in the *Boston Globe*'s Living section about a reporter's week in jail on a trumped-up drunk-driving charge. The newspaper published it as an apparent don't-drink-and-drive admonition in the five days leading up to New Year's Eve, 1983.[1]

The *Globe* jail series was an exception, but rarely are the undercover stories that come out of these institutions presented as stand-alones. They generally work best as "frosting on the cake of a thoroughly investigated story,"[2] as William Gaines once said, explaining the week he spent working as a janitor in 1975[3] for Chicago's only private hospital, the von Solbrig, and the resulting impact of the series—patients fled; no new ones came. Within just a few months, the hospital was forced to shut down. The von Solbrig was one of a number of undercover assignments Gaines undertook for the *Chicago Tribune* between 1973 and 1979.[4]

The *Tribune,* for years, especially in the 1960s and 1970s, was in the vanguard of newspapers that made prominent, unapologetic use of the techniques of undercover reporting for investigations on these and other topics. "Aggressive and righteous"[5] was Gaines's description of the newspaper's bywords in those years, under editor Clayton Kirkpatrick. Acting on ideas generated by reporter George Bliss, the *Tribune* investigated the suspected collusion of Chicago police and private ambulance drivers to restrict service in low-income areas. Bliss suggested that William Jones take a job as a driver to help confirm the reports, and William Recktenwald, then with the Better Government Association, did, too. The series won a 1971 Pulitzer Prize.[6] The same year, in February 1971, the newspaper premiered its legendary *Tribune* Task Force—"a new concept in comprehensive news gathering"[7]—with a six-week team investigation of twenty-one Chicago-area nursing homes.[8] The newspaper reported in a sidebar that the unit's reporters had fanned out to work briefly as nurse's aides, janitors, kitchen help, drifters, supervisors, and college students looking for temporary jobs. In the process, they engaged in everything from "emptying bed pans, changing sheets, scrubbing floors and painting rooms" to facing "ominous warnings from fellow workers who suspected them of being state investigators."[9] Four years later, Gaines took the janitor's job to confirm a tip from a former custodian about disturbing practices at the hospital. "It wasn't hard to get a job," he later recalled. "The first guy would find out what they [the hospital] wanted. The second guy would be exactly that. In a sense we falsified our backgrounds. We could say we were anything, but we couldn't say we were *Tribune* reporters."[10]

Editors instructed him to collect information "not from overheard conversations or stolen documents,"[11] but from what he could glean from his own workaday experiences. He took notes on paper towels, which he put into his pockets to share later with teammates who then followed up on his leads. For instance, just from working his shift every day for a week, he noticed how routinely the hospital's doctors were recommending tonsillectomies to welfare recipients, a procedure for which Medicaid could be billed. Gaines's investigative colleagues then determined how rare it would be for two members of a family to need the procedure at the same time, let alone as many as five members of the same family. To Michael Miner of the *Chicago Reader,* Gaines later acknowledged that the information actually could have been obtained by other means, since it appears on Medicaid vouchers which are available as public records. Someone could have gone through the vouchers and tallied up the instances, should they have had a notion in the first place that there was a possible abuse worth searching out.[12] That would be the rub.

So what Gaines's performance was able to supply to the series was frosting, but frosting of buttercream, lick-the-bowl-clean quality. His story not only provided the needed eyewitness verification to clinch the investigation and led to important reporting areas to follow up, but it added texture and richness—narrative *pow!*—to the more conventional aspects of the series, such as interviews with patients and medical experts, corroboration from former hospital employees, and deep searches of public records.[13] Plus, his janitorial service enabled him to confirm independently one of the most startling tips to come to the newspaper's attention: that janitors were being instructed to drop their mops and help out with patients who were lying unconscious in the operating rooms immediately after surgery. During that week, in soiled clothes, he was personally ordered into the operating rooms six times. That part of the story, he later said, would have been impossible to verify without having been on the scene, undetected.[14]

Experiential narratives provided by companion stories such as Gaines's sweeten and embellish the more essential, data-laden efforts of an investigative series with facts that have been equally, although differently, hard won. They enrich and enliven a presentation that otherwise would consist of data and statistics supplemented with retold anecdotes, dry expert commentary, and disembodied quotes from officials with long bureaucratic titles— with some descriptive elements sprinkled in as a binding agent. The narrative dimension of most undercover efforts has a way of magnetically attracting attention to the main subject, which is, and should always be, one of the high-value propositions of such an undertaking. It is also the element that generates the buzz. In the von Solbrig case, this meant an overspill of visceral outrage. The undercover dimension adds the readability and storyline to long-form reporting, which, contrary to popular perception, are as important in the information-crowded, click-driven universe proliferating on the web as they have been on paper.[15]

To make this point, Miner in 2001 asked Gaines to compare the radical difference in impact of the two Pulitzer Prizes for the *Tribune* in which Gaines played pivotal roles: the von Solbrig in 1976 and the straight investigative reporting of the *Tribune*'s 1988 win twelve years later. The latter required six months of poring over records and conducting interviews to expose the "self-interest and waste that plague Chicago's City Council." The impact of the von Solbrig investigation was clear. What did the 1988 probe achieve? "That's a tough one," Gaines said. "I'd have to say it just educated people to how the City Council worked. It put it all in one big story people could read. I don't think it reformed one thing."[16]

The risk, of course, is that especially in a time such as the present when serious news articles and broadcasts now compete directly for audiences and resources with pure entertainment vehicles, the push to dramatize presentation for its own sake becomes harder to restrain.[17]

During the period the *Tribune*'s investigative work was at its undercover zenith, other newspapers also embraced the method. The *Nashville Tennessean,* the *Los Angeles Times,*[18] the *Chicago Sun-Times* and *Daily News,* and the *San Francisco Chronicle* all produced similarly memorable work in the genre, and yet all, like the *Tribune,* eventually soured to some extent on the most blatant forms of the practice as others stepped forward to embrace it.

Considered in retrospect, it is significant that the undercover aspect of these investigations invariably becomes the shorthand description for the whole project, the only aspect that anyone can summon from memory. How telling that in common recollection, it is to Gaines' and his janitorial pose that the 1976 Pulitzer Prize for Local Investigative Specialized Reporting is often attributed, even though the award was given to the *Tribune*'s "staff" and was shared with a completely separate project.[19] As Gaines himself once mused to an interviewer, "I always felt that I got the prize for being a good janitor rather than a journalist."[20] It is what readers and other reporters and editors most readily and amazedly recall about the achievement, reminding the public of journalism's potential for impact by being enterprising, resourceful, significant, and attention-getting, straightforward in the telling if not entirely so in the process. "The readers responded to us favorably," Gaines recalled at a symposium in 2007, "the journalism community gave us awards, and even Congress loved us. We had cause to believe that we were on the good side and above criticism."[21]

What does it take to enter what the sociologist Erving Goffman called a "total institution?"[22] As in many other undercover ruses, the alteration of the writer's name is common. This happens most often when the writer's byline is likely to be known. Bly, for the asylum report, became Nellie Brown or Nellie Moreno. Pierre Salinger assumed a full-on alias; for a week he split between two California jails in 1953, he was Peter Emil Flik. Nat Caldwell signed into nursing homes with his middle name, Green. In 1983, Richard H. Stewart became "Richard Leader, convicted felon," for his pre-New Year's drunk-driving sentence on assignment from the *Boston Globe*.[23] In 1997, Ted Conover wrote down Frederick, the given name on his birth certificate, as he applied to be a prison guard at Sing Sing, a position he held for nearly eleven months.

Creating a persona for the assignment is typical. Sometimes, the reporters will costume and create elaborate if fleeting identities in the way that other undercover efforts require. Bly, to get herself committed to the Women's Lunatic Asylum, dressed shabbily and practiced looking deranged in front of a boarding house mirror. Three years later, in 1890, Annie Laurie also dressed down, put belladonna drops in her eyes, and faked a faint on the street to gain admission to a San Francisco receiving hospital, where she was treated rudely and sent home after a "mustard emetic."[24] Salinger drank himself silly on command in 1953 and wandered into a car on a San Francisco street.[25] To be convincing for a week each in three different Nashville nursing homes in 1968,[26] Caldwell grew a beard, dyed his hair white, walked with a cane, and made application at each facility accompanied by two younger reporters who claimed to be distant relatives in charge of his care. Also in Nashville, six years later, Frank Sutherland got coaching from a psychiatrist before his month-long commitment to a mental hospital.[27] In 1998, Kevin Heldman, for the New York City investigative magazine *City Limits,* put on layers of shabby clothes before walking into Woodhull Medical and Mental Health Center in Brooklyn and asking a succession of admitting personnel for help, saying he was depressed, not a drug addict, tired of living, and thinking seriously about killing himself.[28]

But as important as a strategy for entry is a plan for getting out, a far more involved issue in the planning phase of these operations than in attempts to, say, infiltrate a factory or set out on the open road. It starts with devising ways to keep the project secret from as many people as possible. This of course is to avoid influencing the dynamics of what the reporter witnesses and experiences on site; but it is also to help ensure the reporter's personal safety. In jail, "secrets are currency and everyone is selling secrets,"[29] Ray Ring explained. And moreover, anyone found to have entered jail under false pretenses is presumed to be a planted informer. A planted informer, Ben H. Bagdikian once deadpanned, "is an occupation with high mortality rates."[30] Both Ring and Bagdikian went to jail on imagined murder convictions, Bagdikian for the *Washington Post* in 1972 and Ring for the *Arizona Daily Star* a decade later.

No one on site may know what the reporter is really up to, but for the prisoner pose especially, it is almost a given that someone in officialdom sanctions the venture. Since incarceration in these cases is not voluntary, how else could the faux jail sentence eventually be commuted or the record erased?[31] Also, such ruses often require legal cover, as much for authorization as to stave off actual charges against the reporter. Bly in 1887 managed to convince a battery of judges and doctors that she was out of her mind, having confided her plans to no one other than her editors and an assistant state's attorney, who agreed to shield her from prosecution.[32] Salinger reported that his jail experiences for the *San Francisco Chronicle* had been made possible under an undisclosed "secret arrangement"[33] that expressly did not include the knowledge of his jailers or fellow prisoners. Only years later, in his 1995 memoir, did Salinger explain in detail how he went about the assignment. It started with his coverage of a meeting of the American Friends Service Committee to demand more humane treatment of prisoners in California's county jails. Pat Brown, the state's attorney general at the time, was presiding. Salinger was horrified by what was reported at the meeting and decided that a series on the appalling conditions the committee had uncovered would make more sense than a secondhand report on the committee's work. "And the more I thought about it," he wrote, "the more I realized that the best way to do the story would be from the *inside*. If I was to tell this ugly story accurately, I would have to become a prisoner myself."[34]

From previous reporting assignments, Salinger had developed

a professional rapport with Brown and felt comfortable proposing the idea to him. Brown thought about it for a minute or two and then not only agreed but offered to cook up the circumstances that would lead to Salinger's arrest. Several days later, Brown called Salinger and told him to stop shaving for five or six days, start looking a little weird, and then go to a bar in Stockton and stay there drinking beer for at least three hours: "At twelve-thirty-nine, walk down Main Avenue to the hotel and you'll see a brown four-door Hudson parked on the street." Salinger said Brown instructed him to get into the backseat of the car, which would be unlocked, go to sleep, and await arrest. Once in court, Brown told him to insult the judge. Why? Salinger asked. "So that he'll be sure to throw you in jail."[35]

Salinger spent four days in the Stockton jail and then another three days in the Bakersfield facility on a trumped-up speeding charge that had been similarly arranged. Deliberately, the two jails were chosen because they represented typical conditions in California's prison system, rather than the best or worst. Salinger's personal jailhouse stories opened the series but represented only a small but potent portion of his seventeen-article report, which considered numerous other facilities that he visited in the more conventional way.[36]

Again for the *Chronicle* nearly twenty years later, Charles Howe arranged to do a week of guard duty at San Quentin, and Tim Findley spent a week as a would-be convict at Soledad Prison. Their firsthand reports were included in the results of a three-month investigation of the California penal system in 1971, published by the *Chronicle* in fifteen daily installments.[37] The stories Findley wrote were in the third person with almost no direct personal references, both from his jail time at Soledad and from the other prisons he visited as an identified reporter. He described what he observed, quoted what he heard, and characterized what he witnessed. Co-incidentally, Findley endured an actual, more impromptu over-night experience at the Alameda County prison farm at Santa Rita, arrested and roughed up by police during the People's Park demonstrations of May 23, 1969. Once apprehended and herded into the bus, he did not identify himself as a reporter, but quickly handed his press credentials to a colleague and got aboard to be able to report on the experience. INSIDE SANTA RITA: I WAS A UC PRISONER, ran on the front page of the *Chronicle* the following day.[38] The stories in the more comprehensive prison series of 1971 skirted reference to the specifics of how the reporters had gotten inside the facility, but thirty years later, in an interview for this book, Findley explained that the *Chronicle* had gotten permission both from top officials in the penal system as well as from Soledad's warden. Including the warden in the informed circle is unusual in these types of investigations, mostly because of the increased risk it poses for word of the ruse to get out among the prisoners or staff on site.

Also atypically, Findley said that once inside, he did, in fact, make himself known by his real name and occupation to a select number of inmates. Prisons at the time, he said, had "succeeded in becoming the celebrity cause of the Left,"[39] helping to create a generation of inmates, especially among blacks, who considered themselves political detainees. Violence often erupted inside the jails, egged on by political agitation from outside. In the brief time Findley was inside Soledad—"a few days, maybe a couple of weeks"—he needed to interact with as many groups as possible while avoiding being identified as a member of any one of them. "We didn't have the time to leave me in there a year," he explained, "nor was I interested in that." It made no sense to spend the little time he had inside trying to establish a convincing identity, so he didn't try. This was about news, not an academic study. Time was simply too short.

The following year, Bagdikian engineered his own faked murder conviction for the *Washington Post* as part of a major report[40] on the state of the penal system nationally. He expressed gratitude to the "prison administrators in state and local systems that gave me freedom to inspect their institutions and speak at length and in private with inmates." He found them open and enlightened. "The harsh fact is that newspaper reporters are not permitted into the worst penal institutions, except, of course, for the privilege of inspecting that great Potemkin village of American prisons—the stainless steel kitchen—during off hours."[41]

Bagdikian initially planned his incarceration at a prison in Oklahoma, but a warning from a former inmate at the facility forced him to change course. "You'll never get out alive," he was told. "Too many people knew about the project, and the grapevine down there has picked it up." He ended up instead at the state penitentiary in Pennsylvania with the authorization and protection of the state attorney general and a few of his close aides, the only people let in on the plan. In case of emergency, the attorney general gave Bagdikian his home telephone number. What would have happened, Bagdikian later mused, if he had told a guard that he was actually a reporter who needed to reach the attorney general? "Oh, he could do that, all right," he quoted the state's director of corrections as saying at the time. "They'd just think he was crazy."[42]

For two personal pieces in a major 1982 prison series in Tucson's *Arizona Daily Star,* Ring's pose was as a prisoner, again on a murder conviction, and John Long's was as a guard. It took repeated approaches, but Ring and his editors managed to convince the new state troubleshooter to authorize the ruse. He had been hired to overhaul the state prison system and clearly saw he had little to gain from allowing the newspaper reporters in. He had little to gain from refusing, either, so he arranged the conviction and jail sentence for Ring.[43]

Long lasted the fully intended period in his correctional officer's uniform, but Ring had to cut short the two weeks he intended to stay inside. Four days before he planned to leave, a gang of inmates trapped him in a stairwell and demanded he hand over his belt. When Ring refused, the inmates pummeled him, leaving a huge bruise on his torso and breaking six of his teeth. Guards spirited him away for treatment and that became his way out.[44]

For infiltrations that involve applying for a job instead of contriving a jail sentence, approaches have varied. Pamela Zekman reported that in responding to an ad to apply for a nurse's aide position for a *Chicago Tribune* nursing home series in 1971, she provided phony references and a made-up work history that no one checked or challenged—"testimony to the poor administration of a nursing home which receives thousands of dollars every month in welfare payments,"[45] she wrote. Gaines "falsified his credentials"[46] to get the janitorial job at von Solbrig. Ring recalled that Long sought top-level authorization in 1982 to work as a prison guard in Arizona, as Ring had done to be a prisoner. Howe did the same to be a guard at San Quentin a decade earlier, yet he further involved the prison's warden in the ruse—again, one of the few—along with top officials in the California penal system.[47] Gaines revealed his plans to no one when he applied for the janitor position at Chicago's von Solbrig Hospital in 1975. Neither did Recktenwald, reporting for the *Chicago Tribune,* when he got hired as a prison guard for two weeks at the Pontiac Correctional Center in Illinois. That was in 1978 during a lockdown that followed the killing of three guards.[48] For Conover's stint as a correctional officer at Sing Sing some twenty years later, he also kept his real purpose totally secret from just about everyone, except his publisher and his wife.[49]

In cases where officials higher up in the system have been complicit in the ruse, a related issue no one has fully addressed is how on-site administrators have reacted to being left out of the information loop. Bagdikian raised it but didn't comment further in the preface to the paperback book that grew out of his series with Leon Dash, *The Shame of the Prisons*. In thanking the Pennsylvania state director of corrections at the time, the man who had helped him gain entry, he wrote, "I'm sure that [Allyn] Sielaff did not make his wardens happy with the thought that they might be unwitting host to a journalist prisoner."[50]

Over the years, journalism historians, critics, ethicists, and pundits have debated this subset of the undercover exposé, underscoring their approval or disdain. Silas Bent, for instance, in his 1939 book *Newspaper Crusaders,* alluded with apparent admiration to a spate of such investigations in that period, but mentioned specifically only one,[51] a Bly-like venture for the *Chicago Daily Times* in 1935 that was headlined SEVEN DAYS IN THE MADHOUSE. Its eight installments were written by Frank Smith, whom the newspaper described in a boxed item as "a *Times* reporter, former college football player and lifeguard who tips the scale at 200 pounds."[52] Bent said the series both increased the newspaper's circulation and led to a cleanup of the state-run mental asylum that was its target at Kankakee, Illinois.[53] *Time* magazine cited the same series prominently in 1937 in a paean to the newspaper—"Chicago's liveliest sheet"[54]—under the impressive leadership of publisher Samuel Emory Thomason and managing editor Louis Ruppel.

Albert Deutsch, a New York reporter and mental health expert of the period, took a dimmer view of the value of such newspaper exposés as tools of social reform, a subject he explored in two different essays, first, in his 1937 book on the history of the mental health movement in the United States, and again in a 1950 article for a scholarly journal.[55] Like Bent, he, too, remarked on the prevalence of newspaper undercover work. Deutsch described it as an "occasional" phenomenon in the late 1930s that had burgeoned by 1950 into an "epidemic" that was "spreading from paper to paper like a benign infection." He compared the exposé to the surgeon's scalpel, with its capacity to be useful or dangerous, constructive or destructive, depending on the user's skill.[56] Yet for specific examples, he mentioned only one, Bly's from the early years, derisively dubbing it and its many imitators the "nine-day sensation."[57] He noted one major change in 1950 from earlier infiltration attempts: the complicity of institutional administrators in the investigative effort. In the later period, reporters had been able to enter these institutions "not as hostile invaders, threatening the reputation and security of superintendents and other officers, but as welcome allies enlisted in a common cause,"[58] he said.

Deutsch offered few examples but did single out one landmark exposé of the middle years of the twentieth century that won his approval, one that has subsequently been of interest to scholars.[59] Headlined BEDLAM, it appeared in the May 1946 issue of *Life* magazine as a disturbing photographic essay with accompanying text based on the reports of some three thousand conscientious objectors—mostly young Methodists, Quakers, Mennonites, and Brethren—assigned in lieu of military service to work as attendants in a third of all state mental hospitals in the United States. As the writer, Albert Q. Maisel, explained, their work involved not only what they witnessed but questionnaires they filled out and "narratives" they wrote as instructional material for mental hospital workers. Their reports were supported by other official data, including statistics on brutality and the physical abuse of patients.[60]

Their work made them privy to all manner of appalling and inhumane treatment, and the photographic evidence *Life* published was all too reminiscent of pictures coming out of Nazi concentration camps in the same time period. In this instance, the conscientious objectors acted both as authorized whistleblowers and, from a privileged insider position over many months, as informants and surrogate undercover reporters for *Life.* Yet how often can a publication count on such sources to surface and make themselves available for such assignments—sources who combine the qualities of reliable witness, ability to document, and the willingness to share?

Almost always in the presentation of institutional exposés there is follow-up reporting to chronicle the impact of the initial investigation as it unfolds—committee hearings, reform initiatives, closures, indictments, arrests. They report the developments but are also intended to document the longer-term impact of the exposés, and to affirm, underscore, and justify their value. Ten months after Salinger's monumental prison series ran in the *San Francisco Chronicle,* he followed up with a second series, this one three articles that detailed various resulting improvements in the system statewide. An editor's note said the improvements stemmed from the reaction to Salinger's series from an "aroused public."[61] Salinger spoke about his series at more than fifty public gatherings, the newspaper reported, and testified before state legislators as they considered a prison reform bill, which passed.

In his memoir, Salinger remembered the response from the reading public as "electric" in the way it had ignited the calls for hearings and new legislation. He said California's governor at the time, Earl Warren, took personal charge of the investigation into conditions at the prisons "and the result was real reform," including the construction of new prisons for Stockton and Bakersfield, where Salinger had been jailed, "but of even greater importance was that the state of California took a new and enlightened approach to penology—rehabilitation, not just punishment."[62]

Recktenwald of the *Tribune* also waited nearly a year after his tour of guard duty in 1978 before he returned to the Pontiac Correctional Center, this time identifying himself as a *Tribune* reporter.[63] In a clear methodological justification for going undercover, with his newspaper credentials, he could no longer get inside. He resorted to standing at the gates and managed to interview the few guards he still knew from his time among them—turnover was still constant and most that he had worked with less than a year earlier by then had quit. Later, he also tracked down some of those no longer working at the facility. Those who remained on staff reported that some conditions had improved but others not.[64]

For an exposé of horrific conditions at an orphanage in Podolsk, Russia, Diane Sawyer, for ABC's television newsmagazine, *20/20,* put a hidden camera in her purse for the sake of "documenting the institutionalized neglect and abuse of thousands of handicapped children warehoused in Russian orphanages," according to the citation that accompanied the project's duPont-Columbia Award. Called "Forgotten Children of Russia," the investigation, which aired January 13, 1999, also won the Robert F. Kennedy Memorial Award. The duPont citation praised the segment for the way it conveyed the shocking nature of conditions at the orphanage with "intelligence and restraint," producing "fine international reporting in a magazine format, demonstrating that television news at its best can devote prime time programs to important humanitarian issues."[65] Human Rights Watch collaborated on the project.

In a follow-up segment that aired fifteen months later, Sawyer reported that all of the babies the *20/20* team had seen had been adopted, "due to pressure generated by our broadcast,"[66] with the aid of the Russian Orthodox Church, which got assistance from the Russian government.[67]

A further word about impact: Both the *Tribune*'s 1971 investigation into nursing homes and its 1975 series on von Solbrig Hospital generated extremely swift official responses. Within weeks, the nursing home probe triggered city, state, and federal investigations, and even arrests.[68] Recktenwald, who also worked on the project, said in an interview for this book that he still considered that 1971 series the most important work he ever did.[69]

For the von Solbrig investigation, within two days of publication, all but three patients had checked out of the hospital. By two months later, even before a scheduled hearing on license revocation before the Chicago Board of Health—also triggered by the series—the hospital, patientless, was forced to shut down entirely.[70] And then a second hospital came under investigation because of reports on the first.

Both of these *Tribune* investigations point out yet another high value of the method: the reporter as unmediated witness. How else could Zekman have been present when an elderly man and woman, not related, were forced to undress for baths in front of each other, face-to-face, "in helpless humiliation."[71] Gaines later explained that the assignment to get hired as a janitor emanated from a tip to the newspaper from a former janitor who said that custodians who hadn't washed up were being used in surgery to move patients. "There was really no question about what had to be done," Gaines told Steve Weinberg in the *IRE Journal*. "No newspaper reader would be expected to believe such a shocking account by an uneducated and disgruntled janitor." Gaines also said that in lying about his background, he "claimed no special expertise to get the job. Once hired, I only acted under direct orders from my supervisors. I worked hard to make sure that my janitorial skills would not be criticized."[72]

Reporters posing as prison guards have done likewise, investing fully in the tasks assigned on the job. And very soon during the week Gaines worked at von Solbrig, he too was instructed to put down his mop and wheel patients from the surgery table to their beds. He saw plenty else, including the tonsil-removing assembly line.

His reporting, he said, "removed the middleman" ("middle filter" was Anne Hull's phrase more than thirty years later for the Walter Reed investigation). "Now I could tell readers in a first-person account about what I saw." And what he saw was highly instrumental in forcing the shutdown of the multimillion-dollar facility. "I knew I had better be right," Gaines said. "I was." Later, he said, other hospital employees, including the head nurse, corroborated his account.[73]

Recktenwald's series about his stint as a prison guard also advances the notion of eyewitness potency. One day's installment of the series featured side-by-side photographs of what the media saw on October 9 during an organized press tour of a very well-kept West Cell House of the facility and of what Recktenwald saw eight days later as he made his rounds unescorted in the prison's garbage-strewn South Cell House. He had managed to photograph it that day with a concealed miniature camera.[74] "It was the size of a pack of cigarettes," he said. "I was able to bring it in without anyone seeing it."[75]

We also cannot underestimate the importance of the element of wonder, brought to the assignments by the undercover reporter who is experiencing such conditions for the first time, but with forethought, preparation, and intention to share, charged with the responsibility of describing the experience for those who likely never will have the chance.

Immediacy is another value well served by the undercover method. To report from inside one of these institutions fulfills a primary journalistic mission: to provide news or information for publication that ordinary citizens should have but cannot easily or reliably obtain on their own. This is often in response to conditions that cry out for information *right now*, while an issue involving the institution or the system is current. Sometimes, however, such information gains currency because a social reformer or former inmate or worker happens to provide a tip or produce a memoir or other writing that finds its way to publication. Bly, for instance, acted on reports of "shocking abuse" at the asylum that surfaced in summer 1887;[76] Salinger's series responded to reports of severe overcrowding in the California jails in 1953.[77]

In 1971, Findley and Howe's undercover prisoner-guard duet for the *Chronicle* came in the aftermath of major unrest at Soledad and a politicization of the prison population across the state, largely instigated, as Findley explained, by polarizing forces from the outside. From the East Coast and in roughly the same period, Bagdikian investigated the nation's penal system because, in his words, "almost everyone seems to agree that our prisons are terrible."[78] Recktenwald was sent in during a lockdown,[79] and in Arizona, the appointment in 1982 of a new prison system troubleshooter bent on major reform sent Ring and Long inside for a closer look.[80]

Deutsch, back in 1950, likened the journalistic exposé to shock treatment. There is no expectation that the shocks will cure a mental patient; they only open the way for follow-up rounds of psychotherapy. Deutsch went on, mixing the metaphor, saying that the responsible journalist "follows the jolting exposé with discussions illuminating the problem digging toward its roots, helping the reader gain insight," and suggesting solutions. The exposé, he said, represents a calculated risk. Realizing that its failure may cause harm, the reporter also knows that "at best, it is but the opening wedge in arousing public interest that can be transmuted into desired public action."[81]

The decision to "go deceptive" is rarely incidental to the willingness of reporters to undertake the assignments or to their ability to amass great material and put their reports across in an unusually compelling way. Talent and personal disposition matter absolutely. The articles and books these writers have produced showcase gutsy flair. Unapologetically, the expectation in return for the editorial investment in risks, costs, and effort is the creation of a narrative tour de force on a significant social issue, stories that will evoke in readers a call to action, or at least a more subtle expression of amazement, even awe. The writing is often, but not always, theatrical, confessional, more personal than usual, meant to provoke a public connection and reaction with enough force to ignite an official response or government action. Often, the narratives reveal the reporter's thoughts as they react to the disturbingly alien worlds in which they find themselves, sometimes with writing that may seem overly self-involved. More importantly, the stories are meant to give voice to the silenced or the stigmatized, to those who lack credibility even when heard.

Largely, no doubt, because of the early 1980s timeframe in which the *Arizona Daily Star* and *Boston Globe* jail exposés appeared, Tom Goldstein in 1985 happened to single out all three as examples of the undercover genre's inherent deficiencies. Although he found Ring's ten-thousand-word opus "powerfully written," he thought much of it was too self-conscious, in the way undercover narratives can be, filled with "lapses in and out of stream of consciousness" that "bespeaks a rebellious reporter" and that revealed "more about Ring and his feelings than about the prison." In Stewart's case, Goldstein said, his aim had been to present a no-holds-barred view of prison life to those who were unlikely ever to experience it. Yet the *Globe* had primly deleted all the expletives to meet its family newspaper standard and the writer, Goldstein thought, provided too many "bland insights."[82] He also zeroed in on how one of Stewart's reflections in the text revealed a central flaw in the undercover methodology: his admission that because the conviction and jail time were based on no crime, "I would not have to live the rest of my life with the burden of trying to conceal the fact that I was a criminal, a man with a prison record."[83] That led Goldstein to point out the inherent lack of authenticity in the method itself. "Capturing the reality of prison life," he concluded, "is as elusive and difficult for the undercover reporter as it is for the reporter who identifies himself."[84]

Twenty-five years later, Ring could not have disagreed more with the professor. Regardless of how the reporter wound up in the situation, in Ring's view, that very self-consciousness along with the writer's unique narrative force gave the method much of its value. "That's what I think you get with a first person piece—narrative power, the power of the writing; I was there. This happened to me," he said in an interview. "I look for the first person voice because of that power and I think many readers are like me.... It's different than a third person voice. Believe me, for many years after, as I go around, this is the most likely thing I hear. 'You're the guy who did the prison story.' This was very well received in the community. It's good for journalism. It's good for the newspaper. It establishes an authority. People are slipping into your shoes."[85]

At least one other researcher has pointed out that the personal and financial investment required to do this kind of reporting has the potential to contaminate the results, predisposing the reporters to find evidence of wrongdoing that may not exist.[86]

Ring said this tendency can be counteracted with strict adherence to two key principles: First, accuracy—"you never want to be wrong and whatever you can do to move from eighty percent to ninety percent accuracy, you do, digging, and that's where this undercover work fits. It's a highly accurate form of reporting." Second, adherence to the maxim: Do No Harm. "You don't hurt people who don't deserve to be hurt," he said. What costs journalism its credibility is not the free use of the first person or a creative approach to telling a story, Ring said. It is being weak. "If we had more assertive journalists," he said, "we would have people respecting journalism more." Looking back at his brief incarceration, he said, "I wouldn't have done anything differently. Even getting roughed up. Even the chipped teeth."[87]

From the personal standpoint of the writer, undercover reporting on prisons, hospitals, and asylums has consistently meant outstanding payoff in both peer accolades and audience response, going back to the earliest-known examples. Bly and Annie Laurie launched legendary careers on the strength of their undercover assignments in the late 1880s and early 1890s. Salinger's 1953 prison series earned that year's Edward V. McQuade Memorial Award and a commendation from then California governor Warren. The *Chronicle* reported that penologists hailed Salinger's effort as "a great contribution to the public understanding of the problem."[88]

Michael Mok's I WAS A MENTAL PATIENT was an eight-part exposé on the treatment of mental patients at Kings County Hospital in 1961 for the *New York World-Telegram & Sun*.[89] It won both the prestigious Albert Lasker Medical Journalism Award[90] and the Newspaper Guild's Heywood Broun Award. The union honor he shared that year with his colleague on the newspaper, Dale Wright, who won for his migrant series.[91]

Caldwell's 1968 pose as a new resident at three area nursing homes brought an overwhelming reader response to the *Nashville Tennessean*. In a follow-up story, Caldwell described the flood of letters as "the largest I have seen in thirty-six years as a reporter."[92] Only 2 of the 162 letters received by two weeks after the series ran were "unqualifiedly unfavorable."[93] Thirty-five years later, at Caldwell's induction into the Tennessee Newspaper Hall of Fame, a press release mentioned the series on a very short list of the major achievements of his long, outstanding career, saying the series had led to the state licensing of such privately owned facilities.[94]

Findley and Howe won a San Francisco Press Club[95] Award for their California prison series in 1971, and the Bagdikian-Dash series for the *Washington Post* placed second with an honorable mention at the 1973 Robert F. Kennedy Memorial Awards behind a landmark mental asylum investigation that employed a different kind of subterfuge. This was Geraldo Rivera's exposé for New York's WABC-TV of appalling conditions for the five thousand residents of the Willowbrook State School, which forced the complete shutdown of a troubled facility for the state's mentally challenged.[96] That subterfuge involved no poseurs. Rivera and his crew entered the facility early one morning in an act of criminal trespass, never prosecuted, with the help of a stolen key.[97] They shot startling footage of feces-smeared patients screaming and fighting. The von Solbrig Hospital exposé, of course, helped land the biggest honor of all for the *Chicago Tribune,* the newspaper's second Pulitzer Prize in five years to have incorporated an undercover aspect.[98]

The awards list goes on. In 1982, Ring's "murder conviction" for the *Arizona Daily Star* prison series received a Scroll Award from the Investigative Reporters and Editors, an American Bar Association Gavel Award, and a first-place finish in state press club's annual investigative reporting contest.[99] As for Reckten-wald, also for the *Tribune,* a prison reform group honored him with its eponymous John Howard Award for 1979 for his Pontiac prison guard series. He also received the *Tribune's* Edward Scott Beck Award, the newspaper's annual internal honor, and several local accolades.[100] The *Tribune's* von Solbrig Hospital series shut down a substandard facility, as did the Willowbrook investigation. Findley said his prison series for the *Chronicle* got important public attention and helped bring about determinant sentencing.[101]

In 2001, Conover's near-year undercover as a corrections officer for his widely acclaimed book, *Newjack: Guarding Sing Sing,* was a Pulitzer finalist in the General Nonfiction category and a winner of the National Book Critics Circle Award.[102]

Even more significantly, these assignments, regardless of the media platform in which they appeared, have often generated substantive civic action. Of all the very early efforts, nothing topped the most frequently cited of all reportage in this genre, Bly's jaw-dropper of a debut as a New York City reporter in fall 1887. As a "girl reporter" in her early twenties, she accepted a life-imperiling, man-size assignment to feign insanity and get herself committed to the Women's Lunatic Asylum on Blackwell's (now Roosevelt) Island. On release, she quickly filled two pages of the *World's* Sunday feature section with her heavily detailed account, starting with her step-by-step preparation for the ruse and then her encounters with the judges and doctors who sent her across the river to endure inedible food, filth, harsh treatment, and stark-raving boredom. Interestingly, the conditions Mok described at King's County seventy years later sounded horrifyingly much the same.

Bly's performance was so convincing—and this part remains wholly unique—that unwitting beat reporters from competing newspapers who had encountered her in court as her insanity determination was being made covered developments daily as a fascinating local mystery. WHO IS THIS INSANE GIRL? the rival *New York Sun* asked in a headline. The *World* followed up day after day with news of the story's impact: an immediate grand jury investigation, which included her testimony, followed. Soon after, the city Board of Estimate and Apportionment approved an increase in the appropriation to the dilapidated facility.[103]

Even Annie Laurie's one-day wonder for the *San Francisco Examiner* in 1890 was credited, at least by her newspaper, with prompting an official investigation that led to the dismissal of some hospital staff, and other reforms.[104]

For Bly personally, as for Annie Laurie, going undercover was the moment of celebrity coronation. For undercover reporting more generally, it gave the method instant credence as a sure-fire circulation-building gimmick for any other publication that could manage to hire as capable and fetching a stunt girl. Bly's work, especially, burnished a weapon long stored in the journalistic armory: not just the undercover sensation for sensation's sake but the undercover sensation with a clear civic or social agenda, a notion completely in tune with the sensibilities of the Age of Reform. The trick then and thereafter was to use the construct selectively, and for high purpose, so as not to wear it out.[105] It was a mark that would often be hit in the years to come, but one that was just as often missed, and one that also would repeatedly invite controversy.

Recktenwald's prison series, too, was one of his many hits. A new warden appointed just before Recktenwald's story ran praised the series but defended the lax hiring procedure under which Recktenwald got the job, explaining that longer background checks had proved to be a deterrent to hiring for good candidates who could not wait for employment until the process was completed.[106] The same day the Recktenwald series concluded, the lockdown was lifted.[107] Three days after that, the Illinois General Assembly, citing the *Tribune* series, called for a special joint advisory committee to investigate conditions in prisons across the state.[108] Although Recktenwald had come to the *Chicago Tribune* from the Better Government Association, and had been involved with several exceedingly difficult watchdog investigations,[109] he considered his turn as a Pontiac prison guard "his toughest yet."[110]

Late in 1973, as a reporter for the *Nashville Tennessean,* the coaching Sutherland received from a licensed psychiatrist taught him how to pose convincingly as mentally ill. On December 14, he registered, in his formal name of Ernest Franklin Sutherland Jr., as a patient of Nashville's Central State Psychiatric Hospital, where he would remain for the next thirty-one days. He shared with no one on staff or above them why he was really there. The *Tennessean* assured its readers that Sutherland had given a fictitious name to any patient whom he quoted or described in his stories, that the newspaper had double-checked to be sure the hospital had empty beds before he entered the facility, and that it had covered the cost of Sutherland's stay at the regular patient rate. Further, to test security precautions at the facility, Sutherland had simply walked away when he left without announcing his departure to anyone. Concurrently, the newspaper clued local police to his "disappearance" to ensure that no taxpayer-paid time or effort would be wasted in trying to locate him.[111]

On January 20, 1974, a week after his release, Sutherland's opening paragraph in the Sunday newspaper hit hard. He flat-out condemned Central State as "a warehouse for the storage of people—an unaccredited and unclean hospital with more than half its doctors unlicensed to practice in Tennessee." He further charged that patients often were admitted without a comprehensive medical examination or a psychiatric evaluation and rarely received psychiatric treatment during their stays. Security was lax; illegal drugs like marijuana were being smuggled in easily; and although violence was not the rule, violence did occur. He characterized his stay with four *d*-words: *degrading, dehumanizing, dreary,* and *depressing,* and reported with specifics and impressions in a way that escorted reporter's visits, even repeated ones, could never have matched.[112]

Nine long articles devoted to his findings comprised the series, ending with the requisite prescriptions for change. Follow-up reporting continued into February and March, including a report of the conclusions of a blue ribbon committee that had been hastily formed to investigate the hospital in the aftermath of Sutherland's series.[113] Its members recommended a number of improvements, including an increased appropriation to the hospital, accelerated movement toward accreditation, a doubling of its housekeeping staff, a substantial increase in its professional care, and demolition of two of its older structures. Two days later, former officials of the facility—all licensed psychiatrists—issued a statement recommending a total change in the institution's scope and leadership.[114]

A couple of days later, at a panel discussion on which the

hospital's superintendent and Sutherland both appeared, the superintendent defended his own leadership. Other hospital aides criticized Sutherland for blaming aides for some of the hospital's failings, which Sutherland denied he had done. Another aide accused Sutherland of focusing only on the negative aspects of the facility and none of its good programs. Sutherland retorted that his story was confined only to what he personally witnessed and experienced in the part of the hospital where he had been placed. He also flatly denied an accusation that he had been "set up" by the "personal vendetta" of a former psychiatrist at the hospital. Sutherland said he never contacted any of the former hospital doctors until after his investigation was well under way.[115] The newspaper reprinted the series as a special edition, ending with an obligatory analysis and a set of proposals for reform.

Twenty-five years later, in July 1999, Sutherland reflected in print on his own undercover triumph, this time in his then current role as the *Tennessean*'s vice president and editor in chief. By that point, he had been the newspaper's editor for a decade. Writing for the Gannett Company newsletter, he mentioned his and other momentous undercover exposés that the *Tennessean* had sponsored, acknowledging that there had not been more than ten of them in the preceding twenty years. Undercover efforts had produced some of the newspaper's proudest hours, he said, some on Sutherland's own watch. He cited Jerry Thompson's eighteen months undercover as a member of the Ku Klux Klan and the month Susan Thomas and Brad Schmitt had spent "living incognito in a public housing project, observing the drug trade and how it affects the lives of families and children in most of these cases." Yet each of these, he acknowledged, had involved *Tennessean* reporters misrepresenting themselves to news sources, a practice he then decreed against in announcing a set of new "Principles" for the paper.[116]

As editor, Sutherland acknowledged this was a full about-face from the position he consistently had taken as a reporter years before in story brainstorming sessions at the newspaper. In fact, he remembered himself as "the representative of lying, cheating and stealing." Without the subterfuge, he acknowledged, Thompson's KKK reporting would have proved too dangerous. His own mental hospital investigation would have been a no-go altogether. Thomas and Schmitt might have been subject to a greater safety risk had their identities as reporters been known, but, Sutherland surmised, they could have avoided misrepresenting themselves. As it happened, they were never asked to reveal who they really were, what they were doing, or why. Then he said, "Weigh those stories, some of which resulted in major changes in the fabric of our society, against the credibility issues raised by readers to us every day." He said that readers put inaccuracy, printing falsehoods, and slanting the news at the top of the list and followed up in the next sentence with, "Would I trade all my undercover stories for a favorable credibility rating from my readers today? You betcha." Some, he said, could still be done within these principles. Some veteran reporters and editors no doubt would question his decision to take away these reporting tools. To them, he said he would reply: "It doesn't matter how many tools we have if our readers don't believe us. And they are only going to believe us if we have a set of Principles that say we don't lie, cheat, or steal, and that we are honest in the way we gather the news."[117]

With a curious logic not uncommon among editors at the time, Sutherland conflated the methods used for the *Tennessean*'s very occasional undercover exposés over two decades—roughly one every other year—with the more generalized reader disgruntlement and distrust that had developed during that period—not so much over the gathering of the news, but over the way the news was being presented. And yet, in the same breath, he acknowledged how those same few undercover exposés had served one of the profession's highest callings and had encouraged "major changes in the fabric of our society."[118]

None of the undercover stories the *Tennessean* published in those years appears to have been fairly accused of inaccuracy, falsehood, or slanting—the top reader complaints Sutherland set out to address. Yet his statement appeared to hold only this small handful of outstanding pieces to account for the industry's much wider failings.[119]

In 2001, the city's alternative weekly, the *Nashville Scene,* reported out another view of what had happened to the newspaper. The article based its reporting on responses it had solicited from more than 130 community leaders and "many of those who were once so close to it." Its conclusion was that the newspaper's real problem was not trust or believability but ennui, nothing like its "story book history—an epic chapter in Southern journalism filled with crusades for black men and women, for open government, disenfranchised voters, the poor and infirm, and the otherwise dispossessed."[120]

Newspaper alumni quoted at other points in the series included illustrious *Tennessean* alumni such as Caldwell, David Halberstam, Jim Squires, Tom Wicker, and Bill Kovach. In interviews, several of them waxed nostalgic about what it had meant to be on the *Tennessean*'s staff in its glory days under John Seigenthaler.[121] Halberstam described it as "an addiction for us. It was like eating. We couldn't live without it" and Kovach as "like breathing pure oxygen."[122]

Sutherland countered calmly that circulation had grown "substantially and consistently" during his years at the paper. "The rest," he said, "is subjective."[123]

Nonetheless, it is also true that to send a reporter undercover has never been the only route to the effective journalistic exposé. Both reporters and social reformers have been highly effective using more conventional means to investigate closed institutions. Such an exemplar was Deutsch himself, who won the George Polk Award in 1948 and the Albert Lasker Award in 1949[124] for his mental health reporting. At his death in 1961, an obituary in the leading psychoanalytic journal described him as a "journalistic leader" known for his advocacy of the "scientific and humane treatment" of the mentally ill.[125] Deutsch had the great advantage of an insider's view. He had been a New York welfare department employee for four years before he became a reporter and columnist for New York City's *PM* and then *Compass* newspapers. In his essays, he defined the word *exposé* broadly, à la *Webster's,* as "an exposure or revelation of something discreditable."[126] He singled out a number of contemporaneous reporters whose conventionally reported work in the mental health area he admired.[127] But for Deutsch, the true "apostle of the insane"[128] was Dorothea Lynde Dix, who in the 1840s took up the cause of getting the mentally ill out of the jails and almshouses and into specially designed asylums. Dix collected facts and data by visiting institution after institution, information she then presented as memorials to state legislatures. Deutsch was especially enamored of the way her version of the exposé, which sometimes appeared in local newspapers, was able to "prick the public conscience and to prod the conscience-stricken into constructive action through the press and other media, in state after state."[129] He considered her work a model for any modern-day reporter. What, for any writer, he asked rhetorically, could top Dix's unembellished, staccato presentation to the Massachusetts State Legislature in 1843, which began:

> LINCOLN: A woman in a cage.
> MEDFORD: One idiot subject chained, and one in a close stall for seventeen years.[130]

Ironically, in 1887, it was an investigation of abuses and deterioration at exactly the kind of facility Dix had championed that Bly set out to expose in her two-part series that fall.[131] Dix died that very year.

Still others have been successful at bringing closed institutions into view without going undercover. The tell-all memoirs of bona fide former inmates or former employees also figure under the rubric of the exposé and have been extremely effective over the centuries in rousing public sentiment and sometimes a meaningful response.

Up to a point, but only up to a point, the journalist's role in these cases can resemble that of the social reformer or even the inmate or worker turned memoirist. Over the years, writers who do not identify as journalists have effectively turned what they have witnessed or personally experienced in these situations into words for publication. Their writing has been successful at unleashing a flood of public sympathy as well as civic or legislative interest. The fact is, save the limits of talent, timing, access to an effective publishing venue, and the force of will, there are no bars on entry to journalism or authorship or to success. In principle, anyone can attempt it, so patients and incarcerates who have the ability to write effectively for wide audiences—before release and after—are among them.[132]

But the role of the memoirist differs from the role of the reporter, just as the social reformer's role differs. In the journalistic case, there is a much higher priority on dispassionate observation as well as on urgency and timeliness, even, as already noted, at the expense of thoroughness. In fact, Deutsch in 1937 was highly critical of this aspect of the journalistic practice at the time. He considered the "nine day sensation" froth at best, perhaps with laudable motives and perhaps providing accurate facts, but facts that would be "lost to sight as suddenly as they had flared up,"[133] facts that would not generate meaningful reforms.

Actually, the record does not support this. Even the seven- or nine-day undercover effort has been very effective in instigating changes, especially when combined with other investigative strategies. But even worse, in Deutsch's view, was that the early efforts were often "hastily conceived and superficially executed," and more likely had the net effect of widening the gap between the institution and the community in the way they generated more undifferentiated fear and horror than context and understanding.[134] Deutsch argued that an exposé without proposed solutions can actually cause more harm than good by conditioning the "frustrated reader to an acceptance of a situation that initially shocked him."[135]

Deutsch acknowledged that in the postwar period, especially, reporters had been going to concerted lengths to provide adequate analysis and to propose solutions. And it is true that almost every undercover investigation from the late 1930s onward concludes with a finale piece that provides prescriptions and suggestions for meaningful reform, as Jack London had offered in *Abyss* as far back as 1902. Yet, these finale pieces are usually the weakest element of any such series. They often seem editor ordered, perfunctory, obligatorily tacked on.

Furthermore, Deutsch's position loses sight of the reporter's primary function of creating awareness. Follow up for the reporter or for the publication almost always means more stories—reports on actions taken as well as editorial and opinion-page advocacy. But by engagement, news organizations do not mean for the activists' business of organizing or fundraising for a movement to become an editorial function. Journalists typically stop at the rallying cry that is the exposé itself, the presentation of the problem, along with reporting on whatever the reporting itself generates. Reporters and editors move on to other subjects, to newer news. They do this without apology; that is the nature of the job.

Then, there is the question of timing. If and when the work of memoirists might happen is serendipitous at best, wholly dependent on the presence of such an individual in such a newsworthy situation—and one who can write at that. No one can predict or direct when such an opportunity will come along, or when a writer will find him- or herself a bona fide patient or inmate with the presence of mind to document the experience and then write about it as if that were the intention. Barbara Ehrenreich in *Harper's* on her own breast cancer treatment comes to mind,[136] or Sallie Tisdale, also for *Harper's,* on working as a nurse in an abortion clinic.[137] What could be more explicitly or starkly moving than William Styron's examination of his own depression for *Darkness Visible, a Memoir of Madness*?[138] There are many other similar efforts, too, self-consciously conceived ones such as Norah Vincent on her self-directed "year lost and found in the loony bin," for a book she titled *Voluntary Madness.* It followed her year-long impersonation of a man, another book idea, that she had crafted two years earlier.[139]

Conover's turn as a prison guard at Sing Sing began by approaching prison officials for access as a reporter as far back as 1992. He wanted to follow a recruit through the training process but permission was denied. Plan B some years later was to try again by applying to be a guard himself. To apply, he presented a résumé that omitted his authorship of three books and his position as a contributing writer to the *New York Times Magazine.* He did however list his bachelor's degree from Amherst and a job he once held as a reporter for the *Aspen Times.*[140]

For this book, Conover has said he was less interested in being a character, as he had been in *Rolling Nowhere,* than he was in being a "narrative presence."[141] The exceptionally long duration of his stay relative to his fellow journalist-guardsmen contributes greatly to this ability, providing the chance for a broad familiarity with staff, the inmates, and the institution itself, its recent and longer-ago history. While short-term guards can describe another officer or an inmate they encounter, they can't really tell you how typical the person is, nor can they comment on it. Recktenwald, for example, talks about how many guards in his group had departed by the time he returned to Pontiac ten months later. As he interviewed the few who remained as well as those who had left, he reported that many were reacting to racial tensions and feared for their lives. At Sing Sing, Conover watched the exodus as it took place. Two-thirds of his class dropped out during the months he was on the job.

Another obvious difference would be the time it naturally takes in any situation to get to know people reasonably well. Just as an interview is not long enough, neither is a week or two. "With officers you do it by carpooling with them, by having beers after hours," Conover said. "With inmates you do it by encountering them day after day, week after week, month after month."[142]

And more than that, he said, was the opportunity that the much longer stay afforded to allow him to identify personally as a correctional officer. "The work was intense and demanding and stressful," he said. "I took it home with me; it made me different from my friends who were not working in prison, and had no idea what I was going through. So a distance grew between me and my old friends whom I couldn't tell about my secret work, and distance shrank between me and my new associates who knew a lot about what I was going through every day, even though I was very different from them in terms of education, previous experience, etc. I still catch myself saying 'we' when I am telling somebody about what it was like for 'us' CO's to work in Sing Sing. Because I was one."[143]

Conover retold an incident from *Newjack* in which an inmate accidentally ran into him, but in a way that seemed to a fellow officer that Conover had been attacked. He saw his colleague ball up his fists as he sized things up. "You okay?" he asked. Conover said he was, and as the inmate apologized, both Conover and his fellow guard accepted that it had been an accident. "But in that split second, where I saw him ready to defend me, I was filled with love (exactly the right word) for that officer," he said, adding that it was "the kind of qualitatively different experience" made possible by the longer stay.[144]

"Let me make it clear," Conover said. "I admire all of these journalists for the chances they took. The result, in each case, was fascinating journalism in the public interest. But if you're asking me, *did they do the same thing as you?* I'd have to say no. They visited a scary foreign country for a few days. I was an ex-pat there."[145]

As editorial hands began to wring over the ethics of misrepresentation in the 1980s, a common argument in favor of abandoning the practice of undercover reporting was that great insider journalism could be produced just as effectively without misrepresentation or subterfuge. As evidence, Goldstein offered a regular column about prison life that the *Nevada Appeal* of Carson City was running at the time, the work of Gerald Crane, a high-school dropout who was serving a thirty-five-year sentence for kidnapping and bank robbery in a local jail. And, what Goldstein described as "probably the best contemporary picture of prison life"[146] had arrived in 1972 in the form of the paperback edition of the official New York State report on the 1971 Attica prison riots and the police takeover that followed. He also mentioned an excellent and lengthy investigative piece with no undercover dimension,[147] an examination of the main jail in Los Angeles, published in 1980 by *Corrections,* a short-lived magazine about the prison system. The writer was William Hart, who at the time was covering the criminal justice beat for the *Detroit Free Press.* Thirty years later, Hart was on the research staff at the Morrison Institute for Public Policy at Arizona State University, still working mainly on criminal justice issues.

Hart never engaged in undercover reporting himself but turns out to be one of its great advocates. "However well you think you are doing as a journalist," he said in an interview for this book, "and I thought I was doing pretty well, especially after a year or so of going to prisons, of having interviewed five hundred inmates, gaining some sense of what to expect, what they're like, and how to report on them and the staff and everyone else, I still think there are things that you don't find out that way.

"Prisons are such unusual and special places," he went on. "Inmates are one hundred percent vulnerable individuals; I think it's relatively rare when they are as candid as they could be. I can't point to anything in particular that I didn't get or that I've read that I wouldn't have gotten from someone because he knew he was speaking to a journalist. I've learned that people lie—good guys, bad guys, people lie. There is just no substitute for being there yourself. I saw this. I experienced this. There are subtleties in communications that won't come through from an event reported later."[148]

He said another benefit, smaller but measurable, is in "letting institutions know that this *could* be happening—a deterrent, in a sense. I would be pleased if prison wardens and police chiefs and corporate CEOs and packinghouse executives knew it was possible that a reporter could come in there undercover. It would keep them honest."[149]

Another hard-to-refute argument in favor of the reported personal experience under guise was one that Bagdikian offhandedly offered in the *Washington Post* piece he wrote about his own jail time, a passage repeated in the paperback reprint of his series, also in 1972: he had researched and reported on the American prison system as an outsider for three months, interviewing prisoners, former prisoners, corrections administrators, and research scientists, and "observing men behind bars and talking about them the way a tourist visits a zoo." None of that had prepared him "for the emotional and intellectual impact of maximum-security incarceration."[150]

THE SHAME OF THE PRISONS was the headline on the eight-part series in the *Post*.[151] From the standpoint of perceived reader appeal, what the newspaper's promoters emphasized about the series in a house ad says it all: "Ben H. Bagdikian of the *Washington Post* spent a week behind bars as part of his four months' research into The Shame of the Prisons."[152]

## TWELVE

## CRUSADERS AND ZEALOTS

Almost no clandestine group has escaped the disloyal scrutiny of infiltrators who gained access to its secrets and then shared them for publication against the organization's wishes. Going back as far as the early 1800s and forward to the present, from the Masons to the theocrats of the Washington elite, from the Nazis and neo-Nazis to the Ku Klux Klan, undercover reporting on dozens of U.S.-based religious organizations, secretive societies, and extreme social movements has been a constant. Ideological passions or deep-seated personal encounters can be the inspiration for these efforts, as they have been for investigations into other broad subject areas, too, such as human and animal rights. The writers in some cases have played a role more akin to official investigator or informant than independently minded journalist, sharing the information they collect as they collect it with opposition groups or law enforcement agencies, often in exchange for payment. This is less true for the newspaper reporters and magazine writers who generally steer a straighter journalistic watchdog path, with the public as their only master, presenting the information they gather as soon as possible for readers, listeners, or viewers.

For scores of years, journalists have used deceptive tactics to penetrate these and other secretive societies, religious groups, and organized social and political movements, especially those perceived to wield insidious power, to have mind control over their followers, or to be suspected of malevolent intent. Often this is to provide a way to frame the reporting in graphic storybook details, in classic journalistic "show" rather than "tell," as Craig Unger put it, in his explanation of why he signed up for a tour of the Holy Land with a group of Christian fundamentalists without telling any of his travel mates that he had an ulterior objective.[1] Other times, the purpose of the ruse is to verify information that would be difficult if not impossible to obtain otherwise.

The subgenre's most startling antecedent, the exposé with perhaps the furthest reaching impact of all, had no such narrative clay packed onto its armature. It is the 1827 case of the stonecutter William Morgan and the Masonic lodge in Batavia, New York, to which he at a certain point sought to belong. In retaliation for his eventual rejection, Morgan enlisted David Cade Miller, a local printer and newspaper publisher, to typeset a straightforward catalog of Masonic rites, rituals, and secret practices, with intent to publish. The consequences of that intention alone could not have been more devastating, for Morgan and soon after for the entire Masonic movement.

Morgan went out for a walk early one morning and wound up arrested on shoplifting charges. That evening, he was released on bail into the hands of a group of men he did not know. In the days that followed, Freemasons contacted his wife, Lucinda, offering to help locate her husband if she would turn over his manuscript and any notes about the society. Afraid to relinquish her leverage, she offered them a portion of Morgan's notes, hoping to at least see her husband in exchange. But the Freemasons rejected her compromise and Morgan was never seen or heard from again.

Miller, the publisher, then defiantly printed the manuscript, adding to Morgan's text a damning introduction that ridiculed the Freemasons as a superfluous institution, kept alive not by its merits but by misplaced self-importance and an unfounded obsession with secrecy. In a way, the Mason's extreme reaction to the impending publication lends weight to Miller's assertion that the source of the society's perceived power lay in its secrecy, the very element that Morgan's manuscript threatened to destroy.

After Morgan's disappearance and the release of the manuscript, an outraged public demanded justice. But despite more than forty separate trials and numerous state and local inquests over several years, only a few of the conspirators were convicted. Not only that, but the details of Morgan's disappearance and the thwarted efforts at prosecution inflamed public opinion against Freemasonry and gave rise to a full-blown movement against it.[2]

Perhaps the most unique element of Morgan's story is that the impetus for his exposé was not rooted in journalistic fervor, activism, or social reform—he wanted to become a Freemason—nor did a traumatic or curious childhood encounter pique his interest in the subject. The motivator was revenge. The power and success of Morgan's work, despite being almost completely devoid of ideology, politics, or even narrative, lies in its undercover nature. Only by gathering information as an insider was he able to expose Freemasonry's closely guarded secrets.

Homegrown Nazi activity generated two memorable journalistic probes in the 1930s. One involved a year's worth of planning but took only a few months to execute in traditional tabloid newspaper style; the other was a full four-year undercover exploit. Both grew out of efforts intended to illuminate for readers far more than could be learned by more conventional means, such as scouring movement literature and publications, interviewing known leaders, or reporting on rallies or other publicly staged events. For what would become a major undercover exposé in 1937, the managing editor of the *Chicago Daily Times,* Louis Ruppel, devised a plan to get an inside view of the inner workings of several U.S.-based bunds. The project was borne of his own prior background as an agent for the U.S. Narcotics Bureau, the already well-established affection of Chicago newspaper readers for a daringly executed undercover exposé, and the availability of three of the newspaper's reporters who happened to be of German origins and German speaking.[3]

Under immense headlines, the results of their investigation ran in the newspaper over fourteen straight days, starting on September 9, 1937. On the opening day of the series alone, the reporting covered ten full pages with its rich detail and photographs of bund activity, including snapshots of the reporters in Nazi mode, decked out as storm troopers. It explained how they had gone about gaining access and what they had learned.[4] *Time* magazine found the reporting impressive enough to feature the series nationally in its media column, lauding Ruppel for this and for his other imaginative successes during two short years at the paper. The column also singled out the newspaper's 1935 SEVEN DAYS IN A MADHOUSE asylum exposé, another Ruppel brainchild. More to the point, perhaps, for Ruppel, *Time* went on to report that for the first time, reader interest in the series had sent the Chicago and suburban circulation of the *Times* "rocketing above its evening rivals," the *News* and *Hearst American*.[5]

Soon after the Chicago splash, a young journalist named Arthur Derounian styled an undercover project of his own, this one without major institutional backing. The accident of ancestry again played a role in his fit for the project, but not in the way that a German heritage had made the Nazi reporting possible for the *Chicago Times.* Derounian was an Armenian who grew up in Bulgaria and Turkey before immigrating to the United States with his family,[6] but he was born in Alexandropolis, Greece, a place he identified with the aside, "Hitler and Himmler now rule it."[7] It was appalling to him that a Nazi-esque movement could take root in his adopted country. While doing freelance research and editorial work for *Fortune,* he became obsessed with "the idea of investigating these people who seemed intent upon destroying every vestige of freedom in America."[8]

As a cover, Derounian set out to become "the finest synthetic Italian-American in New York,"[9] an ostensible young tough named George Pagnanelli. He took a room for a week in New York's Italian neighborhood near Mulberry Street and immersed himself in the local ways—Italian food, Italian movies, Italian music, the way Italian housewives bargained with pushcart peddlers. Through the thin walls of his tiny tenement room, he listened to family quarrels. George dressed and spoke like Tony, a young Italian his own age, right down to the pointy-toed shoes and the copy of the Italian-American newspaper, *Il Progresso,* tucked into his back pocket.

In his Pagnanelli guise, Derounian approached Peter Stahrenberg, head of the Nationalist Press Association, who introduced himself as editor and publisher of the *National American,* the official organ of the American National-Socialist Party. Initially, Derounian ingratiated himself by offering to hand out pamphlets and copies of the organization's newspaper to students on the Columbia University campus.[10]

Soon, Derounian left his job at *Fortune* to spend the next four years "plunged into the opportunity to repay America in a humble way, for her kindness and generosity"[11] by living "the harried existence of an independent under-cover man" for a number of "grueling and abnormal years" "in a sunless world, under conditions which have impaired my health."[12] He infiltrated any number of fascist organizations and also became familiar with their antifascist counterparts, to whom he turned over carbon copies of his notes in exchange for small retainers. This gave him the financial backing to focus on his project full time. "My former secrecy became even deeper," he said, "as from that moment on I became a 'Nazi,' moving mysteriously through the subversive underworld with my employers, the only ones who knew every move."[13]

Derounian later described his years undercover as a time of "self-denial and social ostracism, of late hours and constant personal danger. I could lean on no official agency such as the FBI for help."[14] The payoff was his book about the experience, published by E. P. Dutton in 1943, under the pseudonym John Roy Carlson. A *New York Times* reviewer could not have been more dismissive. Edward N. Jenks described the book as "a sordid one, rather sensationally told, and perhaps dated by its sensationalism. Most of it had been told before and told better."[15] Yet the negative treatment in the *Times* did nothing to undercut the book's success. *Undercover: My Four Years in the Nazi Underworld of America* ranked first on the most important best seller lists for that year and hovered at fourth place for all of its second year in print.[16] It also subjected Derounian to harassment of various kinds, including libel suits and published accusations that he was a Communist, citing his previous writings. There was also a scurrilous rape charge, later dismissed as a frame-up in a trial that led to conviction and a jail sentence for Edward P. Banta, whom Derounian had identified as a Klan and bund member. The young woman who accused the author admitted under questioning that Banta had offered to pay her $1,000 to accuse him falsely.[17] All of this served to enhance rather than diminish Derounian's reputation,[18] and he went undercover twice again, for a 1946 book on American bigots, called *The Plotters,* and then again, for his 1951 book, published by Knopf, titled *Cairo to Damascus.* Dashingly, during his twenty-two months of reporting in 1948 and 1949, he stormed Jerusalem with the Arab forces and then switched to the Jewish side to report further.[19]

Latter-day undercover investigations of this type have not been as extensive as Derounian's, but they have had their own appreciable impact. Among them was one for the ABC newsmagazine *Prime Time Live,* broadcast May 14, 1997. Reporters spent more than a year undercover with David Duke's National Association for the Advancement of White People for a report that, in the estimation of the Southern Poverty Law Center,[20] helped bring about the NAAWP's rupture and ultimate demise. The broadcast documented the relationship between members of the Ku Klux Klan and members of the NAAWP and also exposed the NAAWP's companion militia, which, the report said, was poised to wage race war with illegally purchased weapons to advance its white supremacist cause.[21]

Extreme personal risk is a common threat and thread in most of these accounts, as it was for Timothy K. Smith of the *Wall Street Journal* during his week undercover in 1985 for paramilitary training at a private camp operated by Frank Camper in the Alabama woods. Smith's experience could well have been deadly had his real intentions been exposed, his editor, Paul Steiger, later recalled.[22] In an unrelated development two years later, Camper and one of the camp's instructors were prosecuted and convicted on federal charges of conspiracy and racketeering for firebombing two cars in

Orange County, California. Paroled in December 1991, Camper served five years of a fourteen-year prison sentence before returning to Alabama to open a computer business.[23]

In August 2000, disclosure of an undercover operation of a different sort brought on the publicly stated outrage of every major journalistic association or organization. This was in response to the pose of FBI and Alcohol, Tobacco, and Firearms agents as would-be photojournalists during the civil trial in Coeur d'Alene, Idaho, of Richard Butler, the leader of the Aryan Nations. Thomas Clouse of the *Spokane Spokesman-Review* broke the story[24] that agents had been given credentials as press photographers so that they could shoot pictures and gather information on pro-Butler activists who had massed in protest outside the courthouse. Public statements condemning the FBI action poured in from all areas of the media, among them the Society for Professional Journalists, the American Society of Newspaper Editors, and the Radio-Television News Directors Association.[25] They decried as anathema even the very notion of law enforcement or any other official impersonating a journalist because it discourages the public from cooperating with the media, thus jeopardizing the newsgathering process and media independence. Clouse pointed out that by impersonating journalists in this particular case, the agents had created other unwelcome complications for the reporters assigned to cover it: "They're putting us in danger," he said. "The Aryan Nation is not somebody you want to mess with."[26]

Yet, in the context of undercover reporting in general, the vociferous reaction to the good-for-the-gander move of these federal agents does prompt an additional question: if law enforcement or intelligence operatives should be forbidden under any circumstances from posing as journalists as they gather information to help keep the public safe, are there also poses that should be absolutely off-limits to journalists as they gather information to help keep the public informed?

The only known exceptions[27] are innocuous ones—reporters making fleeting appearances at active crime scenes, hoping to be mistaken in the moment by the cut of a rumpled trench coat or the bulge in a breast pocket, so as not to be shooed away during a critical information-gathering moment, as described later. Yet in instances when the reporting is taking place in tense or dangerous situations, war zones, or countries under oppressive rule, striking such a pose, even momentarily, would be a really bad idea.

All of this is by way of saying that the red lines of undercover activity—by law enforcement or by journalists—are easily drawn at the points of illegality or presupposed harm. No government investigator, no journalist should be engaged in a ruse that by its very design can inflict harm or undermine innocent individuals or that could, by design, break the law, or have wider-ranging adverse impact on an entire category of occupation. An FBI agent's pose as a journalist is unacceptable because it jeopardizes the journalist's role in the larger society. Likewise, a journalist or an agent or anyone else performing the role of, say, a physician or an electrician without adequate training or a license to practice similarly presupposes harm, not only to the individuals they might be obliged to treat or to serve, but to that profession itself.

The fact is, most poses are innocuous enough not to presuppose unintended harm. This does not, however, provide any sort of guarantee that harm will not be inflicted; it can be, particularly if a role is enacted irresponsibly, without common sense or the observance of strict ethical ground rules, or without full preparation, training, or even licensing if that should apply; or, when the information released embarrasses or jeopardizes or endangers the innocent in its wake by virtue of the identification by name, description, quotation, or picture of those individuals. Even conventional reporting methods can do this.

Those whose actions the investigation is meant to expose or to observe at close range are, of course, always at risk. In these situations, especially, that is the point of the pose. But if the reporters are fully trained and prepared and if they observe the law, journalists can function responsibly as, say, prison guards or hospital janitors or factory workers, as bureaucrats or barkeeps. In the FBI-as-journalist case, the pose itself is the wrong; a journalistic pose can turn out to be dangerous or undesirable, but not wrong or harmful prima facie in quite the same way—unless, again, it can harm others because of the lack of adequate training or preparation, or because it can cause damage to the profession or craft itself.

With Germany's defeat in World War II and the increasing momentum of the civil rights movement in the United States, the Ku Klux Klan soon grew into a more menacing national presence than the locally based Nazis.[28] Notable among early efforts to penetrate the organization was the 1954 memoir of the folklorist Stetson Kennedy, titled *I Rode with the Ku Klux Klan,* but renamed for its reprint, *The Klan Unmasked.* The book reports that under the fictional identity of John S. Perkins, Kennedy insinuated himself into the Klan's inner circles with an offer to distribute hate literature through an approach to Eugene Talmadge,[29] a three-term Georgia governor with strong Klan support. By casually dropping Talmadge's name, Kennedy said, he was able to establish his bona fides and got a sales job with a pro-Klan publication called *Southern Outlook.*[30]

Like Derounian, Kennedy came to his choice of subject matter naturally, from a fascination that grew out of a very personal experience, in his case, a deeply Southern one. He discovered a "Halloween ghost costume"[31] tucked away in the closet of his late uncle, Brady Perkins. It was that uncle's surname he appropriated for the ruse. "In the South," he explained, "one must have not only a name, but kinfolks; and the name of Perkins had the advantage of linking me with my Klansman uncle—who by this time had passed on 'from the Invisible Empire to the Empire Invisible,' as the Klan says of its deceased brethren."[32]

There was another deeply affecting memory that led Kennedy to the idea for his pursuit. As a child, he boarded a trolley with Flo, the family retainer who had nurtured and cared for him since birth. When the driver gave her back change for a quarter for the half-dollar piece she had handed him, she protested and asked for correct change. The driver pulled the heavy iron steering handle from its socket and struck her in the head, opening a gash on her forehead that required stitches. Kennedy's mother drove Flo to the county hospital for care. A week later, when she didn't appear for work, Kennedy's mother brought him along when she drove to Flo's home to find out what had happened. There was Flo, laid up in bed and hideously bruised. He remembered her saying that Klansmen had come to her home in the night, tied her hands around a big pine tree in her front yard, and belted her around the legs. After they left, one came back alone and, he recalled her saying, "had to do with me right there . . . pulled my womb down so I don't know if I'll be able to walk."[33] Kennedy said even though he didn't quite understand her words, the sight of her and the tone of her expression moved him. That, along with a number of disturbing encounters to come, turned him against the Klan forever.

Noting how much editorializing there was against the Klan, but how little hard evidence that could hold up in court, Kennedy soon formulated his own plan "to score a knockout."[34]

Sympathetic syndicated columnists of the day, such as Drew Pearson, he said, benefitted from Kennedy's frequent insider tips about Klan activity, as did the office of the attorney general of the state of Georgia and the Atlanta office of the FBI.[35] Kennedy worked with an automatic camera no bigger than a cigarette lighter that produced negatives the size of a fingernail. Kennedy used the camera to photograph secret documents, reams[36] of which are held in established archives at the Schomburg Center of the New York Public Library and in a repository in Atlanta. He even reported making common cause with the producers of the *Superman* radio serial, which tauntingly incorporated revealing tidbits from his investigative efforts into the program's scripts.[37]

Many years later, Kennedy's work came under sudden scrutiny. The journalist, Stephen J. Dubner, and the economist, Steven D. Levitt, who had paid tribute to Kennedy in their best-selling book, *Freakonomics,* then reversed that opinion in a column that appeared in the *New York Times Magazine* in January 2006,[38] detailing the results of their examination of documents in the various Kennedy archives that did not square with what he had told them when they interviewed him for their book. For instance, actual interviews with Klan leaders appeared in the book "in different contexts with different facts."[39] Events that Kennedy covered openly as a reporter he recast for publication as if they had been undercover efforts. Also, Dubner and Levitt concluded, as previous researchers surmised, that much of the infiltration Kennedy claimed as his own was the work of someone who worked for him, whom he identified pseudonymously in memos as "John Brown."[40] This led the *Freakonomics* authors to revise their earlier assessment, honoring Kennedy's fight of the good fight but not the liberties he clearly took with data and facts.[41]

Three weeks after the Dubner–Levitt reassessment appeared in the *Times Magazine,* Jacksonville's *Florida Times-Union* weighed in with its own examination of the archives, reaching much the same conclusion. It added comment from Kennedy saying that he had always been open about the intermingling of facts and sources into a single narrative and that he regretted not writing an introduction to his 1990 edition that would have clarified his methods. He also explained why he found it necessary to recast and embellish his account: to get the story published, and read. The political climate was such in 1948 that it took rewriting his story as a thriller to find a publisher—a French one, as it happened, and not until 1954. Only a tiny press would publish it in the United States. "I wanted to show what was happening at the time," he told the *Times-Union.* "Who gives a damn how it's written? It is the one and only document of the working Klan. . . . Everything that the Klan does in that book, they did in life. The book is a document of our times."[42]

Yet another resurgence of Klan activity spurred two rounds of journalistic response in the late 1970s. Patsy Sims, shortly after leaving the *Philadelphia Inquirer,* set out to write a book about the Klan, not as a history but "rather to try to get at the hearts and minds of its members."[43] And the *Nashville Tennessean,* under the leadership of editor John Seigenthaler, put together a task force whose objective, the editor later explained, was to expose the Klan for what it really was "and hope the exposure rubs it out."[44]

For the *Tennessean* a crucial part of the attempt at exposure was the assignment that fell to Jerry Thompson, one Seigenthaler made to complement and extend the work of the task force. Thompson had been a reporter and editor on the newspaper's staff for twenty years. His assignment was to create a new identity for himself, join "the new Klan," and spend a few months observing it from the inside. As a Tennessee "farm boy" who shared a middle-class, rural background with many Klan members, Thompson was someone in Seigenthaler's view who could easily be accepted into the Klan's "beer-drinking, joke-cracking, race-baiting conversations because he seemed so much like them."[45] Thompson may have seemed a lot like them, but there were distinct differences. He later said it took two full months of rehearsal for him to learn to salt his speech with racial epithets "and not just in discussing the state of the world, but in casual chatter."[46]

As events unfolded, Thompson's anticipated few months undercover stretched into a year and a half in all, despite the extraordinary burden this placed on his wife and four children—one newly born as he left—and a farm. He was able to sneak home for visits only once every three weeks. The newspaper series ran from December 7 to 15, 1980, but the pressure on Thompson and his family continued for a good while after that. There were real, substantiated death threats, and the necessity of bodyguards, both when he traveled and at the farm, where he had to install security alarms and floodlights for his family's protection. After the book came out, a nuisance libel suit was lodged against Thompson and the book's original publisher, G. P. Putnam's Sons, but it was quickly dismissed.[47]

In the preface to the book, Seigenthaler's introductory praise for Thompson was unstinting. The editor also offered his justification for the act of deception that he had obliged Thompson to perpetrate: "To get behind their pious platitudes and expose what they really stood for, it was necessary for Thompson to misrepresent who he was. Had there been any other way to expose the Klan, Thompson's underground role would not have been necessary." It is a view Seigenthaler maintains to this day.[48]

The book Thompson wrote thereafter, *My Life in the Klan,* provides the opportunity for a useful comparison to the work of Sims, whose conventionally reported book, *The Klan,* came out in 1978 and covers roughly the same period in Klan resurgence. Her book was originally published at about the time Thompson began his reporting.

Both Sims and Thompson were veteran newspaper reporters of Southern lineage—hers with the Klan in the closet; his, Southern liberal, without.[49] They worked in a similar timeframe and held similar objectives, even as their approaches varied widely. She actually left to do the book after a long career with the *Inquirer.* Thompson gave off the appearance of having left the *Tennessean*'s staff to go into rehab—a cover story meant to head off questions from his newsroom colleagues during the eighteen months he was with the Klan. Both projects lasted about the same length of time, in her case what she described as "four months on the road constantly,"[50] and then another year and a half to research further and write the book.

Seigenthaler and Thompson were convinced that it was essential to get inside the organization to witness and record Klan violence and hate speech, yet Sims's above-board interviews produced remarkably unfiltered comments from her subjects. To her, they say many of the same things for quotation that Thompson went to more questionable, and far riskier, lengths to gather. To both reporters, the Klansmen express their hatred of blacks and Jews without apology. Also, Thompson gives over a good part of his narrative to concern for his own safety and the burden he has placed on his family; his choice to go undercover shifts much of the focus of his book to himself. Sims had no such complications.

Sims, even without the dramatic device of an undercover ruse, also manages to achieve a stronger, and far more affecting narrative. In the end, Thompson's self-obsessed approach disappoints. As Don Black, a former KKK grand dragon, pointed out in Thompson's account, "He found out that I was anti-Semitic, but he didn't have to infiltrate the Klan to find that out. He found out that our members have guns. Big deal."[51] Sims, by positioning herself as a journalist only, stayed well in the background of her account, which allowed her full focus to stay on what she unearthed while reporting. Concern for her personal safety or paranoia over the possibility of being discovered do not derail her story with constant self-justification. None of the fears or neuroses that plagued Thompson got in her way. And she seems to have effectively captured the personalities of many of the Klansmen she encountered.[52]

Could she be assured that what she presented was the real "truth" about the Klan? It's at least correct to say she amassed a great deal of disquieting commentary. Also, some of the admissions the Klansmen made, such as Virgil Griffin's stated willingness to kill for the Klan[53] undercuts the assertion that going underground was necessary to uncover the Klan's real and violent aims. As a more conventional reporter, Sims also managed to glean this kind of information from the peripheral figures—neighbors, local business people—who have a place in her narrative.

Finally, freed of the constraint on Thompson to recount only what he witnessed directly during his involvement with the Klan, Sims could play around with the structure of her narrative, to imply a broad portrait of the organization as she incorporated historical information about the progression of the Klan and its many continually splintering offshoots in the various locations she visited. For this reason, her book is more complex than Thompson's, but it also manages to provide a more personal, more intuitive sense of the organization at the time.

Thompson died in 2000, but Sims replied to an emailed request to compare her own project with Thompson's. She said she believed that her objective of surveying the national scope of the Klan was well served by her conventional upfront approach. Indeed, hers is the only one of these three Klan-related journalistic efforts—hers, Kennedy's, and Thompson's—to remain in print.[54] She thinks the decision to stay fully above board actually gave her more freedom and improved her access to Klansmen. "I think if I'd been undercover, I'd have been confined to one area," she said. "I think my circle of what I would have been observing would have been a lot smaller." Also, she said, because Thompson had to be very careful not to blow his cover, this likely restricted the amount of material he was able to amass. By having been open about her intentions, Sims thought, she had managed to get more, thus enabling her to create a more detailed picture.[55]

In 2002, Jeff Sharlet spent night and day for nearly a month among the brothers of Ivanwald, the men who live and pray in a house outside of Washington, DC, that sits at the end of a quiet cul-de-sac amid a cluster of houses whose residents are "all devoted, like these men, to the service of Jesus Christ."[56] The brothers of Ivanwald, Sharlet explained, are the next generation of The Family, adherents of the "the secret fundamentalism at the heart of American power," its "high priests in training." For a magazine piece published by *Harper's,* Sharlet shared meals, work, and games with the brothers and participated in their ministry to get deeper inside their mission. "I have wrestled with them and showered with them and listened to their stories," he later wrote, recounting generally some of the intimate details he gathered, among them who resented his father's wealth, who had strayed sexually, and who was such a good dancer he feared he would be mistaken for gay. He also explained the relative ease with which he won entry into this inner sanctum. A banker he knew recommended Sharlet for membership when he mistook the reporter's interest in Jesus for belief. They knew he was half Jewish and that he was a writer who lived in New York, which, he said, they considered only slightly less wicked than Amsterdam or Baghdad. "I told my brothers I was there to meet Jesus, and I was; the new ruling Jesus, whose ways are secret."[57]

The *Harper's* 2003 piece that resulted, titled "Jesus Plus Nothing: Undercover Among America's Secret Theocrats," led Sharlet to research the topic further for a second piece that appeared in the magazine in 2006[58] and for the publication in 2008 of his bestselling book, *The Family: The Fundamentalism at the Secret Heart of American Power.* Two years after that, he followed up with a shorter but related volume, titled *C Street: The Fundamentalist Threat to American Democracy,* keyed to several contemporary sex scandals involving high-level Republican figures, all members of this same theocratic clique. Sharlet's method is a perfect synthesis of conventional research and reporting approaches buttressed heavily by immersion and submersion techniques. He does it all.[59]

For this book, he was asked to reflect in a general way on the relative merits of the various reportorial tools. On-site immersion, he said, whether or not it involves blatant subterfuge, is essential to any and every reporting assignment he undertakes. This has especially been true of the sustained reporting he has been doing since 2002 on fundamentalism and the Christian right. Riffing off of William Gaines's characterization of undercover techniques as the "icing on the cake" of more ranging and in-depth journalistic investigations, Sharlet sees the role of submersive techniques as more intrinsic to the process. "As for icing on the cake—for me," he said, "immersion is the flour, regardless of how much narrative space it occupies."[60]

Unger expressed a similar view. He too has used transgressive tools to help him apprehend more fully, and unobserved, the inner workings and motivations of members of the religious right. His journey to the Holy Land in 2005 for *Vanity Fair* was such an effort. He traveled with a group of ninety Christian followers of Tim LaHaye, the best-selling author and evangelical leader, an experience Unger described in detail for the magazine's readers, under the headline AMERICAN RAPTURE, and again in his 2007 book, *The Fall of the House of Bush.* In neither case did he explain how he had insinuated himself into the tour group, but later, in a blog entry for the *Huffington Post,* he characterized his method as "undercover."[61]

In a later interview for this book, Unger explained that he grew up in Dallas, the son of a transplanted New York Jewish doctor, ever fascinated by those whom he lived among but could never really be "of." As a writer, he wanted to get behind a common liberal perception. "It's stupid and wrongheaded," Unger said, "that evangelicals had to be ignorant or crazy to get so caught up in such a belief system. Given the role of evangelical Christianity in the Bush era aura, it seemed especially important to explore at the time."[62]

LaHaye publicized his "Left Behind" tour of the Holy Land as open to the public. Unger applied to join the tour over the transom, as instructed, and, also as instructed, he gave his name exactly as it appears on his passport: Roger Craig Unger, which, he said, "had the advantage of being true." The nametag he wore for the duration read "Roger Unger."[63]

"I wasn't going to lie," he said. "Anyone who asked me what I did, I said I was a writer." That did not raise nearly so many eyebrows as the fact that he came from New York. "But if I had said I'm doing this as a reporter for *Vanity Fair,* people, I think would have behaved very differently. And I do think reporters should be able to use material that is open to the general public."[64]

On the trip, there were a couple of close calls, one even before he boarded the plane. He stopped himself from picking up a couple of mainstream magazines for the long trip ahead, realizing that his choice of reading matter would be a giveaway. When his tour mates asked, he did acknowledge that he wrote for the "secular press," knowing that "secular" in this company would have the ring of "satanic." And he knew how close he came to blowing his cover when falafel was served at lunch one day, and only he happened to know that it was made of fried chickpeas.[65]

Unger also was careful never to mention his Dallas roots. "There were people on the trip who probably knew my friends," he said, "so I didn't want to go there." And although neither during the trip nor afterward did he share his actual purpose, he was careful in the piece only to quote the public figures by name. He received word of no subsequent reaction to the piece from LaHaye or any of the other tour mates.[66]

He has no regrets about the approach he took. "If I had announced myself," he said, "I wouldn't have gotten this information. If there is one basic rule, it is show don't tell. You have to see these people in a scene, in location, to see how they respond among themselves, to try to understand the culture. I'm not saying I got to the bottom, but I learned more than if I had called people up and said, 'Hi, I'm a reporter for *Vanity Fair.*'"[67]

A few years later, *Rolling Stone* published an excerpt from Matt Taibbi's 2008 book, *The Great Derangement,* describing his time under the name of "Matt Collins" at John Hagee's Cornerstone megachurch in the Texas Hill Country. Like Unger, Taibbi's effort was "to get a look inside the evangelical mind-set that gave the country eight years of George Bush,"[68] gaining understanding of who these people really were and how they behaved when the cameras were off.

Taibbi's time among them was short lived, consisting of an unspecified number of weeks attending church at this bastion of the "Christian Zionists" as a lead-up to a church-sponsored "Encounter Weekend," a spiritual retreat meant to change a person's life. By the end of that three-day experience, Taibbi began to understand how even his own "unending regimen of forced and fake responses," external demonstrations of faith and belief, could have a transformational effect—and, to some extent, did. The more he shouted the Lord's praise, he said, the more he told people how blessed he felt, "the more a sort of mechanical Christian skin starts to grow all over your real self." And he could understand, however fleetingly, how under other circumstances "it would be easy enough to bury your 'sinful' self far under the skin of your outer Christian and to just travel through life this way." He worried that the assignment might prove more than unusually tiring. As he put it, "I feared for my normal."[69]

Arms in the air! Hallelujah! By the end of the third and final day of the retreat, Taibbi felt that he understood the meaning of the words *beyond suggestible*.

> It's not merely the informational indoctrination, the constant belittling of homosexuals and atheists and Muslims and pacifists, etc., that's the issue. It's that once you've gotten to this place, you've left behind the mental process that a person would need to form an independent opinion about such things. You make this journey

precisely to experience the ecstasy of beating to the same big grisly heart with a roomful of like-minded folks.[70]

Around the same time, Kevin Roose, who was a college sophomore in spring 2007, left Brown University for a term and transferred with similar intentions to Jerry Falwell's Liberty University. He had a publisher already lined up for *The Unlikely Disciple: A Sinner's Semester at American's Holiest University,* which came out in 2009.[71] Contrary to the expectations of this son of liberal Quaker parents, he found the students to be in many ways much like those he knew at Brown. He joined the school choir and as many other activities as he could manage. He went to Daytona Beach on a missionary excursion over spring break and even checked out a campus support group for chronic masturbators. Rather than blow his cover, he ended a relationship with a girl he was dating on campus. He revealed himself on a return visit, assuaging the guilt he had felt throughout his Liberty sojourn. He found forgiveness.

The Associated Press, in writing about Roose's adventure, quoted a former student body president as saying he was less troubled than he might have been about Roose's deception because Roose had been fair. The university administration, however, found Roose's view of the campus to be "distorted," despite his generally positive tone, given that he came from a culture "with very little tolerance for conservative Christianity and even less understanding of it."[72] As for Roose, he said the encounter had made a Bible-reader out of him and had started him praying regularly.[73]

However flawed the understanding may or may not be of an informed outsider like a Sharlet or a Taibbi or an Unger or even a young Roose, to readers who are ignorant of these practices, uncommitted, or skeptical, their reports from the vantage point of outsiders still would likely be more credible than the work of a committed disciple in whatever form. For the reader who is also on a journey of discovery, the contrarian position in and of itself, the journey of the stranger into this alien midst, can actually add a layer of believability, which creates a validity of its own, especially with that intended audience in mind.

# THIRTEEN

Beyond slavery and its near relations, beyond sexual predators, tramping, homelessness, factories, food, migrants, prisons, hospitals, asylums, fanatics, extremists; beyond the startling practices featured in the chapters just ahead, plenty of other subject areas and issues have lent themselves to undercover treatment. Some highlights:

The social change-oriented 1960s yielded a number of award-winning undercover exposés, especially those for which reporters took on the role of public watchdog. The decade's one Pulitzer winner for the genre was Edgar May's fourteen-part series in 1960, described by his newspaper, the *Buffalo Evening News,* as a full examination of "one of the most pressing and costly problems of 1960—public welfare." It took six months of research to complete and involved the effort of the newspaper's staff in Buffalo, Albany, and Washington as they interviewed authorities and reviewed the "detailed private surveys of New York State welfare agencies."[1] And yet the Pulitzer went to May by name, singling out his three-month pose as an Erie County welfare caseworker.[2]

To get the job, May took a leave from the newspaper[3] and identified himself as "E. Pratt May,"[4] concealing his actual employment status by referring to his work for the Buffalo paper as "previous."[5] This very finesse of the truth was one that editors would shun by the time Tony Horwitz was filling out his employment applications in 1994, insisting on particular care to avoid that kind of misstep. The shift signified a tightening of ethical standards as public criticism of journalistic practices heightened generally. Undercover practice, in particular, also evolved in the aftermath of those costly courtroom reviews, such as the Food Lion case. This was also a period during which journalism professionalized as a field. For example, David H. Weaver and colleagues report progressively in their three studies of the American journalist that in the thirty-one years between 1971 and 2002, the proportion of full-time U.S. journalists at mainstream news outlets who had at least a college bachelor's degree rose by about a third, from 58 percent to 89 percent.[6]

For May, the very experience of doing casework as a regular county employee was not only essential to the detailed reporting he was able to produce, but the experience transformed him personally. Within just a few weeks of being "simply a newspaper reporter masquerading as a welfare worker," he lost the need to pretend. "I fully became a caseworker," he wrote. "I found myself thinking like a caseworker. I became annoyed and angry like a caseworker."[7] He did not inform the Erie County Department of Social Welfare of his real intent, nor did anyone at the welfare department find out that he was a reporter until the first article appeared. Several years later, May built on the passion for the subject that his undercover reporting had piqued and did an even more thorough examination of welfare policy in a book called *The Wasted Americans*.[8]

Based on reporting from the late 1950s into the early 1960s, at least three books in addition to May's grew out of award-winning undercover newspaper investigations, all the work of journalists for the *New York World-Telegram & Sun*. George N. Allen's *Undercover Teacher* appeared in 1960, the year after his award-winning newspaper investigation, but the others took longer to reach publication as books. Dale Wright's *They Harvest Despair* was published in 1964, three years after his 1961 newspaper series, and Woody Klein's *Let in the Sun* came out four years after his newspaper series in 1959. A fourth undercover investigation by the *World-Telegram & Sun* in this period was Michael Mok's exposé of the mistreatment of mental patients at King's County Hospital in Brooklyn. Although it won the most prestigious national award of the four, the Albert Lasker Prize, it did not evolve into a book. In fact, not since Nellie Bly's *Ten Days in a Madhouse* did a blockbuster newspaper or magazine asylum exposé develop into a book—not the *Chicago Daily Times'* in the 1930s, *Life's* in the 1940s, Mok's in 1961, or the *Tennessean's* in the 1970s.

Klein's book, "the tragic story of a New York tenement—the landlords and tenants, the politicians and social reformers who made it a national disgrace,"[9] grew out of three months[10] of reporting in summer 1959 as an undercover tenant of 311 East One Hundredth Street, where he endured the "overpowering stench"[11] of what at the time was considered the worst slum tenement on the worst slum block in New York City, a place of "animal-like overcrowding, prostitution, gambling, drunkenness, fire and building violations, petty thievery, lack of water, air, heat and light," not to mention "filthy buildings, unscrupulous rent-gouging and exploitation."[12] By centering his narrative on one East Harlem building, Klein hoped to symbolize the conditions under which a fifth of the U.S. population was living at the time, some 38 million people, and to attempt to understand the how and why of an American blight.[13] His series won a Page One Award from the

Newspaper Guild of New York and a Sigma Delta Chi Award for outstanding journalistic achievement in the New York metropolitan area.[14] Telling is a detailed academic critique of the strengths and weaknesses of Klein's work. Published almost a decade later by a housing policy expert,[15] it questioned Klein's implications and presumptions about, for example, the impact of constant turnover on property conditions, and if gross rental receipts, which appeared to be sizeable, actually translated into large profits for slum owners. The writer's wider assessment of Klein's work pinpointed a paradox inherent in many undercover assignments of this kind: "Written from the gut; it provides an emotional catharsis, nonstatistical and nonacademic." But that same "emotionalism and crusading zeal" becomes both the work's greatest strength and its greatest limitation.[16]

In 1966, Jay McMullen, on assignment for CBS, undertook a similar project for which his team lived for more than a year in a low-income tenement in Chicago. McMullen's strategy was more onion peel than undercover. The team members waited three months to start disclosing their actual purpose to local residents and did not even think about starting to film until they sensed they had a reasonable level of acceptance.[17] McMullen later recalled how much he wanted to avoid the errors of other television and radio reporters who stuck microphones in the faces of people they did not know, or who confined their interviewing to the most accessible and media savvy members of a given community, usually the activists, who, it soon became clear, did not necessarily represent the local majority. As McMullen explained to Irv Broughton, the team's black cameraman and soundman moved into the ghetto first, both to get to know people and to assimilate into the local scene, so as to attract less attention. They told people they were interested in making a film around the neighborhood. Gradually,

McMullen joined them and introduced the idea of the involvement of CBS. "We found that as we got to know them, the easier it was to talk to them and the more frank they would be in what they had to say," McMullen recalled. "But it took a long period of time."[18] His central purpose, he said, was to make white people more familiar with the predicament of poor black people who were living in tenements "at a time when the two races were at a point of extreme frustration." The documentary, called *The Tenement*, won the Sidney Hillman Award in 1967,[19] one of the many honors McMullen received over the years.

The cover blurb on the book jacket of *Undercover Teacher*, published in 1960, described what Allen had done as an effort "to report on a crime-ridden school from the inside."[20] In fall 1957, the year before Allen went undercover, New York's public schools had been "engulfed by a wave of violence the like of which had never before been experienced by any school system in the nation," involving a range of crimes from vandalism, arson, robbery, and extortion to assaults on children and teachers, stabbings, rapes, and death threats.[21]

His sixteen-part series ran in the *New York World-Telegram & Sun* from November 12 to December 1 of 1958 and earned him a Newspaper Guild's Heywood Broun Award for that year and an alumni award from Columbia University.[22] Allen's is the earliest known of a number of undercover looks at educational institutions for which reporters have posed as teachers, administrators, or students. The duration of these excursions has varied from a few days to a semester to as long as a full school year. Allen spent about two and a half months as an English teacher at John Marshall Junior High School in Brooklyn, credentialed a few months earlier as part of the assignment. He prepared by taking three education courses at Columbia Teachers' College and obtaining a substitute teacher's license with a falsified employment history.[23]

Apropos the blithe willingness of journalists in the pre–Food Lion days to concoct lies on applications, Allen was no exception. Without a hint of apology, he explained that under instructions from his editor, he invented a background that contained no reference to his employment as a newspaper reporter, present or past. He convinced Levering Tyson, his future wife's employer, of the project's merit and got him to serve as a faux employment reference for a job Allen never held at Columbia University, his college alma mater. At the time, Tyson, a former college president and university chancellor, was special assistant for alumni relations to the university's president.[24] As for Allen's expenses during the assignment, his editor instructed him to submit them under the heading of "air pollution feature" to keep the accounting department and others in the dark.[25]

The impact of the newspaper series was huge. Allen devoted the whole of the book's last twenty pages to the "swift and outspoken" public reaction the series generated.[26] *Time* magazine covered the project twice, admiring Allen's findings about a school that had become notorious the preceding winter "after a month of hoodlum invasions, assaults and an alleged knife-point rape in a school basement ended in the suicide of Principal George Goldfarb."[27] The judge presiding over a Kings County grand jury investigating the school offered lavish praise.[28]

Public response to the series, which Allen reprised and documented in his book, was overwhelmingly positive, but it also included some scathing attacks on Allen's method. Classroom teachers, although prohibited by public school policy from allowing their names to be published, were nearly unanimously favorable, as evidenced by the calls and letters Allen said he received. Two national newsmagazines in addition to *Time* reported on Allen's ruse, prompting an influx of mail from teachers, parents, educators, and school board members elsewhere that indicated similar conditions in their home districts. He heard the same from teachers in Canada and England. Allen testified for three days before the Brooklyn grand jury—it had been investigating the school for more than a year—effectively allowing him to put the articles into the judicial record. As a consequence of the series, he said, the jury asked to have its term extended.[29]

Allen's detractors included the New York City school board, the superintendent of schools, and the administrators at John Marshall Junior High. All roundly rebuked the newspaper for having "invaded the sanctity of the classroom."[30] After the first piece in the series appeared, Allen said School Superintendent John J. Theobald charged that the story was unfair and would damage the school system. He demanded that no further articles run. Editors at the *World-Telegram & Sun* offered to print alongside the series any comments he or the school's principal cared to make, even volunteering to make the next day's installment available twenty-four hours in advance, but Theobald declined and then threatened Allen with indictment for perjury because of the fictionalized job history on his application to teach. Investigators looked into Allen's brief teaching career, the circumstances surrounding his assignment, and the school conditions he described. It led to a revocation of Allen's teaching license and a resolution to condemn his actions for seriously violating the moral and ethical standards of the teaching profession and for effectively invading the privacy of students by "using the special privilege of the position of teacher as a vehicle for sensationalism." The resolution was never implemented and there was never any indictment.[31]

In 1988, Emily Sachar, after two years of award-winning coverage of the Board of Education for *New York Newsday,* used her
own name to apply for a teaching license in May of that year. She
expressed a desire to get beyond "the splashy front-page stories
and nods of praise from senior editors" and into the schools themselves. She hoped to penetrate, in ways her reporting had not, the
"ongoing human and civic disaster" that was the New York City
public school system of the late 1980s. Deciding to teach, she later
said, was an opportunity to trade "a vicarious existence for a desperately consequential one," and if it didn't work out, she could
always write a series of articles about the experience. As it happened, she returned to the newspaper at the end of the 1988–1989
school year, which she spent as an eighth grade math teacher at
Walt Whitman Intermediate School in the Flatbush section of
Brooklyn. The newspaper held her place for that year of unpaid
leave, with no obligation for her to write about the experience,
a courtesy for which she thanked her bosses in her acknowledg-
ments. Her newspaper series, MY YEAR AS A TEACHER, ran from
November 27 to December 6, 1989, and became the basis for her
book, *Shut Up and Let the Lady Teach.*[32]

A number of journalists have looked or been young enough to
bring off convincing poses as students. As a twenty-eight-year-old,
*New Yorker* writer David Owen joined the class of 1980 for the fall
semester "at a large public high school forty-five minutes outside
New York City" (in another rendering, the distance was given
as two hours). Owen presented himself as a seventeen-year-old
senior, a transfer student, who was then admitted to the school on
the strength of a fabricated transcript. His purpose? To find out
"if I could rediscover something of the old hormonal intensity
of adolescence," if he could come to understand the connections

between being a teenager and being an adult—from the vantage point of the adult he now was—and could find out what the teenagers of 1980 were all about in the process. Only his wife was in on the secret.[33]

The same year, Cameron Crowe's *Fast Times at Ridgemont High* chronicled the year he spent with the permission of the principal at a public high school, one that he had attended for summer school seven years earlier. Crowe's efforts also became a film.[34] In 1986, as a very young reporter for the *Milwaukee Journal,* Vivian S. Toy, just a year out of college, posed as a high school student for three weeks for a series the newspaper ran in the newspaper's Sunday magazine in October 1986.[35] Toy, who moved on to report for the *New York Times,* recalled that her articles attracted both praise and criticism—criticism from the newspaper's ombudsman, too—because of their undercover dimension. In the end, she said, the reader representative approved of the project because it wasn't intended to be a "gotcha" exposé, but rather an inside look at the Milwaukee high school student experience of 1986, and because the newspaper had taken careful pains to obtain prior authorization. Toy said the newspaper had gotten advanced permission from the school district and that the superintendent was very supportive. All the teachers had been told in advance, and their names were used when quoted. Students, however, were given pseudonyms to protect their privacy. "There was one first-person piece," she said, "but the rest was a fly-on-the-wall perspective. We didn't use [the first person] as a device, which was the point. We wanted to show people what high school in the 1980s was like. We got tons of feedback from readers."[36]

Toy said the *Journal* was especially careful in preparing for the assignment in light of a story making the journalistic rounds at the time. Leslie Linthicum, a twenty-four-year-old reporter for the

*Albuquerque Tribune,* presented herself with falsified documents as a seventeen-year-old transfer student named "Leslie Taylor"—"my graying brown hair freshly dyed, fingernails youthfully nibbled, clutching a new, red, three-subject binder"—to spend eleven days as a student at Eldorado, the city's "best" and "biggest" high school.[37] Registering was no problem; her cover story was that she needed a few credits to graduate. A gas bill verified her residency in the district and although she was asked to provide a transcript from her Pennsylvania high school, the admistrator allowed her to start classes without it by having her jot down the credits she had earned.[38]

Public reaction to the articles Linthicum based on her experiences was "swift and vehement," she later recalled for an ethics report. The newspaper published letters to the editor for days. "Students, teachers, parents and school administrators reacted with shock and anger, not to the meat of the articles but to the ethics of the method. They felt violated, intruded upon, and tricked into trusting an individual who lied for no good purpose."[39] Major complaints beyond the false identity included the judgments she made after so brief a period of observation and the conclusions she drew from isolated incidents, such as her report of a teacher asking her to read *To Kill a Mockingbird* in class rather than assigning it as homework and devoting class time to discussion. The principal, in a later interview with the newspaper, explained that the teacher in question, an exceptionally fine one, had resorted to the technique that day because she was suffering from a case of severe laryngitis. "You can almost anytime catch someone picking their nose if you look at them long enough," he quipped.[40] Linthicum stood by her approach and her results, but with little affirmation from the public or her peers. The major issues appear to have been two: a questionable purpose for the project and harm done to people who were identifiable and unfairly subjected to ridicule.

The pitfalls have not stopped production. In 1992, the *San Francisco Chronicle* created strict guidelines for Shann Nix, a reporter who went undercover at a local high school during a "growing crisis in the public schools and the crippling effect of the budget cuts on education,"[41] as did the *Minneapolis Star Tribune* for its reporter's sojourn as a student in women's studies at a local college.[42] Later iterations of the scheme have largely been focused on the novelty of the experience. These include Jeremy Iverson's 2007 book, *High School Confidential: Secrets of an Undercover Student,* and at the college level, Rebekah Nathan's 2005 *My Freshman Year: What a Professor Learned by Becoming a Student.*[43]

Television, although still in its early years, already had pioneered the undercover documentary by 1961 when McMullen produced *Biography of a Bookie* for CBS, giving him the reputation of being television's first investigative reporter.[44] By focusing on a bookie joint run out of a key shop in Boston, McMullen was said to have captured not only "the look and feel and smell"[45] of the illegal gambling industry, but its magnitude.[46] CBS not only traced the various complaints against the shop that had been squelched by the Boston Police but triggered a crackdown by giving the information it gathered to the U.S. Justice Department.[47] McMullen later told his interviewer that the show took eight months to produce and then more than a year after that to defend the documentary's every frame, including charges that the men in police uniforms caught going in and out of the shop actually were actors, or that the footage was stock. (To film, McMullen used a lunch box to conceal the hidden cameras and microphones[48] that documented police entering and leaving the shop and ignoring a small curbside stove that the gamblers used to destroy evidence of their bets.) Asked if he considered himself a "subtle or sneaky" person, someone who "approaches things obliquely," McMullen said he didn't think so, and that his preference was always to sit down and talk things over with someone. "But," he said, "there is no way you could do that with this kind of story." He said *Bookie* was the first time he had ever attempted this sort of thing on television.[49]

William Jones won a Pulitzer in 1971 for the *Chicago Tribune* for an investigation of private and public ambulance services that involved his pose as a driver. In 1973, the newspaper's expansive voter fraud investigation also won a Pulitzer,[50] largely on the strength of evidence collected with elaborately surreptitious tactics during the 1972 election season. Twenty-five years later, Clarence Page, the *Tribune* columnist, was moved to recall his role in that project in a piece he wrote in reaction to the initial $5.5 million judgment against ABC in the Food Lion case, which was later so dramatically reduced. Page recalled working undercover as a poll watcher as part of the investigative team,[51] actually one of twenty-five people the newspaper assigned to become poll watchers for the project, seventeen of whom were *Tribune* reporters along with eight independent investigators. Over four weeks, they had access to forged signatures on applications for ballots and other documents that verified fraud. Another journalist was reported to have concealed his identity to get a job at the Chicago Board of Election Commissioners, and yet another holed up in an apartment across from a polling place to monitor activity, exposing the systemic nature of the fraud. The series prompted a change in state election law.[52]

Page, much earlier in his career, as an intern at the *Dayton Journal Herald* in Ohio, posed as an apartment buyer to uncover any racial bias in the local housing market, a test since performed by various newspapers dozens of times. Of Food Lion, Page pointed out that the jurors, when interviewed after the trial, reacted negatively to the notion of journalist misrepresentation in general and seemed to imply that they wanted undercover reporting to stop. To this, Page's reply was, "Never say never." He elaborated by musing on whether the first juror, who happened to be African American, would have reacted as negatively to misrepresentation had the case been about fair housing. For black and white teams of "testers" to pose as homebuyers in efforts to expose racial bias in real estate practices had all the marks of "lying, fraud, misrepresentation and trespassing," Page wrote. And yet the practice is one that federal regulators routinely employ.[53]

In between the Pulitzer Prizes won by the *Tribune* for voter fraud in 1971 and for von Solbrig four years later, the 1974 prize went to William Sherman of the *New York Daily News* for his series on abuses in the administration of Medicaid. That project pivoted on Sherman's pose as a Medicaid recipient, aided by a photographer who presented himself as Sherman's cousin. Support for the project came from both the city's Health Department and its Human Resources Administration, two agencies with a vested interest in "fighting hard to stem abuse of the Medicaid system."[54] Officials involved with the project helped arrange a temporary Medicaid card for Sherman for the duration of the probe.

On publication, the *Daily News* told its readers that the project had involved "not only a lengthy field inquiry, but an exhaustive examination of city records and candidate interviews with public officials."[55] For the first of fourteen installments that appeared in late January and early February 1973, Sherman disguised himself as a welfare client complaining of nothing more serious than a common cold for visits to three different medical offices in the Ozone Park neighborhood of Queens. (Nellie Bly did something similar in 1889. With the complaint of a migraine, she visited seven doctors and got seven different diagnoses.)[56] Similarly, physicians at the offices Sherman visited referred him to a foot doctor, an internist, and a psychiatrist, from whom he cumulatively received six different prescriptions with instructions in some cases to have them filled at a specific pharmacy. He also underwent an electro-cardiogram, three blood tests, two urine tests, and a chest x-ray.[57] A COLD? a first-day headline in the series asked, TAKE 3 DOCTORS EVERY HOUR.[58]

In August 1983, Philip Shenon of the *New York Times* randomly picked out a welfare hotel and moved in for three days and nights to get a sense of what life was like for New York City's thousands of displaced families. It was a far shorter duration of assignment than McMullen's Chicago tenement sojourn of 1966, but Shenon used an accelerated version of the same strategy of entry. He didn't introduce himself to anyone right away. In an internal publication of the *Times,* Shenon explained the freedom it gave him not to have to reveal himself too soon. For one thing, the manager didn't kick him out and for another, it gave him time over the first day and a half just to wander around the hotel, watching the tenants and observing the conditions in which they were living as they lived them. Interviewing started in the afternoon of the second day and at that point he identified himself as a *Times* reporter. "I wore a Walkman, which often sparked conversation," he said. "The young kids kept pulling the earphones from my neck to listen to the music. As they listened, I talked to their parents."[59] Although he did not use the first person, and plenty of people were quoted by name, Shenon's piece included what only could have been his personal observation: the stifling heat and smell of overcrowded rooms without air conditioning or fans, the bugs crawling on the bed sheets, the thin walls, the wakeful children, and the men in flipflops that "bat against the stairs, making a noise like gunfire."[60]

And, he later pointed out that a huge advantage of not disclosing his affiliation—and by extension a big advantage of reporting undercover in similar circumstances—is that he knew for certain that nothing had been staged expressly for the benefit of a reporter for the *New York Times*.[61]

Abortion, too, has resurfaced periodically since August 23, 1871, when *New York Times* editor Louis Jennings assigned a reporter, Augustus St. Clair, to pose with a "lady friend" as a couple seeking someone to perform the procedure. The would-be couple spent several weeks visiting all of the relevant offices in the city. EVIL OF THE AGE was the headline over St. Clair's story, which described how human flesh, supposed to have been the remains of infants, was found decomposing in barrels of lime and acids[62] and how extravagantly the practitioners were living.[63] In one instance, St. Clair reported that he drew a revolver (!) to escape from one doctor who suspected the couple's real motive. Four days after St. Clair's story ran, a woman's nude body, bruised around the pelvic region, was found inside a trunk at a railway baggage station, leading to the arrest two days later of one of the doctors St. Clair mentioned in his first article. St. Clair followed up with a report in which he said he had seen the young woman at the doctor's Fifth Avenue clinic. She was later identified as an orphan named Alice Mowlsby,[64] whose "seducer," Walter Conklin, committed suicide. The doctor, Jacob Rosenzweig,[65] was sentenced to seven years in prison. Soon after, the state passed stricter abortion laws.[66]

The huge success of the Nell Nelson factory life articles in the *Chicago Times* in 1888 gave the publisher, James J. West, another idea, as the circulation spike prompted by her stories began to flatten. He wanted Charles Chapin to assign a man and a woman to pretend to be sweethearts and to find out from various doctors in the city, à la St. Clair, where they could get abortion services. Chapin flatly refused, declaring it was the "yellowest suggestion ever made in a newspaper office" and that he would quit before assigning it. Chapin thought his refusal ended the discussion and paid no mind when West a few weeks later asked him to send a male and female reporter to see him for some special instructions. It wasn't until Chapin walked into the composing room on December 11 to find the abortion series being set into type that he understood what the publisher had done. Chapin confronted West and demanded that the series be pulled. West refused, the series ran, and Chapin quit in protest as threatened.[67]

Later undercover abortion projects included a 1976 sting published by the *New York Post*. Two researchers for a New York–based advocacy group submitted male urine specimens for testing at two different abortion clinics and were told they were pregnant. Once confronted, the operators of the facilities blamed human error.[68] Two years later, in 1978, the *Chicago Sun-Times* produced a major series by Pamela Zekman and Pamela Warrick with the Better Government Association, headlined THE ABORTION PROFITEERS.[69] The catalog of findings included dozens of procedures performed on women who were not pregnant or were over the legal twelve-week limit; women who became sterile because of haphazard care and an unsterile clinic; women who suffered from internal damage, debilitating cramps, infections, and damage to their reproductive organs that required removal; incompetent or unqualified practitioners; and the performing of the procedure in an excruciating two minutes instead of the proper ten to fifteen minutes.[70] The stories also focused on the profiteers themselves, naming names, and in counterweight, profiled two safe, compassionate clinics. The series prompted the newspaper to announce that it would stop publishing ads for abortion clinics, as it was not in a position to "determine safe and sanitary conditions at all the abortion counseling services and clinics which advertised in our classified pages."[71] As for results, the *Sun-Times* later reported that one doctor had his license revoked,[72] various members of Congress on both sides of the aisle called for an investigation,[73] and a permanent injunction was issued against one of the clinics, prohibiting it from performing abortions.[74] Later, *Sun-Times* reports mentioned "business as usual" at clinics that had been investigated as part of the series.[75]

In 1987, Sallie Tisdale, writing in *Harper's,* explored the subject by describing graphically her personal experience as a nurse in an abortion clinic. "We do abortions here; that is all we do," she wrote. "There are weary, grim moments when I think I cannot bear another basin of bloody remains, utter another kind phrase of reassurance."[76] And in 2008, a student named Lila Rose, writing for an antiabortion magazine she started on the campus of the University of California, Los Angeles, secretly taped an employee of the on-campus health center "encouraging a student to get an abortion."[77] She also posted a YouTube video of herself pretending to be a fifteen-year-old girl seeking counsel from a Planned Parenthood employee, who encouraged her to lie about her age to avoid statutory rape charges against the twenty-three-year-old boyfriend she claimed had impregnated her. The school newspaper, the *Daily Bruin,* questioned Rose's journalistic ethics[78] for the sting she had planned with the help of James O'Keefe, who was a UCLA law student at the time. O'Keefe posted audio recordings of Planned Parenthood staffers agreeing to earmark his proffered donations to finance abortions for African American women.[79]

This was the first of a number of stings O'Keefe has orchestrated in support of a clearly conservative political agenda—waging "culture war," as the media critic Jay Rosen has called it, with a "gotcha!" dimension to the work that aims to ferret out any morsel of damning evidence against his investigative targets. Rosen sees him as a "performance artist who profits from the public wreckage and institutional panic his media stunts seek to create."[80] In summer 2009, O'Keefe and Hannah Giles posed as pimp and prostitute for visits to various offices of ACORN, the Association of Community Organizations for Reform Now, ostensibly interested in arranging a loan for their brothel. A hidden camera captured the advice ACORN employees offered them at one office, from how to launder their money to where to lie on their loan application.[81] By August 2010, ACORN had lost all of its federal funding[82] and within three months had been forced into bankruptcy.[83]

In March 2011, a day after Vivian Schiller, the president of NPR, made her case for continued federal funding for public radio, O'Keefe released a surreptitiously recorded video in which NPR's chief fundraiser, Ron Schiller, was featured courting two men who had identified themselves falsely both as prospective major donors and as representatives of a U.S.-based group with ties to the Muslim Brotherhood. Under O'Keefe's direction, ruses with a similar aim also were tried on employees of the Public Broadcasting Corporation and of its various local affiliates. Ron Schiller was recorded making disparaging remarks that he prefaced as personal against the Tea Party movement, evangelical Christians, and the Republican Party. Before the video was released, NPR declined interest in this purported $5 million gift. Nonetheless, the Ron Schiller remarks were inappropriate enough to bring the wrath of the NPR leadership down on both Schillers, forcing their immediate departures. The two are not related, but Vivian Schiller had recruited Ron Schiller to the organization.[84]

O'Keefe's work puts in stark light the question of whether undercover stings produced by advocacy groups, especially those with unswervingly ideological intent, can or should ever qualify or be regarded as journalism. Mary Sanchez, a columnist for the McClatchy newspaper chain, thinks not. "These gotcha recordings are the stock-in-trade of ideological operatives," she wrote about the NPR sting and an incident just two weeks earlier in which a reporter for *Buffalo Beast,* a website at the other end of the political spectrum from O'Keefe's *Project Veritas,* placed a prank call to the Republican governor of Wisconsin, Scott Walker. The caller posed as David Koch, a wealthy and influential funder of conservative causes. The transcript quoted Walker making disparaging comments directed at the state public employees union, whose collective bargaining rights the governor was in the process of trying to strip.[85]

Sanchez wrote, "The point is not to uncover actual corruption, but to move public opinion on an issue by creating bad 'optics'— which puts the opposition on the defensive. Gotcha artists don't help the public to think, only to feel."[86] Edward Wasserman, in the *Miami Herald,* objected to the lack of any tests of fundamental accuracy on the part of mainstream media before they willingly and indiscriminately disseminate such reports. He questioned if editors even bothered to ask themselves "if the information is important enough and unobtainable enough to warrant waiving the usual strictures on honest questioning." He said he could discern no standard being applied before accepting the material other than crass "reader appeal."[87] In the *Los Angeles Times,* James Rainey condemned "the new fakery" that has arrived "on the backs of something real and winning—the influx of an untold number of new voices into journalism as computers and the Internet have lowered the cost of entry to zero."Yet some of those in the new crowd, he said, operate like "lone wolves—without oversight, rules or even a solid definition of what game they are playing."[88]

First of all, for advocacy and better government-type groups to partner with mainstream news organizations for investigative purposes or to provide the results of independently conducted investigations is nothing new, as the preceding pages make clear. Key is if—and it is a big if—it is possible to verify the truth of the material through supporting documentation, including notes and raw footage, and expert or independent analysis, and the forthrightness of the editing of the report, tape, or transcript. In the end, these considerations, I think, matter more than the impetus for its creation.[89] In the Ron Schiller instance, these standards were not met before the video got wide mainstream play. Although *Project Veritas* described the footage as "largely the raw video" redacted only in one brief section to ensure the safety of an NPR correspondent overseas, analysis by others (interestingly, the most impressive was done by fellow conservatives at Glenn Beck's *The Blaze*) pinpointed instances of highly selective editing of the two-hour hidden camera taping—discrediting it, even though the slanted finesses did not concern the key comments that forced the two Schillers out.[90]

Leaving the theatrics of O'Keefe aside, if it can be determined conclusively that the work meets exacting journalistic standards and that the report as presented is sound and unskewed—again, this is an all-important if—what would be the difference between these two types of operations: stings produced by those with blatant political alignments who aim to wage culture war on matters on which public opinion remains divided, and stings produced by advocacy groups whose aim is to stop intolerable practice in instances where a broader national consensus already has formed? Consider an example from roughly the same time period: the widely favorable reaction to the inhumane treatment of pigs by the world's largest pork producer as shown in the pig gestation video obtained undercover by the Humane Society of the United States and posted in December 2010. The undercover footage was reported on, discussed, and linked to via local and national media, as described in chapter 10.[91]

The public relations blowback on Governor Walker, on NPR, and on Smithfield Foods, Inc., were comparably disastrous and, many would say—have said—equally deserved, given what transpired and what was recorded and shared.[92] In the NPR and Walker cases, the instigators stepped right into another equally contentious area in journalism debates over the practice—the more ethically *verboten* tarpit of blatant, outright lies told to perpetrate an undercover journalistic ruse. In the NPR sting, there is also the matter of discreditable editing, as noted above.

In the case of the Humane Society, a legend on one screen of the highly produced—clearly edited—video reads, "Undercover at Smithfield Foods," but no further explanation was publicly provided of how the investigator obtained the footage.[93] Paul Shapiro, senior director of the organization's factory farming campaign, said later in a telephone interview that the Humane Society sends investigators to work undercover at the factory farms for up to a month. They use their real names but without disclosing their Humane Society affiliation. They are able to film both with hidden and handheld cameras. The facilities are mostly automated, so it is possible to shoot openly without being detected. In Smithfield's case, the society released the report on its own site, backed by companion reports from scientists and other experts. The society even offered the company advance access to extended segments of the video, without the narration or music, and offered to hold a joint press conference. "Our goal is not 'gotcha,' but to prevent animal cruelty," Shapiro said. Smithfield declined to participate.[94] For previous investigations, the society has partnered with major media outlets, such as the *Washington Post,* giving them exclusive first rights to the information. In those cases, the organization also has provided elaborate backup material for verification.[95] Shapiro said the Humane Society resorts to these techniques because factory farming is very secretive because of the cruelty involved. "There isn't another way to find out what's happening," he said. "Whistleblowing is really the only way to get the information."[96] Apropos, within months there were committee moves in four state legislatures—Iowa, Minnesota, Florida, and New York—to ban undercover access to factory farms. Dubbed the "ag-gag" bills, none passed in 2011 but could potentially be reintroduced in subsequent sessions or in other states.[97]

In the realm of boundary-shaking journalistic exposés against unacceptable practices, stings that provide information the public might need to inform its decision making, it seems only fair to conclude that what is good for the goose is good for the gander. Compare O'Keefe's lies to Ken Silverstein's 2007 lies for his similarly deceptive sting on Washington's powerful lobbyists for *Harper's,* as detailed in the final chapter, which appeared to have wide public support if not a consensus among prominent journalistic arbiters. It leads me to venture that what is most important in these cases is the exercise of sound journalistic judgment: to establish first if the deception was important enough to perpetrate, and after that, if accepted journalism standards have been fully adhered to and met, and if that can be reliably verified. In the end, method matters more than the provenance of who performed the act.[98]

Some fresh arenas for undercover treatment have emerged in the twenty-first century: The 2008 Democratic primary provided an opportunity for reporters from the *Philadelphia City Paper* to infiltrate the local political campaign operations of Barack Obama and Hillary Clinton[99] for an insider's view of the candidate's disparate approaches to managing their volunteers. And airport security, especially in the aftermath of the attacks on New York and Washington, DC, of September 11, 2001, has become an important and attention-getting area of inquiry, for both newspapers and television stations.[100]

In short, the best of all these undercover reporting efforts exemplify how the method can effectively serve the public interest, providing a hard-to-refute "show" to the "tell" of C. Thomas Dienes, a law professor, media lawyer, and legal consultant who succinctly explained why this is so in both the public and private sector. His remarks at a symposium came in 1999, well after the major controversies of the late twentieth century had put a pall on the practice. He wrote:

> In the public sector, it allows the media to perform its role as the eyes and ears of the people, to perform a checking function on government. Especially at a time when citizens are often unable or unwilling to supervise government, this media role is critical to self-government. In the private sector, when the government fails in its responsibility to protect the public against fraudulent and unethical business and professional practices, whether because of lack of resources or unwillingness, media exposure of such practices can and often does provide the spur forcing government action.[101]

In 1998, in response to the legal implications for journalists in the Food Lion case, John P. Borger, an attorney and legal expert, offered the view that undercover reporting persists because of "elementary facets of human nature," the propensity of wrongdoers to avoid comment or lie until confronted with specific evidence to the contrary. He went on:

> Even well-intentioned people may be less candid when they believe that their remarks will be widely disseminated than when they are speaking to a small group of trusted confidants. Yet these same persons usually make little or no effort to protect their comments from being overheard or repeated by nonjournalists. Many journalists who pose as "ordinary people" see no reason to place themselves at a special disadvantage by assuming an affirmative obligation to disclose their journalistic role.[102]

# FOURTEEN

# MIRAGE

Of all the known attempts of journalists going undercover to expose things gone wrong, none quite rivals the ingenuity and imaginative flair of the Mirage exposé. More than thirty years after the *Chicago Sun-Times* published "this tale of cold beer and hot graft, in which a team of investigative reporters ran a Chicago tavern to probe corruption—and pulled off the greatest sting in the city's history,"[1] Mirage remains among the most ambitious, most celebrated, but then most sharply contested of undercover reporting efforts ever attempted. No discussion of journalism's role as public watchdog, or the place of undercover work within that mandate, would be complete without first taking a seat on a corner stool of the bar that flourished at 731 North Wells Street in late summer and fall 1978, and then was gone.

By 1976, Pamela Zekman had been fantasizing for five years about buying a tavern to witness firsthand, gain a clear understanding, and then explain in print how graft in Chicago worked.[2] As a member of the *Chicago Tribune*'s investigative task force since 1971 and then as its leader, she had been involved in most of the twenty major investigations the team undertook during those years, many of which involved the prominent, deliberate use of undercover techniques.

In her desk at the *Tribune,* Zekman kept a folder marked "Tavern," filled with notes of anonymous shakedown complaints she had received from readers over the years and the memos that she and George W. Bliss had drafted in efforts to convince editors to back the idea. They never managed to get beyond the dream stage. Year after year, there was no green light. Editors stymied the project because of too tight a budget or concern over crackdowns on the press from the state's attorney's office or a more generalized journalistic unease. It was one thing, the reporters later wrote, for a newspaper to infiltrate an institution as "a useful method of last resort." But to create its "own little institution" was something quite apart, laden as it would be with "possible legal burdens and entanglements."[3] At about the same time, James Hoge became editor of the rival *Chicago Sun-Times,* saw an opportunity to hire Zekman away, and did. The tavern folder came with her.

On a February afternoon in 1976, Zekman and her new boss returned to the office on foot from a downtown luncheon seminar about law enforcement, chatting amiably about possible investigative projects as they walked back across the Michigan Avenue Bridge to the *Sun-Times* building. Zekman told Hoge of the many complaints she had heard over the years about demands for payoffs and shakedowns from fire and building inspectors and from the police. If the *Sun-Times* owned and staffed a tavern, however briefly, reporters could witness this as it happened, she recalled telling Hoge. It would be a way to investigate and document the city's time-honored system of "government by envelope," not for the larger payoffs it took to snag a choice piece of property or a harbor mooring, but at street level, where traffic in ten-, twenty- and hundred-dollar denominations was known to be robust—a "supermarket approach to graft: low prices, high volume."[4] Also, taverns were heavily regulated social bastions of easy talk about the shadow workings of city life, a perfect stage set to see an illicit system in action.

Hoge seemed more intrigued with the idea than Zekman could have dared to expect, given the responses she had received at the *Trib.* He quickly calculated the potential outlay as perhaps as high as $50,000 or $60,000—enough to buy a three-bedroom house at the time in one of the city's middle-class suburbs.[5] After a long pause, he added that such an undertaking would need to be budgeted a year ahead, and a number of challenges would first have to be overcome before she could proceed. "Entrapment for one," she later recalled him saying in that first conversation. "Security. We'd have to go at it very carefully."[6]

Beyond ethics and logistics, there were other complications, too. First, there was no major personality to target. The city's mayor, Richard J. Daley, "wasn't about to get caught grabbing envelopes. He just ran the stationery store."[7] And second, most small business owners either had grown complacent about the system or were too fearful of repercussions to risk more than some anonymous grousing. For small businessmen to identify themselves as whistle-blowers could mean all manner of unwanted attention, from a plague of repeated inspections up and down the scale of quasi-official harassment.

Ten months later, the day before Christmas Eve, 1976, Hoge gave Zekman the go-ahead to proceed with the project, to be joined by the Chicago NBC affiliate, WMAQ, and the Better Government Association,[8] which had been keen on the idea since Zekman's *Tribune* days. Joining forces with the BGA again brought William Recktenwald to the team, who, since 1968, had been partnering with various Chicago news outlets for major investigations. It was he the *Tribune* sent to work as a prison guard at the Pontiac Correctional Center.[9]

With so many players, Zekman's first task was to keep the project totally secret, so as not to see months of work and expense go to total waste because of a published leak in any of the city's other news outlets. These included the *Chicago Daily News,* which shared not only the same floor in the *Sun-Times* building, separated only by a glassed-in room for the rackety teletype machines, but Hoge as editor. With one head attached to two bodies, how could Hoge be expected to keep one's secret from the other? Somehow he did. Zekman and Zay N. Smith would later describe the security operation as something akin to "keeping a salt lick secret from a community of deer."[10] With the *Tribune* only a few streets away, loose reporter talk over too many beers at the Billy Goat or Boul Mich could fell months of planning in a night. To hide her purpose inside the *Sun-Times* newsroom, she created a maze of false trails, cryptic expense account notations, and requests for clippings from the newspaper morgue that she submitted under assumed names. Then, yet another concern emerged with the death of Mayor Daley on December 20, 1976, just days before Hoge approved the plan. What impact would the city power transition have on the project, which would likely take the whole of the coming year to plan and execute?

At a meeting with the *Sun-Times* attorneys, Zekman and the editors considered all the pitfalls, ethical and legal, as the lawyers laid them out. From the start, concern over any appearance of entrapment headed the list. The team reviewed Illinois law:

> A person is not guilty of an offense if his conduct is incited or induced by a public officer or employee, or agent of either, for the purpose of obtaining evidence for the prosecution of such a

person. However, this Section is inapplicable if a public officer or employee, or agent of either merely affords to such person the opportunity or facility for committing an offense in furtherance of a criminal purpose which such person has originated.[11]

Zekman later explained that Illinois courts tended to interpret the law liberally, citing a case in which the conviction of a subject held firm even though a Chicago narcotics officer had approached the dealer twenty times before the man agreed to sell him dope. The *Sun-Times* would take a far more conservative approach. "The only act would be to open a tavern—and then let the visitors take it from there," Zekman and Smith later explained. "This was a matter of news judgment as well as ethics. The aim of the project was to catch Chicago in the act of being itself."[12]

More protocols had to be established. To avoid invasion of privacy, the *Sun-Times* would protect the identity of anyone who told a personal story. If a criminal act were committed, the newspaper would reveal names, dates, places, and amounts. Since Illinois law required a court order for the use of secret sound-recording devices, the *Sun-Times,* for documentation, would rely only on hidden photographers, multiple witnesses, and detailed memos. The newspaper also agreed to assume all general liability.[13]

Still another problem remained: how could the *Sun-Times* finance the project and fill out the tavern's license application honestly and legally but still keep its involvement under wraps? The lawyers found the means through the device of a straw buyer who got financing through an investment company to whom the *Sun-Times* loaned the money. That way the newspaper's role could be obscured.[14]

In the meantime, Zekman met with the incoming director of the Illinois Department of Law Enforcement, Tyrone C. Fahner, a former federal prosecutor who had jurisdiction in this area. Zekman later recalled telling him in carefully selected words: "All we want is the chance to fulfill our obligation, as citizens, to report crimes to an appropriate law enforcement agency. That has to be the extent of our involvement. We can't be your agents, in any sense." Fahner agreed and enlisted one of his top aides to accept crime reports from Zekman and her team. He also promised to keep their secrets.[15]

Recktenwald and Zekman made the real estate rounds as the ostensible Mr. and Mrs. Ray Patterson in search of an affordable tavern to lease. They met with bar owners, leasing agents, and crooked accountants who gave them a much clearer sense of what had eluded them again and again in their roles as crack investigative reporters: detailed how-to information about everything from the payoff system to shadow accounting. And they found an affordable bar, $18,000 for the trade and fixtures and $300 a month in rent[16] for a seedy little North Side joint called The Firehouse, which, despite its rotting drain boards, broken bathroom faucets, vermin-infested basement, trash-strewn walkways, and backed-up sewer, had never been cited for a code violation. Perfect.

Then came more hurdles. WMAQ hit a legal barrier imposed by both the television station's own attorneys and those at the NBC network and had to pull out of the project. Its lawyers warned that if a television station was involved in infiltrating Chicago's payoff system, even in the role of victim, it could be accused of taking part in the commission of a crime, thus jeopardizing its federal license.[17] (In time, CBS's newsmagazine *Sixty Minutes,* led by Mike Wallace, would become involved, but as observers only, to do a television segment about the project that aired as the series launched.)[18] The BGA agreed to provide $5,000, but that left a shortfall of at least $18,000; WMAQ had initially committed to cover half the estimated costs of $46,000. With the project woefully underfinanced,

Zekman and Recktenwald convinced the owner to sell them the bar on the installment plan and deferred the issue of how to make the next payments.

After about six weeks of renovation, The Firehouse receded into memory and in its place, on August 17, 1977, appeared the Mirage.[19] What followed for the *Sun-Times* reporters was two and a half months of bartending; waitressing; short-order cooking; chatting up the likes of jukebox salesman, inspectors, and cops; keeping the books; and surreptitiously taking notes for the eventual series. They sold a lot of beer, enough to cover the rent and all of their expenses other than salaries, since the *Sun-Times* was covering those.[20] Photographers documented dubious transactions, aiming their camera lenses through a peephole—actually a vent—in a cramped covered loft above the bar. At some points, cameramen from *Sixty Minutes* joined them in the space above, collecting footage for that program's eventual segment. The reporters closed down the bar on Halloween night.[21]

The series itself rolled out in twenty-five parts, from January 8 to February 5, 1978,[22] instantly capturing national attention, much as Dana Priest and Anne Hull would do thirty years later when the Walter Reed investigation broke in the *Washington Post*. One week into the series, the *Washington Post* described the Mirage exposé as "remarkable."[23] As the second week of stories unfolded, the *New York Times,* under a Chicago dateline, detailed the pervasiveness of the corruption the series was exposing and even raised the possibility of adverse political repercussions for Daley's successor, Mayor Michael Bilandic.[24] As Recktenwald would later say, taken incident by incident, the individual acts of corruption may indeed have been petty; but the cumulative burden the illicit system placed on Chicago's small business owners was not. The *Sun-Times* estimated the annual toll in lost tax revenue at up to

$16 million at the time.[25] Not only that, but the reporting heightened consciousness; Chicagoans followed it closely. Recktenwald recalled for Michael Miner how he reviewed page proofs for the series each night as the newspaper went to bed, "so I knew where the funny parts were," and then had the delight the next morning of watching *Sun-Times* readers commuting on the el and laughing at all the right places.[26]

On February 1, John D. Moorhead, writing from Chicago for the *Christian Science Monitor,* wondered in print whether real reform could come from such a "jazzy journalistic coup."[27] He quoted the response of local skeptics who said it would take much more than a hard-hitting, attention-demanding newspaper series to cure the systemic ills of a city as corrupt as Chicago, an attitude Hoge dismissed as "apathetic cynicism," adding, "You cannot move toward reform until you know in detail what needs to be reformed. Institutions do not reform themselves from within but because of pressure from outside."[28]

Applying that kind of outside pressure, in fact, is what newspapers are supposed to do. In this case, it also seemed to work. A year after the series launched, in winter 1979, as the impact of the project was still unfolding, leaders of the Mirage investigative team cataloged their project's results. These included the firing of more than a dozen city and state employees, including health and fire inspectors; the indictment of two state liquor inspectors for bribery and official misconduct; the conviction of eighteen of thirty-one indicted electrical inspectors accused of bribery, including one named in the series; and the creation of city, state, and federal task forces and several new internal investigating units.[29]

Back a year earlier, as news of the series spread in winter 1978, the common reaction among journalists could be summed up in the four syllables it takes to say Pulitzer Prize. And yet at the same time, a parallel response started to brew among the cognoscenti, presaged in an article by Deirdre Carmody, the second of two pieces the *New York Times* published about the sting around the time of its publication. Her piece appeared on Feburary 23, more than two weeks after the last installment of the Mirage series ran. By then the *Sun-Times* had moved on to covering the indictments, task force creations, and institutional reforms its reporting had spawned.[30] Rarely—and again, the *Chicago Tribune*'s von Solbrig Hospital and the *Washington Post*'s Walter Reed exposé are two other spectacular cases in point—have the impact and results of such a journalistic investigation been so concrete, so sweeping, *and* so swiftly obtained.

Carmody focused her inquiry on the undercover methodology itself. As it turned out, her article would become an early entrant among the many media self-examinations of the period of "Journalism Under Fire" angst of the 1980s and 1990s. She opened in a general way with a description of a number of typical undercover scenarios, such as journalists who go to work on assembly lines to experience what conditions are like for the workers, or reporters who take their cars in for servicing but really to check for fraud, or reviewers who make reservations in assumed names and then arrive at the restaurants in disguise to avoid preferential treatment. Rhetorically, she asked, "Are these reporters being unethical? Or are they using the only effective means they can to uncover conditions that their readers should know about?"[31]

Her question, of course, was a device to showcase the dazzling response to the undercover story of the hour. "As a result of the *Sun-Times* series, federal, state and county investigations are underway," Carmody wrote, "the Mayor has announced a new office of inspections, the building code is being rewritten, about one hundred jukebox and pinball machines have been confiscated and fourteen officials have been suspended." But she also reflected on the views of those who, although equally entranced by the potency of the sting, had begun to have questions about it "that were difficult to answer."[32]

She brought up the matter of entrapment and elicited a response from Zekman, who explained, as she would again later, that the reporters did not initiate the bribes—those came only at the suggestion of inspectors or business brokers—and that the Mirage crew reported every payoff to the Illinois Department of Law Enforcement. "Technically," Carmody wrote, "entrapment can be committed only by a law enforcement agent, not by a journalist. Entrapment involves luring someone into the commission of a crime as opposed to allowing him to conduct himself in a normal manner." She quoted Fred W. Friendly, who said the key words in avoiding an accusation of entrapment were "not planting the idea,"[33] which the *Sun-Times* reporters had taken extra care not to do.

The most salient of these early responses to the ethics questions raised by Mirage came from Robert P. Clark, then executive editor of the *Louisville Courier-Journal and Times.* At the time, he also chaired the ethics committee of the American Society of Newspaper Editors. "The public is the master, so to speak, and at least we have to level with them," he told Carmody. "If they feel we shouldn't have done it by masquerading, they will probably let us know."[34]

In fact, the public did let the *Sun-Times* know. A telephone survey the newspaper released on January 29, 1978, a few days before the series had finished its formal run,[35] showed that 85 percent of more than 200 Chicagoans interviewed believed the events reported in the series were true. Nearly a third of them, 31 percent, said that either they themselves had been approached for payoffs or they knew someone who had been.[36] Readers, in short, were comfortable with the questionable machinations that resulted in the Mirage exposé and expressed satisfaction with its results. Two years later the newspaper's readers reaffirmed their approval of the methodology in an even more extensive reader survey. It followed the newspaper's 1980 undercover investigation of a racket that was inflating the insurance rates of Illinois drivers by as much as a third as it put some $3 billion a year in the pockets of the ambulance chasers, doctors, and operators of clinics involved in the scheme.[37] The second survey included 603 Chicagoans—a group three times as large as those surveyed after Mirage—77 percent of whom expressed support for the use of undercover reporting devices and tactics, including hidden cameras, microphones, and the concealment of identity. A full 77 percent of respondents considered investigative reporting of this nature "very important" over against a mere 2 percent who did not see its value. Also, the great majority—again, 77 percent of those surveyed—said "exposure" was more important than "corrective action" as the most worthwhile reason for undertaking such an investigation. As to how often such enterprises lead to corrective action, 39 percent said "frequently" and 49 percent said "sometimes." Sixty percent of the respondents approved of reporters actively assuming identities, as opposed to concealing their identities. Thirty-five percent disapproved of the practice.[38]

The overwhelmingly favorable reaction of Chicago readers was not shared by most of the twelve men[39] who gathered in April 1979 to choose the winners of that year's Pulitzer Prizes. When Mirage came up for discussion, it precipitated "the most fascinating debate ever heard at Pulitzer,"[40] in the words of one of the judges, Eugene Patterson of the *St. Petersburg Times*. His remarks appeared in a near-forensic examination of the ensuing controversy by a *Washington Post* reporter, Myra McPherson, featured on the front page of the newspaper's Style section. In the headline, "debate" became, more accurately, "donnybrook."

MacPherson recalled the many squabbles of Pulitzer seasons past and how they had marred the annual announcement of the results, especially in the categories of arts and journalism. More than once, she reported, critics had chastised the board over a selection process that Robert Bendiner, a former editor of the *Nation*, characterized as "private lobbying, personal whim and a genial sort of logrolling."[41] Despite a concerted effort to quell criticism by amending the rules, the 1979 season turned out to be no exception.[42] The board[43] overturned the confidential choices of its jurors in six of twelve categories: four in journalism and two in the arts. Of course, as one board member explained, this was the board's absolute right; jurors nominate, the board selects.[44] Still, in light of the focus put on improving the process, to rebuff the choices of the judges in fully half of the cases did not seem to indicate meaningful reform.

Mirage was the obvious frontrunner among the four entries the jury put forward for consideration in the now-defunct category of "local investigative specialized reporting." Three undercover investigations had won in that category between 1971 and 1976 alone.[45] Yet the award went to a small Pennsylvania newspaper, the *Pottsville Republican*, for its series on the role of organized crime in the demise of a local coal company.

How could they not have chosen Mirage? In comments to MacPherson, Patterson explained that a mood of new moral stringency was aloft and that even though almost everyone on the board had either personally sanctioned or personally participated in undercover episodes at various points in their careers, a shift in the zeitgeist had made the use of ethically ambiguous reporting methods a far less appealing prospect. Not only that, but Patterson thought the Mirage exposé "had an element of entrapment."[46] Ben Bradlee of the *Washington Post,* also a board member, offered this quote to his reporter: "We instruct our reporters not to misrepresent themselves, period."[47] To award a Pulitzer to the *Sun-Times* for Mirage, Bradlee said further, "could send journalism on a wrong course."[48]

In comments to McPherson, Clayton Kirkpatrick, another board member, took an opposing view, acknowledging the number of Pulitzers the *Tribune* had won for investigations that involved reporters working undercover over the years. Repeating the standing litmus test even then for deciding to go deceptive, he said the results the *Sun-Times* achieved in this instance could not have been attained in any other way. Asked about the new moral stringency that both Patterson and Bradlee alluded to, Kirkpatrick scoffed. "A new morality as far as Pulitzer Prizes,"[49] he said.

Jack Nelson of the *Los Angeles Times,* not a member of the Pulitzer board at the time, agreed with Kirkpatrick. Recalling his own days reporting on the civil rights movement in the South, he told McPherson, "When you covered the KKK you damn well didn't let the KKK know you were a reporter. I passed myself off as a textile worker to see if Georgia state officials would buy my vote, and they did. I passed myself off as a client in a whorehouse to find out about bribes." The actions of the *Sun-Times,* he said, seemed "perfectly legitimate."[50]

Hoge, of course, concurred with Kirkpatrick and Nelson, although he expressed reluctance to say much, concerned not to be perceived as spewing sour grapes. To McPherson, he did offer this: "The board's capriciousness and arbitrariness is mystifying and profoundly disappointing. There was nothing in the board's advisory to indicate they were judging from a different set of rules than in the past."[51]

This unannounced wave of new thinking reflected wider cultural currents, crystallized a year earlier in Sissela Bok's book, *Lying: Moral Choices in Public and Private Life,* which quickly became, and has remained ever since, a favorite of journalism's ethical arbiters.[52] Bok framed a problem as old as society in ways that "hit the mind like a spanking offshore breeze"[53] and even singled out journalism directly at specific points in her wider-ranging text.[54]

As a guide for journalists, she posed three questions, those, in fact, often prescribed and followed in responsible journalistic quarters. Paraphrased, they are: Is there another way to get the information without the lie? If not, then what moral reasons might excuse the lie, and what counterarguments might be raised in opposition? And third, how might "a public of reasonable persons" react to the lies?[55]

By the end of summer 1979, the controversy triggered by the Mirage judging had not abated. The *Columbia Journalism Review* found the decision of the Pulitzer board irritating enough to write about it twice. In its Chronicle section, its writer repeated much of the earlier reporting on the subject, adding that during the board's deliberations, James Reston had helped to clarify the board's thinking by drawing a distinction between "pretense" and "deception." "Pretense," he ventured, was a passive act in which the reporter allows someone to draw the wrong conclusion, but "deception" was active, a deliberate effort to mislead.[56] This kind of hair-splitting became the commonly applied means of separating acceptable from unacceptable practices.

As to the entrapment bugaboo, *CJR* reported that other board members had discounted this suggestion from Patterson and actually were comfortable with the safeguards the *Sun-Times* had put in place to avoid such an accusation. (And yet interestingly, media critiques in the years since then often point to the odor of entrapment as the reason why Mirage did not prevail at prize time.)[57] The real difference of opinion, the writer indicated, had come down to whether the *Sun-Times* could have achieved the same result without the erection of such an elaborate stage set. Patterson and Bradlee prevailed in their belief that the subterfuge was unnecessary; a minority, including Kirkpatrick, disagreed. Still others, whom the writer, Steve Robinson, did not name, expressed the hope that the rebuff from the Pulitzer board would not deter editors and reporters from resorting to the journalism of last resort when stories important to the public interest legitimately warranted the use of more extreme measures.[58]

In *CJR*'s next issue, the magazine went even further. Its founder and publisher at the time, Edward W. Barrett, questioned the board's wisdom in the case of Mirage, expressing the belief that the project had been executed "well within the bounds of responsible, defensible conduct." He amplified his thoughts with the common argument of the project's defenders: "The central issue is: how else could such corruption be exposed? If the reporters had simply quizzed bar owners, none would have provided documented evidence on the record. If one had, he'd soon have been out of business." On behalf of the magazine, Barrett then offered the *Sun-Times CJR*'s "own imaginary award" for service to its community.[59]

Eighteen years later, Jack Fuller summoned Bok, as others so often had done and would do when pondering similar issues.[60] This was for a chapter of his 1996 book *News Values: Ideas for an Information*

*Age,* in which he explores the use of deception and other "confidence games,"[61] his term for the sketchier tactics he once fully embraced, but by then was questioning deeply, citing their role in eroding media credibility as his reason.[62] (Once again, that curious conflation of two separate events that happened in roughly the same time period: the controversy over Mirage and the publication of the first of a succession of national surveys that confirmed the public's increasing distrust of and disappointment in the media's performance.)

Fuller expressed particular concern for those on the periphery of an investigation who might be inadvertently hurt by an undercover effort. To Bok's three-point guide, he added that the decision to go deceptive be subject to full deliberation by an organization's top leadership and that measures be taken—such as inviting an informed outsider into the conversation—to avoid the moral blindness that group thinking can engender. And regardless of whether the deceptive act produces publishable work, he said, readers should be told what was done.[63]

Yet he also said that journalists are not obliged to "give Miranda warnings" or to reveal their affiliations "when a building inspector solicits a bribe at the reporter's own home, for example, or a city work crew goes to sleep on the job along his route to the office." He did cite examples of the cases in which "the requirement of candor" must be met, including job applications (the post–Food Lion rule) or when reporters are questioned by authorities or even "perhaps" when another person asks.[64] And yet in a much earlier iteration of some of these ideas in a slightly different context, Fuller was very clear on where a journalist's fundamental obligations should lie: "Pare away the hyperbole, though," he wrote, "and there remains the intriguing question of whether a journalist owes anyone besides his readers a duty of truth."[65] In short, although it likely was not his intention, he made the ultimate case for going undercover when warranted.

Fuller is among the many who share the view that Mirage "pretty much put an end"[66] to undercover reporting or that the technique had gone "out of fashion"[67] by the mid-1990s. Indeed, successive surveys of "U.S. newspeople" across all media between 1991 and 2007 give the same impression. Rank-and-file journalists expressed increasingly heightened discomfort with the use of deceptive techniques, with support remaining strong among a minority of reporters the researchers described as younger, better educated, more liberal, more adversarial, more likely to get more feedback from news sources, and who worked for publicly traded companies.[68] Television journalists mirrored their print counterparts opposing falsification and masquerade, although they continued to support the use of hidden cameras and microphones in increasing numbers;[69] Food Lion did not prove to be the deterrent so widely predicted when the first verdict against ABC came down.

Reaction in the years since Mirage among the field's most influential figures has been mixed. While some important pundits have consistently opposed or severely questioned the resort to undercover techniques,[70] just as many have continued to defend the practice under highly controlled conditions, as noted elsewhere in this text.[71]

And what of Bok's "public of reasonable persons"? The most authoritative surveys of the period since Mirage, particularly one by the National Opinion Research Center (NORC) that *Time* cited in its 1983 cover story, "Journalism Under Fire," focused on many other reasons for the public's diminishing approval of the media. These included falsification and embellishment of the facts, lack of concern about accuracy, bias, the prevalence at the time of libel suits, the use of unidentified sources, and a perception that journalistic power and presumption of importance had increased to a point of arrogance and insensitivity. None of these are undercover's natural sins, and in fact, in *Time*'s assessment, the use of surreptitious techniques did not really figure. Halfway through an article of nearly eight thousand words appeared a reference to the Wolin and Mirage defeats during the Pulitzer judging, but the writer failed to mention that the rebuffs did not result from public rebuke, which was what the piece was about. Quite the contrary: the public was in obvious thrall of those two enterprising projects. Interestingly, the only known complaints against these stories came during the Pulitzer deliberations—not from the public, but from the profession's top rung.[72]

Likewise, an article in Harvard's *Nieman Reports* in summer 2005 cited a number of surveys—those conducted by NORC over the years, those by the Pew Research Center for the People and the Press, and an early one released in 1986 that Times Mirror commissioned from the Gallup Organization. All of these confirmed the continued and steady erosion of public confidence in the press that studies had been documenting since the early 1980s. Why? Respondents over the years variously cited undue influence from powerful individuals, from government, from corporations, from advertisers, or from labor unions. By the end of the 1990s, respondents had added—in steadily increasing numbers—immorality, questionable values, believability, and partisanship.[73] Again, undercover reporting, hidden cameras, or the use of surreptitious techniques got no specific mention.[74]

So given this largely unfettered public support, how did undercover reporting become the designated culprit, the fall guy, for journalism's much more pervasive troubles? How did the decision at some outlets to swear off the practice entirely become the palliative, the major corrective action taken, as a way to cure journalism's unrelated ills? Why the response of eliminating a highly selective but popular course of action that addressed none of the red-button issues? Was it to strike a more generalized blow for honesty in the simplest, least painful, and most concrete and most promotable way possible? There is no clear answer.

Speaking of the public, not only is there evidence of its abiding support for undercover projects that bring significant information and meaningful results to public light, but the public also has more tacitly affirmed the use of subterfuge by journalists who pursue significant but difficult-to-obtain information by other unconventional means. Witness the public response to the Pentagon Papers of 1971 and Watergate in 1972.[75] Fuller, for one, acknowledged this reliable public affirmation. Yet he offered his own three reasons for shying away from deceptive practices more generally, even when the public approves: First, because they represent a "shortcut" to information that can be obtained in other ways; second, because it is dangerous for journalism to function in an environment that tolerates lying; and third, because a publication's "strongest bond with its audience is the simple truth." (And yet, I would ask, how often is truth a simple thing to establish?) To depart from those principles, he said, even when audiences understand and accept the reasons for the departure, "can hardly help but erode the confidence that forms the very basis of the enterprise."[76] From the data, it appears that audiences indeed are focused on "the simple truth," but by that they seem to mean the simple truth as it ultimately appears on the page or screen, and that at the point of publication they expect to be told the simple truth about how the information was obtained and the way decisions were made about its presentation.

Despite years of pontification suggesting the contrary, the Mirage supporters actually prevailed. However squeamish about undercover tactics the Pulitzer board suddenly became in spring 1979; however reticent to do undercover reporting the profession professes to have become in the years that followed; however often reporters, analysts, and critics have since stated as fact that the dead hand had dropped on a century's worth of zeal for going undercover, the evidence tells a different tale. Based on a reasonably thorough review of the available record,[77] there has been no letup in the cumulative rate or use of undercover techniques across all media, not before or since Mirage, and not before or since Food Lion. Taking the nation's top journalistic award as an indicator, it is true that fewer undercover projects received the recognition of a Pulitzer Prize for a good while, and none at all won it in the years between the Mirage controversy of 1979 and Tony Horwitz's chicken-processing win for the *Wall Street Journal* in 1995. It is also true that some newspapers that once enthusiastically embraced the practice of going undercover in time decided to forbid it, the *Chicago Tribune* and the *Nashville Tennessean* notably among them.

And yet there has been a good deal of honor bestowed on undercover efforts in the years from Mirage to the end of the first decade of the twenty-first century—honor beyond the Pulitzers that the *Wall Street Journal,* the *New York Times,* and the *Washington Post* received in 1995, 2001, and 2007, respectively. The Pulitzer board named the *Tennessean* a finalist in 1981 in the prestigious Public Service category for its reporting on the national resurgence of the Ku Klux Klan. (Jerry Thompson's eighteen months as a card-carrying Klansman may or may not have been submitted as part of the prize consideration packet but was prominently published during the period under review.)[78] That same year, the *Sun-Times,* clinging rather defiantly to the cherished method despite the snub of two years before, also was named a Pulitzer finalist in the "local specialized or investigative category"[79] for its accident swindlers series,[80] the insurance project mentioned above for which Gene Mustain, with purported injuries invented for him by the Associated Physicians' Clinic, checked into Community Hospital of Evanston, where nearly all of the patients were "equally phony." (The headline homage: OUR OWN PHONY PATIENT IS HOSPITALIZED AND DISCOVERS THE HOSPITAL IS A MIRAGE.[81]) For the project, Zekman and Mustain teamed up with the local ABC affiliate, WLS-TV, which won a 1981 duPont-Columbia Silver Baton for the same project.[82] Also in that period, in 1982 as noted, the Pulitzer board named as a finalist Merle Linda Wolin's Latina sweatshop series for the *Los Angeles Herald Examiner,* and in 1984, George Getschow made the finals for his *Wall Street Journal* series, DIRTY WORK, which included his pose as a day laborer.[83]

Other newspapers have continued openly to support the practice of undercover reporting, although sparingly, and not always for projects that have drawn significant national attention. They have done so when the methods were most effective for obtaining the information or for telling the story. Just a sampling: in the fifteen years between 1979 and 1995, at least twenty-three mainstream newspapers sponsored notable undercover projects, some newspapers more than once.[84] Some projects were misfires, too.[85] Television has produced as much undercover and hidden-camera activity as ever, including the NBC *Dateline* series *To Catch a Predator*[86] in 2006 and its various clones. Magazine and book projects also have been plentiful.[87]

In the fourteen years between 1996 and 2010, a difficult period for newspapers economically, at least nine newspapers mounted major investigations with an undercover dimension.[88] Still others from 1979 on have been more careful in crafting and framing the way they explain the execution of their projects, sometimes massaging the definition of what constitutes deception. In Recktenwald's view, despite the *Chicago Tribune*'s ban, at least a couple of its major latter-day investigations have undercover markings.[89]

By the same token, at the twentieth century's end, there was no record of the Pulitzer judges or Pulitzer board raising a ruckus over the way Horwitz conducted himself in 1994, or LeDuff in 2001 (2001 was the same year Ted Conover's *Newjack* was a Pulitzer finalist in the general nonfiction category), or with how the *Washington Post* reporters comported themselves at Walter Reed in 2007. What this suggests is that elaborate, highly stretched identity finesses—and no disclosure of the reporters' affiliation or actual intent until confronted or until they deliberately reveal their purpose at the point of publication—meet the profession's parameters of permissibility. Outright lies, spoken or written, do not.

More to the point, in the years since Mirage, the use of such techniques by respectable outlets of all description remained—and remains—a highly selective but still acceptable editorial course of action. That is the way it always has been and should continue to be. Attitudinally, some influential journalists may believe the practice went out of favor with Mirage because it seems like it did, or because they think it should have, or because they have picked up that sense from earlier punditry, or because the practice has gone out of favor with them personally or with people whose opinions they respect.

While in fact, the post-Mirage years have produced some of the most stunning undercover exposés in memory and at the same steady, discriminating clip as ever before. The only bow to the attitudinal change has been greater sensitivity to the ethical concerns and, perhaps, a more deliberate explanation in published stories, or in sidebars to the stories, or in prefaces, or in letters of nomination to prize boards, of how and why the resort to undercover techniques was necessary and how the reporter and publication endeavored to minimize harm. And reporters, for the most part, have taken far more care not to write down or verbalize outright lies during the reporting process. Others have simply been more calculating in their explanations of how they got that story, distancing the investigation from the distasteful tactics that helped to make it possible and from the taint of the undercover label. And yet despite protestations from many quarters, despite the opposition and expressed disdain in some camps, effective and responsible reporting that involves undercover techniques has continued to have significant impact on the journalism that matters; and the public has continued to support it, even in cases that involved the telling of outright lies.

No wonder nearly a quarter of a century after the Mirage disappointment, the insult of 1979 to those involved in the project still stung. As Hoge told Michael Miner of the *Chicago Reader* in 2002, he still believed the Mirage exemplified "dramatic investigative journalism that made a difference," one that was undertaken only as a last resort. He again explained how much effort had gone into avoiding accusations of entrapment and that he had reviewed these steps thoroughly in the submission cover letter to the Pulitzer board, but "apparently to no avail. I think the *Sun-Times,* its editors and reporters who were involved ought to be forever proud of the Mirage project."[90]

Proud they remain. In late August 2006, gathered at the Brehon Pub at 731 North Wells were Zekman, Smith, Recktenwald, and Jim Frost, one of the two photographers who had holed up in the loft above the bar, when the Mirage appeared within those same walls. The local chapter of the Society of Professional Journalists sponsored the event to commemorate the thirtieth anniversary of the legendary exposé. In fact in November 2010, *Chicago*

*Magazine* placed Mirage at nineteenth on its fortieth anniversary list of the forty most "OMG!" moments in the city's recent history.[91] "OMG!" as in "mouth wide open, stop, blink, and say, 'Oh My God!'"

Recktenwald reminded the crowd at the Brehon that every word in the series was right, every fact the team presented was documented; every source identified. "There's no Jimmy-the-eight-year-old in there," he said, referring to the Pulitzer the *Washington Post* had been obliged to relinquish in 1981 because the story's central figure, an eight-year-old heroin addict, turned out to have been imagined, a mirage. Smith pointed up the singular value of an undercover investigation as a work with special narrative power. Mirage was far more than an investigative series, he told the crowd, harkening to its appeal as a story. "A tavern," he said, "is a city writ small."[92]

# FIFTEEN

# TURKMENISTAN AND BEYOND

In 2008, the New Press published *Submersion Journalism,* a collection of fifteen relatively contemporaneous articles from *Harper's* magazine, compiled and edited by Bill Wasik, then one of the magazine's longtime senior editors and an advocate of the technique. As described in the book's table of contents, the articles, many reported undercover, ranged across subjects, from politics to violence to illness to vice to arts to the confessions of war.[1] Among the pieces selected for inclusion were Jeff Sharlet's "Jesus Plus Nothing"; Wells Tower's foray into campaigning with the Florida Republications for the reelection of George Bush in 2004 (there would be several similar efforts during the Obama-Clinton presidential primary campaign season of 2007);[2] Barbara Ehrenreich's personal encounter with the funded fight against breast cancer movement; Kristopher A. Garin's efforts to buy a Ukrainian mail-order bride; Jake Silverstein's participation in a poetry slam; and Willem Marx's summer as a military propagandist in Iraq. If Ehrenreich's *Nickle and Dimed* hadn't become a cottage industry all its own, one could imagine it would also have been included, as could any of the dozens of other pieces of this ilk that

*Harper's* published in this century, the last century, or the century before. *Harper's* is and has always been "heart" undercover.

Prominent among the selections was the undercover reportage of 2007 that caused the loudest cymbal clash in the profession since Food Lion. It was the work of the magazine's then Washington editor, Ken Silverstein, who had been writing for *Harper's* as a contributing editor going back to the early 1990s. In between, he became a reporter for the *Los Angeles Times,* where the questionable activities of the city's most powerful lobbyists had also been a leitmotif of his reporting from Washington. By 2007, more than a dozen lengthy takeouts on this or closely related themes had appeared under his byline in one publication or the other. Yet much to Silverstein's disappointment, none of these pieces had generated significant interest, considering the extent of the influence the most powerful firms were exerting, however quietly, in the public sphere.[3]

In consultation with Wasik and the magazine's then editor, Roger Hodge, Silverstein began to dream up ways of drawing broader attention to the ever more powerful band of Washington lobbyists and the means they and their firms had developed for promoting even the most thuggish of client-states, for lobbying policymakers, for putting together conferences and Congressional junkets, for getting op-ed pieces placed that featured the work of knowledgeable, prominent academics or experts from prestigious think tanks. Silverstein's first thought was to expose the system of winning earmarks by dummying up a phony firm to win one with the help of a powerful lobbyist, but he ultimately abandoned that plan. It would have meant a huge pileup of fees owed to the lobbying firm as the bill made its way through Congress, not to mention the waste of congressional time and resources for a phantom endeavor. "Deceitfully seeking money for a genuinely important use,"[4] he later wrote, raised both ethical and legal issues too thorny to surmount.[5]

Silverstein willfully ignored what he perceived to be the disfavor into which undercover reporting had fallen, at least among the Washington-based reporters he knew. In his view, the disdain could be "traced in part to the transformation of journalism from a profession for cynical, underpaid gumshoe reporters into (in Washington at least) a highbrow occupation for opinion-mongers, Sunday talk show yakkers, and social climbers." To this group, he considered himself an outsider. He soon came up with another plan: to pose as a representative of a "small, mysterious overseas firm with a major financial stake in the country in question" and see what interest top Washington lobbying firms might have in representing a dictatorial government known for its abuses of human rights.[6] He chose Turkmenistan.

What Silverstein wanted to know, as he later explained in his book about the sting, was "just how low would a well-heeled Washington lobbying firm sink" to represent a pariah regime? What sort of promises do the firms make to win the contracts? How closely do they scrutinize potential clients and what means do they use for orchestrating support for these clients? How visible is their hand in what Congress and the public can see? How much of this, he wondered, could thus be subject to more public scrutiny and debate?[7] But how would it be possible to find all that out?

He set up virtual shop with little more than a new set of calling cards in the name of not Ken Silverstein but Kenneth Case, a rudimentary website, and a London-based cellular telephone number. Wasik and Hodge knew that Silverstein's use of the method would "take heat,"[8] but they were willing to authorize the project anyway.

Despite the additional risk of exposure, Silverstein decided to hide a tiny tape recorder in the inside pocket of his expensive new suit jacket, both to document the conversations should the need for a record ever arise, and also to have a verbatim account of what transpired, so as not to have to rely on memory or his notes in shorthand when it came time to write or if he had to corroborate his reporting.

He and the editors also made a decision that left him vulnerable to criticism. He did not call the firms for comment before the story ran. Silverstein later explained that given the magazine's lead time to publication of more than six weeks, the risk was simply too great that the firms would use the lag to disseminate an alternative spin before his story even had a chance to get into print. "There is no way to do anything for the magazine at the last minute," he said. "And editorially, we decided there wasn't a lot to be gained by calling them. We could have put something on the Web. We could have called and posted a comment online. I acknowledge that you can see this as self-serving. But what was I going to ask them precisely? What was I going to gain? It was an undercover story. You either like that, or you don't."[9]

By mid-June, the article appeared in the magazine's July 2007 issue. "Their Men in Washington: Undercover with D.C.'s Lobbyists for Hire,"[10] brought the attention on the lobbyists and their moral acrobatics that Silverstein so long had sought. Reaction to the piece also focused a good deal of attention on Silverstein himself and the lengths he had gone to expose the lengths lobbyists would go to land lucrative deals with questionable clients. He was braced for some negative response to his methodology from his colleagues in the profession and had a clear sense beforehand that undercover reporting "in polite journalism circles is generally frowned upon—at least it seems that way to me."[11] He also anticipated the harsh reaction he indeed received from the lobbyists he had named. But the article also provoked far more positive attention than he expected from readers and from the larger media establishment. For the next month, Silverstein found himself fielding questions and comments about what he had done. These mostly positive reverberations echoed out through the media-centric blogosphere.[12] Silverstein did have detractors. Both Howard Kurtz, then media columnist for the *Washington Post,* and Mark Lisheron, writing for the *American Journalism Review,* were among the few media writers to go on the attack. Kurtz quoted Silverstein as saying he was comfortable weighing his ethics against those of a firm that would agree to represent and whitewash the record of a Stalinist dictatorship, but Kurtz also cited the controversies emanating from Mirage and Food Lion to assert that the undercover tradition had faded in recent years because "no matter how good the story, lying to get it raises as many questions about journalists as their subjects."[13]

Silverstein fired back, both on his *Harper's* blog and in an op-ed piece for the *Los Angeles Times,* defending his use of the questionable tactics that enabled him to "gain an inside glimpse into a secretive culture of professional spinners only by lying myself." He said he disclosed his deceptions clearly in the resulting piece—in contrast to the lobbyists he met who "boasted of how they were able to fly under the radar screen in seeking to shape U.S. foreign policy." Readers uncomfortable with his methods, he said, were free to dismiss his findings.[14] Could he have accomplished the same end without the subterfuge? "Impossible,"[15] he said.

Silverstein was given a number of national platforms from which to explain his actions. NPR programs featured him in interviews,[16] and Bill Moyers invited him onto his PBS program, *Bill Moyers Journal.* Moyers, in his introduction to the piece, called Washington "an occupied city, a company town, whose population of lobbyists constitute the permanent government."[17] He said the number of lobbyists registered to do business in Washington had more than doubled in the past six years to twenty-five lobbyists for every member of Congress[18] and that Silverstein would be a tour guide for his viewers into the inner workings of their world.

Moyers also asked readers to respond to questions in an online reader poll on his blog, in which he asked, "Do you think undercover investigations like those used in Ken Silverstein's recent report compromise journalistic credibility?" Readers overwhelmingly responded "no."[19] In a count taken in 2007 shortly after the program aired, 88 percent of respondents expressed support for the practice.

Nevertheless, in the October 2007 issue of *American Journalism Review,* Lisheron focused on the way Kurtz had reignited the "longstanding and unresolved debate about the ethics of undercover journalism."[20] Lisheron posed the issue much as Kurtz had posed it several months earlier and then asked if journalists lying or misrepresenting themselves was really the way to restore public faith in the newsgathering process—even if, as Silverstein said, people who doubt the efficacy of the undercover method were free to dismiss the findings. "But how much trust should one place in a journalist who lies or the publication that endorses such behavior?" Lisheron asked. Further, he said, "If lying is a superior tool in some instances, what is to stop reporters from using it indiscriminately? In Silverstein's world, it is left to the reader to determine whether the lying is being done in the service of the truth or self-interest."[21]

Lisheron acknowledged Silverstein's many supporters and the hundreds of emails he received praising both the story and the sting. He also cited a column on the subject by Edward Wasserman that appeared both in the *Miami Herald* and on Wasserman's personal blog.[22] In it, Wasserman questioned Silverstein's approach and acknowledged his respect for those who opposed it. He also repeated a prevailing impression that no one goes undercover any longer, saying, "There's something anachronistic about it, as if reporters suddenly started using pay telephones and Remington typewriters. That's not how we get news nowadays."[23] But then Wasserman zigzagged. He asked his readers if Silverstein was the right trickster for them to be worried about: If it is right to demand that public deliberations be held in public view, "don't we need to challenge the sanctity of backroom discussions that are intended to have no less impact than a mere public hearing? Trickery has its costs, but they need to be weighed against the harm of keeping those backrooms locked."[24] Four years later, Wasserman replied by email to a question put to him after his column on the James O'Keefe NPR sting appeared in the *Miami Herald*. He was asked if his condemnation of the O'Keefe exposé represented his change of heart on the allowability of deceptive techniques more generally, as he seemed to suggest in the earlier column. He replied that he was "indeed tougher" on deception in his 2011 column than he had been in the past, but that

> I had tried to be clear in the Silverstein affair that such entrapment is highly problematic ethically. You are tricking people, robbing them of their time, denying them the fundamental right to choose their words in view of whom they're talking to, setting them up to look bad. Of course that's all wrong. Nevertheless, I do also believe there are important realities that cannot be forced into light without engaging in such techniques. Here, I think, the SPJ's [Society of Professional Journalists'] rules work, and *Harper's,* to me, met that test. The new era ignores the obligation to subject such work to any discernible test whatsoever.[25]

Wasserman, incidentally, made a similar appeal in 2005 for a more nuanced evaluation of the appropriateness of the use of subterfuge. This was in response to the *Spokane Spokesman-Review*'s use of a computer expert in an online sting to support its allegation that the mayor "had used positions of public trust—as a sheriff's deputy, Boy Scout leader, and powerful politician—to develop sexual relationships with boys and young men."[26]

At the time, Wasserman took issue with the reaction against the Spokane sting of some major news executives, notably the then editor of the *Philadelphia Inquirer,* Amanda Bennett. "I don't permit deception," she told a reporter for *Editor & Publisher.* "Undercover is a method of the past."[27] To this, he hotly disagreed, pointing to the Spokane investigation as a case in point. He then responded more expansively in his *Miami Herald* column to the larger question of the method's appropriateness. To his mind, the "affair" had "disquieting elements," but deception was not one of them. The newspaper's deception had been well thought out and fair, he said. "I'm bothered more by the possibility that such stories are being eyed by journalists elsewhere and ignored because editors despise the reporting that the stories might require."[28]

Responding to the Turkmenistan sting, Bob Steele, the Poynter Institute's resident ethicist, made a similar point. Saying he was no "absolutist on these matters of truth versus lies," he believed that there were "rare, exceptional cases—when deception may be justified, providing the reporter and the publication meet multiple thresholds." Silverstein, he said, had provided "yeasty material to renew the debate on when, if ever, deception is justified in pursuit of truth."[29]

Kurtz persisted in his opposition, telling Lisheron that he still could not grasp, as a matter of fairness, why Silverstein did not seek comment from the lobbyists before *Harper's* published his piece and that "I stand by what I said about impersonating being wrong."[30]

Looking back several years later to that summer of renewed consternation over the ethics of undercover reporting, neither Spokane nor Turkmenistan would become the new Food Lion or the new Mirage. Nor did Ian Murphy's prank call to the governor of Wisconsin during a major labor dispute with the state's union of public employees[31] or James O'Keefe's NPR sting, both in winter 2011.[32]

The impact of these episodes on the way journalists view undercover reporting has been transitory at best. Silverstein, in a 2010 interview for this book, said that he was told that one of the firms he contacted had turned down a contract to represent Pakistan and he wondered if his story might have influenced the decision. He hoped to spur Congress to push for reform legislation to address the reach of foreign lobbying, but that was not to be. The piece's most far-reaching impact came courtesy of Gary Trudeau who riffed off the article in a series for his *Doonesbury* comic strip. "I have to say that made me pretty happy," Silverstein said. "It's not that it changed the world, but it does count for something. That's a pretty mass audience."[33] Silverstein, for his part, did not drop the subject; in subsequent as in prior years, he revisited the lobbyist theme several times, albeit conventionally, on the Washington blog he wrote for *Harper's* website.

Silverstein subtitled the last chapter of his book "Aftermath: The Death of Undercover Reporting," a premature pronouncement, to be sure. Since 2008, when *Turkmeniscam* was published, I count at least forty undercover efforts of significant enough virtue to be listed.[34] Witness *Harper's,* for one. Undaunted by the Turkmenistan blowback, it published Matthieu Aikins's article about his cloaked

and long-bearded stint as a supposed member of the Afghani border police in December 2009, a report that two months later was
being handed to members of the entering class of U.S. intelligence
analysts to acquaint them with a situation in the key border town
of Spin Boldak, along the drug-smuggling route of southern Afghanistan. Between Aikins's seventy-five hundred words in a magazine and a six-page classified military intelligence report, there was
no contest; the agents were meant to conclude that Aikins's report
was more useful.[35] With mainstream journalists, it is fair to say the
practice of reporting undercover has continued to thrive. Not even
its pulse has slowed.

One distinguishing characteristic of Silverstein's ruse that aligns
it, at least to some extent, with the excesses of Food Lion is the
issue of overt misrepresentation, the deliberate, verbalized or written act with the intention to mislead. In this case, the target was
the lobbying firms via Silverstein's use of the additional cell phone
number, the false identity, the dummy website, and the printed
calling cards; in other words, the lies. In our interview, I asked
Silverstein to compare his approach to the lengths that latter-day
prize-winners for the *Wall Street Journal,* the *New York Times,* and
the *Washington Post* had gone to in efforts to avoid the need to
speak or write a lie or to overtly misrepresent what they were
doing—if not in actions, at least in words.

He pondered the notion, but only for a moment. Clearly, he
said, if the lobbyists had gotten even a sniff of what he was up to,
and had called him on it, he would have acknowledged his actions
and aborted the project immediately, much as Horwitz described
being prepared to do for his chicken-processing story. But to Silverstein, the very idea of developing an elaborate subterfuge to
cover a story based on subterfuge sounded preposterous. "That's
a ridiculous distinction," he said. "If editors want to feel better,

fine. But it's a totally ridiculous distinction. The whole pretense of this was that it was an undercover sting," he said. "We lied. I misrepresented myself. I think the piece was legitimate. If others don't, that's fine. We didn't think about how we could make this legitimate, how we could make this something that was not quite a lie. It's under–fucking–cover reporting! What's the point of trying to save your ass? That's an outrage. I think that's outrageous. To make it *appear* that you've been fully forthcoming? It's either you do it or you don't. If you do, what's the point of making up deceptions to justify your deception?"[36] (Bill Kovach and Tom Rosenstiel expressly allow for journalistic masquerade under tight controls[37] but they also give the lie to another common form of journalistic deception, the "unprincipled, dishonest, and biased"[38] technique of selecting sources to express a reporter's own point of view but then using a neutral voice to make the information seem objective. Journalism's arbiters are not known to have prescribed any concrete actions against this common practice.)

Indeed, Silverstein's point is a key one: Where is the honor in covering a deception with yet another deception to justify an effort to accomplish a public good? What is the sense in going to such convoluted lengths to avoid what amounts only to avoidance of the letter of the lie?

This book has sought to demonstrate not only the indisputable staying power of undercover reporting, and to argue on the strength of the historical record that despite the acknowledged ethical complications and compromises it necessitates, despite its misuses, its importance and value as a journalistic form should not be in doubt. Few narrative strategies are as effective at exposing wrong, engaging public interest, and generating action.

True, there have been missteps. Yet much of the criticism leveled at undercover reporting applies to one degree or another across journalism's many and varied forms. On the whole, because of the careful consideration, long-term planning, and expense that serious undercover efforts require, the misfires may be colossal when they happen, but they appear to happen less often than in other types of reporting. Of the hundreds upon hundreds of examples reviewed for this project, the real embarrassments would fill only a child's hand. Minor successes and major triumphs outpace the embarrassments by the dozens. Of all the journalistic practices in need of reform or rejection, the indignation undercover reporting has drawn in response to its blatant use—but not to its just-as-frequent unstated use—seems to me to be wildly misplaced.

True, the unique performance aspect of undercover reporting is a strength as powerful as it is a potential weakness. The frequent reliance on the reporter persona can produce in readers a vicarious, even voyeuristic thrill that brings an issue alive. And yet putting the writer in the center of the narrative requires caution, for the risk is great, as John Hersey once warned in another context, that the writer can become more important than the subject he or she seeks to picture, allowing what matters most to recede into the backdrop, dissolving out of focus into something "fuzzy, vague, unrecognizable and false."[39]

There is also the pitfall of "improperly speaking for others,"[40] as Philip Brian Harper has observed about cross-racial undercover narratives, making a point that easily can apply more broadly to other subject areas for which reporters have used disguise. His reflection raises another question: If reporting of this nature can result in no more than the portrayal of one reporter's unique experience, rather than a true representation of the people or situation he or she hopes to convey, does value enough remain to justify the subterfuge? Do such performances invalidate the very information they seek to reveal, the possibility of sharing those experiences widely, and a virtual forum for generating informed discussion about it? Is the form too limiting, is the picture it creates too distorted for it to achieve anything close to what the writer may have set out in earnest to convey? My question is, would we challenge an affecting, effective writer of fiction who seeks to reveal larger truths through specific fictional examples in a specific fictional narrative setting that may well be drawn from actual lives? We would not.

When undercover reporting is done well, when the method is deployed sparingly by exceptional reporters operating under strict and thoughtful editorial and ethical controls, the work soars. It performs journalism's all-important watchdog or "audit" function. It can provide important, hard-to-get, difficult-to-penetrate information to a mass audience in a highly readable way. As a narrative device, it can be stunningly effective. The drama, the sense of theater, it lends to the journalistic enterprise not only can bring important issues to wider attention but it can sustain the attention it attracts and even catalyze reform, as all great storytelling can do.

It also reminds us of the importance of reaffirming the role of the journalist as outsider—but just as importantly, never as outlaw. It underscores the need for journalists to be in, but not of, the worlds they inhabit as reporters. Best practice and the prevailing consensus about journalism's role in a democratic society require a higher level of personal remove than is often the case any longer. Essential is the detachment that allows one to point an accusing finger when necessary and to amass the evidence needed to support that charge, unencumbered by personal or social connections or ambitions. Necessary is the possibility to find out how people think and know and act, without the "middle filter," as Anne Hull called the layer of spun fuzz between reality and its projection by

those with vested interests. Like journalism's investigative counterparts in other disciplines and professions—ethnography and
law enforcement come to mind—strict bounds must be placed on
the ethically challengeable behavior such work at times requires;
and reporters must be obliged to disclose the way they have gone
about their reporting—and their editing—as part of their initial
presentations, rather than in interviews or memoirs that often appear well after the fact. As part of their work, they should provide
avenues of response to the targets of their investigations. But at
the same time, undercover reporting needs much wider latitude of
acceptance than currently provided for what the work sometimes
obliges its reporters and producers to do.

As to undercover's ethical conundrums, if navigating them were
simple, they wouldn't continue to be so perplexing. "You can't lie"
is the thick red line most often drawn between what is and what is
not journalistically acceptable. To be sure, those three words seem
to provide a fine and unambiguous place to begin. But as often
as not, they have led to pretzel-like ethical contortions, elaborate
work-arounds, and dubious bouts of self-justification—in other
words more deception, as Silverstein put it, to cover the deception.
To me, it is an effort to mislead all the same. Reporters so carefully
constricted indeed do not lie. But what they do instead bears very
little resemblance to truth, even though projecting an image of
truthfulness is the point of these sometimes very elaborate machinations.

When is undercover the right course of action? The long-
accepted starting points are still the right ones: when the subject
at hand really warrants it, when the project has been considered
carefully and thoughtfully reviewed first, and when there is no
other way to get the information. I would suggest that the latter
part of the formulation be amended to say, when there is no other

timely and equally effective means of getting and presenting the information. It is also critical that the work be undertaken with extreme care to avoid any unintended peripheral harm and that the actions involved be performed and explained transparently and fully within the bounds of law. Awful as it may sound, as awful as it does feel, deception for journalists, whether they work above board or undercover, is often just a given in the quest to change some systems or to get some wrongs righted, at least for a little while.

# NOTES

## CHAPTER ONE

1. Dana Priest and Anne Hull, "Soldiers Face Neglect, Frustration at Army's Top Medical Facility," *Washington Post,* 18 February 2007, A01; Hull and Priest, "The Hotel Aftermath," *Washington Post,* 19 February 2007, A01; Priest and Hull, "Hospital Investigates Former Aid Chief," *Washington Post,* 20 February 2007, A01; Hull and Priest, "'It Is Just Not Walter Reed,'" *Washington Post,* 5 March 2007, A01; Priest and Hull, "The War Inside," *Washington Post,* 17 June 2007, A01; Priest and Hull, "Soldier Finds Comfort at Dark Journey's End," *Washington Post,* 17 June 2007, A13; Hull and Priest, "Little Relief on Ward 53," *Washington Post,* 18 June 2007, A01; Priest and Hull, "Almost Home, But Facing More Delays at Walter Reed," *Washington Post,* 15 September 2007, A01; Hull and Priest, "A Wife's Battle," *Washington Post,* 14 October 2007, A01; Priest and Hull, "A Patient Prosecuted," *Washington Post,* 2 December 2007, A01; and Michel duCille, "The Invisibly Wounded," *Washington Post,* 14 October 2007, also duCille photographs 2 December 2007.

2. Hull and Priest, "Army Fixing Patients' Housing," *Washington Post,* 20 February 2007, A01.

3. Steve Vogel and William Branigin, "Army Fires Commander of Walter Reed," *Washington Post,* 2 March 2007, A01; Michael Abramowitz and Steve Vogel, "Army Secretary Ousted," *Washington Post,* 3 March 2007, A01; Josh White, "Surgeon General of the Army Steps Down," *Washington Post,* 13 March 2007, A01.

4. Priest and Hull, "Recovering at Walter Reed," *Washington Post,* 20 February 2007, http://www.washingtonpost.com/wp-dyn/content/discussion/2007/02/23/DI2007022302220.html. In this online Q&A with the reporters, there was minor criticism of the newspaper's decision

not to acknowledge the earlier published work on the same subject by Mark Benjamin for Salon.com. To this, Priest said, "We weren't the first to bring these issues to the attention of the WR command. The last in a long line, in fact. That's why we were contacted. Apparently no or little action was taken when others stepped forward." See also Mark Benjamin, "Insult to Injury," Salon.com, 27 January 2005; and "Behind the Walls of Ward 54," Salon.com, 18 February 2005.

5. Len Downie, Jr., executive editor, *Washington Post,* to Pulitzer Prize Committee, New York, 25 January 2008, Category 1, Public Service. Letter of Introduction, dated 25 January 2008. Courtesy of the Pulitzer Prize Committee, New York.

6. Downie to Pulitzer Prize Committee. "They proceeded carefully, without identifying themselves to military authorities as they learned about the wounded soldiers' experience and gathered the detail that gave their stories such poignancy." Also, author email exchange with Len Downie, 19 December 2011, who emphasized his opposition to misrepresentation and undercover reporting, which, he said, Walter Reed was not.

7. Priest and Hull, "Soldiers Face Neglect," A01.

8. Howard Kurtz, "The Army's Preemptive News Briefing," *Washington Post,* 24 February 2007, C01. Kurtz, the *Post*'s media columnist, said Priest "declined to explain how she and Hull had repeatedly signed into Walter Reed without the knowledge of the Army brass. Every patient or family member quoted by name, she said, had agreed to be on the record. 'We never lied to anyone about who we were,' Priest said. 'We just tried not to be in a position to identify ourselves to anyone who would report us to public affairs and have us kicked off the base.'" Priest, responding to criticism from Maj. Gen. George Weightman, Walter Reed's soon-to-be-ousted commander, that the reporters should have alerted the army earlier in the process, said it was "ridiculous" and told Kurtz, "You find wrongdoing and you don't report it to the public first? You report it to them first? That's not our role."

9. Lori Robertson, "Uncovering Misery at Walter Reed," *American Journalism Review* 29.2 (April/May 2007): 10. An italicized entry in this Q&A reports: "They say they didn't ask permission before they began reporting but never lied about who they were. They won't elaborate."

10. "Reporters Who Broke Story on Conditions at Walter Reed," narrated by Neal Conan, *Talk of the Nation,* NPR, 6 March 2007. Hull

refers to the successful, hospital-sanctioned two weeks she spent on Walter Reed's amputee ward in 2003 for a two-part series, a 2003 Pulitzer Prize finalist in feature writing, saying that as the war dragged on and both casualties and pressure on the hospital increased, Walter Reed had become "stingy with what they let you see. So, we decided to remove the filter, as it were, and just sort of freelance." Conan asked her to clarify. "Sure," she went on. "I mean we didn't go through the Army for permission, nor did we go through Walter Reed. We went to the soldiers, removing that middle filter, because we wanted to hear what their lives were like, and we wanted to witness these problems firsthand, and that required lots of time with these people as they went through their days."

11. Deborah Howell, "A Powerful Story at Walter Reed," *Washington Post,* 4 March 2007, B6.

12. John Irvine, "Hospitals: Army Pledges Fixes at Walter Reed," *Health Care* (blog), 21 February 2007; Douglas Watts, "The Thing Which Is Not," *Talking Points Memo Reader* (blog), 26 February 2007, http:// www.talkingpointsmemo.com/talk/blogs/douglas_watts/2007/02/the -thing-which-is-not.php; and Andrew Stephen, "Iraq: The Hidden Cost of War," *New Statesman,* 12 March 2007, http://www.newstatesman .com/world-affairs/2007/03/iraq-war-wounded-bilmes-cost.

13. Hull and Priest, "Anne Hull and Dana Priest on Their Walter Reed Stories," *Nieman Reports,* 4 July 2008, http://niemanwatchdog.org/ index.cfm?fuseaction=showcase.view&showcaseid=85. The presentation was March 14–16, 2008, at the 2008 Conference on Narrative Journalism. The Pulitzer Prize announcement was April 8, 2008. See also Al Tompkins, "Anatomy of a Pulitzer: Q&A with Hull and Priest," *Poynteronline,* 8 April 2008, http://www.poynter.org/latest-news/top-stories/88125/ anatomy-of-a-pulitzer-qa-with-hull-and-priest/.

14. Six days before publication of the first *Washington Post* article, Hull and Priest presented officials at Walter Reed with a list of thirty questions in writing.

15. Hull and Priest, "Their Walter Reed Stories"; and Tompkins, "Anatomy of a Pulitzer."

16. Tompkins, "Anatomy of a Pulitzer."

17. Dan Gross, "VA Pokes CBS 3 in the Eye," *Philadelphia Daily News,*

2 April 2007, 41. The story also quoted Rich Manieri, spokesman for the U.S. Attorney's office, saying a CBS 3 crew had been "caught in an area of the nursing facility where they were not allowed to be," resulting in fines to a photographer of $150 for disorderly conduct, $50 for trespassing, and $50 for unauthorized photography, plus two lesser fines to a producer. VA officers confiscated a videotape, a copy of which was returned to the station.

18. There are two relevant points in the *Washington Post*'s Code of Ethics. B1, "The Reporter's Role": "Although it has become increasingly difficult for this newspaper and for the press generally to do so since Watergate, reporters should make every effort to remain in the audience, to stay off the stage, to report the news, not to make the news. In gathering news, reporters will not misrepresent their identity. They will not identify themselves as police officers, physicians or anything other than journalists." J2, "The *Post*'s Principles": "As a disseminator of the news, the paper shall observe the decencies that are obligatory upon a private gentleman." See http://judicial-discipline-reform.org/6TextAuthorities %20Cited%20toeC71/J%20Prof%20respon%20lawyrs%20journlis/19Wash Post%20Ethics17feb99.pdf .

19. Sissela Bok, *Lying: Moral Choice in Public and Private Life* (New York: Vintage Random House, 1999), esp. 8–9, 18, 31, 32–46, 49, 71, 75–106, 112, 117–19, 121, 130–31, 132–45, 138, 177, 179, 181, 213–19. Commonly listed synonyms for "mislead" are "give the wrong impression about," "misinform," "deceive," "lie to," "hoodwink," "delude," and "take in."

20. Vogel and Branigin, "Army Fires Commander."

21. Bill Kovach and Tom Rosenstiel, *The Elements of Journalism: What Newspeople Should Know and the Public Should Expect* (New York: Crown, 2001, 2007), 5–6.

22. John Howard Griffin, "Life as a Negro: Journey into Shame" pts. 1–6, *Sepia* (April 1960): 12–18; (May 1960): 44–52; (June 1960): 32; (July 1960): 30–35; (August 1960): 28–34; (September 1960): 28–34; Griffin, "White Man Turned Negro is Praised and Damned," *Sepia* (October 1960): 11–18.

23. Nellie Bly, *Ten Days in a Mad-House* (New York: Ian L. Munro, n.d. [1887]). http://digital.library.upenn.edu/women/bly/madhouse/madhouse.html.

## CHAPTER TWO

1. James Redpath [John Ball Jr.], "Southern Notes for Northern Circulation," *New York National Anti-Slavery Standard,* 9 December 1854, quoted in John R. McKivigan, ed., *Roving Editor or Talks with Slaves in the Southern States by James Redpath* (University Park: Pennsylvania State University Press, 1996), 143.

2. See Northrop, "Slave Dealing in New Orleans—An Auction," *New York Daily Tribune,* 11 February 1846, 1; W., "Visit to a Slave Auction," *Tribune,* 30 January 1855, 3; Hopper, "A Northerner in New-Orleans," *Tribune,* 16 February 1855, 6; Hopper, "Scenes at a Slave Auction," *Tribune,* 24 March 1855, 6; V., "A Virginia Slave Auction," *Tribune,* 28 March 1856, 6; "From Virginia," *Tribune,* 12 March 1856, 6.

3. Revolutionary figures sometimes used several pseudonyms in the same edition of the same publication to obscure both their identities and their sources; sometimes the device was more of a literary conceit than a disguise (e.g., John Dickinson's "Letters from a Farmer in Pennsylvania," the first of which appeared in the *Pennsylvania Chronicle* the week of November 30, 1767. See R. T. H. Halsey, introduction to *Letters from a Farmer in Pennsylvania,* by John Dickinson [New York: Outlook, 1903]). See also Eran Shalev, "Ancient Masks, American Fathers: Classical Pseudonyms During the American Revolution and Early Republic," *Journal of the Early Republic* 23.2 (2003): 151–72.

4. John R. McKivigan, *Forgotten Firebrands: James Redpath and the Making of Nineteenth Century America* (Ithaca: Cornell University Press, 2008), 6, 196n34.

5. See Traveler, "Facts of Slavery," *New York Daily Tribune,* 17 January 1854, 3; "Facts of Slavery," *Tribune,* 18 August 1854, 2; Kentuckian, "Facts of Slavery in Kentucky," *Tribune,* 1 May 1855, 5; Traveler, "Facts of Slavery," *Tribune,* 17 January 1854, 3.

6. McKivigan, *Roving Editor,* 19.

7. Ibid.

8. Ball, "Southern Notes," quoted in McKivigan, *Roving Editor,* 143.

9. Redpath to Sydney Howard Gay, 6 and 17 November 1854, and 23 January 1855, Gay Papers, quoted in McKivigan, *Roving Editor,* xvii. See also Hopper, "Northerner in New-Orleans," 6; and Hopper, "Scenes

at a Slave Auction," 6; and McKivigan, *Roving Editor,* 143n1. Redpath hastily left Augusta, Georgia, when the newspaper's editor, James Garner, happened to open a letter Redpath received from his sister in Michigan in which she referred to the John Ball letters of November 17 and December 8, 1854.

10. Albert D. Richardson, *The Secret Service: The Field, the Dungeon and the Escape* (Hartford: American, 1865), 121–22. "By rare good fortune, all its correspondents escaped personal harm, while representatives of several other New York journals were waited upon by vigilance committees, driven out, and in some cases imprisoned."

11. Ibid., 20.

12. Ibid., 28, 44, 57–58.

13. Ibid., 57–58.

14. Ibid.

15. Prof. Perri Klass, M.D., email exchange with author, 2 February 2011. See also "Health Information Privacy," *U.S. Department of Health and Human Services,* n.d., http://hhs.gov/ocr/privacy.

16. Pierce Butler was born in Philadelphia. His grandfather, Maj. Pierce Butler, was a senator from South Carolina who wrote the fugitive slave clause.

17. Mortimer Thomson [Q. K. Philander Doesticks, P. B.], "American Civilization Illustrated," *New York Daily Tribune,* 9 March 1859, 5, and various reprints. See also "People and Events: The Weeping Time 1857 [*sic,* actual date is 1859]," PBS, *Africans in America,* n.d., http://www.pbs.org/wgbh/aia/part4/4p2918.html; "Home Summary," *Evangelist* 30.10 (10 March 1859): 5; "A Great Slave Sale at Savannah: Chattels at Public Auction," *Independent* 11.536 (10 March 1859): 1; Dean, "Pierce Butler's Slave Sale," *Independent* 11.537 (17 March 1859): 1; "The Wanderer and the Slave Sale," *Independent* 11.537 (17 March 1859): 1; "Summary of News," *Friends' Review: a Religious, Literary and Miscellaneous Journal* 12.28 (19 March 1859): 448; and Sigma, "Valor for the Church," *Independent* 11.540 (7 April 1859): 2.

18. W., "Visit to a Slave Auction," 3. See also Hopper, "Northerner in New-Orleans," 6; and Hopper, "Scenes at a Slave Auction," 6.

19. "A Slave Auction in Virginia," *New York Daily Tribune,* 10 March 1853, 6; "From Virginia," 6; F., "Virginia Slave Auction," 6.

20. See particularly "A Scene in St. Louis—Slave Auction," *Tribune,* 15 January 1850, 4 ("The critters, after having their mouths examined like horses, and their limbs pulled about to test their soundness."); "A Slave Auction in Virgenia [*sic*]," *Tribune,* 15 January 1850, 6; "Richmond, Va.," *Tribune,* 3 March 1853 ("You really cannot conceive that men in human form could conduct themselves so brutally; each scar or mark is dwelt upon with great minuteness—its cause, its age."); "Visit to a Slave Auction," 6 ("The poor frantic mother begged and implored of 'masser' to 'buy little Jemmie, too'"); and "Virginia Slave Auction," 6. See also Richardson, *Secret Service,* 66–70.

21. These tactics are still in use and have enabled some of the best-remembered reporting ever done, e.g., Hull and Priest at Walter Reed; the tactics white reporters used in the South to cover the civil rights movement a century later; and the investigation at Chappaquiddick. See David Shaw, "Deception—Honest Tool of Reporting?" *Los Angeles Times,* 20 September 1979, B1.

22. Joan D. Hedrick, *Harriet Beecher Stowe: A Life* (New York: Oxford University Press, 1994), 223. The book's publication came in March 1852 as the serial ended in the *National Era.* It sold ten thousand copies in the first two weeks and three hundred thousand in the first year.

23. Harriet Beecher Stowe, letter to Gamaliel Bailey, 9 March 1851, quoted in Hedrick, *Stowe,* 208.

24. Hedrick, *Stowe,* 222: "Even southern critics did not guess how slim was Stowe's firsthand knowledge of the South. . . . Yet Stowe's lack of realism was more than made up for by her ability to manipulate cultural icons. Little Eva aroused sympathy even among southern readers."

25. Harriet Beecher Stowe, *A Key to Uncle Tom's Cabin: Presenting the Original Facts and Documents upon Which the Story Is Founded. Together with Corroborative Statements Verifying the Truth of the Work* (Boston: Jewett, 1853).

26. See Hedrick, *Stowe,* 202–32. At one point during the development of the series, Stowe sought information with unknown results from horses'-mouth sources such as Frederick Douglass and other former slaves turned activists such as Henry Bibb and Josiah Henson, on whose riveting escape experiences she drew.

27. Thanks to Richard R. John for insights and source suggestions.

28. See W., "Visit to a Slave Auction," 3; John Ball Jr., *Boston Liberator,* 4 August 1854 ("Nota Bene—The place I have above described, I should have before mentioned, is the scene of 'Uncle Tom's' sale after the death of St. Clair. Mrs. Stowe has painted it well and faithfully," and references in other letters to "Legree," "Topsy," "Miss 'Phelia"). See also Thomson, "American Civilization Illustrated," 5; and "The Sale of the Butler Slaves," *Tribune,* 30 April 1859, 5.

29. Redpath trained as a stenographer in Scotland. "Kagi was a remarkably skillful phonographer, Redpath a very rapid stenographer, while I brought up the rear." George W. Martin, ed., *Transactions of the Kansas State Historical Society, 1897–1900* (Topeka: W.Y. Morgan, State Printer, 1900), 379.

30. McKivigan, *Roving Editor,* 19.

31. Ibid., 229n10. Redpath worked as a reporter at the Savannah newspaper from mid-April to June 1854.

32. *Dictionary of Literary Biography,* 2005–06 ed., s.v. "Thomson, Mortimer," by David E. Sloane, quoted in *Dictionary of American Biography,* s.v. "Thomson, Mortimer," by Franklin J. Meine, who writes, "He brought to American humor terse, vigorous, quick-moving phrases and vivid slang, and became the most popular humorist writing in the period before that of C.F. Browne."

33. Archibald Henderson and Alvin Langdon Coburn, *Mark Twain* (New York: Stokes, 1910), 47. "Mr. Clemens once remarked to me: 'I succeeded in the long run, where Shillaber, Doesticks, and Billings failed, because they never had an ideal higher than that of merely being funny.'"

34. J. Louis Kuethe, "Q.K. Philander Doesticks, P.B., Neologist," *American Speech* 12.2 (1937): 111–16.

35. "Great Auction-Sale of Slaves, at Savannah, Georgia," *Atlantic Monthly* 4.23 (September 1859), 386–87.

36. His books were titled *Doesticks: What He Says* (1850), *Plu-ri-bustah* (1856), *The History and Records of the Elephant Club* (with Edward F. Underhill) (1856), *Nothing to Say* (1857), and, the most recent before being sent to Savannah, *The Witches of New York* (1858). See also "The Doesticks Letters," *New York Daily Tribune,* 23 January 1855.

37. "The Witches of New-York," nos. 1–16, *New York Daily Tribune,* 22 January 1857, 6; 23 January 1857, 6; 24 January 1857, 3; 27 January 1857,

5; 28 January 1857, 7; 31 January 1857, 5; 6 February 1857, 5; 13 February 1857, 6; 14 February 1857, 5; 24 February 1857, 7; 25 February 1857, 7; 2 April 1857, 6; 4 April 1857, 10; 25 April 1857, 9; 9 May 1857, 10; and 20 May 1857, 7.

38. *Dictionary of Literary Biography,* s.v. "Thomson, Mortimer."

39. Thomson, *The Witches of New York* (Philadelphia: T. B. Peterson, 1858), 22–23.

40. "Arrest of the Fortune Tellers," *New York Daily Tribune,* 23 October 1858, 5.

41. "Crackdown on Quackery," *Life,* 1 November 1963, 72. Two *Life* magazine staffers collaborated with the office of the Los Angeles County District Attorney to gain access to the home of Antone Dietemann, one posing as a patient's husband. With a hidden camera and concealed audio equipment, they photographed and recorded the visit, which included a diagnosis of a breast lump that Dietemann said was caused by consuming rancid butter exactly eleven years, nine months, and seven days earlier. The recordings were turned over to the district attorney in exchange for the right to publish the photographs. Dietemann was convicted of fraud in criminal court, but subsequently brought a civil action for invasion of privacy and was awarded $1,000. The case was one of the first to debate the use of hidden recording devices and has since served as an important precedent for hidden-camera cases.

42. Fletcher Daniel Slater, "The Life and Letters of Mortimer Thomson" (M.A. diss., Northwestern University, August 1931), 176.

43. Thomson, "American Civilization Illustrated," 5. Special thanks to Patricia O'Toole for pointing out the piece. See O'Toole, *Money and Morals in America: A History* (New York: Potter, 1998), 113–42.

44. Thomson, "American Civilization Illustrated," 5.

45. The time is approximated from 1855 timetables of the South Atlantic Coast railroad. Without waits, the time involved would have been at least thirty-six hours.

46. "Notice," *New York Daily Tribune,* 11 March 1859, quoted in Malcolm Bell Jr., *Major Butler's Legacy* (Athens: University of Georgia Press, 1987), 331.

47. "Sale of the Butler Slaves," 5.

48. "Great Auction-Sale," 386.

49. "Sale of the Butler Slaves," 5.

50. Horace Greeley, *Aunt Sally, Come Up! Or, the Nigger Sale* (London: Ward and Lock, 1859). See also Mortimer Thomson [Q. K. Philander Doesticks], *What Became of the Slaves on a Georgia Plantation? Great Auction Sale of Slaves, at Savannah, Georgia, March 2d and 3d, 1859. A Sequel to Mrs. Kemble's Journal* (n.p.: American Anti-Slavery Society, 1863).

51. "Reviews and Literary Notices," *Atlantic Monthly* 4.23 (September 1859).

52. *Savannah Daily Morning News,* 15 March 1859, quoted in Bell, *Major Butler's Legacy,* 330.

53. *Savannah Republican,* 15 March 1859, quoted in Bell, *Major Butler's Legacy,* 330.

54. "Great Auction-Sale," *Atlantic Monthly* 4.23, 386.

55. See Fanny Kemble, *Journal of a Residence on a Georgia Plantation in 1838–1839* (Athens: University of Georgia Press, 1984). See also Catherine Clinton, ed., *Fanny Kemble's Journals* (Cambridge: Harvard University Press, 2000); and Deirdre David, *Fanny Kemble: A Performed Life* (Philadelphia: University of Pennsylvania Press, 2007). Kemble spent time on both plantations with her then husband after he inherited the properties. The journals—written not in the haze of memoir but as actual correspondence while she was living the experience—covered her two years as plantation mistress. For a quarter of a century, protective of her children though the marriage was long over, she only shared the journals privately. By 1863, she agreed to publication in book form.

56. See Joe Lockard, *Watching Slavery: Witness Texts and Travel Reports* (New York: Peter Lang, 2008), xv.

57. Bell, *Major Butler's Legacy,* 332–33. To Thomson's credit, Bell points out the following: "When reporter Thomson remarked on the absence of 'light mulattoes' with very few of the Pierce Butler slaves being 'even a shade removed from the original Congo blackness,' he cast light on the division process in which the many mulattoes known to have been on the plantations were purposely left behind as the property of the John Butler estate. He gave his reason, citing that pure-blooded Negroes were more readily marketable, they being 'more docile and manageable' than those of mixed blood."

58. Lockard, *Watching Slavery*, viii, xxii. Lockard observes what he calls Thomson's "racist preconceptions," his "objectification and stereotyping of blacks" and his "observational location atop white privilege."

59. Brooke Kroeger, "Journalism with a Scholar's Intent," *Zoned for Debate*, 16 October 2002, NYU Arthur L. Carter Journalism Institute Faculty Web Forum, http://journalism.nyu.edu/publishing/archives/debate/forum.1.essay.kroger.html.

60. West Virginia did not become a state until 1863.

61. A check of indexed *Tribune* articles datelined Charlestown in 1859 shows none with bylines.

62. Henry S. Olcott, "How We Hung John Brown," in *Lotos Leaves: Original Stories, Essays, and Poems,* ed. John Brougham and John Elderkin (Boston: Gill, 1875), 233–49. See also Charlestown-datelined but un-bylined correspondence in the *New York Daily Tribune,* 28 November–10 December 1859: "John Brown's Invasion," 28 November 1859, 6; "Further from Charlestown. Additional Troops Expected," 29 November 1859, 5; "From Charlestown. A Visit to the Prisoners," 30 November 1859, 5; "John Brown's Invasion," 30 November 1859, 6; "From Charlestown. A Pro-Slavery Clergyman," 1 December 1859, 5; "John Brown's Invasion," 1 December 1859, 6; "From Charlestown. The Visits of Clergymen," 2 December 1859, 5; "The Execution of John Brown. He Makes No Speech," 3 December 1859, 7; "John Brown's Invasion," 5 December 1859, 5; "John Brown's Invasion. Further Interesting Incidents of the Execution," 6 December 1859, 6; "John Brown's Invasion. The Fugitives—Cooke and Virginia in Kansas," 7 December 1859, 3; "John Brown's Invasion. The Martial Law Illegal—Reaction against Wise," 8 December 1859, 6.

63. Olcott, "How We Hung John Brown," 233–49.

64. Ibid.

65. Ibid.

66. Merrill D. Peterson, *John Brown: The Legend Revisited* (Charlottesville: University of Virginia Press, 2004), 46: "Edward F. Underhill, the erstwhile *Tribune* correspondent, said he had written the story in the New York office from secondhand reports. An alternate attribution was to the *Tribune*'s Henry S. Olcott." See also Cecil D. Eby Jr., "Whittier's 'Brown of Ossawatomie,'" *New England Quarterly* 33.4 (1960): 452–61 n13.

## CHAPTER THREE

1. Doug Munro, "The Origins of Labourers in the South Pacific: Commentary and Statistics," in Clive Moore, Jacqueline Leckie, and Doug Munro, eds., *Labour in the South Pacific* (Townsville: James Cook University, 1992), xxxix–li.

2. "Slavery by another name," *Sioux Valley News,* 6 October 1892, 1.

3. Lo Hui-min, ed., *The Correspondence of G. E. Morrison,* vol. 2 (Cambridge: Cambridge University Press, 1976), 2.

4. George Morrison [A Medical Student], "The Contributor: A Cruise in a Queensland Slaver," *Leader* (Melbourne), 21 October 1882, 36.

5. Morrison, "The Contributor," 36.

6. Editorial, *Age* (Melbourne), 10 May 1883, 4. See also *Australian Dictionary of Biography,* vol. 10, ed. 1986, s.v. "Morrison, George Ernest (Chinese) (1862–1920)," by J. S. Gregory.

7. George Morrison, "The Queensland Slave Trade," *Age,* 9 May 1883, 7.

8. Morrison, "Queensland Slave Trade," 9 May 1883, 7.

9. Editorial, *Age,* 4.

10. Letter to the Editor, *Age,* 10 May 1883, 7; 14 May 1883, 1.

11. "The *Lavinia* Outrages," *Brisbane Courier,* 9 February 1884, 5.

12. "Occasional Notes," *West Australian* (Perth), 11 March 1884, 3. As it happened, Morrison does not appear to have followed up on his willingness to carry his charges to Britain. He went immediately on a two-month walk to Melbourne, chronicled in the *Argus.* The trip took him 2,000 miles in 123 days. See Peter Thompson and Robert Macklin, *The Man Who Died Twice* (Crows Nest, NSW: Allen and Unwin, 2004).

13. "Occasional Notes," 3, which read in part: "The Governor, in his dispatch, states he regrets that he is unable to agree with Mr. Griffith in his opinion that the evidence taken at the enquiry elicited no facts corroborated in the slightest degree Mr. Morrison's serious accusations. His Excellency observes that the evidence is that of witnesses more or less implicated in the offences charged, and that a simple denial of the accuracy of Mr. Morrison's statements by no means amounts to a disproof, while a good deal that is distinctly admitted is not inconsistent with Mr. Morrison's narrative."

14. "The Pacific Labor Trade—Report of the Western Pacific Commission," *Age,* 10 March 1884, 5.

15. For more about Morrison, see Thompson and Macklin, *Man Who Died Twice,* and *Australian Dictionary of Biography,* s.v. "Morrison, George Ernest (Chinese)."

16. "The Brig Was Bottom Up," *New York Tribune,* 30 November 1891, 1. The postmortem reports that on August 19, the brig was "caught in a squall. The topsails were blown into shreds and both foresail and mainsail were carried away. The vessel lurched in the heavy seas, and the islanders, cooped up in the hold, were thrown into deadly terror."

17. "The News This Morning," *New York Daily Tribune,* 8 September 1891, 6.

18. "The *Tahiti*'s Passengers Not Slaves," *New York Daily Tribune,* 9 September 1891, 7.

19. "Is It a Cargo of Slaves?" *New York Daily Tribune,* 8 September 1891, 1.

20. Ibid.

21. Ibid.

22. Ibid., 7. See also, "The *Tahiti* Carried No Slaves," *Daily Tribune,* 1 December 1891, 5. After the tragedy, Humphrey Leavitt's family and friends continued to insist to the *Tribune* the ship was not a slaver.

23. "Brig Was Bottom Up," 1.

24. "*Tahiti* Disaster: Another Chapter in the Mishaps That Befell the Slave Trading Vessel," *Hamilton Daily Democrat,* 21 July 1892, 1.

25. See Arthur Inkersley and W.H. Brommage, "Experiences of a Blackbirder Among the Gilbert Islanders," *Overland Monthly* 23.138 (June 1894): 565–75; also, Inkersley, "A Trip to the Kingsmill Islands on a Labor-Vessel," *Travel* 1.6 (January 1896): 443–46.

26. Melvin's ship, also known as *The Bundaberg,* left the Burnett River on July 30 and returned on November 18, 1892. Brommage's voyage on *The Montserrat* began from San Francisco April 23 and returned October 14. See also J. D. Melvin and Peter Corris, eds., *The Cruise of the Helena: A Labour-Recruiting Voyage to the Solomon Islands* (Melbourne, AU: Hawthorn Press, 1977); W. H. Brommage, "A Sale of Souls," *San Francisco Examiner,* 15 October 1892, 1; and "A Representative on a Recruiting

Schooner, the Kanaka Labour Traffic: Special Investigation by *The Argus*," *Argus*, 3 December 1892, 9.

27. David McCreery and Doug Munro, "The Cargo of the *Montserrat*: Gilbertese Labor in Guatemalan Coffee, 1890–1906," *Americas* 49:3 (January 1993): 271–95.

28. "Representative on a Recruiting Schooner," 3 December 1892, 9.

29. Ibid., 9.

30. *Australian Dictionary of Biography*, vol. 10, ed. 1986, "Melvin, Joseph Dalgarno (1852–1909)," by Peter Corris. See also source references.

31. "Representative on a Recruiting Schooner," 3 December 1892, 9.

32. "The Kanaka Labour Traffic: A Full Ship. The Nineteenth 'Boy' Obtained," *Argus*, 19 December 1892, 5–6.

33. "Sale of Souls," 1–2.

34. Ibid., 1–2.

35. Brommage, "The Blackbird Cruise: Further Details of the Slaver '*Montserrat*'s' Expedition to the Gilbert Islands," *San Francisco Examiner*, 16 October 1892, 1–2. "They have a careless way of leaving things just where they use them last. If they want water to bathe they draw it over the side of the vessel in a bucket. They take a rope's end and make fast to the bucket and heave it over. The first rope's end they reach suits them; no matter how much importance it may have as part of the running gear of the vessel it makes no difference to them. After they have hauled up the water they drop the bucket then, and it is still attached to the rope's end. It may be a buntline, halliard, or any other important line. Suppose the sails are set, and a squall arises which makes it necessary to take in the sails quickly. The ropes are let go in an instant. Up fly the buckets and pails like a flock of birds and as they are made fast to the ropes and cannot pass through the holes in the fair leads, the sails are still set, and the entire crew must devote its attention to untying the buckets and the old clothes and thousand and one articles that the sailors found tied to the ropes' ends. By that time a quick squall could capsize the vessel."

36. "Sale of Souls," 15 October 1892, 1–2.

37. "Ferguson's Story," *San Francisco Examiner*, 16 October 1892, 2.

38. Ibid.

39. Ibid.

40. Brommage, "Blackbird Cruise," 15 October 1892, 1–2.

41. "Ferguson's Story," 16 October 1892, 2.

## CHAPTER FOUR

1. W. T. Stead, "The Maiden Tribute of Modern Babylon" pts. 1–4, *Pall Mall Gazette,* 6 July 1885, 1–6; 7 July 1885, 1–6; 8 July 1885, 1–5; 10 July 1885, 1–6.

2. For more on the Stead investigation and links to the articles and significant ancillary material, see Owen Mulpetre, W. T. Stead Resource Site, http://attackingthedevil.co.uk.

3. It was not the first undercover effort of the *Pall Mall Gazette,* which sent reporter James Greenwood to spend a night in a London workhouse as far back as 1867. See James Greenwood, "A Night in a Workhouse," in Peter Keating, ed., *Into Unknown England, 1866–1913: Selections from the Social Explorers* (Manchester, UK: Manchester University Press, 1976), quoted in Michael Robertson, *Stephen Crane, Journalism, and the Making of Modern American Literature* (New York: Columbia University Press, 1997), 95.

4. Stead, "Modern Babylon," pt. 1, 6 July 1885.

5. Ibid.

6. Stead, "Modern Babylon" pt. 1, 8 July 1885: "We knew that we had forged a thunderbolt; but even we were hardly prepared for the overwhelming impression which it has produced on the public mind. The great monopoly of railway bookstalls that bears the name of one of the members of an Administration which had just declared in favour of amending the law to deal with the criminals we have exposed, forbade the sale of the most convincing demonstration of the necessity for such legislation. This helped us somewhat by reducing a demand which we were still utterly unable to meet. In view of the enormous result that has followed the simple setting forth of a few of the indisputable facts which the public has hitherto been afraid to face, we are filled with a new confidence and a greater hope. With all humility we feel tempted to exclaim with the martyr Ridley, 'Be of good cheer, for we have this day lighted up such a flame in England as I trust in God shall never be extinguished.'"

7. Jennifer Doyle, *Sex Objects: Art and the Dialectics of Desire* (Minneapolis: University of Minnesota Press, 2006), 58–59n51, 162.

8. "Social Crime in London," *Independent,* 16 July 1885, 1911.

9. Doyle, *Sex Objects,* 58–59n51, 162.

10. "Social Crime in London," 16 July 1885, 1911.

11. Ibid.

12. One domestic documentary project involved some undercover segments: *Very Young Girls,* directed by David Schisgall, Nina Alvarez, and Priya Swaminathan (Showtime Independent Films, 2007).

13. Special thanks to Ryann Liebenthal for culling and helping to synthesize the collected research on contemporary iterations of this topic.

14. Rebecca Leung, "Rescued from Sex Slavery: *48 Hours* Goes Undercover into the International Sex Slave Trade," *48 Hours,* CBS, 23 February 2005.

15. Leung, "Rescued from Sex Slavery."

16. "Girls for Sale," narrated by Cynthia McFadden, Diane Sawyer, and Charles Gibson, *20/20,* ABC, 2 June 1999.

17. Ric Esther Bienstock, "Sex Slaves: Director's Notes," *Frontline,* PBS, 7 February 2006, http://www.pbs.org/wgbh/pages/frontline/slaves/making/>. For more details on the project, see Ric Esther Bienstock, "Sex Slaves: Transcript," *Frontline,* PBS, 7 February 2006, http://www.pbs.org/wgbh/pages/frontline/slaves/etc/script.html; and "Sex Slaves: The Making of This Film—An Interview with Ric Esther Bienstock," *Frontline,* PBS, 7 February 2006, http://www.pbs.org/wgbh/pages/frontline/slaves/making/bienstock.html>.

18. Bienstock, "Sex Slaves: Transcript."

19. "Sex Slaves: Join the Discussion," *Frontline,* PBS, 7 February 2006, http://www.pbs.org/wgbh/pages/frontline/slaves/talk/.

20. "2006 Silver Baton: HBO, 'Real Sports with Bryant Gumbel: The Sport of Sheikhs,'" Alfred I. duPont Columbia University Awards in Broadcast News, n.d., http://www.dupontawards.org/year/2006#2009_goldbaton.

21. "The Sport of Sheikhs," *Real Sports with Bryant Gumbel,* produced by Joseph Perskie, Correspondent, and Bernard Goldberg, HBO, 19 October 2004.

22. "Sport of Sheikhs."

23. Simon Hattenstone, "Undercover and Overexposed," *Guardian,* 5 December 2007.

24. Wallraff's books in English translation include the following collection of articles: *The Undesirable Journalist* (Woodstock: Overlook Press, 1979), and *The Lowest of the Low* (London: Methuen, 1985). The few other sources in English on Wallraff include: Abbie Hoffman, "Undercover in the New Germany: The Many Cloaks and Daggers of Günter Wallraff," *Mother Jones,* February–March 1979, 44–54; Victoria Tschirch, *The Sphere of Rigour Reporting: An Essay on Investigative Journalism and Its Importance: In General and In Some Respects to New Zealand* (Germany: Grin Verlag, 2008), 19; Wolfgang Beulin, *A History of German Literature: From the Beginnings to Its Present Day* (London: Routledge, 1993), 608–609. John Pilger, ed., *Tell Me No Lies: Investigative Journalism That Changed the World* (New York: Thunder's Mouth Press, 2005), 158–59; and A. Sivanandan's introduction to selections from Wallraff's investigation of Germany's immigrant workers' culture, *Lowest of the Low,* 159–73.

25. Wallraff, *Undesirable Journalist,* 1.

26. Wallraff, *Lowest of the Low,* xi–xii.

27. Ibid., xi.

28. Sivanandan, introduction to Wallraff, *Lowest of the Low,* xiv.

29. Abbie Hoffman, "Undercover in the New Germany" (also available via Google books).

30. Ibid.

31. Fabrizio Gatti, "I Was a Slave in Puglia," trans. Wolfgang Achtner, *L'Espresso* (Rome), 4 September 2006. Gatti describes how he pretended to be a South African migrant worker in order to join a group of other Africans working in horrifying conditions for fifteen to twenty euros a day and often less or nothing at all.

32. Roberto Saviano, *Gomorrah* (New York: Picador, 2006).

33. Giles Tremlett, "Carlos the Jackal Was My Friend," *Guardian,* 10 October 2010.

34. Nicholas Schmidle, "Smuggler, Forger, Writer, Spy," *Atlantic,* 16 October 2010, 110–14.

35. Department of State, *Trafficking in Persons Report* (Washington, D.C.: Government Printing Office, June 2008), http://www.state.gov/documents/organization/105655.pdf.

36. "Anas Is Journalist of the Year," Myjoyonline.com, 19 August 2010, http://news.myjoyonline.com/news/200708/7748.asp.

37. "Winners of the 2008 Kurt Schork Awards in International Journalism," Institute for War and Peace Reporting, n.d., http://iwpr.net/special/winners-2008-kurt-schork-awards, accessed 8 February 2011.

38. "Every Human Has Rights Media Awards," Internews Europe, n.d., http://www.internews.eu/projects/every-human-has-rights-media-awards, accessed 8 February 2011.

39. Schmidle, "Smuggler, Forger, Writer, Spy."

40. Anas Aremeyaw Anas, "Sex Ghetto Raided," *Crusading Guide* (Ghana), 28 January 2008.

41. Anas, "Sex Ghetto Raided."

42. Michael Haddon, "I Have Chosen to Belong to the Remedy," Journalism.co.uk, 25 November 2008, http://www.journalism.co.uk/news-features/-i-have-chosen-to-belong-to-the-remedy—ghana-s-anas-aremayew-anas-on-undercover-journalism/s5/a532917/. Anas was speaking to a meeting of the Centre for Investigative Journalism on November 24, 2008.

43. Peter Johnson, "*Dateline* Roots Out Predators; Men Seeking Teens for Sex via Internet," *USA Today,* 15 February 2006, B9.

44. Scott Collins, "CBS Blog Takes Some Swipes at NBC's *Dateline,*" *Los Angeles Times,* 31 March 2006, E27.

45. Jesse Wegman, "Dateline: To Kill a Predator," *Huffington Post,* 23 February 2007.

46. Deborah Potter, "Over the Line: The Questionable Tactics of 'To Catch a Predator,'" *American Journalism Review* 29.4 (August/September 2007): 54.

47. Paul Farhi, "*Dateline* Pedophile Sting: One More Point; NBC Collaboration Raises Eyebrows as Well as Awareness," *Washington Post,* 9 April 2006, D01.

48. Douglas McCollam, "The Shame Game," *Columbia Journalism Review* 45.5 (January/February 2007): 28–33.

49. Collins, "Swipes at NBC's *Dateline,*" 31 March 2006, E27.

50. Paul Farhi, "*Dateline* Pedophile Sting."

51. McCollam, "The Shame Game," 28–33.

52. Farhi, "*Dateline* Pedophile Sting"; Chris Hansen, "Ethics of NBC's Sting Show 'To Catch a Predator,'" NPR, 16 January 2007; McCollam, "The Shame Game," 28–33.

53. Peter Franceschina and Jon Burstein, "TV Sting Prompts Ethics Debate: Prosecutor's Arrest Spurs Discussion of Journalists' Roles, Authorities, Disclose Details of Investigation," *South Florida Sun-Sentinel,* 23 January 2003, 1B.

54. "Social Crime in London."


## CHAPTER FIVE

1. Helen Campbell, *The Problem of the Poor: A Record of Quiet Work in Unquiet Places* (New York: Fords, 1882), 23.

2. Weeks was her married name before divorce. See American Periodical Series Online via Proquest under search terms author "Helen C. Weeks" and dates "January to December 1871," which shows regular publication in both magazines, *Our Young Folks* and *Youth's Companion.* See biographical entries, "Working Women, 1800–1930," Harvard Open Collection Program, n.d., http://ocp.hul.harvard.edu/ww/people_campbell.html, accessed 8 February 2011; Frances E. Willard and Mary A. Livermore, ed., *A Woman of the Century: Fourteen Hundred-Seventy Biographical Sketches Accompanied by Portraits of Leading American Women in All Walks of Life* (Buffalo: Moulton, 1893), 147; Ross E. Paulson, "Helen Stuart Campbell," in *Notable American Women, 1607–1950* (Cambridge: Belknap, 1974), 280–81; and Robert W. Dimand, "Nineteenth-Century American Feminist Economics: From Caroline Dall to Charlotte Perkins Gilman," *American Economic Review* (May 2000): 480–84.

3. Helen Campbell, "The City of the Simple," *Lippincott's* 24.144 (December 1879): 698–706.

4. The social reform work appeared first between January and July 1879 in Sunday *Afternoon* magazine in a series of six prose sketches, followed by six more pieces the following year for *Lippincott's* under the common header, STUDIES IN THE SLUMS. That too ran serially, from

May to October 1880. Campbell, "An Experience Meeting in Water Street," *Sunday Afternoon,* January 1879, 53–61; Campbell, "Sunday in Water Street, II," *Sunday Afternoon,* February 1879, 167–74; Campbell, "The Tenement House Question," *Sunday Afternoon,* April 1879, 317–23; Campbell, "Six Stories in One," *Sunday Afternoon,* May 1879, 393–98; Campbell, "An Experiment and What Came of It," *Sunday Afternoon,* June 1879, 537–44; Campbell, "Max," *Sunday Afternoon,* July 1879, 624–30; Campbell, "Studies in the Slums," pts. 1–6, *Lippincott's,* May 1880, 568–73; June 1880, 740–45; July 1880, 103–109; August 1880, 213–17; September 1880, 362–67; October 1880, 498–502.

5. Campbell, preface to *Problem of the Poor.*

6. Campbell, "Mrs. Herndon's Income," pts. 1–27, *Christian Union,* 12 March 1885, 9–11; 19 March 1885, 9–11; 26 March 1885, 9–11; 2 April 1885, 9–11; 9 April 1885, 13–16; 16 April 1885, 9–11; 23 April 1885, 9–11; 30 April 1885, 9–11; 7 May 1885, 9–11; 14 May 1885, 9–11; 21 May 1885, 10–11; 28 May 1885, 10–11; 4 June 1885, 9–11; 11 June 1885, 9–11; 18 June 1885, 9–11; 25 June 1885, 9–11; 2 July 1885, 9–11; 9 July 1885, 9–11; 16 July 1885, 9–11; 23 July 1885, 9–11; 30 July 1885, 9–11; 6 August 1885, 9–11; 13 August 1885, 9–11; 20 August 1885, 9–11; 27 August 1885, 9–11; 3 September 1885, 10–11; and 10 September 1885, 10–11. See also Campbell, *Mrs. Herndon's Income: A Novel* (Boston: Roberts, 1886).

7. Review of *Mrs. Herndon's Income,* by Helen Campbell, *New York Times,* 22 November 1885, 5. Of the novel, this critic wrote: "A great many incidents in the story seem to have been taken from actual facts." See also review of *Mrs. Herndon's Income,* by Helen Campbell, *New-York Tribune,* 22 November 1885, 8: "Much of it [the novel] indeed is so strong that we find ourselves wondering where Mrs. Campbell got her ample experience of life. Its variety is not less remarkable than its truthfulness."

8. "From Home Economics to Human Ecology: A One Hundred-Year History at the University of Wisconsin-Madison—Campbell, Helen Stuart (1839–1918)," University of Wisconsin-Madison's School of Human Ecology, n.d., http://www.sohe.wisc.edu/depts/history/bios/campbell .htm, accessed 8 February 2011.

9. Campbell, "Prisoners of Poverty," pts. 1–21, *New York Daily Tribune,* 24 October 1886, 13; 31 October 1886, 13; 7 November 1886, 13; 14 November 1886, 13; 21 November 1886, 13; 28 November 1886, 13;

5 December 1886, 13; 12 December 1886, 13; 19 December 1886, 13; 26 December 1886, 10; 2 January 1887, 10; 9 January 1887, 10; 16 January 1887, 10; 23 January 1887, 10; 30 January 1887, 10; 6 February 1887, 10; 13 February 1887, 9; 20 February 1887, 10; 27 February 1887, 10; 6 March 1887, 10; and 13 March 1887, 10.

10. Susan Henry, "Reporting Deeply and at First Hand: Campbell in the Nineteenth-Century Slums," *Journalism History,* 11.1–2 (Spring/Summer 1984): 18–25, quoted in Patricia Bradley, *Women and the Press: The Struggle for Equality* (Evanston: Northwestern University Press, 2005), 144.

11. Campbell, *Prisoners of Poverty Abroad* (Boston: Roberts, 1889).

12. William Dean Howells, "Editor's Study," *Harper's,* August 1889, 479.

13. "The Prisoners of Poverty," *New York Daily Tribune,* 17 October 1886, 4.

14. Campbell, *Prisoners of Poverty: Women Wage Workers, Their Trades, and Their Lives* (Boston: Little, 1900), 10.

15. Ida Tarbell, "Women in Journalism" *Chautauquan,* April 1887, 395. For other positive reviews of *Prisoners of Poverty,* see *New-York Tribune,* 14 April 1887, 6; *Literary World,* 28 May 1887, 169; *Chautauquan,* June 1887, 573; *Critic: A Weekly Review of Literature and the Arts,* 11 June 1887, 294; *Overland Monthly and Out West,* March 1889, 327; *Church Review,* June 1887, 688; *Independent,* 28 April 1887, 12; and *Washington Post,* 17 April 1887, 4.

16. Tarbell, "Women in Journalism," 395.

17. Author telephone interviews and email exchanges with Steve Weinberg, Tarbell's biographer, 27 November 2007, 27 August 2009, and 8–10 June 2010. See also Steve Weinberg, *Taking on the Trust: The Epic Battle of Ida Tarbell and John D. Rockefeller* (New York: Norton, 2008).

18. See Hazel Dicken-Garcia, *Journalistic Standards in Nineteenth-Century America* (Madison: University of Wisconsin Press, 1989), 183–222. Although press criticism was lively in this period, the matter of the undercover method appears not to have been addressed directly.

19. Brooke Kroeger, *Nellie Bly: Daredevil, Reporter, Feminist* (New York: Times Books, 1994), 507.

20. Nellie Bly, "Nellie Bly Again—She Interviews Emma Goldman and Other Anarchists," *New York World,* 17 September 1893, 1–5; and

Bly, "Nellie Bly in Pullman—She Visits Homes of Poverty in the 'Model Workingman's Town,'" *New York World,* 11 July 1894, 5.

21. Kroeger, *Nellie Bly,* 85–99, 139–73.

22. Bly's personal columns for the *New York World* were unsuccessful, but her later column in 1919–1922 for the *New York Evening Journal* was better received. See Kroeger, *Nellie Bly,* 278.

23. Bly, "The King of the Lobby," *New York World,* 1 April 1888, 19.

24. Bly, "What Becomes of Babies," *New York World,* 6 November 1887, 10.

25. Bly, "Wanted—A Few Husbands," *New York World,* 4 December 1887, 25.

26. Bly, "Visiting the Dispensaries," *New York World,* 2 December 1888, 9.

27. Bly, "Nellie Bly as a Mesmerist," *New York World,* 25 March 1888, 19.

28. Bly, "Trying to Be a Servant," *New York World,* 30 October 1887, 9.

29. Bly, "The Girls Who Make Boxes," *New York World,* 27 November 1887, 10.

30. Bly, "Nellie Bly on the Stage," *New York World,* 4 March 1888, 15.

31. Bly, "Shadowed by a Detective—Nellie Bly Makes a Test of the Private Spy Nuisance," *New York World,* 28 April 1889, 13.

32. Bly, "Magdalen Home," *New York World,* 12 February 1888.

33. Bly, "In the Biggest New York Tenement," *New York World,* 5 August 1894, 21.

34. Bly, "Nellie Bly A Prisoner—She Has Herself Arrested to Gain Entrance to a Station-House," *New York World,* 24 February 1889, 9.

35. "The Plain Facts," *Minneapolis Tribune,* 13 May 1888, quoted in Elizabeth Faue, *Writing the Wrongs: Eva Valesh and the Rise of Labor Journalism* (Ithaca: Cornell University Press, 2002), 9. A typical passage from Gay's reporting: "When I got to the factory, I found myself breathing an atmosphere whose distinguishing characteristics were a smell of new cloth, dust, heat and sewer gas. Where does the sewer gas come from? I asked as an extra-strong whiff made me feel faint. A stout German girl nearby said, 'Oh, tisn't very bad now, but most every day the water be not running in the toilets for an hour or so at a time, but of course they are used just the same. The smell is awful then: some of the girls get sick almost every day.'"

36. James McGrath Morris, *The Rose Man of Sing Sing* (New York: Fordham University Press, 2003), 83–88n377.

37. Nell Nelson, "City Slave Girls," *Chicago Daily Times,* 30 July 1888, 1, 2; 31 July 1888, 1, 2; 1–4 August 1888, 1, 2; 5 August 1888, 17; 6–11 August 1888, 1, 2; 12 August 1888, 17; 13–18 August 1888, 1, 2; and 19 August 1888, 17.

38. Nell Nelson, *The White Slave Girls of Chicago* (Chicago: Barkley, 1888).

39. "Thanks 'The Times,'" *Chicago Daily Times,* 21 August 1888, 1.

40. Mary McGray, letter to the editor, "*Chicago Daily Times,* 27 August 1888, 1.

41. McGray, letter to the editor, 1.

42. Ibid.

43. Nelson, "City Slave Girls," 27 August 1888, 1.

44. "A Libel Suit for $50,000," *Dunkirk Observer-Journal,* 1 August 1888, 1.

45. *Evening Gazette,* 16 October 1888, 2.

46. Nell Nelson, "White Slave Girls," *New York World,* 23 September 1888, 17; 14 October 1888, 17; 21 October 1888, 20; 11 November 1888, 12; 18 November 1888, 9; 25 November 1888, 21; 2 December 1888, 20; 16 December 1888, 22; as cited in Kroeger, *Bly,* 550, notes to pp. 120, 121.

47. The *Weekly Sun* series ran from October to December 1893, titled IN CAP AND APRON. For a fuller treatment of Elizabeth L. Banks's career, see chapter 3 of Seth Koven, *Slumming: Sexual and Social Politics in Victorian London* (Princeton: Princeton University Press, 2004), 141–80. See also Banks, *Campaigns & Curiosity: Journalistic Adventures of an American Girl in Late Victorian London* (London: Cassell, 1894); and Banks, *The Autobiography of a "Newspaper Girl"* (London: Methuen, 1902).

48. Banks, *Autobiography.*

49. William L. Alden, "London Letter: Written for The *New York Times Sunday Review of Books* by William L. Alden," *New York Times Sunday Review of Books,* 18 October 1902, BR6. Alden also took exception to Banks's characterization of herself as a "newspaper girl," writing, "The male reporter who has reached the age of Miss Banks does not call himself a 'newspaper boy.'"

50. Lucy Hosmer, "Factory Girls in a Big City," *St. Louis Post-Dispatch,* 26 November 1896, 1, quoted in Morris, *Rose Man,* 133n383.

51. "Tramps with the Genius of London," *Toronto Daily Mail,* 12 March–16 April 1892, 5, first cited in Barbara M. Freeman, *Kit's Kingdom: The Journalism of Kathleen Blake Coleman* (Carleton: Ottawa University Press, 1989), 83–84n98.

52. "Tramps" 5.

53. Judith Adler, "Youth on the Road: Reflections on the History of Tramping," *Annals of Tourism Research* 12.3 (1985): 335–54. She notes how tramping was the middle class equivalent of the Grand Tour for many, separating the tourists from those who saw their travels as an actual or ersatz sociological study, though both often saw publication.

54. See Jill Downie, *A Passionate Pen: The Life and Times of Faith Fenton* (Toronto: HarperCollins, 1996).

55. Charles H. Garrett, "Lived Three Months on Five Cents a Day," *New York Evening World,* 18 July 1898, 1.

56. Catherine King, "Girl Toilers of the City," *New York Evening World,* 26 July 1898, 7, quoted in Morris, *Rose Man,* 144.

57. For a much fuller treatment of tramping, see such works as Adler, "Youth on the Road," 335–54; Todd Depastino, *Citizen Hobo: How a Century of Homelessness Shaped America* (Chicago: University of Chicago Press, 2003); Koven, *Slumming;* and Kenneth L. Kusmer, *Down and Out, On the Road: The Homeless in American History* (New York: Oxford University Press, 2002).

58. Earle Labor, Robert C. Leitz III, and I. Milo Shepard, eds., *The Letters of Jack London* (Stanford: Stanford University Press, 1988), 260, quoted in Louise E. Wright, "Talk about Real Men: London's Correspondence with Maurice Magnus," *Journal of Popular Culture* 40.2 (April 2007): 366.

59. Josiah Flynt, "The American Tramp," *Contemporary Review* 60 (August 1891): 253–61; "Club Life Among Outcasts," *Harper's,* April 1895, 712; "Two Tramps in England," *Century* 50.2 (June 1895): 289; "How Men Become Tramps: Conclusions from Personal Experience as an Amateur Tramp," *Century* 50.119 (October 1895): 941–45; and "Jamie the Kid," *Harper's,* October 1895, 776–83 (fiction). Except for "American Tramp," these appear in *Tramping with the Tramps* (New York: Century, 1899). In the 1900s, Flynt pieces, sometimes coauthored with Francis Walton, appeared in *Every-*

*body's* (November 1900), *Munsey's* ("Policing the Railroads," February 1900), *McClure's* ("True Stories from the Under-World," August and September 1900), and *Cosmopolitan* (March, June 1907, on pool rooms and gambling). Later books included *The Powers that Prey* (1900), *Notes of an Itinerant Policeman* (1900), *The World of Graft* (1901), and a volume of short stories, *The Little Brother* (1902). His tramping as "Cigarette" was during the 1890s.

60. Philip Morse, "The Tramp," *Century* 51.2 (December 1895): 320.

61. Flynt, *Tramping with the Tramps,* ix.

62. Ibid., ix.

63. Arthur Symons, introduction to *My Life,* by Josiah Flynt (New York: Outing, 1908), xi–xxi, quoted in Toby Higbie, "Crossing Class Boundaries: Tramp Ethnographers and Narratives of Class in Progressive Era America," *Social Science History* 21.4 (Winter 1997): 569–70.

64. Flynt, *Tramping with the Tramps.*

65. "Best Books of 1899," *New York Times,* 21 April 1900, BR13.

66. "The Natural History of the Vagabond," *New York Times,* 31 March 1900, BR19.

67. Ibid.

68. "Josiah Flynt's Own Life Story," *New York Times,* 24 October 1908, BR619.

69. John Berryman, *Stephen Crane: A Critical Biography* (New York: Cooper Square Press, 1950), 82. Also, Stephen Crane, "An Experiment in Misery," *New York Press,* 22 April 1894; "An Experiment in Luxury," 29 April 1894.

70. Kusmer, *Down and Out,* 171.

71. Fredson Bower, ed., *Stephen Crane: Tales, Sketches, and Reports* (Charlottesville: University of Virginia Press, 1973), 283–301.

72. Michael Robertson, *Stephen Crane, Journalism, and the Making of Modern American Literature* (New York: Columbia University Press, 1997), 95–97.

73. Alvan Francis Sanborn, *Moody's Lodging House and Other Tenement Sketches* (Boston: Copeland and Day, 1896), quoted in "Among the Poor," *Bookman* 25.736 (28 March 1896): 214.

74. Walter Wyckoff, *The Workers* (New York: Charles Scribner's Sons, 1898), vii.

75. Ibid., vii.

76. Ibid., viii–ix.

77. "A New Volume of Tenement Sketches," *Bookman* 2.5 (January 1896): 425.

78. Ibid.

79. "Among the Poor," *Critic* 25.736 (28 March 1896): 214.

80. Ibid.


CHAPTER SIX

1. See such as Mark Pittenger, "A World of Difference: Constructing the 'Underclass' in Progressive America," *American Quarterly* 49.1 (March 1997): 26–65; also, Toby Higbie, "Crossing Class Boundaries: Tramp Ethnographers and Narratives of Class in Progressive Era America," *Social Science History* 21.4 (Winter 1997): 559–92.

2. Jack London, *People of the Abyss* (Cornwall: Diggery Press, 2008), 16.

3. London, *Abyss,* 16.

4. Alex Kershaw, *Jack London: A Life* (New York: Thomas Dunne Books, 1997), 115.

5. London, *Abyss,* 60.

6. Brooke Kroeger, *Nellie Bly: Daredevil, Reporter, Feminist* (New York: Times Books, 1994), 90.

7. London, preface to *Abyss.*

8. London, *Abyss,* 7.

9. Ibid., 9.

10. Ibid., 10–11.

11. Ibid., 32–33.

12. Ibid., 28.

13. Ibid., 64–104. The change proposals came under such headings as PROPERTY VS. PERSON; INEFFICIENCY; WAGES; THE GHETTO; COFFEE-HOUSES AND DOSS-HOUSES; THE PRECARIOUSNESS OF LIFE; SUICIDE; THE CHILDREN; THE VISION OF THE NIGHT; THE HUNGER WAIL; DRINK, TEMPERANCE AND THRIFT; and THE MANAGEMENT.

14. Kershaw, *Jack London,* 122.

15. "Jack London's People of the Abyss," *Current Literature* 36.4 (April 1904): 413–16.

16. Edward Clark Marsh, "Jack London's People of the Abyss," *Bookman* 18.6 (February 1904): 647–48.

17. Review of *People of the Abyss,* by Jack London, *London Daily News,* 28 November 1903, quoted in Kershaw, *Jack London,* 120.

18. Marsh, "People of the Abyss," 647–48.

19. Kershaw, *Jack London,* 119.

20. Upton Sinclair, *Love's Pilgrimage* (New York: Mitchell Kennerley, 1911), 556, quoted in Leon Harris, *Upton Sinclair: An American Rebel* (New York: Thomas Y. Crowell, 1975).

21. Morris Dickstein, introduction to *The Jungle,* by Upton Sinclair (New York: Bantam Books, 1981), xiv.

22. Sinclair, "Is *The Jungle* True?" *Independent* 60.2998 (17 May 1906): 1129–33.

23. Sinclair, "What Life Means to Me," *Cosmopolitan* (October 1906): 594.

24. Sinclair, "What Life Means," 592. Sinclair noted George Moore as an English exponent of the school, but listed no French writers, such as Gustave Flaubert or Honoré de Balzac.

25. Ibid., 591–95.

26. Ibid., 594.

27. Anthony Arthur, *Upton Sinclair: Radical Innocent* (New York: Random House, 2006), 59.

28. Arthur, *Radical Innocent,* 69.

29. Sinclair, "What Life Means," 591–95.

30. Ibid., 593.

31. Among those that appeared in the years before Sinclair's novel was Charles Edward Russell's exposé of the Beef Trust, titled "The Greatest Trust in the World," and published serially in *Everybody's* magazine through August 1905. Russell did not go undercover.

32. Arthur, *Radical Innocent,* 41.

33. Sinclair, "What Life Means," 591–95.

34. Sinclair, "Is *The Jungle* True?" 1129–33.

35. Ibid.

36. Ibid.

37. Ibid. After the book's release, he acknowledged one error of mis-

calculation that was not his own. He had immigrants paying $8.40 in a rental arrangement, when the correct figure was $7.00. (Although, he mused, given the way the information came to him—from an agent responsible for the calculations—the higher figure might actually have been what the locals were paying.)

38. Sinclair, "Is *The Jungle* True?" 1129–30.

39. Food Lion, Inc., v. Capital Cities/ABC, Inc., Brief of Investigative Reporters and Editors, Inc., as Amicus Curiae, p. 5, refers to Sinclair as having depicted "gruesome practices he witnessed while working under-cover at a Chicago meat-packing plant." Repeated latter-day references to *The Jungle* use the term *undercover* in the clear suggestion of Sinclair's having posed as a wage worker to get his information.

40. Sinclair, "Is *The Jungle* True?" 1131.

41. Ernest Poole, *The Bridge: My Own Story* (New York: MacMillan, 1940), 95–96, widely cited, including reference to Jack London's book blurb for *The Jungle* published in 2005 in *Appeal to Reason* during the story's magazine serialization: "Here it is at last! The book we have been waiting for these many years! The *Uncle Tom's Cabin* of wage slavery!" quoted in Upton Sinclair, *My Lifetime in Letters* (Columbia: University of Missouri Press, 1960), 20, and various.

42. Arthur, *Radical Innocent,* 48. Local guides included Ernest Poole, who told of the "Hello!" moment in his 1940 memoir and took Sinclair on an authorized tour of the plant. Poole was a Princetonian who had been doing settlement house work and had written about the recent Chicago stockyards strike for the *Independent,* the story that initially caught Sinclair's eye. He also relied on Mary McDowell, known as the "angel of the stockyards" for her devotion to the workers; the social worker Jane Addams of Hull House; and an English medical writer named Adolph Smith, who was researching the meatpacking industry for the *Lancet.*

43. Sinclair, "Is *The Jungle* True?" 1131.

44. Sinclair, "What Life Means," 593.

45. Upton Sinclair, *American Outpost: A Book of Reminiscences* (New York: Farrar and Rinehart, 1932), 154. Sinclair repeats the same informa-tion in *The Autobiography of Upton Sinclair* (New York: Harcourt, Brace, 1962), 109.

46. Arthur, *Radical Innocent,* 71.

47. Sinclair, "What Life Means," 594.

48. Arthur, *Radical Innocent,* 83–84.

49. Ibid., 36.

50. Ibid., 74.

51. Ibid., 81.

52. For example, "Twenty-five Years of Pure Food Law," *New York Times,* 13 July 1931, 9, quotes W. G. Campbell, chief of the federal Food and Drug Administration at the time, saying, "The years immediately preceding and succeeding the passage of the pure food law were marked by an awakened public consciousness of the evils and malpractices of the time. Lincoln Steffens was exposing the shame of misgovernment in large American cities. Upton Sinclair had written *The Jungle,* pillorying the meatpackers. Ida M. Tarbell was uncovering the cynicism and dishonesty of early Standard Oil operations. It was an age of exposure of unethical and demoralizing practices, and a wave of public indignation against the evils of food and drug manufacturing brought the Federal food and drugs act into being."

53. Harris, *American Rebel,* 2. In this period, the United States adopted the minimum wage, maximum working hours, employer liability for accidents, subsequent pure food and drug laws, collective bargaining rights, and support for strong unions.

54. Harris, *American Rebel,* 2.

55. Ronald Gottesman, introduction to *The Jungle,* by Upton Sinclair (New York: Penguin Classics, 1985), xxv.

56. Gottesman, introduction to *The Jungle,* xxv. Gottesman explains further that the novel highlighted "the structural, interlocking nature of corruption in American life: the interdependence of urban politics and urban crime; the symbiosis of corporate graft and precinct patronage; the direct linkage of the disintegration of the family, alcoholism, ill health, and despair. Efficiency, competitiveness, and materialism, Sinclair showed, were worshiped at great social cost."

57. Dickstein, introduction to *The Jungle,* v.

58. Jane Jacobs, introduction to *The Jungle,* by Upton Sinclair (New York: Modern Library, 2006), xii.

59. Sonia Orwell, *The Collected Essays, Journalism and Letters of George Orwell* (Jaffrey, N.H.: David R. Godine, 1968), 232, from a re-

view of *The Jungle,* inter alia, *New English Weekly,* 24 September 1936. See also George Orwell, *The Road to Wigan Pier* (New York: Harcourt, 1958), 84.

### CHAPTER SEVEN

1. Bessie Van Vorst, "The Woman That Toils: Experiences of a Working Girl," *Everybody's,* 7.3 (September 1902): 211–25; 7.4 (October 1902): 361–77; 7.5 (November 1902): 413–25; 7.5 (December 1902): 540–52; 8.1 (January 1903): 3–17. See also Mrs. John Van Vorst and Marie Van Vorst, *The Woman Who Toils: Being the Experiences of Two Ladies as Factory Girls* (New York: Doubleday, 1903).

2. "Books People Are Reading," *New York Tribune,* 2 November 1903, 8; "The Publishers," *New York Times,* 28 March 1903, BR14; C.A. H., "Chicago Letter," *Literary World,* 1 May 1903, 127.

3. See also Mrs. John Van Vorst, "The Woman of the People," *Harper's,* May 1903, 871–75.

4. See, for examples, reviews of *Woman Who Toils* in *Christian Advocate,* 23 April 1903, 677; *Overland Monthly and Out West,* May 1903, 397; *Literary World: A Monthly Review of Current Literature,* April 1903, 78; *Bookman* 17.2 (April 1903): 187; and *San Francisco Chronicle,* 22 March 1903, 18.

5. Lillian Pettengill, "Toilers of the Home: A College Woman's Experiences as a Domestic Servant," *Everybody's,* March 1903, 273–79; April 1903, 375–84; May 1903, 471–79; and June 1903, 561–68.

6. Lillian Pettengill, *Toilers of the Home: The Record of a College Woman's Experience as a Domestic Servant* (New York: Doubleday, 1903), viii.

7. Pettengill, *Toilers of the Home.*

8. Van Vorst, "Woman of the People," 872.

9. Rheta Childe Dorr, *A Woman of Fifty* (New York: Funk, 1924), 165–208.

10. Ibid., 194.

11. Ibid., 194.

12. Ibid., 197.

13. Ibid., 202.

14. Cornelia Stratton Parker, *Working with the Working Woman* (New York: Harper, 1922), ix.

15. Adela Rogers St. Johns, *Honeycomb* (New York: Doubleday, 1969), 235–36.

16. Ibid., 236.

17. Ibid., 240.

18. Ibid., 242.

19. Ibid., 243.

20. Ibid., 244.

21. Emmeline Pendennis, "Where Can a Girl Alone in New York Find Assistance?" *New York Evening World,* 4 February 1905, 8; 6 February 1905, 3; 7 February 1905, 3; 8 February 1905, 3; 9 February 1905, 14; and 10 February 1905, 8. Also quoted in James McGrath Morris, *The Rose Man of Sing Sing* (New York: Fordham University Press, 1999), 165.

22. Among those not detailed: See Neda M. Westlake, preface to *An Amateur Laborer,* by Theodore Dreiser (Philadelphia: University of Pennsylvania Press, 1983), vii–viii, on his attempt to write about his experiences as a day laborer while recuperating at a sanitarium from an emotional breakdown; Dr. Ben Reitman (the "king of HoBodom"), "Good Samaritans Few in Chicago," *Chicago Daily Tribune,* 12 May 1907, 1, and "Tramp King Plans Union," *Washington Post,* 15 December 1907, M16; George Meek, *Bath Chair-Man* (New York: E. P. Dutton, 1910); Percy F. Bicknell, "The Life Story of an Odd-Job Man," *Dial* 49.581 (1 September 1910): 110–11; and Edwin A. Brown, *Broke, the Man Without the Dime* (Chicago: Browne and Howell, 1913).

23. "Getting at the Worker's Mind," *New York Tribune,* 10 October 1920, H10.

24. Whiting Williams, *What's on the Worker's Mind: By One Who Put on Overalls to Find Out* (New York: Charles Scribner's Sons, 1920), v.

25. Williams, *Worker's Mind,* v.

26. "Getting at the Worker's Mind," H10.

27. George Orwell, *The Road to Wigan Pier* (New York: Harcourt, 1958), 152.

28. Jeffrey Meyers, *Orwell: Wintry Conscience of a Generation* (New York: W. W. Norton, 2000), 73–79.

29. Orwell, *Wigan Pier,* quoted in Jeffrey Meyers, *Orwell,* 79.

30. Orwell, *Wigan Pier,* 153.

31. Orwell, *Wigan Pier,* 12, quoted in Victor R. S. Tambling, "Jack London and George Orwell: A Literary Kinship," in Courtney T. Wemyss and Alexej Ugrinsky, eds., *George Orwell* (New York: Greenwood Press, 1987), 171.

32. Tambling, "Jack London and George Orwell," 171–74.

33. Later, Orwell would go hop-picking in Kent and write about it, but it did not make this manuscript.

34. George Orwell to Leonard Moore, 19 November 1932, in Sonia Orwell and Ian Angus, eds., *The Collected Essays, Journalism and Letters of George Orwell,* vol. 1, *An Age Like This, 1920–1940* (New York: Harvest, 1968), 106.

35. George Orwell to Jack Common, 26 December 1938 in Orwell and Angus, *Collected Essays,* 106.

36. "Book Exposes Destitution in Paris, London," *Washington Post,* 30 July 1933, S8.

37. Herbert Gorman, "On Paris and London Pavements," *New York Times,* 6 August 1933, BR4.

38. Introduction to the French edition of *Down and Out in Paris and London* (1933), in Orwell and Angus, *Collected Essays,* 114.

39. "Book Exposes Destitution," S8.

40. George Orwell to Henry Miller, 28 August 1936, and to Jack Common, 26 December 1938, in Orwell and Angus, *Collected Essays,* 227, 368. Among the titles not otherwise mentioned: Ben Hamper, *Rivethead: Tales from the Assembly Line* (New York: Warner Books, 1992); and Adam Shepard, *Scratch Beginnings: Me, $25, and the Search for the American Dream* (Chapel Hill, N.C.: SB Press, 2008). See also Pete Jordan, *Dishwasher: One Man's Quest to Wash Dishes in All Fifty States* (New York: Harper Perennial, 2007), parts of which appeared previously as "Dishwasher Pete" (November 1998) on the NPR radio program *This American Life;* Alex Frankel, *Punching In: The Unauthorized Adventure of a Front-Line Employee* (New York: Collins, 2007), about work as a service or retailing employee of some of the largest U.S. firms; and Jerry Newman, *My Secret Life on the McJob: Lessons from Behind the Counter Guaranteed to Supersize Any Management Style* (New York: McGraw-Hill, 2007).

## CHAPTER EIGHT

1. Walter F. White, "I Investigate Lynchings," *American Mercury* 16 (January 1929): 81.

2. White, "I Investigate Lynchings," 81

3. White, "The Burning of Jim McIlherron: An N.A.A.C.P. Investigation," *Crisis* 16.1 (May 1918): 16–20.

4. White, "I Investigate Lynchings," 81.

5. Marcel Dufresne, "Judgment Call: To Sting or Not to Sting?" *Columbia Journalism Review* 30.1 (May/June 1991): 49. Several newspapers and television stations sent pairs of reporters undercover—some black, some white—to test local practices.

6. Lee May, telephone interview by author, 17 March 2010.

7. Ella Baker and Marvel Cooke, "The Slave Market," *Crisis* 42.11 (November 1935): 330. Cooke revisited the subject for the *Amsterdam News* two years later, producing a follow-up report on the establishment of a domestic workers' union aimed at bringing an end to this "modern-day slavery." See Marvel Cooke, "Modern Slaves: Domestic Jobs Are Miserable in Hours, Pay. Union Is Seeking to Relieve Their Bad Situation," *Amsterdam News,* 16 October 1937, 13. Cooke was active in the Communist Party.

8. "Marvel Jackson Cooke, 99, Pioneering Black Newspaper Reporter," *New York Times,* 10 December 2000. Cooke made the remark in 1988 in an interview with the *Chicago Defender,* which identified her as the first black woman to get a job as a reporter on a white-owned mainstream newspaper, according to the obituary. See also "N.Y. Daily Gets First Negro Woman," *Chicago Defender,* 28 January 1950, 10, which reports, "The staff is small therefore her duties are not confined to Negro news but compare equally with those of other editorial staffmen."

9. "First Negro Woman," 10. Series by Marvel Cooke appearing in the *Daily Compass (Sunday Compass* magazine): "I Was a Part of the Bronx Slave Market," 8 January 1950, 1, 15; "Where Men Prowl and Women Prey on Needy Job-Seekers," 9 January 1950, 4, 7; "'Paper Bag Brigade' Learns How to Deal with Gypping Employers," 10 January 1950, 4, 21; "'Mrs. Legree' Hires Only on the Street, Always 'Nice Girls,'" 11 Janu-

ary 1950, 4, 21; and "Some Ways to Kill the Slave Market," 12 January 1950, 6.

10. Cooke, "Needy Job-Seekers," 4.

11. Ibid.

12. Cooke's experience did not address, but subtly raised, the specter of if and how often the women reduced to soliciting domestic work from streetside might, in a state of desperation, succumb to prostitution.

13. Robert Castle, comment on Bill Moyers, "Polls: Undercover Journalism," 21 June 2007, http://www.pbs.org/moyers/journal/blog/2007/06/poll_undercover_journalism.html.

14. Series by Ray Sprigle appearing in the *Pittsburgh Post-Gazette:* "I Was a Negro in the South for 30 Days," 10 August–1 September 1948. Individual articles: "Sprigle, Mildly Sun-Tanned, Encounters Many Negros with Lighter Skin Than His," 10 August 1948, 1; "Sprigle Found Life as Negro Was Not Quite Slavery—Not Quite Freedom, Either," 11 August 1948, 1; "Sprigle Finds Negro Parents Face Problem in Teaching Racial Facts to Children," 12 August 1948, 1; "Broken Negro Women Tells Prigle How White Folks Murdered Husband in Jail," 13 August 1948, 1; "10,000 Homestead Projects Needed to Dent South's Evil System of Share-Cropping," 14 August 1948, 1. The subsequent articles in the series (7th through 21st) appeared under the headline "I was a Negro in the South for 30 Days" on August 16–21, 23–28, 30, and 31 and September 1, 1948, all on page 1. See electronic copies at http://post-gazette.com/sprigle/default.asp, accessed 21 February 2011.

15. The series in *Sepia* is listed in note 22 of chapter 1: Introduction.

16. John Howard Griffin, *Black Like Me, Thirty-Fifth Anniversary Edition* (New York: Signet, 1977). See also Robert Bonazzi, *Man in the Mirror: John Howard Griffin and the Story of "Black Like Me"* (New York: Orbis, 1997).

17. For subsequent, now forgotten book projects, Halsell posed as a Native American (*Bessie Yellowhair*) and then as an illegal Mexican immigrant (*The Illegals*) in the early 1970s. No one is known to have tried skin-dyeing again until 1994, when a University of Maryland student, Joshua Solomon, inspired by Griffin's adventure, took the drug Psorlen as Griffin had done to change his skin from white to brown. He then

got on a bus and went to Atlanta, returned, and wrote about his brief experience IN THE HEART OF RACE-CONSCIOUS AMERICA, as the headline read, for the *Washington Post*. See Joshua Solomon, "Skin Deep: Reliving 'Black Like Me': My Own Journey into the Heart of Race-Conscious America," *Washington Post,* 30 October 1994, C01.

18. "Harvest of Shame," narrated by Edward R. Murrow, *CBS Reports,* CBS, 24 November 1960.

19. Dale Wright, "The Forgotten People: I Saw Human Shame as a Migrant Worker," *New York World-Telegram & Sun,* 10 October 1961, 1; "Migrant Pay $4.32 a Day in Florida Tomato Field," 11 October 1961, 1; "Migrants Live Horror Story in Job Travel," 12 October 1961, 1; "Migrant Labor Exploited by Delay Trick," 13 October 1961, 1; "Speed-Up Forces Migrants to Quit Job Before Pay Day," 16 October 1961, 1; "Migrant Workers Need U.S. Protection," 17 October 1961, 25; "Farm Camp Slum Exposed 8 Years Ago, Is Still Hell," 18 October 1961, 33; "Migrant Accepts Gyp as Part of Life," 19 October 1961, 13; "Migrants Exist in Duck Shed," 20 October 1961, 27; and "State Could Remedy Conditions for Migrant Labor," 23 October 1961, 3. See also "Drudgery and Despair," *Newsweek,* 23 October 1961.

20. Robert G. Miraldi, *Muckraking and Objectivity: Journalism's Colliding Traditions* (New York: Greenwood Press, 1990), 105.

21. Miraldi, *Muckraking and Objectivity,* 106.

22. Tom Goldstein, *The News at Any Cost: How Journalists Compromise Their Ethics to Shape the News* (New York: Touchstone, 1985), 127–51, quoted in Miraldi, *Muckraking and Objectivity,* 107.

23. Miraldi, *Muckraking and Objectivity,* 107.

24. Ibid., 106.

25. Dale Wright, *They Harvest Despair: The Migrant Farm Worker* (Boston: Beacon Press, 1965). In pamphlet form the work was called *The Forgotten People.*

26. Wright, preface to *They Harvest Despair.*

27. Ibid.

28. Ibid.

29. Obituaries for Dale R. Wright in the *New York Times* (Associated Press) and the *Riverdale Press,* 24 December 2009. Both cite the series as his most valued work.

30. Ibid.

31. Richard Prince, "Dale R. Wright, 86, Integrated a New York Newsroom," *Richard Prince's Journal-isms,* Maynard Institute, 16 December 2009, http://www.mije.org/richardprince/afro-picks-apology-not -unanimous.

32. Grace Halsell, *Soul Sister* (New York: World, 1969).

33. For consideration of white-for-black investigative passing narratives, see Philip Brian Harper, *Are We Not Men? Masculine Anxiety and the Problem of African-American Identity* (New York: Oxford University Press, 1996), 103–26. Gayle Wald, for example, describes *Black Like Me* as a form of colonial infiltration, "an essentializing piece of anthropological fieldwork designed to assuage liberal white guilt," in her essay "A Most Disagreeable Mirror: Reflections on White Identity in *Black Like Me,*" in Elaine K. Ginsberg, *Passing and the Fictions of Identity* (Durham, N.C.: Duke University Press, 1996), 151–77.

34. Halsell, *Soul Sister,* 143–44.

35. Nella Larsen, *Passing* (New York: Arno, 1969).

36. Halsell, *Bessie Yellowhair* (New York: William Morrow, 1973), jacket copy. See also Halsell, "When You've Walked a Mile in Their Shoes," *New York Times,* 10 November 1973, 31.

37. Halsell, *Bessie Yellowhair,* jacket copy.

38. Halsell, *Bessie Yellowhair,* and *The Illegals* (New York: A John L. Hochmann Books), 1978.

39. Dick J. Reavis, *Without Documents* (New York: Condor, 1978), 215–31.

40. John Davidson, *The Long Road North* (Austin: Texas Monthly Press, 1981), 13. "I was willing to travel as Javier's shadow." (Original article, Davidson, *Texas Monthly Magazine,* October 1977.)

41. Frank del Olmo, "The Borderline Case of America's Illegal Aliens," *Los Angeles Times,* 24 December 1978, L3.

42. Halsell, *Soul Sister,* 206–7.

43. Dorothy Gilliam, "A White Woman in 'Black' Skin," *Washington Post,* 4 November 1959, B4.

44. Gilliam, *Washington Post,* 4 November 1959.

45. Chester Goolrick and Paul Lieberman, "The Underpaid and Under-Protected," *Atlanta Constitution,* pts. 1–6, 1–6 December 1979.

Individual articles are: "Part 1: The Turpentine Men: Hard Woods Toil for Little Pay," 1 December 1979, 1A; "For Many Americans, Work Pays Off in Poverty," 1 December 1979, A1; "'Junior' Sears: A Man Born to Turpentine," 1 December 1979, 4A; "Jim Palmer: He Recalls Bad Days in The Woods," 1 December 1979, 4A; "L. D. Davis: 'Boss Had a Pencil,'" 1 December 1979, 4A; "Part II: Endless Debt Haunts Turpentiners," 2 December 1979, 1A; "Naval Stores Ages-Old, But Few Like Living in Past," 2 December 1979, 32A; "Part III: No Golden Eggs in Georgia's Chicken Sheds, Whole Families Labor on Poultry Farms to Earn Paycheck of a Single Worker," 3 December 1979, A1; "Part IV: Motels, Gas Stations, Motel Maid's Wages Fall Into Crevice in the Law," 4 December 1979, 1A; "Unique Deductions Push Pay Below U.S. Minimum," 4 December 1979, A1; "Some 'Surprised I Pay $2.50 . . .'" 4 December 1979, 10A; "Part V: Ice Toters, Ministore Clerks: Over 40 Years, A Corporation's Pattern of Underpaying Workers," 5 December 1979, A1; "Munford: 'Minimum Wage a Terrible Thing,'" 5 December 1979; "Part VI: Works Ethic Amidst Poverty: They'd Rather Collect Weeds Than Welfare," 6 December 1979, A1; "Wage Law Enforcers Overwhelmed by Complaints," 6 December 1979, A1; and "Pulse of the Public: 'Underpaid . . .' Series 'Excellent Work,'" 7 December 1979, 5A.

46. Paul Lieberman, email interview by author, 15 March 2010, following up telephone interview of 10 February 2010.

47. Lee May, telephone interview by author, 17 March 2010. Lee moved on to the *Los Angeles Times* in 1980, serving as Atlanta bureau chief and White House correspondent during his twelve years with the paper.

48. Paul Lieberman, telephone interview by author, 10 February 2010.

49. Ibid.; and May, telephone interview.

50. Paul Lieberman, telephone interview.

51. Chester Goolrick, telephone interview by author, 15 November 2009.

52. May, telephone interview.

53. Goolrick and Lieberman et al., "Underpaid and Under-Protected."

54. May, telephone interview.

55. Merle Linda Wolin, telephone interview by author, 18 March 2010.

56. Ibid.

57. Merle Linda Wolin, "Sweatshop: Merlina's Job in Oscar Herrera's

Factory," *Los Angeles Herald-Examiner*, 14 January 1981, A1, A10; "Five Days' Work for Felix Mendoza, $38.74," 15 January 1981, A1, A10; "'This Is the Filthiest of All Industries,'" 16 January 1981, A1, A10; "Homework: The Alien's Secret Support System," 18 January 1981, A1, A12; "Seven Hours in a Union Shop for $2.50," 19 January 1981, A1, A8; "Merlina Faces the Labor Commissioner—And Wins," 20 January 1981, A1, A10; "'I'm Not Joan of Arc. I'm a Garment Manufacturer,'" 21 January 1981, A10; "The Work Is 'Killing' Martha and Oscar," 22 January 1981, A10; "The Fading of Felix Mendoza's Dream," 23 January 1981, A1, A8; "Employer Meets Employer—Merlina, Melton, Mendoza," 25 January 1981, A1, A12; "'It's Another Mike Wallace Trick!'" January 1981, A8; "The Retailers' Side of the Story," 27 January 1981, A10; "Who Are the Players? What Are the Problems?" 28 January 1981, A8; "Bradley:'I Wouldn't Want to Speculate . . . ,'" 29 January 1981, A12; "Brown:'It's Wrong for Civilized Society . . .'" 30 January 1981, A1; "What It Will Take to 'Outlaw Slavery,'" 1 February 1981, A12; and "What to Do About 'Sweatshop,'" 8 February 1981, F2.

58. Pulitzer Prize finalist for Public Service: http://www.pulitzer.org/finalists/1982.

59. The previous year, the *Nashville Tennessean*'s series on the resurgence of the Ku Klux Klan, discussed in chapter 12, also was named one of two finalists in the Public Service category. Whether the packet included the reporting of Jerry Thompson, who went undercover as a Klansman to report on the organization's initiation rites and practices, is not clear. The Pulitzer Prize records do not include those of finalists and the records of the submission could not be located at the newspaper's offices.

60. See John J. Goldman, "Times' Bernheimer Wins Pulitzer for Music Criticism," *Los Angeles Times*, 13 April 1982, B1.

61. *Reemergence of Sweatshops and the Enforcement of Wage and Hour Standards: Hearings on H.R. 6103, Before the Subcommittee on Labor Standards of the Committee on Education and Labor*, 97th Cong. 169 (1981–82) (statement of Merle Linda Wolin, reporter, and Mary Anne Dolan, managing editor, *Los Angeles Herald-Examiner*).

62. Wolin and Dolan, *Reemergence of Sweatshops*, 169.

63. Merle Linda Wolin, telephone (Skype) interview by author, 18 March 2010.

64. The series over twelve consecutive days began with Neil Henry, "Exploring the World of the Urban Derelict: Inside the Crumbling Walls of Baltimore's Helping-Up Mission, Where Men Recount the Legend of Old Louie, Eat Macaroni, and Mumble in Their Sleep," *Washington Post,* 27 April 1980, A01; "Street People Share Secrets of Survival," 28 April 1980, A01; "'Work!' Brings Cheers at Local 194's Hiring Hall," 29 April 1980, A01; "'Holy Roller' Resounds with Joy, Wrath," 30 April 1980, C01; "Learning the Tricks of Walking a Md. Throwaway Paper Route," 30 April 1980, A01; "Money Brings a Taste of 'Real Living,'" 1 May 1980, A01; "All-Night Café: A Classroom on How to Survive," 2 May 1980, A01; "Snug Haven But No Sleep at Crisis Center," May 1980, A01; "In D.C., Raw and Threatening Things," 4 May 1980, A01; N. Henry, "A Washington Winter's Tale: Fear, Hunger, Loathing, Abuse," 5 May 1980, A01; "Tapping 'The Bank,'" 6 May 1980, A01; "'What's In It For Me?' In Washington," 7 May 1980, A01; "Mozart-Playing New Yorker Learns a Secret, and Laughs," 8 May 1980, A01.

65. N. Henry, *American Carnival: Journalism Under Siege in an Age of New Media* (Berkeley: University of California Press, 2007), 222–26.

66. Ibid. N. Henry, "The Long, Hot Wait for Pickin' Work," *Washington Post,* 9 October 1983, A01; "Slim Pickin': Taken for a Ride, Sold 'Like Cattle,'" 10 October 1983, A01; "Half a Day Nets $1.50 and 'Supper,'" 11 October 1983, A01; "A Wretched Reality of Life in the Fields," 12 October 1983, A01; "Homeward Bound," 13 October 1983, A01; "Looking for Answers About Workers and Wages," 14 October 1983, A01.

67. N. Henry, *American Carnival,* 222–26.

68. http://www.rfkmemorial.org/legacyinaction/1984/.

69. William A. Henry III, "Journalism Under Fire," *Time,* 12 December 1983, cover story.

70. Athelia Knight, "Drug Smuggling and Hot Goods: A Ride on Prison Visitors' Buses," *Washington Post,* 4 March 1984, A1. See also Knight, "Officials Differ on Depth of Prison Drug Problem," *Washington Post,* 7 March 1984, A1.

71. Knight, "Drug Smuggling."

72. Ibid.; Knight, "Visitors Make Drug Deliveries to Inmates," *Washington Post,* 5 March 1984, A1; Knight, "Threat of Violence Haunts Drivers," *Washington Post,* 6 March 1984, A1; and Knight, "Prison Drug Problem." See also mentions in Henry, *American Carnival,* 222–26. Henry and Tom Goldstein are both former deans of the Graduate School of Journalism at the University of California at Berkeley. Goldstein also was dean of the Columbia University Graduate School of Journalism. The book Henry cites is Goldstein's *News at Any Cost,* especially 141–45. Among articles sounding the alarm in this period was Henry III, "Journalism Under Fire," which cited both the Henry and Wolin investigations.

73. Goldstein, *News at Any Cost,* 144.

74. Henry, *American Carnival,* 222–26.

75. Q&A with Neil Henry for Princeton University, 24 October 2001, http://www.princeton.edu/paw/web_exclusives/more/more_102401 .html.

76. N. Henry, *American Carnival,* 223.

77. Ibid., 224.

78. Cited as a 1988 investigation in the *Miami Herald* in John P. Borger, "New Whines in Old Bottles; Taking Newsgathering Torts off the Food Lion Shelf," *Tort and Law Insurance Journal* 34.61 (Fall 1998).

79. Clarence Page, "RIP: Undercover Journalism," *Chicago Tribune,* 29 January 1997, 17.

80. Lyn Bixby et al., "Some Real Estate Agents Discriminate Against Black Home Buyers," *Hartford Courant,* 21 May 1989, A1. See also, Henry McNulty, "White Lies: Bending the Truth to Expose Injustice," *FineLine: The Newsletter on Journalism Ethics* 1.4 (August 1989): 6–7.

81. Gloria Cooper, "Darts and Laurels," *Columbia Journalism Review* 28.4 (November/December 1989): 22.

82. Henry McNulty, "Real-Estate Probe Built on Deception," *Hartford Courant,* 8 June 1989. Special thanks to Mike McIntyre for tracking this down.

83. McNulty, "White Lies," 6–7.

84. McNulty, "Real-Estate Probe"; and McNulty, "White Lies," 6–7.

85. Dufresne, "Judgment Call," 30.

86. Ibid.

87. Lawrence Otis Graham, "Invisible Man: Why did This $105,000-a-Year Lawyer from Harvard Go to Work as a $7-an-Hour Busboy at the Greenwich Country Club—and What Did He Find?" *New York,* 17 August 1992.

88. Lawrence Otis Graham, *Members of the Club* (New York: HarperCollins, 1996).

89. Gloria Steinem, "I Was a Playboy Bunny," *Show,* May and June 1963, reprinted in Jon E. Lewis, ed., *The Mammoth Book of Journalism* (New York: Carroll, 2003), 346–52. Also reprinted in Steinem, *Outrageous Acts and Everyday Rebellions* (New York: Henry Holt, 1995), 32–75, and referenced in pp. vii, xix, 6, 16, and 19–20.

90. Steinem, *Outrageous Acts,* 19–20.

91. Carolyn G. Heilbrun, *The Education of a Woman: The Life of Gloria Steinem* (New York: Ballantine Books, 1996), 105–108.

92. Ibid.

93. Steinem, *Outrageous Acts,* 19–20.

94. Ibid., xix.

95. Katherine Leigh Scott, *The Bunny Years* (Los Angeles: Pomegranate Press, 1999), 2.

96. Ibid., 2–3.

97. Ibid., 1–9. Also, quoted in James K. Beggan and Scott T. Allison, "Tough Women in the Unlikeliest of Places: The Unexpected Toughness of the Playboy Bunny," *Journal of Popular Culture* 38.5 (August 2005): 812.

98. Scott, *Bunny Years,* 4.

99. Ibid., 6.

100. Doug Clifton, "How the *Herald* Covered the Pope's Visit to Cuba," *Miami Herald,* 1 February 1998, 1L. See also Larry Rohter, "With Pope Due, the Cubans Wrest Dollars from Heaven," *New York Times,* 20 January 1998, A1.

101. Clifton, "Pope's Visit to Cuba," 1L.

102. Jane H. Lii, "65 Cents an Hour—A Special Report. Week in Sweatshop Reveals Grim Conspiracy of the Poor," *New York Times,* 12 March 1995, 1.

103. Helen Zia, "Made in the U.S.A.," *Ms.,* January 1996, 66–73.

104. Barbara Ehrenreich, *Nickel and Dimed: On (Not) Getting By in America* (New York: Metropolitan, 2001), 51. Also *Harper's,* January 1999, 37–52.

105. Ehrenreich, *Nickel and Dimed,* 89.

106. James Fallows, "Working Classes: An Exchange with Barbara Ehrenreich, the Author of *Nickel and Dimed: On (Not) Getting By in America,*" *Atlantic Unbound,* 2, 4, and 11 May 2001, http://www.theatlantic.com/past/docs/unbound/fallows/jf2001-05-02/.

107. Fallows, "Working Classes," 2 May 2001.

108. Ibid.

109. Ibid.

## CHAPTER NINE

1. Ted Conover, email interview by author, 18 January 2010. Conover rode the rails from September to December 1980. An Amherst student publication called *In Other Words* published a piece Conover wrote about his experience, which the college alumni magazine, *Amherst,* picked up for its Winter 1981 issue. An Associated Press reporter in Springfield read it, interviewed Conover, and wrote a story about his experience. That led to a *Today Show* interview that in turn piqued interest from the literary agent, Sterling Lord. The book contracts followed.

2. Ted Conover, *Rolling Nowhere: Riding the Rails with America's Hoboes* (New York: Random House Vintage Departures, 2001), 39, 164, 272.

3. Conover, email interview, 18 January 2010.

4. Ted Conover's thesis was titled "Between Freedom and Poverty: Railroad Tramps of the American West."

5. Ted Conover, "A Morning with Pops," *Amherst,* Winter 1981, 14–17, 26.

6. Douglas Harper, *Good Company: A Tramp Life* (University of Chicago Press, 1982). Conover's book followed *Harper's* original work, which had less general notice.

7. Conover, *Rolling Nowhere,* xv.

8. Anatole Broyard, "Fantasy of Freedom," *New York Times,* 13 December 1983, 17, which reads in part: "As we might expect, much of the

book is naïve, and that's all to the good. The reader, too is naïve about the life of a tramp, and the author's candor raises and answers the kinds of questions that might be overlooked by a more sophisticated approach. Where do you sleep? What do you eat? How do you keep warm?"

9. Conover, *Rolling Nowhere,* xv.

10. Robert Boynton, ed., *The New New Journalism* (New York: Vintage, 2005), 3–30. Q&A with Ted Conover.

11. Ted Conover, email interview by author, 1 April 2010. See also John Crewdson, "The Illegal Odyssey of Don Bernabe Garay," *New York Times,* 14 December 1980, A1.

12. Boynton, *New New Journalism,* 3–30.

13. John Davidson, telephone interview by author, 8 April 2010.

14. Ibid.

15. John Davidson, "The Long Road North," *Texas Monthly,* October 1977.

16. Ted Conover, *Coyotes: A Journey Through the Secret World of America's Illegal Aliens* (New York: Vintage Books, 1987), 4.

17. Charlie LeDuff, "The Crossing: A Perilous 4,000 Mile Passage to Work," *New York Times,* 29 May 2001.

18. Sonia Nazario, "Enrique's Journey," *Los Angeles Times,* 29–30 September 2002, A1; 2, 4, 6–7 October 2002, A1.

19. Ruben Martinez, "Promised Land: *Enrique's Journey: The Story of a Boy's Dangerous Odyssey to Reunite with His Mother,*" *Los Angeles Times,* 9 February 2006, R2.

20. Ginger Thompson and Sandra Ochoa, "By a Back Door to the U.S.: A Migrant's Grim Sea Voyage; Dangerous Passage: From Ecuador by Sea," *New York Times,* 13 June 2004, 1.

21. William A. Henry, "Journalism Under Fire," *Time,* 12 December 1983, cover story, http://www.time.com/time/magazine/article/0,9171,921424,00.html. The story cites a 1976 National Opinion Research Center poll which found that 29 percent of the population had "a great deal of confidence in the press." By 1983, that figure had fallen to 13.7 percent. Another excellent examination of the state of play in 1983 can be found in Jonathan Friendly, "Investigative Journalism Is Found Shifting Goals," *New York Times,* 23 August 1983, A16, which describes how attitudes in newsrooms had become more cautious and judicious

in light of the threat of expensive legal challenges and erosion of public trust, which he attributed to the overuse of unidentified sourcing and reports found to be manufactured or plagiarized (but not, interestingly, to the use of misrepresentation in undercover reporting, which he mentioned only as an internal editorial concern of James P. Herman, editor of the *Traverse City Record-Eagle* in Michigan, before publishing an article about a local escort service that involved a reporter who signed a statement at the service without identifying herself as a reporter).

22. Clayton Kirkpatrick and Gene Patterson, "Should Reporters Play Roles," *ASNE Bulletin,* September 1979, 12–13.

23. Gary C. Schuster, "Crashing a Moment in History," *Detroit News,* 27 March 1979, 1A.

24. Lois Timnick, "Despair for the Mentally Ill: Metro Hospital— Place of Little Hope," *Los Angeles Times,* 12 August 1979, A1. The newspaper's front-page explainer reads: "Posing as a graduate psychology student, *Times* Human Behavior Writer Lois Timnick worked for two weeks inside Metropolitan State Hospital, gaining an unprecedented firsthand look at what goes on behind locked doors of the psychiatric wards. This report and other articles on Page 3 reveal a mental-health program that in many ways has no better chance of succeeding than the patients it purports to serve. It is underfinanced, poorly staffed and riddled with conflict."

25. Beth Nissen, "An Inside View," *Wall Street Journal,* 28 July 1978, 1.

26. Quoted in David Shaw, "Masquerades: Deception—Honest Tool of Reporting?" *Los Angeles Times,* 20 September 1979, B1.

27. Michael Cordts, "Title Free Books Sold by Editors: Scandal Embarrasses Newspapers," *Rochester Democrat and Chronicle,* 5 August 1979, 18.

28. Shaw, "Masquerades," B1. See also Jack Fuller, *News Values* (Chicago: Chicago University Press, 1996), 44–68.

29. Mike Goodman, "Youngsters of All Ages Free to Browse Among Hashish Pipes, Obscene Comic Books and Posters," *Los Angeles Times,* 9 April 1972, C1; Goodman, "Juvenile Hall: Powder Keg of Rage, Racism: Youths Subjected to Sexual Degradation, Beatings and Rat-Pack Struggle to Survive," *Los Angeles Times,* 17 May 1974, A3; Goodman, "Workers Complain of Boredom, 'Rip-Off,'" *Los Angeles Times,* 18 November 1975, A2; and Patt Morrison and Mike Goodman, "Mexico's

'Mordida': Bribes Are a Way of Life—and Death: U.S. Families Pay Up to $1,000 to Recover Loved Ones' Bodies," *Los Angeles Times,* 9 February 1977, B3.

30. Dick J. Reavis, email and telephone exchange with author, 2 April 2010.

31. Tom Goldstein, *The News at Any Cost: How Journalists Compromise Their Ethics to Shape the News* (New York: Touchstone, 1985), 132–33.

32. Neil Henry, *American Carnival: Journalism Under Siege in an Age of New Media* (Berkeley: University of California Press, 2007), 222–26.

33. N. Henry, *American Carnival,* 12, 223–24; and Ben Bagdikian and Leon Dash, *The Shame of the Prisons* (New York: Pocket Books, 1972).

34. Shaw, "Masquerades," B1. Similarly, the late A. M. Rosenthal, then executive editor of the *New York Times,* indignant after having reprimanded a reporter for posing as an airline mechanic to get closer to a plane on which authorities had detained the wife of a Russian ballet star, who was defecting, said this: "Reporters should not masquerade." "We claim First Amendment rights and privileges and it's duplicitous for us to then pass ourselves off as something other than reporters. Saying you'll get a better story or perform a valuable public service doesn't change anything. It's still wrong." But even Rosenthal, when pressed, conceded that if "the only way to save someone's life would be to masquerade, I might change my mind." In fact, the *Times,* under other leadership, has authorized these tactics.

35. Goldstein, *News at Any Cost,* 141–45.

## CHAPTER TEN

1. Tony Horwitz, "*The Jungle* Revisited," *Wall Street Journal,* 1 December 1994, A8. See also Horwitz, "9 to Nowhere: These Six Growth Jobs are Dull, Dead-End, Sometimes Dangerous," *Wall Street Journal,* 1 December 1994, A1.

2. Horwitz, "9 to Nowhere," A1.

3. Horwitz, "*The Jungle* Revisited," A8.

4. Charlie LeDuff, "At the Slaughterhouse, Some Things Never Die: Who Kills, Who Cuts, Who Bosses Can Depend on Race," *New York Times,* 16 June 2000, A1.

5. Joseph Lelyveld, ed., *How Race Is Lived in America* (New York: Times Books, 2001), xiv.

6. Horwitz, "9 to Nowhere," A1.

7. Several times since his student days, LeDuff has faced accusations of appropriation of the ideas and words of other writers. See next note.

8. LeDuff, "Who Kills, Who Cuts," A1. The similarity of the cited paragraph to Horwitz's opening paragraph was striking enough for me to seek an opinion from Horwitz, who replied in an email message of 27 May 2010: "Tough to judge this sort of thing, phrases can stick in your head and creep into your copy. I had an image in rough draft of one of my books that I thought lovely and original until I realized it was very similar to a line in a Robert Frost poem. Don't mean to suggest my prose was poetry, but short of blatant copy cat-ism, I'm inclined to give folks the benefit of the doubt." Others throughout the years have responded differently. LeDuff apologized personally and in writing to Ted Conover for repeating phrases and passages from the opening pages of *Rolling Nowhere*. Conover also spoke on the issue in an unpublished talk, "Something Borrowed," delivered at the Bread Loaf conference, 14 August 2004. LeDuff was cited by another author, Blake Gumprecht, for appropriating or distilling ideas and information without credit from Gumprecht, *The Los Angeles River: Its Life, Death, and Possible Rebirth* (Baltimore: Johns Hopkins University Press, 1999). See http://sanfranmag .com/story/los-angeles-river, accessed 18 February 2011, for which the *New York Times* issued an editor's note. See also Jack Shafer, "The Same River Twice," *Slate,* 16 December 2003, http://slate.com/toolbar .aspx?action=print&id=2092708; and "Los Angeles Journal; Los Angeles by Kayak: Vistas of Concrete Banks," *New York Times,* 8 December 2003, appended editor's note, 15 December 2003, http://query.nytimes.com/ gst/fullpage.html?res=990DE1D8103DF93BA35751C1A9659C8B63&sc p=2&sq=%22The%20Los%20Angeles%20River%22&st=cse.

9. Joan Biskupic, Howard Kurtz, "'48 Hours' Wins 11th Hour Case to Show Undercover Videotape," *Washington Post,* 10 February 1994, A10. Story quotes Joe Peyronin, a CBS vice president at the time, saying, "Ironically, we were not even going to identify this particular plant in

South Dakota. It was not until the company decided to take us on that their name came out in court."

10. "Part II: Is Your Food Safe? Bum Steer: Secret Videotape Taken Inside Meat Processing Plant Records Blatant Violations of Health Regulations During Processing: Transcript," *48 Hours,* CBS, 9 February 1994. See also "Man Says He Was Fired over Secret Tape," *Baltimore Sun,* 20 February 1994, 29A.

11. Relevant cases: *CBS Inc. et al. v. Jeff W. Davis,* 510 U.S. 1315 (1994); *Federal Beef Processors, Inc. v. CBS Inc.: CBS News Divison,* CIV 94-5009, 1994 U.S. Dist. LEXIS 6796; *Federal Beef Processors, Inc. v. CBS Inc.,* CIV 94-5009, 1994 U.S. Dist. LEXIS 9980.

12. "Fired over Secret Tape," 29A. In a court affidavit, the by-then (ten days after the segment aired) former employee Ray Lum said he was fired after refusing $3,000 to help Federal Beef with its suit against CBS, and that if he cooperated, he would not be prosecuted. The company argued that the financial reward was offered to all employees for information about who helped CBS get the tape. Lum said he helped CBS because he was aware of the unsanitary practices at the plant and did so out of public concern.

13. "Food Lion Stock Falls After Report," *New York Times,* 7 November 1992, A37. See also Paul Nowell, "Food Lion Stock Falls After ABC Broadcast," Associated Press (*Times-Picayune*), 7 November 1992, C2, inter alia.

14. "Stockholder Sues Food Lion," *Herald,* 14 November 1992, 7B.

15. Frank Swoboda, "Food Lion Faces Huge U.S. Complaint: Labor Dept. to Allege Thousands of Child Labor, Overtime Violations," *Washington Post,* 7 November 1992, A1. Janet Battaile, "Supermarket Chain to Face Child-Labor Case," *New York Times,* 8 November 1992, A36.

16. "Food Lion to Scale Back Expansion Plans for 1993," *Washington Post,* 25 December 1992, C9; "Food Lion Slows Expansion in Wake of TV Report," *New York Times,* 25 December 1992, D3.

17. Linda Brown Douglas and Tim Gray, "Food Lion to Close 88 Stores," *News & Observer,* 8 January 1994.

18. *Primetime Live,* hosted by Diane Sawyer, ABC, 5 November 1992.

19. Ibid.

20. Ibid.

21. Ibid.

22. Annetta Miller, with Verne E. Smith and Marcus Mabry, "Shooting the Messenger," *Newsweek,* 23 November 1992, 51.

23. Relevant Food Lion court decisions include: *Food Lion, Inc. v. Capital Cities/ABC, Inc.,* 887 F. Supp. 811 (U.S. Dist. 1995), 965 F. Supp. 956 (U.S. Dist. 1997); *Food Lion, Inc. v. Capital Cities/ABC, Inc.,* No. 97-2492, No. 97-2564, 1999 U.S. App. LEXIS 26373 (4th Cir.); *Food Lion, Inc. v. Capital Cities/ABC, Inc.,* 887 F. Supp. 811 (U.S. Dist 1995).

24. *Food Lion,* No. 97-2492, No. 972564.

25. *Food Lion,* 887 F. Supp. 811 (U.S. Dist. 1995).

26. Ibid.

27. *Food Lion,* No. 97-2492, 97-2564. The organization of Investigative Reporters and Editors supplied a detailed amicus brief, dated 2 April 1998, for the court case. The brief defended undercover methods in general with a litany of their historic importance going back to the Revolutionary period in U.S. history. But it made no specific reference to ABC or the actions of its producers. "Brief of Investigative Reporters and Editors, Inc. as Amicus Curiae." Incorporated; Richard N. Kaplan; Ira Rosen; Susan Barnett, Defendants Appellants/Cross Appellees. On Appeal from the United States District Court for the Middle District of North Carolina.

28. Explanation courtesy of my colleague, Associate Professor Stephen D. Solomon of New York University, who says further: "Note caution: Food Lion did not sue ABC for libel (damage flowing from injury to its reputation), which would have required that it meet the daunting First Amendment standard of proving that ABC published intentional or reckless falsehoods. Instead it alleged a number of tort violations for which the First Amendment provided no protection for ABC (making it easier for Food Lion to win), including trespass, fraud, and breach of the duty of loyalty. Yet Food Lion still asked for a large monetary award based in part on the damages it said that it suffered (such as lost sales) from the actual broadcast. The appeals court ruled— in a significant victory for ABC and the press—that Food Lion could not collect defamation-type damages for its nonreputation tort claims without also meeting the higher First Amendment standard of inten-

tional or reckless falsehood. Thus, Food Lion was limited to collecting damages assessed for the newsgathering wrongs alone. Here, the damages for trespass and breach of the duty of loyalty were only a token two dollars." Stephen Solomon, email exchange with author, 3 June 2010; 2 February 2011.

29. Howard Kurtz, "Hidden Network Cameras: A Troubling Trend? Critics Complain of Deception as Dramatic Footage Yields High Ratings," *Washington Post,* 30 November 1992, A1.

30. "1992 IRE Awards," Investigative Reporters and Editors, n.d., http://ire.org/resourcecenter/contest/past/1992.html, accessed 18 February 2011. Also mentioned in Brant Houston, "Solid Reporting Defies Last Year's Worst," *IRE Journal* 22.1 (January/February 1999): 2.

31. Susan Banda, "Working Undercover," *IRE Journal* 18.14 (January 1995): 14. The exact quotation is: "But TV investigative producers armed with hidden cameras have gone back to the technique in recent years with stunning results, including revelations about conditions at veterans' hospitals and in supermarket meat departments. Still, many editors have worried about the tangled ethical problems involved in undercover work. How can you do such a story without misrepresentation and lies?"

32. See Kurtz, "Hidden Network Cameras," *Washington Post,* 30 November 1992, A1. Also, Coleman McCarthy, "Getting Truth Untruthfully," 22 December 1992, *Washington Post,* D21, and later, Jonathan Alter, "'Candid Camera' Gone Berserk?" *Newsweek,* 30 August 1993, 36. The earlier court filing summary reports that producer Lynne Neufer Litt had applied for the job in the name of Lynne Neufer and said that she loved and missed her previous job working in a grocery store as a meat wrapper and that she would like to make a career with the company. She quit after eleven days, saying it was to move back to Pennsylvania and care for her grandmother after the death of her grandfather. (The last was not actionable because reasons for quitting were not part of the employment contract.)

33. *Food Lion,* No. 97-2492, 97-2564.

34. Steve McClellan, "Undercover Under Fire," *Broadcasting & Cable* 27.8 (24 February 1997): 37.

35. *Food Lion,* No. 97-2492, No. 972564.

36. The thirteen stories cited were: Nellie Bly's madhouse exposé in 1887 and her women's home expose in 1888; Edgar May's Pulitzer Prize—winning turn in 1960 as a welfare caseworker for the *Buffalo Evening News;* the *Chicago Tribune*'s 1975 investigations where reporters posed as nurses' aids and janitors at nursing homes and hospitals to expose deplorable conditions; a *Chicago Sun-Times* abortion exposé in 1978; a CBS *60 Minutes* soundman's posing as a cancer clinic patient at a bogus California clinic; a *Chicago Sun-Times* farm-loan fraud exposé; the *Nashville Tennessean*'s Ku Klux Klan investigation; a *Miami Herald* investigation into racial discrimination in the real estate market in 1988; Horwitz in 1994; and Helen Zia's *Ms.* magazine sweatshop exposé in 1996.

37. Susan Paterno, "The Lying Game," *American Journalism Review* 19.4 (May 1997): 40.

38. The original $5.5 million verdict was issued on January 22, 1997, reduced to $315,000 on August 3, 1997; and reduced again to $2 on October 20, 1999. Among the stories that appeared: Russ Baker, "In Greensboro, Damning Undercover Tactics as 'Fraud,'" *Columbia Journalism Review* 35.6 (March/April 1997): 28; David B. Smallman, "The Long-Awaited Food Lion Ruling," *IRE Journal* 22.8 (October/November 1999): 5; "Statement of Concern: Committee of Concerned Journalists," *IRE Journal* 21.1 (January/February 1998): 2; Mark Lisheron, "Lying to Get the Truth," *American Journalism Review* 29.5 (October/November 2007): 29; Paterno, "Lying Game," 40; Jane Kirtley, "Don't Pop That Cork," *American Journalism Review* 22.1 (January/February 2000): 84; and Charles C. Schiem, "Trash Tort or Trash TV? Food Lion, Inc., v. ABC, Inc., and Tort Liability of the Media for Newsgathering," *St. John's Law Review* 7.1 (Winter 1998): 185. There was a minor secondary tempest late in 1998 when Food Lion issued a brief for journalism schools on unethical journalism, which an associate professor at the University of Missouri, Sandra Davidson, used as the basis of a piece in the *IRE Journal* without cross-checking with ABC or the staffers involved. Sandra Davidson, "Food Lyin' and Other Buttafucos," *IRE Journal* 2.6 (November/December 1998): 6. The *IRE Journal* subsequently apologized in print to ABC and issued a chapter and verse rebuttal from ABC of statements

in the article. "Apologies to ABC, Producers," *IRE Journal* 22.6 (August 1999): 4.

39. Horwitz, email exchange with author, 25 and 27 May 2010. Horwitz was living in a Virginia village without telephone reception in 1994. "For a journalist," he said, "as you're probably grasping, I've had the perhaps bad habit of not paying much attention to other media, tend to focus tightly on what I'm working on and tune out the rest."

40. Horwitz, telephone interview by author, 21 January 2010.

41. Ibid.

42. Paul Steiger, telephone interview with author, 19 May 2010.

43. Charlie LeDuff, "The Crossing: A Perilous 4,000 Mile Passage to Work," *New York Times,* 29 May 2001.

44. Ellen Bugher, "At Massage Parlors Image Fits," *News-Sentinel,* 17 November 1984, 1A; Bugher, "City Policy Hinders Law Enforcement," *News-Sentinel,* 17 November 1984, 7A; Tony Horwitz and Bugher, "About the Visits," *News-Sentinel,* 17 November 1984, 7A; Bugher, "Nothing Surprises Massage Manager," *News-Sentinel,* 17 November 1984, 7A; Bugher, "Stigma Irks Trained Massagists," *News-Sentinel,* 19 November 1984, 1B; and Nancy Nall, "Studios Offer Varied 'Conversation,'" *News-Sentinel,* 19 November 1984, 1B.

45. Horwitz, telephone interview.

46. Ibid.

47. Ibid.

48. Horwitz: "Yes, Barney was a stickler and put the fear of God in us (almost literally—he's a preacher's son) . . . and in those days, the copy editors were sticklers too and certainly would have quizzed me about wording in the piece." Horwitz, email exchange with author, 2 June 1010.

49. Steiger, telephone interview by author, 19 May 2010. Steiger mentioned several memorable instances: reporters called the hotline of the Internal Revenue Service pretending to be taxpayers in need of information and were able to document the often contradictory information ordinary citizens received when seeking authoritative advice. Byron "Barney" Calame, in a telephone interview by the author on 1 June 2010, recalled several others the *Journal* had authorized.

50. Steiger, telephone interview. See also Alix Freedman, "Peddling Dreams: A Marketing Giant Uses Its Sales Prowess to Profit on Poverty—Thorn EMI's Rental Centers Push Sofas, Rings, VCRs to the Poor at High Rates—Repos and 'Couch Payments,'" *Wall Street Journal,* 22 September 1993, A1.

51. Timothy K. Smith, "War Games: In Alabama's Woods, Frank Camper Trains Men to Repel Invaders—Prep School for Mercenaries Has Notorious Graduates, Seminar in Throat Cutting—A Paramilitary Fantasy Land," *Wall Street Journal,* 19 August 1985, 1. The story does not mention method, but the last third has references to "we" and "our."

52. Steiger, telephone interview.

53. Calame, telephone interview.

54. Ibid.

55. Steiger, telephone interview.

56. Ibid. He had no television in February 1994 during the Federal Beef v. CBS contretemps and was living abroad in 1992 when *20/20* originally aired its Food Lion exposé. The ethics aspects of the story did not garner sustained media attention until the court cases heated up about five years later.

57. Steiger, telephone interview; and Calame, telephone interview.

58. A copy of the application has not survived, but the wording in Horwitz's story, coupled with Calame's explicit instructions, indicates that the application did not ask for his "previous" employer, which, in Calame's view, had Horwitz responded with Dow Jones, would have crossed the line, would have constituted a lie. The question was raised because a reporter's summary of how Horwitz had completed his job application (Banda, "Working Undercover"), published shortly after the story appeared, uses this wording: "'My instructions from the editors were to tell no lies,' he said. On his application form, he listed Dow Jones & Co., publishers of the *Wall Street Journal,* as his previous employer, though he left the job description question blank. He also accurately put down his university education." Susan Paterno ("Lying Game," 40) says he gave "Dow Jones & Co., the publisher of the *Journal,* as his current employer." Claudia Kovar ("Court Judgment Provides Food for Thought," *Tulsa World,* 19 March 1997, 2) interviewed Horwitz in 1997 and writes of the application matter: "He said he listed his actual employer, Dow Jones and

Co., which owns the *Wall Street Journal,* giving the time of his employment there as 1989—on the job application." From what Horwitz wrote in the piece and my subsequent interviews with him and with Calame, it appears the use of the word *previous* in Banda's recounting is in error.

59. Calame, telephone interview.

60. Horwitz, telephone interview.

61. Charlie LeDuff, interview, JournalismJobs.com, March 2001, http://www.journalismjobs.com/interview_leduff.cfm.

62. LeDuff, interview.

63. Michael Winerip, telephone interview by author, 1 June 2010.

64. Ibid.

65. LeDuff, "At the Slaughterhouse," A1.

66. Horwitz, "9 to Nowhere," A1.

67. Ibid.

68. LeDuff, "At the Slaughterhouse," A1. Analysis courtesy of William Marshall.

69. LeDuff, "At the Slaughterhouse," A1.

70. Horwitz, telephone interview.

71. LeDuff, interview.

72. Horwitz, telephone interview.

73. LeDuff, interview.

74. Banda, "Working Undercover," 14.

75. Horwitz, telephone Q&A with author and NYU journalism students, 17 January 2010.

76. LeDuff, interview.

77. Banda, "Working Undercover," 14

78. Horwitz, telephone interview, confirming information in Banda, "Working Undercover," 14, with the exception of the application employment record.

79. Steiger, managing editor, *Wall Street Journal,* to the Pulitzer Committee Judges, 23 January 1995, Pulitzer Prize Archives courtesy of the Columbia University Rare Books and Manuscript Library. The letter, dated not even two months after the first story ran, concludes with the requisite assessment of its impact, which included swift and abundant response from readers; mention by OSHA's director, Joseph Dear, and U.S. Secretary of Labor Robert Reich; and a call for hearings from Kan-

sas Senator Nancy Kassenbaum, then chair of the Labor and Human Resources Committee.

80. Banda, "Working Undercover," 14.

81. Charlie LeDuff, interview by Charlie Rose, *Charlie Rose,* PBS, 25 April 2001, http://charlierose.com/view/interview/3150.

82. Steve Striffler, *Chicken* (New Haven: Yale University Press, 2005). Striffler is an anthropologist who was teaching at the University of Arkansas at the time of publication.

83. Banda, "Working Undercover," 14. The story appeared only a few short weeks after Horwitz's articles from December 1, 1994. The prizes would not be awarded until spring.

84. A more detailed accounting of these projects appears in the companion database to this project at http://undercoverreporting.org.

85. See, for example, Joel Grover, "Produce Market Investigation," KNBC, 1–2 February 2007, 6 February 2007, 12 March 2007, which revealed filthy conditions at the Los Angeles Seventh Street Produce Market.

86. Dave Savini, "Rotting Meat, Security Documents, and Corporal Punishment," *Nieman Reports,* Summer 2009, http://www.nieman.harvard.edu/reports/article/101556/Rotting-Meat-Security-Documents-and-Corporal-Punishment.aspx.

87. Ibid.

88. Ibid.

89. "HSUS Exposes Inhumane Treatment of Pigs at Smithfield," Humane Society of the United States, 15 December 2010 http://www.humanesociety.org/news/press_releases/2010/12/smithfield_pigs_121510.html. See also Philip Walzer, "Humane Society Claims Abuse at Smithfield Foods Farm," *Virginian-Pilot,* 15 December 2010; "Smithfield's Treatment of Pigs Under Scrutiny," *Virginian-Pilot,* 16 December 2010, B1; "Smithfield Foods Fires Three After Complaint of Pig Abuse," 22 December 2010, B3; "Smithfield Defends Handling of Pigs," *Virginian-Pilot,* 23 December 2010, B2; and "Humane Society Claims Pigs Abused at Va. Farm," *Washington Post* via Associated Press, 15 December 2010.

90. Steiger, telephone interview.

91. Steiger, to the Pulitzer Committee Judges.

92. Ibid.

## CHAPTER ELEVEN

1. Richard H. Stewart, "Doing Time" series, *Boston Globe,* Living, 1: "The First Day; Dignity Leaves and Fear Arrives," 27 December 1983; "The Cell Block: Life in a Barren 5-by-8 Space; Second of a Five-Part Series," 28 December 1983; "Rules to Learn; Cigarettes Are Money, Bells Control Life; Salem—Locked in My Cell for the First Time I Began to Sense the Isolation; and the First Pangs of Frustration from the Loss of Freedom," 29 December 1983; "Jail Boredom Biggest Hassle; Fourth of a Five-Part Series," 30 December 1983; "The Final Days in Jail; Last of a Five-Part Series," 31 December 1983.

2. Steve Weinberg, "Interview with William Gaines," *IRE Journal* (November/December 1997): 3, 10.

3. "Filth and Neglect Bared at von Solbrig Hospital," *Chicago Tribune,* 7 September 1975, 1; William Gaines, "Janitor Helps with Patients: Lives Are Held in Grimy Hands," 7 September 1975, 10; "By von Solbrig Physician: Surgery Done on Assembly Line," 8 September 1975, 1; Gaines and Jay Branegan, "Probe Started at von Solbrig," 9 September 1975, 1; Branegan, "Hospital Tour Bears Apparent Violations," 10 September 1975, 10; Pamela Zekman and Gaines, "Von Solbrig Hospital Placed on Probation," 10 September 1975, 1; Zekman and William Crawford Jr., "3 Northeast Hospital Probes Begin," 11 September 1975, 1; Zekman and Branegan, "Delay Will Back Probe of Hospitals," 12 September 1975, 2; "Two Hospitals Take the Cure," 12 September 1975, A2; Zekman and Crawford, "Senate to Hold Hearings on Aid Fraud at Hospitals," 14 September 1975, 3; Arthur Siddon, "Two *Tribune* Reporters Tell Hospital Abuses; Senate Unit 'Shocked,'" 27 September 1975, N1; Charles Mount, "Media-Maneuvering in the Walker Style," 6 October 1975, A2; Zekman, "Hospital on Probation: von Solbrig Hearing Set," 7 October 1975, A1; Zekman and Gaines, "City Is Asked to Close von Solbrig Hospital," 10 October 1975, 1; Zekman and Branegan, "Powers Sought by Health Board," 11 October 1975, S7; "Half a Job Well Done," 13 October 1975, A2; Gaines, "Von Solbrig Hospital Sued for Violations," 16 October 1975, 2; Zekman and Crawford, "Health Violations Found at Northeast Hospital," 31 October 1975, B16; Gaines and Branegan, "Von Solbrig Hospital

Shuts in Wake of Probe," 13 November 1975, 1; "Federal Probe of Two Hospitals Set Here," 14 November 1975, 1; Zekman and Crawford, "Second Hospital in Probe Closes," 20 November 1975, 1; and Zekman and Crawford, "2nd Facility to Stay Shut: Rush Medical Center to Operate Northeast," 22 November 1975, S2. See also Gaines, "Lost Art of Infiltration," *Journalism* 8.5 (October 2007): 495, in which he says he participated in seven undercover investigations.

4. Undercover investigations in which Gaines played a role included the *Tribune*'s bill collection probe in 1974 and its 1975 investigations of trucking school practices.

5. Gaines, "Lost Art of Infiltration," 495.

6. See http://pulitzer.org/awards/1971. Jones won the award in his name, with a citation that read: "For exposing collusion between police and some of Chicago's largest private ambulance companies to restrict service in low income areas, leading to major reforms." William Jones, "Men of Mercy Profit in Pain," *Chicago Tribune,* 7 June 1970, 1; Jones, "Sadism Rides an Ambulance," 8 June 1970, 1; Jones, "Landlady Almost Ruins Probe," 9 June 1970, 2; Jones, "Heart Victim Is Left in Flat; Had Only $2," 9 June 1970, 1–2; Jones, "Police Sell Ambulance Cases; $10 Is Common Fee," 10 June 1970, 1–2; Jones, "Ambulance Quiz Ordered," 10 June 1970, 1–2; Jones, "3 Ambulance Firms Banned in Aid Cases," 11 June 1970, 2; Jones, "Ambulances' Crews Pilfer Hospital Goods for Their Supplies," 12 June 1970, 1–2; Jones, "Ambulance Quiz in Senate Urged," 13 June 1970, 1; Jones, "Report Urges Control over Ambulances," 14 June 1970, 27; Jones, "City Ambulance Reform: Daley Vows More Units, Better Care," 18 June 1970, 1–2; Jones, "City Ambulance Firms Linked to Mob Loans," 21 June 1970, 3; Jones and Edward Schreiber, "City Acts to Aid Poor, Buys 10 Ambulances," 23 June 1970, B11; "City Controls on Ambulance Services Proposed," 24 June 1970, A4; Jones, "Investigators Find Three Linked to Mob Control Ambulance Firm," 25 June 1970, 2; Jones, "2 Ambulance Firms Denied Funds," 26 June 1970, 15; Schreiber and Jones, "Daley Urges Testing of Ambulance Crews," 2 July 1970, 10; Jones, "5 Ambulance Reforms Told: Association Acts to End Mistreatment," 22 July 1970, 1–2; Jones, "Ordinance Seeks Ban on Ambulance Sirens," 25 July 1970, 1, 6; Jones, "Three Ambulance Firms Face City Charges, Loss of Licenses," 6 August 1970, 1, 4; Jones, "State

Ambulance Fee Controls Sought by Public Aid Official," 7 August 1970, 4; Jones, "Police Probed in Ambulance Payoff Plot," 8 August 1970, 12; Jones, "City Council Passes Tough, New Controls on Ambulance Firms," 11 August 1970, 5; Jones, "Calls for City Ambulances Set a Record: Follows Addition of 11 Vehicles to Fleet," 14 August 1970, 18; "Ambulance Hearing Is Told of Violations," 28 August 1970, 6; Jones, "Left by Ambulance, Prober Says at Quiz," 19 September 1970, N19; Jones, "Hearings End in Ambulance Abuse Cases: Licenses of 3 Firms Are in Jeopardy," 22 September 1970, A8; Jones and Schreiber, "Ambulance Firms Suspended for 30 Days," 29 September 1970, A6; Jones, "Probe Finds More Ambulance Abuses," 20 October 1970, A10; Jones, "New Ambulance Service to Begin," 12 November 1970, C16; Jones, "Ambulance Jury Cites 16," 20 November 1970, 1–2; "Plea for Aid Spurs Probe, Jury Action," 20 November 1970, 2; Jones, "4 More Cops Face Possibility of Being Fired," 21 November 1970, 2; Jones, "Ambulance Firm's President Fined $100 in Municipal Court," 24 November 1970, A11; Jones, "3 in Ambulance Quiz Seek Runs in Gary," 9 December 1970, D8; Jones, "Ambulance Probe Firm Folds Here," 10 December 1970, C21; and "Saved Taxpayers $50 Million: B.G.A.," 16 February 1971, A14.

7. "Tribune Task Force Reports from Inside," *Chicago Tribune,* 28 February 1971, 2; and Jones, "Sentence Cop in Ambulance Case," 20 April 1971, 7.

8. The Task Force members were William Jones, Pamela Zekman, Phil Caputo, and William Currie. "Tribune Task Force Reports from Inside," *Chicago Tribune,* 28 February 1971, 2; "Abuses in Nursing Homes: Some Elderly Prefer Death, Reporters Find," 28 February 1971, 1; Zekman, "Cries for Help from Aged Answered with Brutality," 1 March 1971, 1; "Warehouses for Neglected: Nurse Homes Defy Health, Fire Codes," 1 March 1971, 1; Jones, "Simon Will Ask Nurse Home Probe," 1 March 1971, 2; Caputo and Currie, "Halt Nursing Home Funds: State Welfare is Withheld, Probe Begins," 2 March 1971, 1; "Nursing Home's Shaving Time Becomes Torture for Patient," 2 March 1971, 1; Jones, "'Nobody Works Too Hard Here,'" 2 March 1971, 2; Editorial, "Man's Inhumanity," 2 March 1971, 14; Jones and Zekman, "Daley Orders New Laws, Nurse Home Inspections," 3 March 1971, 1; Michael Kilian, "Rangel on Probe," 3 March 1971, 1; "Regulations Fail to Aid 'Living Dead,'" 3 March 1971,

2; Caputo, "Crippled and Elderly Patients Abused in North Side Home," 3 March 1971, 2; Zekman and Caputo, "Subpoena Homes for Elderly," 4 March 1971, 1; Jones, "As 'Patients,' Probers Learn Ordeal of Nursing Home Life," 4 March 1971, 2; "Nursing Home Unit Backs State's Probe," 4 March 1971, 3; Jones and Zekman, "'A Lousy, Horrible Place,'" 5 March 1971, 1; "Nursing Home Investigators Cite Examples of Good Care," 5 March 1971, 2; Jones and Zekman, "Nursing Home Closed," 6 March 1971, 1; Currie, "Reporter 'Directs' Home," 6 March 1971, 1; "State Attacked on Nursing Home Licenses," 7 March 1971, 5; Jones and Caputo, "Some Nursing Homes Jeer at Law," 8 March 1971, 1; Zekman, "City's Health Chief Closes 3 Nursing Homes for Abuses," 9 March 1971, 1; John Elmer, "3 Call for Tightening of Nursing Home Laws," 9 March 1971, 3; Philip Warden, "Senate Sets Hearings on Nurse Homes," 10 March 1971, 1; Jones and Zekman, "Crisis in Nursing Homes Is Blamed on State Policy," 10 March 1971, 3; Jones and Zekman, "Nurse Home Bars Transfer of Patients," 11 March 1971, 1; "Delay Asks Nurse Home Change," 11 March 1971, 4; Elmer, "House Panel O.K.'s Rest Home Probe," 11 March 1971, 5; Jones and Zekman, "State Vows Cleanup of Nursing Homes," 12 March 1971, 1; Zekman, "Chicago Board of Health Calls Nurse Home Staffs to Account," 13 March 1971, 5; Zekman and Caputo, "Flay Nursing Home Chiefs: Legislators Charge Lack of Standards," 16 March 1971, 1; John Davies, "Aged Homes Shut, Patients Moved," 21 March 1971, 4; Jones, "Percy Predicts Wide Rest Home Reforms," 22 March 1971, 1; Jones and Zekman, "Court Action Sought Against Rest Homes," 23 March 1971, 1; Jones, "Delay Predicts City to File Suit Against More Nursing Homes," 26 March 1971, 1; Jones and Caputo, "Reveal Recommendations to Improve Nursing Homes," 1 April 1971, 1; and "The Tribune Task Force Goes to Work: Case No. 1: Chicago's Nursing Homes," 28 February 1971–5 March 1971, and reactions and response through May 1971. Of the Task Force launch, the newspaper said, "The concept of using a team of reporters enables *The Tribune* to present to its readers, quickly and comprehensively, stories that will analyze the major concerns of society today.... The task force will have varied assignments which will take it into the complexities of government, the maze of social programs and the dilemmas of urban affairs."

9. "Tribune Task Force Reports from Inside," *Chicago Tribune,* 28 February 1971, 2.

10. Michael Miner, "When Undercover Was King: More Bleeding at the *Sun-Times,*" *Chicago Reader,* 9 August 2001.

11. Steve Weinberg, "Interview with William Gaines."

12. Michael Miner, "When Undercover Was King."

13. Weinberg, "Interview with Gaines."

14. Miner, "When Undercover Was King."

15. See David Remnick, "Big Think Interview," *BigThink,* 20 April 2010, http://bigthink.com/davidremnick; and Choire Sicha, *The Awl,* 2 June 2010, which quotes Remnick as saying, "One of the great Web orthodoxies was that no one would read anything of length on line. Bullshit. Yes! It's one of the most pleasing and surprising facts of the Internet! Anyone who says that long-form writing doesn't perform well online is working for some MSN celeb picture site or just hates words." http://www.theawl.com/tag/david-remnick, accessed 21 February 2011.

16. Miner, "When Undercover Was King."

17. This was the suggestion of Kurt Andersen in a letter to Northwestern University Press, dated 20 December 2007, commenting on the proposal for this project.

18. Lois Timnick, "Despair for the Mentally Ill: Metro Hospital—Place of Little Hope," *Los Angeles Times,* 23 August 1979, A1. The newspaper's front-page explainer reads: "Posing as a graduate psychology student, *Times* Human Behavior Writer Lois Timnick worked for two weeks inside Metropolitan State Hospital, gaining an unprecedented firsthand look at what goes on behind locked doors of the psychiatric wards. This report and other articles on Page 3 reveal a mental-health program that in many ways has no better chance of succeeding than the patients it purports to serve. It is underfinanced, poorly staffed and riddled with conflict."

19. The citation reads: "Local Investigative Specialized Reporting: Staff of *Chicago Tribune* for uncovering widespread abuses in Federal housing programs in Chicago and exposing shocking conditions at two private Chicago hospitals." http://pulitzer.org/awards/1976.

20. Weinberg, "Interview with Gaines."

21. Gaines, "Lost Art of Infiltration."

22. Erving Goffman, *Asylums: Essays on the Social Situation of Mental Patients and Other Inmates* (New York: Anchor Books, 1961), 16. Goffman said total institutions in our society can be listed in five rough groupings: those established to care for the incapable and harmless; to care for people felt to be unable to look after themselves but also a threat to the community; sanitaria and asylums; those organized to protect the community against perceived dangers to it (jails and prisons; POW and concentration camps); institutions established to "pursue some work list task" (boarding schools; army camps; servants' quarters on large estates); and retreats such as monasteries and convents.

23. Stewart, "Doing Time" series, *Boston Globe,* Living section, 27 December 1983–31 December 1983, 1. Stewart went to jail for six days in Salem, Massachusetts, on an ostensible drunk-driving conviction. He was "confined at hard labor" on a "phony but official-looking court order," which he described as "part of the deception to get me into jail as a 'legitimate' inmate without anybody knowing my true identity."

24. Annie Laurie, "A City's Disgrace: Sample of Civilization of the Nineteenth Century; Brutality of Public Servants; The 'Examiner's' Annie Laurie in the Receiving Hospital; An Emetic Given for Hysterics," *San Francisco Chronicle,* 19 January 1890, 11. Laurie also reported that hospital staffers made lewd comments to her. After her report was published, an official investigation led to dismissal of some hospital staff and the opening of that city's first ambulance service.

25. Pierre Salinger, *P.S.: A Memoir* (New York: St. Martin's Press, 1995), 32–35.

26. Nat Caldwell, undated full series in a reprint issue, "The Abandoned Generation," *Nashville Tennessean,* ca. March 1968. In the newspaper: Nat Caldwell, undated full series in reprint, "The Abandoned Generation," *Nashville Tennessean,* 31 March–9 April, 1968. "Reporter's Inside Story: Nursing Homes Crowded, Dirty," 31 March 1968, 1; "'Old Man' Headed Team in 6-Week Investigation," 31 March 1968, 1; "'For 85 Years ... And This Is All He Had to Show,'" 1 April 1968, 1; "Fire Danger for Aged Ever Present," 2 April 1968, 1; "Residents Are 'Guests': Belcourt Terrace Living's Good," 3 April 1968, 1; "Nursing Home's 'Pride' Pays Off," 4 April 1968, 1; "'Take Us Fishing,' Doctors Can't Cure Boredom,"

9 April 1968, 4. Follow-up articles: Caldwell, "Nat Caldwell Reports: Public Shows Deep Concern For Nursing Home Patients," 12 April 1968, 4.

Two younger reporters who also worked on the series posed as distant relatives arranging for his care and, a week later in each instance, his release. For his six-part series in the *Tennessean,* Caldwell reported graphically on "overcrowding and deprivation," old buildings "that were firetraps," and "revoltingly unsanitary" conditions.

Caldwell first flew to Charlotte, North Carolina, to secure his cover story and was admitted to a home in that city first to avoid having his identity questioned once he was back in Nashville. In explaining the methodology, the newspaper reported that Caldwell never used a false name or address and even offered as identification his real Social Security number and Tennessee driver's license. The license gave his correct name, Nathan G. Caldwell, his correct address, and age. It even identified him as a reporter. Nonetheless, none of the operators of the homes showed any interest in confirming his identity. He was admitted to the first home in the space of half an hour and without a doctor's examination. "I have been called a hard-boiled reporter," Caldwell wrote in his opening piece. "Often in those three weeks, I cried. And not at anything that happened to me."

The six-week investigation included above-board visits by Caldwell and his fellow reporters to all twenty-six of Nashville's private nursing homes. Although most of the administrators were cooperative, some refused access to kitchens and bathrooms and others said inspection could happen only after a patient's admission. A few denied access entirely. At least one or two stood out as excellent facilities and stories about them featured prominently in the series, too.

27. Frank Sutherland, "Personal Experience: Central State Conditions Found Poor," *Nashville Tennessean,* 20 January 1974, 1; "Reporter Finds Hospital Stay Demoralizing," 21 January 1974, 1; "Aides, Many Untrained, Run Central State," 22 January 1974, 1; "Christmas Means Joyless Tension in Locked Ward," 23 January 1974, 1; "Skimpy, Unprofessional Patient File Reveals Inadequate Treatment," 24 January 1974, 1; "'Ward Meeting' Breaks Silence," 25 January 1974, 1; "Hospital Complex Old, Battered, But in Use," 26 January 1974, 1; "State Help Dire Need at Hospital," 27 Janu-

ary 1974, 1; "Officials Agree Central State Needs Reform," 28 January 1974, 1; "State Mental Hospitals 'Could Lose Millions,'" 29 January 1974, 1; "Central State Woes Reflected at East State Hospital," 10 February 1974, 10; "Report Urges Central State Improvements," 19 February 1974, 1; "Change in Central State Role, Scope Advised," 21 February 1974, 1; Doug Hall, "Tragle Raps Hospital Critics," *Nashville Tennessean,* 24 February 1974, 4; and Sutherland, "Central State Needs Action Right Now!" 3 March, 1974, 1B. Commentary: Editorial, "State's Mentally Ill Deserve Better Care," *Nashville Tennessean,* 22 January 1974, 6; John Hale, "Mental Health Fund Needed," 31 January 1974, 1; and Editorial, "Mental Health Deserves Top Assembly Priority," 31 January 1974, 14.

28. Kevin Heldman, "7 ½ Days," *City Limits,* June–July 1998, http://journalismworksproject.org/psych_hosp01.html.

29. Ray "R. H." Ring, telephone interview with author, 1 July 2010.

30. Ben H. Bagdikian, "No. 50061, Inside Maximum Security: Six Days in State Prison Through the Eyes of a 'Murderer,'" *Washington Post,* 31 January 1972, A1.

31. Albert Deutsch, in "The Exposé as a Progressive Tool," *Mental Hygiene* 341.1 (1950): 80–89, writes: "The recent epidemic of exposés, spreading from paper to paper like a benign infection, has been unique in at least one respect: the reporters, in most instances, have entered the institutions not as hostile invaders, threatening the reputation and security of superintendents and other officers, but as welcome allies enlisted in a common cause" (80).

32. Brooke Kroeger, *Nellie Bly: Daredevil, Reporter, Feminist* (New York: Times Books), 89–90n546.

33. Pierre Salinger, "Exclusive! Brutal, Filthy Jails Exposed: *Chronicle* Reporter Does Time, Tells Inside Story of Cruel, Crowded Cells," *San Francisco Chronicle,* 26 January 1953, 1. Salinger explains that the jails were selected not because they were the worst, but because they were representative of dilapidated, overcrowded conditions across the system, and that "by secret arrangement," he was "'arrested' on a small side street in Stockton, where I was asleep in an automobile. After being frisked by two police officers, I was hustled into a police car and taken to the jail. . . . After being booked at the jail as 'drunk and hold' I was shoved into Tank 8 to spend my first night in jail" in a cell with seventeen other men. The

Salinger series continued on the following dates and under the following headlines: "Youths Cooped Up with Older, Hardened Crooks," 27 January 1953; "Ugly Violence Behind Bars: Reporter Tells How Cellmate Blew His Top," 28 January 1953; "The Slip at 18 . . . Al's in a Cell: He Met Thieves, Cons, in S.F. Jail . . . 'Dismal' System, Says Expert," 29 January 1953; "Sex Perverts, Extortionists Run the Cells," 30 January 1953; "Honor Rancho in L.A. Better Than Others," 31 January 1953; "Honor Rancho Has Its Faults: One of the Best—But: No Medical Care, Not Enough Rehabilitation," 1 February 1953; "Inside Story of Kern Jail: Reporter's Hitch at Bakersfield Reveals Bad Food, Crowding," 2 February 1953; "A Beating in Jail: In the Pre-Dawn, a Man Is Marked Up for Life," 3 February 1953; "Alameda Jail—'Best in Nation'—County Prisoners Work to Go to School, Eat Well," 4 February 1953; "Shame of County: Degradation in Stinking Cells," 5 February 1953; "S.F. County Jail Is Too Much Like a Penitentiary," 6 February 1953; "Men in S.F. Jails Get Helping Hand," 7 February 1953; "County Jail Reform Urged: Warren, Brown Tell How Conditions Can Be Improved," 8 February 1953; "Worst Institutions: Poor Jails Cause Crowding in Prison," 9 February 1953; and "A Fight for Reform: Modesto Aroused by Its Rotten Jail," 10 February 1953.

34. Salinger, *P.S.: A Memoir,* 32–35.

35. Ibid.

36. Salinger, "Brutal, Filthy Jails Exposed."

37. *San Francisco Chronicle,* "Behind Prison Bars" series: Tim Findley, "Reporter's Story—'I'm in Soledad,'" *San Francisco Chronicle,* 22 February 1971, A1; Charles Howe, "California Penal System—World's 3rd Biggest," 22 February 1971, A1; Findley, "Con's Main Street," 23 February 1971, A1; Findley, "Soledad's 'Hole'—A Setting for Death, Revenge," 24 February 1971, A1; Findley, "The Soledad 'Games,'" 25 February 1971, A1; Findley and Howe, "Behind Prison Bars: Sex Fears Among the Cons," 1 March 1971, A1; Howe, "The Prison Clientele Is Tougher," 1 March 1971, A13; Howe, "Cons Get It Together," 2 March 1971, A1; Findley, "Folsom—Where the 'Elite' Meet," 2 March 1971, A16; Findley, "The Men Without Hope," 3 March 1971, A1; Findley, "Behind Prison Bars," 4 March 1971, A8; Howe, "I Was a Guard at San Quentin," 8 March 1971, A1; Howe, "Vacaville, the First Stop," 8 March 1971,

A10; Howe, "Why Prisoners Keep Coming Back," 9 March 1971, A14; Howe, "The Day We Shook the Yard Down," 9 March 1971, A14; Howe, "San Quentin's Elite Force in Action," 10 March 1971, A1; Findley, "The Men Who Dictate Prison Terms," 10 March 1971, A18; Findley, "The Men Who Can Set a Con Free," 11 March 1971, A8; Howe, "Loneliness, Unemployment: Problems of Parolees," 12 March 1971, A8; and Howe, "How Experts Want to Change Prisons," 15 March 1971, A1. See especially Howe, "I Was a Guard," 1, where he writes, "My cover story was that I had transferred to San Quentin from a prison in Southern California after spending about six months there. Prior to that, I said, I had spent twenty years in the Marine Corps, mainly working in brigs and stockades, retiring as a Master Gunnery Sergeant." The Findley Soledad pieces are dated 22, 23, 24, and 25, February 1971.

38. Findley, "I Was a UC Prisoner," *San Francisco Chronicle,* 24 May 1969, A1.

39. Tim Findley, telephone interview by author, 26 July 2010.

40. Ben H. Bagdikian and Leon Dash, "The Shame of the Prisons" series, *Washington Post:* "A Human Wasteland in the Name of Justice," 30 January 1972, A1; "Inside Maximum Security" 31 January 1972, A1; "Bureaucratic Overload Turns Justice to Misery," 1 February 1972, A1; "Female Homosexuality Prevalent," 2 February 1972, A1; "Juvenile Prison: Society's Stigma," 3 February 1972, A1; "Rehabilitation: A Frayed Hope," 4 February 1972, A1; "The Drive for Inmates Rights," 5 February 1972, A1; and "An Agenda for Reform of a Hell Behind Walls," 5 February 1972, A1. Also, in book form, see Ben H. Bagdikian and Leon Dash, *The Shame of the Prisons* (New York: Pocketbooks, 1972).

41. Bagdikian and Dash, *Shame of the Prisons,* 5.

42. Bagdikian, "Inside Maximum Security."

43. Ring, telephone interview. Ring recalled that Arizona's prison system was deeply troubled in the early 1980s, "under one court order, bad conditions, riots, oppressive regime—typical menu." Ellis MacDougall, a troubleshooter and prison reformer, had been brought in to turn things around, or, as Ring put it, "someone who could satisfy the judges." Tucson's *Arizona Daily Star* decided to produce a major package of stories that looked at the system historically, in terms of its overcrowding, election year issues, racism, and reform. As an anchor to the series, Ring took

an assignment from his "life list—like hitchhiking to Alaska or visiting a Mexican whorehouse"—to go undercover as a prisoner. For a companion piece in the long supplement, another reporter, John Long, posed as a guard. Ring said MacDougall was very reluctant to agree to the ruse—as Ring soon understood, there could be no good outcome for him—and he delayed and delayed before giving an answer. When it seemed clear he was going to refuse the request, Ring walked out of a meeting with him, accusing him hotly of having strung the paper along. Ring knew he had played an important card. No one in MacDougall's position wants to alienate a major newspaper, and even if the story worked out badly for him, it would only be one piece in a major series that served the prison system's larger interest. MacDougall followed Ring out to the elevator and relented.

44. R.H. Ring, "Convicted," *Arizona Daily Star,* 8 August 1982.

45. Zekman, "Cries for Help," 1.

46. Gaines, "Lost Art of Infiltration."

47. Howe, "I Was a Guard," 1.

48. William Recktenwald, telephone interview by author, 23 December 2010. Also, the series: Recktenwald, "'I Was a Guard in Pontiac Prison,'" *Chicago Tribune,* 29 October 1978, 1; "How *Tribune* Investigator Was Hired," 29 October 1978, 22; "Working the Cells Where Three Died," 30 October 1978, 1; "'Just Keep 'Em Locked Up, That's All,'" 31 October 1978, 1; Mitchell Locin, "Pontiac Disclosures No Shock—Thompson," 31 October 1978, 10; Recktenwald, "New Pontiac Warden Moves to End Deadlock," 1 November 1978, 1; "How He Read Prison Story," 1 November 1978, 16; "Judge to Rule Friday on Suit to End Lockup," 1 November 1978, 16; Bob Wiedrich, "Charles Rowe's Sudden Discovery," 1 November, 1978, B4; Wiedrich, "Prisoners Get Exercise: Pontiac Deadlock Ending," 2 November 1978, C14; Wiedrich, "Special Committee: Assembly Leaders Act to Probe Prisons," 5 November 1978, 5; Recktenwald, "Asked $500,000 for Prosecuting Prison Rioters," 26 November 1978, B7; "One Visitor's Return," *Tribune,* 22 July 1979, A1.

49. Conover, various email and telephone exchanges with author, 2009–2011.

50. Bagdikian and Dash, *Shame of the Prisons,* 5.

51. Silas Bent, *Newspaper Crusaders: A Neglected Story* (New York: Whittelsey House, 1939), 197–98.

52. Frank Smith, "Seven Days in the Madhouse: Reporter's Experience at Kankakee," *Chicago Daily Times,* 15 July 1935, 1, 3; "Reporter Takes Kankakee 'Water Cure,'" 16 July 1935, 3; "Reporter's Night of Terror at Kankakee," 17 July 1935, 3; "'Death Cup' Perils Kankakee Inmates," 18 July 1935, 3; "'Railroaded to Kankakee as Insane,'" 19 July 1935, 3; "Haunted by Kankakee Fire Hazards," 22 July 1935; "Crazy Rhythm! Dance at Kankakee," 23 July 1935, 3; "Attempted Suicide at Kankakee Hospital," 24 July 1935, 3; "Water Perils Inmates at Kankakee," 25 July 1935, 3; "Freedom! Reporter Leaves Kankakee," 26 July 1935, 3.

53. Bent, *Newspaper Crusaders,* 197–98.

54. "The Press: Chicago Thorn," *Time,* 20 September 1937. *Time* credited managing editor Louis Ruppel's formula for the newspaper's success, under publisher Samuel Emory Thomason, who went to the newspaper in 1935 and led off with the Kankakee revelations. The complimentary report mentioned another sting for which the newspaper's photographers had disguised themselves as clergymen "so they could sneak into a hospital [and] scoop a picture of an injured motorman after an 'L' crash."

55. See both Deutsch, *The Mentally Ill in America* (New York: Columbia University Press, 1937), 300–330, and Deutsch, "Exposé as a Progressive Tool," 80–89.

56. Deutsch, "Exposé as a Progressive Tool," 80–81.

57. See both Deutsch, *Mentally Ill in America,* 300–330, and "Exposé as a Progressive Tool," 80–89.

58. Deutsch, "Exposé as a Progressive Tool," 80–83.

59. See, for example, Steven J. Taylor, *Acts of Conscience: World War II, Mental Institutions, and Religious Objectors* (Syracuse: Syracuse University Press, 2009), 263; Alex Sareyan, *The Turning Point: How Men of Conscience Brought About Major Change in the Care of America's Mentally Ill* (Washington, D.C.: American Psychiatric Press, 1994), 270; and Gerald N. Grob, *The Mad Among Us: A History of the Care of American's Mentally Ill* (New York: Free Press, 1994), 205.

60. Albert Q. Maisel, "Bedlam," *Life,* May 1946.

61. Salinger, "Prisons Revisited," *San Francisco Chronicle,* 29–31 December 1953. The series highlighted improvements at several facilities, including new dormitory units, completion of construction plans, and new appropriations for improvements at other facilities.

62. Salinger, *P.S.: A Memoir,* 32–35.

63. Recktenwald, "How *Tribune* Investigator Was Hired," 22. See also Recktenwald, "One Visitor's Return," A1.

Three guards were slain at Pontiac Correctional Center in Illinois on 22 July 1978. Two and a half months later, prisoners were still on lockdown, confined to their cells virtually all day, denied exercise, showers, and family visits. Recktenwald applied for a guard job at the prison, hired after a twenty-minute interview in which he was asked to confirm he knew about the killings but without a background check. He reported for work on October 10, heeding the only advice he was given: that he would need a pair of comfortable shoes. "That was it," he wrote in a preface to his series, describing life in lockdown as an existence as hellish for the guards as it was for the prisoners. "No identification check. No tests. A background check wasn't initiated until a week later, when I was already working in Pontiac." On his second day, he was assigned to the segregation unit, where the "worst" prisoners were housed.

64. Recktenwald, "One Visitor's Return," *Chicago Tribune,* 22 July 1979, A1. For example, since his stories ran, background checks for prospective guards had been reinstituted. (When he applied, no action was taken on background checks until a week after hire.) But in most other ways, guards he interviewed reported, conditions at Pontiac remained about as bad as before.

65. "The Unwanted Children of Russia," *20/20,* ABC, 13 January 1999, Alfred I. duPont Columbia University Awards in Broadcast News, http://duPontawards.org/year/2000.

66. Ibid., and "Russia's Unwanted Children; Update on Russia's Orphans Living in Institutions," *20/20,* hosted by Charles Gibson and Diane Sawyer, ABC, 26 April 2000.

67. "Unwanted Children of Russia."

68. Philip Caputo, "2 Aides Arrested for Striking Elderly Nursing Home Patients," *Chicago Tribune,* 29 May 1971, 6.

69. Recktenwald, telephone interview.

70. Tribune Task Force, Von Solbrig series, *Chicago Tribune,* 7 September 1979–14 November 1975.

71. Zekman, "Cries for Help," 1.

72. Weinberg, "Interview with Gaines."

73. Ibid.

74. "What the Press Tour Saw Oct. 9; What Our Reporter Saw Oct. 17," *Chicago Tribune,* 29 October 1978, 22.

75. Recktenwald, telephone interview.

76. See *New York World,* 7 May 1893, 56; and *New York Times,* 14 August 1887, 9.2; 16 August 1887, 8.2.

77. Salinger, "Brutal, Filthy Jails Exposed," 1.

78. Bagdikian, "Human Wasteland," A1.

79. Recktenwald, "'I Was a Guard,'" 1; "How *Tribune* Investigator Was Hired," 22; "Working the Cells," 1; "'Just Keep 'Em Locked Up,'" 1; and "New Pontiac Warden," 1.

80. John S. Long, "Holding Down the Fort," *Arizona Daily Star,* 8 August 1982, 36; and Ring, "'This Ain't That Kind of Prison,'" *Arizona Daily Star,* 8 August 1982, 23.

81. Deutsch, "Exposé as a Progressive Tool," 86.

82. Tom Goldstein, *The News at Any Cost: How Journalists Compromise Their Ethics to Shape the News* (New York: Touchstone, 1985), 135–36.

83. Stewart, "Final Days in Jail."

84. Goldstein, *News at Any Cost,* 137.

85. Ring, telephone interview.

86. Elliott Parker, "Undercover Reporting, Hidden Cameras and the Ethical Decision-Making Process: A Refinement" (conference paper, Association for Education in Journalism and Mass Communication conference, Chicago, Ill., 11 October 1997), 2.

87. Ring, telephone interview.

88. Salinger, "Prisons Revisited," 1.

89. Michael Mok, "I Was a Mental Patient" series, *New York World-Telegram & Sun:* "Scared Children, Depraved Men Jammed in Wards, Reporter Reveals Overcrowding and Inadequate Staff," 15 March 1961; "Inmates Sleep on the Floor, Mutter, Stare Into Corner," 16 March 1961; "Ward 51, Nightmare of Violence," 17 March 1961; "Crowd Turns Vis-

iting Hours into Bedlam," 18 March 1961; "In Ward 33 Only Delusion Is Bearable," 20 March 1961; "Outside World Helps Lessen Boredom," 21 March 1961; "Entering Hospital Easier Than Exit," 22 March 1961; and "Ward Miseries Are Worse for Women," 23 March 1961.

90. See the Lasker Awards site: http://laskerfoundation.org/awards/formaward.htm, accessed 19 February 2011, top entry for Medical Journalism Awards, 1961.

91. For the Newspaper Guild's Heywood Broun Award winners, judges, 1960–1979, see http://www.newsguild.org/index.php?ID=986, accessed 19 February 2011.

92. Caldwell, "Nat Caldwell Reports," 4.

93. Caldwell, full series reprinted as a standalone issue, "Public Shows Deep Concern for Nursing Home Patients: The Abandoned Generation." In the newspaper, see note 26 for full citations.

94. Press release, University of Tennessee, "Petry, Caldwell in Press Hall of Fame," *Tennessee Today,* 11 November 2003. The release also notes that Caldwell shared a 1962 Pulitzer Prize with Gene Graham for six years of reporting that exposed the collusion of the United Mine Workers with mine company management.

95. Findley, telephone interview.

96. For the full list of 1973 winners, see http://rfkmemorial.mediathree.net/legacyinaction/1973/, accessed 19 February 2011.

97. For informed speculation on why Rivera was not prosecuted, see Goldstein, *News at Any Cost,* 116.

98. See http://pulitzer.org/awards/1976 and http://pulitzer.org/awards/1971. The citation reads: "Staff of *Chicago Tribune:* For uncovering widespread abuses in Federal housing programs in Chicago and exposing shocking conditions at two private Chicago hospitals." The category "Local Investigative Specialized Reporting" appears to have been dropped after the 1984 awards. See http://pulitzer.org/awards/1971. Jones won the award in his name, with a citation that read: "For exposing collusion between police and some of Chicago's largest private ambulance companies to restrict service in low income areas, leading to major reforms." As of 2010, the *Tribune* had won two more Pulitzer Prizes for investigative reporting, one in 1988 and a second in 2008.

99. Ray Ring to author, 23 June 2010.

100. "Two Tribune Writers Cited," *Chicago Tribune*, 9 May 1979, 5.

101. Findley, telephone interview.

102. See http://pulitzer.org/awards/2001. Ted Conover, *Newjack: Guarding Sing Sing* (New York: Vintage, 2001). See also http://tedconover.com/book-newjack/reviews-of-newjack/.

103. Nellie Bly, *Ten Days in a Madhouse* (New York: Munro, 1887). See also UPenn Digital Library, http://digital.library.upenn.edu/women/bly/madhouse/madhouse.html; Bly, "Among the Mad," *Godey's Lady's Book*, January 1889; and Kroeger, *Nellie Bly*, 79–103. For coverage of Bly in other New York newspapers, see *New York Sun*, 25 September 1887, 1:7; *New York Times*, 26 September 1887, 8:3; *New York Evening Telegram*, 26 September 1887, reprinted in *New York World*, 9 October 1887, 26:5; *New York Herald*, 25 September 1887, reprinted in *New York World*, 9 October 1887, 26:5. See also *New York Sun*, 7 October 1887, 5:5; *New York Times*, 7 October 1887, 8:2; *New York Sun*, 14 October 1887, 1:6–7, 2:1–4; and various in the *New York World*, 17 October 1887, 5:4, 16 October 1887, 26:4, and 17 October 1887, 5:4.

104. "The Real Annie Laurie: A Personal Introduction to a Famous and Talented Lady," *San Francisco Examiner*, 18 December 1892, 13.

105. Of Bly's dozens of subsequent undercover exploits, none of this particular ilk was as elaborate or as lengthy as her stay on Blackwell's Island. In one case she got herself arrested and spent one night in jail to experience for herself how jailers and matrons treated common women prisoners, and in another instance she visited an array of doctors complaining of the same set of symptoms and getting as many diagnoses. But for her subsequent reports on clinics for alcoholics, homes for wayward women, and the like (also in Chicago during her very short stint as a reporter for the *Chicago Times-Herald* in 1895; see Kroeger, *Bly*, 255–58), she had become far too well known not to present herself at the outset as reporter Nellie Bly.

106. "Prison Boss Says Findings 'Inexcusable,'" *Chicago Tribune*, 29 October 1978, 22.

107. "Prisoners Get Exercise," C14.

108. Wiedrich, "Special Committee," 5.

109. Recktenwald, telephone interview. Recktenwald said he also was

involved with several *Tribune* investigations that used undercover tactics, among them the newspaper's nursing home investigation, its vote fraud investigation, and its ambulance bias investigation, two of which—vote fraud and ambulance bias—won Pulitzer Prizes. For the ambulance series, Recktenwald said, "Bill Jones gave me half the money."

110. "Tribune Employees Win 1978 Beck Awards," *Chicago Tribune,* 9 December 1978, N4.

111. Sutherland, "Personal Experience." See full series at note 27.

112. Ibid.

113. Sutherland, "Central State Improvements," 1.

114. Sutherland, "Change in Central State," 1.

115. Hall, "Tragle Raps Hospital Critics," 4.

116. Sutherland, "Undercover Reporting Discouraged: The Practice Usually Is Not Necessary to Get a Story," *Editorially Speaking* 53:4 (July/August 1999).

117. Ibid.

118. Ibid.

119. Ibid.

120. Willy Stern, "Grading the Daily Part I—The Way Things Were," *Nashville Scene,* 26 April 2001.

121. Goldstein, *News at Any Cost,* 138. Responding to a questionnaire, Goldstein quotes Seigenthaler on undercover reporting, saying, "I would limit role-playing to situations where the information to be gained is of substantial public interest, and when the information sought would not be available in the same form if reporters were required to use second hand accounts."

122. Stern, "Grading the Daily Part I."

123. Ibid.

124. Deutsch won both the George Polk Award in 1948 (Science Reporting, *PM* and the Albert Lasker Award in 1949 (given by the National Committee Against Mental Illness) for his beat coverage of the mental health system. In addition to his newspaper work, he wrote a major history of the mental health movement, *Mentally Ill in America,* and various articles in scholarly journals. See Obituary, "Albert Deutsch, Critic of Social Ills in U.S.," *Washington Post,* 19 June 1961, B2.

125. Albert Deutsch's obituary (1905–1961), *Bulletin of the American Psychoanalytic Association* 18, 442–43.

126. Deutsch, "Exposé as a Progressive Tool," 80.

127. Deutsch, writing in 1950, mentioned Walter Lerch of the *Cleveland Press;* Peter Lisagor of the *Chicago Daily News;* Al Ostrow of the *Cleveland Press* and the *San Francisco News;* Mike Gorman, whose "Oklahoma Attacks Its Snake Pits" became the basis for a novel and classic film; Odom Fanning of the *Atlanta Journal;* Howard Norton of the *Baltimore Sun;* Albert Q. Maisel of *Life;* and Edith Stern, the heiress and social activist who wrote for *American Mercury.* Deutsch, "Exposé as a Progressive Tool," 85.

128. Deutsch, "Dorothea Lynde Dix: Apostle of the Insane," *American Journal of Nursing* 36.10 (October 1936): 987–97.

129. Deutsch, *Mentally Ill in America,* 307.

130. Deutsch, "Exposé as a Progressive Tool," 81.

131. Ibid.

132. Deutsch mentions two, Clifford W. Beers, *A Mind That Found Itself* (New York: Longmans, Green, 1910), and Elizabeth Parsons Ware Packard, *Mrs. Packard's Prison Life* (n.p.: Chicago, 1867), and later in two volumes, *The Prisoners' Hidden Life; or Insane Asylums Unveiled* (n.p.: Chicago, 1868, 2 vols.), republished later as *Modern Persecution* (Hartford, Conn.: n.p., 1885–87, 2 vols.). Mrs. Packard, whose husband had her committed for three years, wrote melodramatically about her experiences in *Mrs. Packard's Prison Life,* a book published in 1867, four years after her release from a public asylum in Illinois. Largely on the strength of her advocacy, a poorly considered state law was enacted to require a jury trial before a person could be committed (see Deutsch, *Mentally Ill in America,* 307). Deutsch said the requirement, widely opposed in the professional mental health community, did not protect the insane since it left the decision about mental state to a lay jury and caused families to hesitate to go through commitment proceedings because of the attendant publicity and humiliation. This in turn lessened the chance of recovery that early attention to the relative's mental state might have brought. As for Beers, he became a more formidable advocate after the publication of his book. He captured the public imagination with details of his gruesome asylum experiences

and his complete recovery. Deutsch was particularly impressed that Beers went to the trouble of enlisting psychiatrists, psychologists, and other leaders in the mental health field to vet his manuscript before publication. The book did not come out until a full five years after his asylum release.

133. Albert Deutsch, *Mentally Ill in America,* 307.

134. Ibid.

135. Albert Deutsch, "Exposé as a Progressive Tool," 86.

136. Barbara Ehrenreich, "Welcome to Cancerland: A Mammogram Leads to a Cult of Pink Kitsch," *Harper's,* November 2001, 43−53.

137. Sallie Tisdale, "We Do Abortions Here," *Harper's,* October 1987, 66−70.

138. William Styron, *Darkness Visible: A Memoir of Madness* (New York: Modern Library, 2007).

139. Norah Vincent, *Voluntary Madness: My Year Lost and Found in the Loony Bin* (New York: Viking, 2008), and Vincent, *Self-Made Man: One Woman's Journey into Manhood and Back Again* (New York: Viking Adult, 2006).

140. Norman Oder, "In the Belly of the Beast," *Publishers Weekly* 247.19 (8 May 2000): 200−201.

141. Ibid.

142. Conover, email interview by author, 17 July 2010.

143. Ibid.

144. Ibid.

145. Ibid.

146. Goldstein, *News at Any Cost,* 137, cites *Nevada Appeal* of 16 July 1984 and *The Official Report of the New York State Commission on Attica* (New York: Bantam Books, 1972).

147. "L.A.'s Giant Jail Is a Giant Headache," *Corrections,* December 1980, 32−37.

148. William Hart, telephone interview by author, 21 July 2010.

149. Hart, telephone interview.

150. Bagdikian, "Inside Maximum Security," A1. See also Bagdikian and Dash, *Shame of the Prisons,* 35.

151. Bagdikian and Dash, "Shame of the Prisons" series.

152. Advertisement, *Washington Post,* 29 January 1972, B11.

## CHAPTER TWELVE

1. Craig Unger, telephone interview by author, 15 October 2010. See also Unger, "The Fool on the Hill," Huffingtonpost.com, 13 December 2007; Unger, "American Rapture," *Vanity Fair,* December 2005, also appeared in Unger, *The Fall of the House of Bush* (New York: Scribner, 2007).

2. There are numerous early documentary sources on the Morgan case, including: Capt. William Morgan, *Illustrations of Masonry by One of the Fraternity Who Has Devoted Thirty Years to the Subject* (n.p.: David C. Miller, 1827), available online at http://utlm.org/onlinebooks/ captmorgansfreemasonrycontents.htm, accessed 19 February 2011; David C. Miller et al., *A Narrative of the Facts and Circumstances Relating to the Kidnapping and Murder of William Morgan and of the Attempt to Carry off David. C. Miller and to Burn and Destroy the Printing-Office of the Latter for the Purpose of Preventing the Printing and Publishing of a Book, Entitled "Illustrations of Masonry" Prepared Under the Direction of the Several Committees Appointed at Meetings of the Citizens of the Counties of Genessee, Livingston, Ontario, Monroe and Niagara in the State of New York* (Chicago: Ezra Cook, 1827); and Henry Brown, Counsellor at Law, Batavia, N.Y., "A Narrative of the Anti-Masonic Excitement in the Western Part of the State of New-York, During the Years 1827, 1827, 1828, and Part of 1829," *American Quarterly Review* 7.13 (March 1830): 162. See also the account of Morgan's kidnapping and the rise of the anti-Freemasonry movement in Daniel Walker Howe, *What Hath God Wrought* (Oxford: Oxford University Press, 2007), 266–70.

3. "The Press: Chicago Thorn," *Time,* 20 September 1937, http://www .time.com/time/magazine/article/0,9171,758226,00.html; and The Editors, "Behind the Scenes!" *Chicago Daily Times,* 9 September 1937, 3. During a two-month probe, the brothers Metcalfe, John C., the newspaper's real estate editor, became Hellmut Oberwinder, and James J., a former "G" man, also became an Oberwinder, but kept his first name. John C. joined a German American organization based in Astoria, New York. He quickly gained the trust of its leaders and within months was charged with traveling the country to speak to other American Nazi organizations. James J., posing as a Berlin-born son of a German father

and American mother, joined a local Chicago bund reserved for German citizens only. A third reporter with Teutonic roots, William Mueller, gained access by feigning interest in the bunds as a prospective recruit.

4. William Mueller, "Nazi Army in U.S.," *Chicago Daily Times,* 9 September 1937, 3; Mueller, "Children 'Heil'!" 10 September 1937, 3; "Nazis' Merger Scheme," 12 September 1937, 3; "Swastika in Flames," 13 September 1937, 3; "Nazis—and Church," 14 September 1937, 3; "Nazi Toys Teach War," 15 September 1937, 3; "Bund Push Jewish Boycott," 16 September 1937, 3; "Storm Troopers Develop Skill on Rifle Range," 17 September 1937, 3; and "Nazis in U.S. Boast German Consul Control," 19 September 1937, 3.

John C. Metcalfe, "I Am a U.S. Nazi Storm Trooper," *Chicago Daily Times,* 9 September 1937, 3; 10 September 1937, 3; 12 September 1937, 3; 13 September 1937, 3; 14 September 1937, 3; 16 September 1937, 15; "I Am a Nazi Storm Trooper in the U.S. Army," 15 September 1937, 14; "Storm Trooper Learns of Black Shirts' Plans," 17 September 1937, 22; "I Am a Storm Trooper in U.S. Nazi Army," 19 September 1937, 22; 20 September 1937, 14; "Boasts Rabbis Aid U.S. Nazis," 22 September 1937, 21; "Fuehrer Kuhn Travels Secretly on His Tours," 23 September 1937, 14; and "'It Can Happen Here'; Nazi Torturer Tells How," 24 September 1937, 20.

James J. Metcalfe, "Ex G-Man in U.S. Alien Nazi Army!" 15 September 1937, 3; 16 September 1937, 15; "Ex G-Man Learns Nazi Drill Plans," 17 September 1937, 21; "Ex G-Man in U.S. Alien Nazi Army," 19 September 1937, 19; "Ex G-Man Hears Bund Edict on Kenosha March," 20 September 1937, 14; "German Citizens Join U.S. Bund, Ex G-Man Learns," 21 September 1937, 19; "Ex G-Man Finds Friction in Nazi Ranks," 22 September 1937, 20; "Chicago Police 'with Us,' Ex G-Man Hears Nazi Boast," 23 September 1937, 14; and "Nazis Spy on 'Reds' Here, Ex-G Man Told," 24 September 1937, 20.

5. "Chicago Thorn."

6. Glenn Fowler, "Arthur Derounian, 82, an Author of Books on Fascists and Bigots," *New York Times,* 25 April 1991, B14.

7. John Roy Carlson, *Undercover* (Philadelphia: Blakiston, 1943), 17.

8. Carlson, *Undercover,* 28. His proud immigrant background and two affecting events in New York City also heavily influenced him in deciding to take on such a dangerous pursuit. First, there was the utter shock

to members of the Armenian community of the assassination of their primate, Archbishop Leon Tourian, who was stabbed to death with butcher knives in the culmination of a months-long internecine struggle. The attack came while Tourian was leading a processional through the Church of the Holy Cross in the Washington Heights neighborhood of New York City on December 24, 1933. See "Slain in 187th St. Church: Assassins Swarm About Armenian Prelate and Stab Him," *New York Times*, 25 December 1933; and "Nine Found Guilty in Church Murder: Two Convicted of Murder and Seven of Manslaughter in Prelate's Death," 14 July 1934. Five years later, while riding on a subway car, Derounian happened to pick up a tract titled "Why Are Jews Persecuted for their Religion?" The disturbing answer sparked the idea. The publishing company identified itself as the Nationalist Press Association and the proximity of its uptown offices beckoned him further into an elaborate plan of discovery. Derounian began his investigation in the fall 1938 and did not stop until spring 1943.

9. Carlson, *Undercover*, 28.

10. Ibid., 25.

11. Ibid., 28.

12. Ibid., 519.

13. Ibid., 70.

14. Ibid.

15. Edward N. Jenks, "Fifth Column—with American Labels," *New York Times*, 18 July 1943, BR8. Jenks says the story is "a sordid one, rather sensationally told, and perhaps dated by its sensationalism. Most of it had been told before and told better. As an account of the author's personal experiences, it is sometimes hair raising, but those who turn to it as a source of additional information about the activities of subversive groups in the United States will find it disappointing."

16. See Alice Payne Hackett and James Henry Burke, *80 Years of Best Sellers: 1895–1975* (New York: R. R. Bowker, 1977). See also Keith L. Justice, *Bestseller Index: All Books, "Publishers Weekly" and the "New York Times" Through 1990* (Jefferson, N.C.: McFarland, 1998). According to Justice, the book came onto the best seller list of *Publishers Weekly* at no. 5 on August 7, 1943, and shot to first place by September 4, where it remained for the next twenty-five weeks. In all, it spent forty-four weeks on the *PW*

list. It had a similar showing on the *New York Times* list, which it entered at no. 13 on the general list on August 8, 1943. It reached its peak position of no. 1 on September 12, 1943, and stayed at no. 1 for twenty-eight weeks. It was on the *NYT* list for a total of forty-eight weeks.

17. "Banta Sentenced; Called a Traitor," *New York Times,* 1 December 1944, 16.

18. Leonard Lyons, "Broadway Bulletins," *Washington Post,* 14 February 1944, 11.

19. Carlson, *Cairo to Damascus* (New York: A. A. Knopf, 1951). See also Quentin Reynolds, "Danger at Every Step," *New York Times,* 14 October 1951, 213.

20. "N.A.A.W.P.," *Primetime Live,* ABC, 14 May 1997 (transcript available through LexisNexis). See also "The Year in Hate, 1998: Hate Group Count Tops 500, Internet Sites Soar," *Intelligence Report* 93 (Winter 1999).

21. "N.A.A.W.P." See also the award summary provided by Investigative Reporters and Editors, on its website, no. 14595, subject: hate groups, authors: Phyllis McGrady, Robert Lange, Robbie Gordon, Sarah Walker, Sam Donaldson, *Primetime Live,* ABC, 14 May 1997. http://www.ire.org/resourcecenter/stories.php?pageNum_Recordset1=25&action=search&year=none&keywords=%22ABC%20NEWS%22&order=Descending&sort_order=Score, accessed 30 September 2011.

22. Paul Steiger, telephone interview by author, 19 May 2010.

23. Timothy K. Smith, "War Games: In Alabama's Woods, Frank Camper Trains Men to Repel Invaders," *Wall Street Journal,* 19 August 1985, 1. See also Jane Applegate, "Mercenary Offers Tales of Secret U.S. Missions at Firebombing Trial," *Los Angeles Times,* 9 November 1986, 1; Applegate, "Two Mercenaries Convicted of Bombing Cars," 14 April 1987, 1; Applegate, "Ex-Teacher Is Given 2 Years in Bombings," 9 June 1987, 4; Jay Reeves, "Ex-Mercenary Frank Camper Trades Guns for Computers," *Birmingham News,* 12 June 1995, 1B; Kristi Lamonth Ellis, "Writer-Adventurer Backs Venture," 29 July 2001; "Mercenary Tales of Espionage / This Vietnam Veteran Sells Computers and Writes Books. But His Former Life was Tied Up with Intrigue and Secret Work for the FBI," *Chattanooga Free Press,* 12 August 1995. See also *Camper, Franklin J. v. United States,* No. 89-5034, 493 U.S. 857. LEXIS 4109 (2 Oct. 1989).

Prior History: On Petition for Writ of Certiorari to the United States Court of Appeals for the Ninth Circuit. Reported below: *Franklin Joseph Camper v. United States of America,* No. 91-55747, 977 F. 2d587, 1992 U.S. App. LEXIS 36207 (9th Cir. 22 Sept. 1992).

24. Thomas Clouse, "ATF, FBI Agents Pose as Journalists: Sheriff Pulls Media Credentials After Learning of Undercover Operation at Aryan Nations Trial," *Spokane Spokesman-Review,* 31 August 2000, A1.

25. "SPJ Demands FBI Discipline Agents for Posing as Journalists," Society of Professional Journalists, 1 September 2000, http://www.spj.org/news.asp?ref=97; Richard A. Oppel, "Government Relations, Past and Present," American Society of Newspaper Editors, 27 July 2000, http://asne.org/kiosk/editor/00.nov-dec/oppel1.htm; and "SPJ, RTNDA Protest FBI Agents' Posing as Journalists," Associated Press and Freedom Forum Online, 5 September 2000, http://www.freedomforum.org/templates/document.asp?documentID=3695.

26. Louis Rolfes, "FBI Agents Pose as Photographers During Aryan Nation Trial," *News Media and the Law* 24:4 (Fall 2000): 11–12.

27. This is an aside, but there are a number of situations in which reporters would be highly unlikely to pose as law enforcement personnel or official informants of any kind, a taint that can be too compromising and too hard to shake off. It is for certain that no reporter in a dangerous or heavily politicized situation abroad, or in a war zone, would risk a pose as an investigator or a spy, an association always to avoid. Even the mention of a reporter's name in the same sentence with the words CIA or FBI or the like can be injurious, compromising not only the reporter's safety, but his integrity, his standing with colleagues, his ability to gather information in the future—above board or below—and even his life.

28. Patsy Sims, *The Klan* (Lexington: University Press of Kentucky, 1996), 1–3.

29. Stetson Kennedy published frequently during the 1940s and '50s in the *Pittsburgh Courier,* the *Amsterdam News,* the *Atlanta Daily World,* the *Baltimore Afro-American,* and occasionally on other topics in the *New York Times.*

30. Stetson Kennedy, *I Rode with the Ku Klux Klan* (London: Arco, 1954), 28–29.

31. Ibid., 17.

32. Ibid., 21.

33. Ibid., 18.

34. Ibid., 20–21.

35. Ibid., 85.

36. Ibid., 81.

37. Ibid., 92–94.

38. Stephen J. Dubner and Steven D. Levitt, "Hoodwinked?" *New York Times Magazine,* 8 January 2006, 26. See also Charles Patton, "Investigation of Stephen J. Dubner & Seven D. Leavitt Article," *Florida Times-Union,* 29 January 2006.

39. Ibid.

40. Kennedy, *The Klan Unmasked* (Boca Raton: Florida Atlantic University Press, 1990), 6. "Brown" has never been identified, but Kennedy did pay homage to "Bob" in a fleeting, oblique acknowledgment on the page facing the table of contents in the 1990 edition of his book. The sentence reads in part: "In the preparation of this book, however, special contributions have been made by my fellow anti-Klan agent 'Bob,' who has risked his life many times." Three other people who had studied the archival record closely, one of whom had interviewed Kennedy extensively for her dissertation, came to the same conclusion: that Kennedy had liberally bent the facts, placing himself "Zelig-like, at the center of the action." Dubner and Levitt quoted the head of the imprint that published all four of Kennedy's books as calling Kennedy "an entrepreneurial folklorist." Ben Green, who examined the archives for a tangentially related book of his own, came to the same conclusion, but also understood the reason why no one, until the publication of *Freakonomics,* had called Kennedy out. "It would be like killing Santa Claus," Green told the two authors. "To me, the saddest part of this story is that what he actually did wasn't enough for him, and he had felt compelled to make up, embellish or take credit for things he didn't do."

41. Dubner and Levitt, "Hoodwinked?" See also Patton, "Investigation of Stephen J. Dubner."

42. Patton, "Investigation of Stephen J. Dubner."

43. Patsy Sims, *Klan,* ix.

44. John Seigenthaler, introduction to *My Life in the Klan,* by Jerry Thompson (Nashville, Tenn.: Rutledge Hill Press, 1988), 14–17.

45. Seigenthaler, introduction to *My Life in the Klan,* 14–17.

46. Steve Sonsky, "Under the Cloak of the Klan," *Miami Herald,* 18 January 1983, 1C.

47. Seigenthaler, introduction to *My Life in the Klan,* 14–17.

48. Ibid. Also, author Seigenthaler, telephone interview by author, 14 January 2011.

49. Sims, *Klan,* 1.

50. Patsy Sims, email exchange with author, 18 June 2008.

51. Thompson, *My Life in the Klan,* 305.

52. Thanks to Ryann Liebenthal for her close reading of these works and contribution to these insights.

53. Sims, *Klan,* 65.

54. Sims describes finding as a young girl a black box of valuables in a bedroom closet that contained a picture postcard of "fifty or so robed and hooded men marching down Main Street in Beaumont, Texas, in the early twenties" (1).

55. Patsy Sims, email exchange.

56. Jeff Sharlet, "Jesus Plus Nothing," *Harper's,* May 2003, 53–64.

57. Ibid.

58. Sharlet, "Through a Glass, Darkly: How the Christian Right is Reimagining U.S. History," *Harper's,* December 2006, 33–34.

59. See Roger D. Hodge, introduction to *Submersion Journalism: Reporting in the Radical First Person from "Harper's Magazine,"* ed. Bill Wasik (New York: New Press, 2008).

60. Jeff Sharlet, email exchange with author, 29 August 2010.

61. Unger, "The Fool on the Hill," Huffingtonpost.com, 13 December 2007. See also Unger, "American Rapture," later in Unger, *House of Bush.*

62. Craig Unger, telephone interview by author, 15 October 2010.

63. Ibid.

64. Ibid.

65. Ibid.

66. Ibid.

67. Ibid.

68. Matt Taibbi, "Jesus Made Me Puke and Other Tales from the Evangelical Front Lines," *Rolling Stone,* 1 May 2008, 69+; and Taibbi, *The*

*Great Derangement: A Terrifying True Story of War, Politics, & Religion at the Twilight of the American Empire* (New York: Spiegel and Grau, 2008).

69. Taibbi, *Great Derangement,* 75.

70. Ibid., 75–86.

71. Kevin Roose, *The Unlikely Disciple: A Sinner's Semester at America's Holiest University* (New York: Grand Central Publishing, 2009).

72. Eric Tucker, "Ivy Leaguer 'Infiltrates' Falwell's University," Associated Press via Yahoo! News, 22 April 2009.

73. Ibid.

## CHAPTER THIRTEEN

1. "What Welfare Means to You," *Buffalo Evening News,* 7 June 1960, 1.

2. The 1961 Pulitzer Prize citation for "Local Reporting; No Edition Time," reads, "Edgar May of *Buffalo (NY) Evening News*: For his series of articles on New York State's public welfare services entitled, 'Our Costly Dilemma,' based in part on his three-month employment as a State case worker. The series brought about reforms that attracted nation-wide attention."

3. Edgar May, "Way Out of the Welfare Mess," *Harper's,* October 1961, 37–42.

4. Ed May, "Welfare—Our Costly Dilemma," *Buffalo Evenings News,* 7–25 June 1960 (signed, "By a Welfare Caseworker"). See also Edgar May, "Welfare Mess"; May, *The Wasted Americans* (New York: Signet, 1965); John Fischer, "Edgar May," *Harper's,* July 1971, 4; John McMahon, "'Our Costly Dilemma' and Welfare Revisited, 50 Years Later," *Buffalo News,* 13 June 2010.

5. See John P. Borger, "New Whines in Old Bottles: Taking News-gathering Torts Off the Food Lion Shelf," *Tort and Law Insurance Journal* 34.61 (Fall 1998); C. Thomas Dienes, "Symposium: The Media's Intrusion on Privacy: Panel, Protecting Investigative Journalism," *George Washington Law Review* 67.1139 (June/August 1999). Dienes, a law professor at George Washington and former corporate counsel to a number of major media companies, asserts: "Undercover journalism often serves the public interest. In the public sector, it allows the media to perform

its role as the eyes and ears of the people, to perform a checking function on government. Especially at a time when citizens are often unable or unwilling to supervise government, this media role is critical to
self-government. In the private sector, when the government fails in
its responsibility to protect the public against fraudulent and unethical
business and professional practices, whether because of lack of resources
or unwillingness, media exposure of such practices can and often does
provide the spur forcing government action."

6. See David H. Weaver et al., *The American Journalist in the Twenty-First
Century* (Mahwah, N.J.: Lawrence Erlbaum Associates, 2007), 31. The
book notes, incidentally, that in the same period, the number of college
graduates in the profession who had a journalism degree increased only
negligibly by 2 percent.

7. Ed May, inter alia, "Welfare—Our Costly Dilemma," *Buffalo Evenings News,* 7–25 June 1960. See also Edgar May, "Welfare Mess," 37–42;
and May, *Wasted Americans.*

8. May, *Wasted Americans,* ix.

9. Woody Klein, *Let in the Sun* (New York: Macmillan, 1964).

10. Woody Klein, email interviews by author, 7, 8, 9 July 2008 and
18 September 2010. See also Michael A. Stegman, "Slumlords and Public
Policy," *Appraisal Journal* (April 1968): 204–6; and Nathan Glazer, "Letter
from East Harlem," *City,* Autumn 1991.

11. Klein, *Let in the Sun,* xiii. See also Klein, "I Lived in a Slum" series:
Robert H. Prall, "I Lived in a Slum: Sickening Story Unfolds in City's
Blighted Areas," *New York World-Telegram and Sun,* 22 June 1959, 1; Klein,
"'At Home' in a Filthy Cage, Family Is Trapped in West Side's Jungle,"
23 June 1959, 1; "Bugs Reign in Squalor," 24 June 1959, 1; "Tenants Battle
to Survive in Lower East Side's 'Korea,'" 25 June 1959, 1; "'We Ain't
Alive, Just Hangin' On,'" 26 June 1959, 1; "At the End of the Road—
Welfare," 29 June 1959, 1; "Tenant Rights Lost in Ignorance," 30 June
1959, 1; "Lack of Inspection Brings Squalor," 1 July 1959, 1; "City Aids
Admit Blight Is Gaining," 2 July 1959, 1; and "Boy on the Brink: Miguel
Is Trapped in Slum Jungle," 6 July 1959, 1. See also "Out of the Rubble
and Filth, An Addict's Cry of Despair," 17 June 1963, 1; and "I'm Frightened When I Rob; I'm Sick . . . Got to Get Money," 18 June 1963, 6.

12. Klein, *Let in the Sun,* xiii.

13. Ibid.

14. Klein, *Let in the Sun,* jacket copy.

15. Stegman, "Slumlords and Public Policy," *Appraisal Journal* (April 1968): 204–5. At the time of this writing in 2010, Stegman was director of Policy and Housing for the John D. and Catherine T. MacArthur Foundation.

16. Stegman, "Slumlords and Public Policy," 204–5.

17. Irv Broughton, *Producers on Producing* (Jefferson, N.C.: McFarland, 1986), 151.

18. Ibid.

19. See Hillman Award, 1967, http://www.hillmanfoundation.org/ hillman-prizes/hillman-prize-broadcast-journalism?order=field_prize_ year_value&sort=asc, accessed 18 February 2011.

20. George N. Allen, *Undercover Teacher* (New York: Doubleday, 1960).

21. Ibid., 11.

22. The Newspaper Guild site, listing Heywood Broun Award winners, 1941–59, http://newsguild.org/index.php?ID=910, accessed 19 February 2011.

23. Allen, *Undercover Teacher,* 24–38.

24. Ibid., 33. See also "Dr. Levering Tyson Dies at 77; Muhlenberg's Former President," *New York Times,* 11 June 1966. Tyson was also the chancellor of the Free Europe University in Exile at Strasbourg, France.

25. Allen, *Undercover Teacher,* 32.

26. Ibid., 171.

27. "Education: Undercover Teacher," *Time,* 24 November 1958.

28. See Adam Bernstein, "George N. Allen: Undercover, He Exposed School's Disorder," *Washington Post,* 16 November 2007, B7; "Undercover Teacher"; "Education: Undercover Uproar," *Time,* 8 December 1958; "Kings Jury Praises Series on Schools," *New York Times,* 20 February 1959, 9; and "Alumni Honor 5 in Journalism," *New York Times,* 7 May 1959, 34.

29. Allen, *Undercover Teacher,* 171–72.

30. Ibid., 171.

31. Ibid., 172, 176, 177, 197, 183.

32. Emily Sachar, *Shut Up and Let the Lady Teach* (New York: Poseidon Press, 1996), 26–27.

33. David Owen, "Shouts and Murmurs: Passing," *New Yorker,* 2 April 2007, x–xi.

34. Cameron Crowe, *Fast Times at Ridgemont High* (New York: Simon and Schuster, 1981). Universal produced the film version in 1982, http://www.imdb.com/title/tt0083929/.

35. Vivian S. Toy, in a telephone interview on July 18, 2008, said the stories appeared in the *Milwaukee Journal Sunday Magazine,* ca. October 1986.

36. Vivian S. Toy, telephone interview by author, 18 July 2008.

37. Leslie Linthicum, "Undercover Student," *Albuquerque Tribune,* 7–14 March 1983. See also Tom Goldstein, *The News at Any Cost* (New York: Touchstone, 1985), 140–41; Leslie Linthicum, "When to Go Undercover? As Last Resort to Get a Story," National Ethics Committee, Society of Professional Journalists, Sigma Delta Chi, 1983. Journalism Ethics Report, 20, as cited in Goldstein, 141; and Deni Elliott, "End vs. Means: Comparing Two Cases of Deceptive Practices," Society of Professional Journalists, Sigma Delta Chi Ethics Committee, 1985, 15–16, quoted in Ron F. Smith, *Groping for Ethics* (Iowa: Iowa State University Press, 2003), 285.

38. Linthicum, "High School Revisited: Reporter Gets an Education in Paperwork," *Albuquerque Tribune,* 7 March 1983, 1.

39. Linthicum, "When to Go Undercover?" 141.

40. "Eldorado Principal Speaks About 'Undercover Student,'" *Albuquerque Tribune,* 17 March 1983, A5B.

41. Shann Nix, "Why *Chronicle* Reporter Posed as a Student," *San Francisco Chronicle,* 16 November 1992, A7. Nix's series ran in the *Chronicle* from November 16–22, 1992.

42. The *San Francisco Chronicle* and *Minneapolis Tribune* episodes are cited in Linthicum, "When to Go Undercover?"; in Elliott, "End vs. Means," 15–16; and in Smith, *Groping for Ethics,* 285.

43. Both books became paperbacks after their initial printing. Jeremy Iverson, *High School Confidential: Secrets of an Undercover Student* (New York: Atria Books, 2007), and Rebekah Nathan, *My Freshman Year: What a Professor Learned by Becoming a Student* (New York: Penguin Books, 2006).

44. For a lengthy and informative Q&A with McMullen, see Brough-

ton, *Producers on Producing*, 143–60. Specifically about the bookie documentary, see esp. 143–48.

45. Greg Vitiello, "Where Are the Documentaries of Yesteryear?" *Television Quarterly* 36.3–4 (Spring/Summer 2006): 7–8.

46. Ibid.

47. Ibid.; and Broughton, *Producers on Producing*, 143.

48. Erik Barnouw, *The Image Empire: A History of Broadcasting in the United States from 1953* (n.p.: Erik Barnouw, 1970, 1977), 182.

49. Broughton, *Producers on Producing*, 147.

50. For the series, reporters first mailed out registered letters to more than five thousand voters in precincts where fraud was suspected and found that 13 percent of regular voters were dead or never existed. George Bliss carried out surveillance in one polling place from outside, and a total of seventeen *Tribune* staffers and eight outsiders engaged as election judges and poll watchers (James L. Aucoin, *The Evolution of American Investigative Journalism* [Columbia, MO: University of Missouri Press, 2005] 96–97). William Mullen, who orchestrated the series with Bliss, spent three months as a clerk in the office of the Board of Elections Commissioners following the March primary elections "in which *The Tribune* had already disclosed massive irregularities" ("Task Force Report," *Chicago Tribune*, 10 September 1972, 1): Bliss and Mullen, "Reveal Huge Vote Fraud," 10 September 1972, 10, 1; Mullen, "Election Board Infiltrated by *Chicago Tribune*'s Reporter," 10 September 1972, 1; Bliss and Mullen, "Dem-Ruled Polls Kill 2-Party System," 11 September 1972, 1; Mullen and Bliss, "Poll Judge Violations Condoned in Election," 12 September 1972, 2; Mullen, "Loose Controls Permit Vote Judges to Switch Parties," 13 September 1972, 2; Bliss and Mullen, "20,000 Seek U.S. Marshals in Polls," 13 September 1972, 6; "Task Force Report," 14 September 1972, 2; Mullen and Pamela Zekman, "Mass Vote Fraud Arrests: 40 Reported Cited by U.S. Grand Jury," 16 September 1972; Bliss and Mullen, "U.S. Acts to Protect Vote," 17 September 1972, 1; Editorial, "Just as We Said," 28 September 1972, 20; Bliss and Mullen, "Phony Election Judges on Kusper's Nov. 7 List," 29 September 1972; Mullen and Bliss, "Kusper Crony Draws Big Fee from Vote Board," 9 October 1972, 1; Bliss and Mullen, "Kusper Office Vote Records Are Missing," 10 October 1972,

1; Bliss and Zekman, "14668 on North Side Vote Lists Are Called Ineligible," 12 October 1972, 1, 14; Bliss and William Currie, "Kusper Asks Specifics: Vote Board Blocks G.O.P. Election Judges: LEAP," 25 October 1972, 1; Bliss and Currie, "Vote Canvass Fails; Ghosts Haunt Rolls," 30 October 1972, 2; Vincent Butler, "*Chicago Tribune* Exposé Wins a Pulitzer: Chicago Vote Fraud Disclosures Earn Top Local Reporting Award," 8 May 1973, 1.

51. Clarence Page, "RIP: Undercover Journalism," *Chicago Tribune,* 29 January 1997, 17.

52. James H. Dygert, *The Investigative Journalist: Heroes for a New Era* (New York: Prentice-Hall, 1976), 126–28. Dygert further notes that the newspaper collected conclusive evidence that voter fraud was occurring before it decided to go undercover. Reporters mailed registered letters to a sampling of 5,495 voters in precincts where fraud was suspected (Dygert, 1976, 126).

53. Page, "Undercover Journalism," 29 January 1997, 17.

54. "The City's Medicaid System: Still Sick, Sick, Sick," *New York Daily News,* 23 January 1973, 7; William Sherman, "Medicaid Probe—A Cold? Take 3 Doctors Every Hour," 23 January 1973, 7; "Our 'Patient' Gets More Tests on 2nd Visit," 24 January 1973, 2; "How Medicaid Paid $757,000 for Sesame Oil," 25 January 1973, 2; "You Don't Need Glasses to See Thru This," 29 January 1973, 5; "How a Physician Can Prescribe Pure Dollars," 30 January 1973, 5; "Foot Docs Wearing a 35M Golden Slipper," 31 January 1973, 5; "Pair of Medicaid Kings With a Midas Touch," 1 February 1973, 3; "Medicaid Loses as Docs Play Beat the Clock," 2 February 1973, 3; "In Race for Medibucks, the City's Poor Lose," 5 February 1973, 5; "How Medicaid Dentist Pulled City's 800G," 6 February 1973, 5; "Medicaid's Deaf Ear to Hearing Aid Dealers," 7 February 1973, 7; "City Gives Dr. Hi Billmore Shot of Comedownance," 8 February 1973, 5; "Drawing a Map of Land of Nod," 10 February 1973, 3; and "Bureaucracy Choking in Attempts at Control," 11 February 1973, 5.

55. "The City's Medicaid System," 23 January 1973, 7+.

56. Nellie Bly, "Nellie Bly's Doctors, Seven Well-Known Physicians Disagree About Her Case," *New York World,* 27 October 1889, 13. Bly's numerous corruption-exposing reports are detailed in Brooke Kroeger,

*Nellie Bly: Daredevil, Reporter, Feminist* (New York: Times Books, 1994), 79–148.

57. "The City's Medicaid System," 23 January 1973, 7+.

58. Ibid.

59. "Winners and Sinners," *New York Times,* 24 November 1983, 1, quoted in Goldstein, *News at Any Cost,* 142.

60. Philip Shenon, "Welfare Hotel Families: Life on the Edge," *New York Times,* 31 August 1983, B1.

61. "Winners and Sinners," 1, quoted in Goldstein, *News at Any Cost,* 142.

62. Marvin Olasky, *The Press and Abortion, 1838–1988* (Hillsdale, N.J.: Lawrence Erlbaum Associates, 1988), 26.

63. Augustus St. Clair, "The Evil of the Age," *New York Times,* 23 August 1871, 6; 27 August 1871, 1; 28 August 1871, 8; 29 August 1871, 8; 30 August 1871, 4, 8; 2 September 1871, 8; 6 September 1871, 8; and 3 September 1871, 8, quoted in Olasky, *Press and Abortion,* 160.

64. Olasky, *Press and Abortion,* 28.

65. Oddly, from first reference and for two weeks worth of coverage, Rosenzweig was referred to repeatedly only by his last name, until this reference: "Rosenzweig the Abortionist—His Fruitless Attempt to Get Out on Bail," *New York Times,* 8 September 1871, 2.

66. Olasky, *Press and Abortion,* 30.

67. James McGrath Morris, *The Rose Man of Sing Sing* (New York: Fordham University Press, 1999), 86–87. The unsigned series runs in the *Chicago Daily Times* from 12 December 1888 to 5 January 1889. "Infanticide," 12 December 1888, 1, 2; 13 December 1888, 1, 2; 14 December 1888, 1, 2; 15 December 1888, 1; 16 December 1888, 1; 17 December 1888, 1; 18 December 1888, 1; 19 December 1888, 1, 7; 20 December 1888, 1, 5; 21 December 1888, 1, 3; 22 December 1888, 1, 5; 23 December 1888, 9; 24 December 1888, 1, 5; 25 December 1888, 1, 5; 26 December 1888, 1, 5; "The Remedy" 27 December 1888, 1, 5; 28 December 1888, 1, 8; 29 December 1888, 5; 30 December 1888, 1; "Seeking the Remedy," 31 December 1888, 5; 1 January 1889, 1, 3; 2 January 1889, 5; 3 January 1889, 5; 4 January 1889, 5; 5 January 1889, 8.

68. "Survey: 2 Abortion Clinics Found 'Pregnancy' in Men," *New York*

*Post,* 16 December 1976, 9, quoted in Olasky, *Press and Abortion,* 133n189. Note that this was not the *Post*'s project, but that of the New York Public Interest Research Group, according to the article, which described itself as a "nonpartisan research and advocacy organization established, directed and supported by New York State college and university students."

69. Pamela Zekman and Pamela Warrick, "The Abortion Profiteers— Making a Killing in Michigan Av. Clinics," *Chicago Sun-Times,* 12 November 1978, 1; "Meet the Profiteers: Men Who Profit from Women's Pain," 13 November 1978, 1; "The Abortion Lottery: Women Take Chances with 'Tryout' Doctors," 14 November 1978, 1; Zekman and Warrick, "Dr. Ming Kow Hah: Physician of Pain," 15 November 1978, 1; "Nurse to Aide: 'Fake That Pulse!'" 16 November 1978, 1; "Soft Voices, Hard Sells—Twin Swindles," 17 November 1978, 4; "12 Dead After Abortions in State's Walk-in Clinics," 19 November 1978, 1; "Big Kickbacks to Abortion Mills," 20 November 1978, 1; "Infamous Doctor Is Detroit Connection," 21 November 1978, 8; "Pregnant or Not, Women Given Abortions," 22 November 1978, 8; "Counseling the Patient: Buy This Abortion," 24 November 1978, 5; "Hot Line Deceptions Sell Most Abortions," 25 November 1978, 4; Ellen Warren, "The Politics of Abortion—a Big Business," 27 November 1978, 6; and Zekman and Warrick, "Inside Story of City's Pro-life Movement," 28 November 1978, 6.

The following stories were published under the running headline THE ABORTION PROFITEERS REACTION: Karen Koshner and Pamela Zekman, "Other Officials' Reactions—Jury Subpoenas Records of Abortion Clinic," *Chicago Sun-Times,* 12 November 1978, 5; Zekman and Koshner, "State to Act on Abortion Clinics," 13 November 1978, 3; "Thompson Orders Clinic Check Step-Up," 14 November 1978, 3; Koshner, "State Inspects Abortion Clinics," 15 November 1978, 5; Zekman and Koshner, "Doctor Loses out in 2 Court Battles," 16 November 1978, 5; "2 Abortion Referral Firms are Subpoenaed," 17 November 1978, 5; Koshner and Dolores McCahill, "Court Revokes Dr. Hah's License," 21 November 1978, 3; Charles N. Wheeler III and G. Robert Hilman, "Medic Blames State for Abortion Clinic Abuses," 29 November 1978, 7; Zekman and Koshner, "Report of Record Changing at Abortion Clinic Probed," 30 November 1978, 8; Lynn Sweet, "Indiana Abortion Clinic Is Thriving," 1 December 1978, 3; Ellen Warren, "Probe Abortions, House

Asked," 2 December 1978, 4; Koshner and Zekman, "Closed Clinic Oks Appointments," 23 November 1978, 3; and "Health Chief Defends His Clinic Curbs," 5 December 1978, 4.

Other abortion-related articles by the same staff members who wrote the "Profiteers" series: Zekman and Warrick, "Abortion Peril Greater Before Legalization," *Chicago Sun-Times,* 12 November 1978, 6; "Probe Michigan Av. Abortion Clinic Death,'" 17 November 1978, 1; "Mom Has Abortion, and Another Child," 19 November 1978, 10; "For 'Babies Who've Died'—His Mission," 28 November 1978, 7; and Ellen Warren, "State Aid Chief Raps HEW on Abortion Issue," 1 December 1978, 26.

Published under the headline THE ABORTION PROFITEERS ANALYSIS: Zekman and Warrick, "Hospital Abortion Issue 'Hot,'" *Chicago Sun-Times,* 2 December 1978, 4; published under the headline THE ABORTION PROFITEERS BACKGROUND: "Profiteering Shocks These Abortion Pioneers," 3 December 1978, 10. See also Olasky, *Press and Abortion,* 134.

70. Zekman and Warrick, "The Abortion Profiteers," 1.

71. Zekman and Warrick, "Found: Safe, Compassionate Care," *Chicago Sun-Times,* 1978, 35.

72. Ibid., 31.

73. Ibid., 44.

74. Ibid., 46.

75. Olasky, *Press and Abortion,* 137.

76. Sallie Tisdale, "We Do Abortions Here: A Nurse's Story," *Harper's,* October 1987, 66.

77. Brett Noble, "Ethics Apply to Indie Media, Too," *Daily Bruin,* 10 March 2008.

78. Noble, *Daily Bruin,* 10 March 2008.

79. Josiah Ryan, "Planned Parenthood Agreed to Accept Race-Motivated Donations," CNS News, 7 July 2008.

80. Jay Rosen, "They Brought a Tote Bag to a Knife Fight," Pressthink .org, 10 March 2011, http://pressthing.org/2011/03/they-brought-a-tote -bag-to-a-knife-fight-the-resignation-of-vivian-schiller/.

81. "'Pimp' in ACORN Video Shares Story," *Washington Post,* 9 September 2009.

82. Tom Hays, "New York Federal Appeals Court Rules Against ACORN," Associated Press, 13 August 2010.

83. Daniel Massey, "Acorn Files for Bankruptcy," *Crain's New York Business,* 3 November 2010.

84. "Judge for Yourself," TheProjectVeritas.com, 8 March 2011, http://theprojectveritas.com/nprjudge. See also Karen Everhart, "NPR Loses CEO, Its Third Exec Swept Away by Political Tornado," Current.org, 9 March 2011; Jack Shafer, "The NPR Body Count," *Slate,* 10 March 2011; and Joel Meares, "Stingers from Our Past: James O'Keefe's Ethics, Their Stings, and Their Ethics," *Columbia Journalism Review,* 10 March 2011.

85. Ian Murphy, "Koch Whore: Wisconsin Governor Scott Walker Answers His Master's Call," BuffaloBeast.com, 23 February 2011, http://www.buffalobeast.com/?p=5045. See also W. Paul Smith, "Prank Call to Governor Was Good Journalism," *Voyager,* 1 March 2011. Murphy posed as David Koch, a billionaire conservative, to elicit questionable responses from Governor Walker about his approach to a dispute with the public employees union over efforts to remove its rights to collective bargaining. Kevin Z. Smith for the Society of Professional Journalists condemned Murphy's deception, saying it violated "the highest levels of journalism ethics. To lie to a source about your identity and then to bait that source into making comments that are inflammatory is inexcusable and has no place in journalism." Murphy said he decided to make the call when he learned that Wisconsin Democrats had been unable to get through to the governor. Asked for comment by the editor of the student newspaper at West Florida University, Murphy replied:

> You've chosen to pursue one of the most ignoble professions in existence. To succeed, you will have to become a mouthpiece of swine, a conduit through which money can speak. To simply make ends meet you will be forced to suffer an endless loss of morality and make countless compromises of character in pursuit of your master's bottom line. Even the most righteous and least successful of you will betray your dignity on a nearly daily basis.
>
> Some of you will look for truth; few of you will find it. Some of you will look for truth and find lies, but not know the difference. And some of you will wind up looking for other jobs in other fields.
>
> The lies of the rich will be tempting and golden, and you'll have to remember to whom you're beholden. It's not that you can't speak the truth if

you dare, but you may end up fired and no one will care. Informing the public is its own reward and that, dear students, is what you have to look forward.

86. Mary Sanchez, "The Ethical Bankruptcy of 'Gotcha!'" *Bellingham Herald,* 11 March 2011, http://www.bellinghamherald.com/2011/03/11/1910885/the-ethical-bankruptcy-of-gotcha.html#ixzz1GNnGgxPF.

87. Edward Wasserman, email exchange with author, 13–14 March 2011, regarding Wasserman, "Journalist Stings Go Mainstream," *Miami Herald,* 13 March 2011. Wasserman was asked if his harsher view of undercover reporting in this column represented a change of heart from earlier columns that indicated support for the practice in specific reference to Ken Silverstein's 2007 sting on Washington lobbyists and the 2005 *Spokane Spokesman-Review* exposé of the city's mayor. (See Wasserman, "Can Trickery by Reporters be Right?" *Miami Herald,* 9 July 2007, A17, and Wasserman, "When Subterfuge is an Acceptable Tool of Reporting," *Miami Herald,* 17 May 2006, 1.) In the email exchange, Wasserman responded charmingly to the question: "I'm a little chagrined to learn I'm being held to standards of consistency," he wrote. "That may have far-reaching effects on the way I do business." He also acknowledged that he was "indeed tougher in the latest column that I had been in the past." See chapter 15 for further elucidation.

88. James Rainey, "On the Media: NPR Video Stings Ethics Too," *Los Angeles Times,* 11 March 2011.

89. Adam Hochberg, "Planned Parenthood Videos, Undercover Recordings Have Roots in Journalism They Challenge," Poynteronline, 23 February 2011, http://www.poynter.org/latest-news/making-sense-of-news/120446/planned-parenthood-videos-undercover-recordings-have-roots-in-journalism-they-challenge/.

90. Scott Baker, "Does Raw Video of NPR Exposé Reveal Questionable Editing & Tactics?" *The Blaze,* 10 March 2011, http://theblaze.com/stories/does-raw-video-of-npr-expose-reveal-questionable-editing-tactics. Also, Emily Esfahani Smith, "Ends Vs. Means: The Ethics of Undercover Journalism," *The Blaze,* 9 March 2011, http://theblaze.com/stories/ednds-vs-means-the-ethics-of-undercover-journalism.

91. "HSUS Exposes Inhumane Treatment of Pigs at Smithfield," Humane Society of the United States, 15 December 2010. See also Philip

Walzer, "Humane Society Claims Abuse at Smithfield Foods Farm," *Virginian-Pilot,* 15 December 2010; "Smithfield's Treatment of Pigs Under Scrutiny," 16 December 2010, B1; "Smithfield Foods Fires Three After Complaint of Pig Abuse," 22 December 2010, B3; "Smithfield Defends Handling of Pigs," 23 December 2010, B2; and "Humane Society Claims Pigs Abused at Va. Farm," *Washington Post* via Associated Press, 15 December 2010.

92. See Peter Catapano, "Opinionator: Masters of Deception," *New York Times* (blog), 11 March 2011, http://opinionator.blogs.nytimes.com/2011/03/11/masters-of-deception.

93. "Inhumane Treatment of Pigs," http://video.humanesociety.org/video/629262638001/Channels/729780781001/Investigations/768491318001/Undercover-at-Smithfield-Foods/.

94. Paul Shapiro, telephone interview by author, 14 March 2011.

95. Ibid.

96. Ibid.

97. See such as Mark Bittman, "Opinionator: Who Protects the Animals," *New York Times,* 26 April 2011; Andrew Duffelmeyer, "Iowa Agriculture Committees Approval Bill That Would Limit Animal Groups' Undercover Investigations," *Los Angeles Times* via Associated Press, 16 March 2011.

98. Adam Hochberg, "Planned Parenthood Videos, Undercover Recordings Have Roots in Journalism They Challenge," Poynteronline, 23 February 2011, http://www.poynter.org/latest-news/making-sense-of-news/120446/planned-parenthood-videos-undercover-recordings-have-roots-in-journalism-they-challenge/.

99. Mike Newall, "I Was an Obama Volunteer," *Philadelphia City Paper,* 16 April 2008; and Tom Namako, "I Was a Clinton Volunteer," 16 April 2008.

100. Examples include Maki Becker and Greg Gittrich, "Weapons Still Fly at Airports," *New York Daily News,* 4 September 2002; Mike Savini, "Fly at Your Own Risk," WMMB-TV, 15 November, 2006; and Lisa Fletcher, "Serious Security Questions at Sky Harbor Airport," ABC, KNXV-TV, 23 July 2007.

101. C. Thomas Dienes, "Symposium: The Media's Intrusion on Privacy: Panel, Protecting Investigative Journalism," *George Washington*

*Law Review* 67.1139 (June/August 1999). Dienes, a professor emeritus on the faculty of George Washington University Law School, is the former general counsel for *U.S. News and World Report* and a legal consultant to *U.S. News, Atlantic Monthly,* and *Fast Company* magazines.

102. Borger, "New Whines in Old Bottles." Speaking of the legal implications, Borger went on to say that the day will come when there will be a "trespass" case in which "the newsgathering justification is so clear and overriding that rigid rules of liability for trespass and similar torts will have to bend or break, because it would be simply outrageous to permit a lawsuit to survive past the very earliest stages when the journalists have revealed that the plaintiffs engaged in election fraud, health care abuses, exploitative employment practices, or violent criminal conduct."

## CHAPTER FOURTEEN

1. Zay N. Smith and Pamela Zekman, *The Mirage* (New York: Random House, 1979), jacket copy.

2. Smith and Zekman, *Mirage,* 5.

3. Ibid., 8–9.

4. Ibid., 6–7.

5. Chicago real estate classified ads for 1976 in the Chicago suburbs of Des Plaines, Palatine, and Libertyville show three-bedroom houses for sale in this range. Courtesy of Gioia Diliberto.

6. Smith and Zekman, *Mirage,* 5.

7. Ibid., 7.

8. For more on the Better Government Association in this approximate period, see William Mullen, "BGA: A Civic Watchdog Under Fire," *Chicago Tribune,* 3 May 1981, A1.

9. Smith and Zekman, *Mirage,* 9–10. See also the recounting of Recktenwald's prison guard pose as detailed in chapter 11.

10. Ibid., 11.

11. Ibid., 12–13.

12. Ibid.

13. Ibid., 13.

14. Ibid., 14, 27–29.

15. Ibid., 15.

16. Ibid., 27.

17. Ibid., 30.

18. Ibid., 55.

19. Ibid., 37. See also James L. Merriner, *Grafters and Goo Goos: Corruption and Reform in Chicago* (Carbondale, Ill.: Southern Illinois University Press, 2004), 5.

20. William Recktenwald, telephone interview with author, 23 December 2010.

21. Smith and Zekman, *Mirage,* 200, 209.

22. Pamela Zekman and Zay N. Smith, "Our 'bar' uncovers payoffs, tax gyps," *Chicago Sun-Times,* 8 January 1978, 1; "It wasn't just a bar, it was a Mirage," *Chicago Sun-Times,* 8 January 1978, 5; Pamela Zekman and Zay N. Smith, "Cheating the taxpayer—'Mr. Fixit' tells how," *Chicago Sun-Times,* 9 January 1978, 1; Editorial, "'College Education' in Fraud,"*Chicago Sun-Times,* 9 January 1978, 37; Pamela Zekman and Zay N. Smith, "Payoff Parade Begins; Mirage clears fire inspection – for $10," *Chicago Sun-Times,* 10 January 1978, 1; Michael Flannery and Karen Koshner, "BGA sees city ombudsman need; Mayor denies payoffs, shakedowns prevalent," *Chicago Sun-Times,* 10 January 1978, 3; Pamela Zekman and Zay N. Smith, "Building code gives muscle to inspectors," *Chicago Sun-Times,* 10 January 1978, 5; Editorial, "4 suspensions aren't enough," *Chicago Sun-Times,* 10 January 1978, 33; Pamela Zekman and Zay N. Smith, "The envelope please; Building aide OKs Mirage for $15," *Chicago Sun-Times,* 11 January 1978, 1; Michael Flannery and Pamela Zekman, "New fire inspector chief vows cleanup," *Chicago Sun-Times,* 11 January 1978, 7; "Three suspended inspectors named," *Chicago Sun-Times,* 11 January 1978, 7; Pamela Zekman and Zay N. Smith, "At the Mirage shakedown time again," *Chicago Sun-Times,* 12 January 1978, 1; Pamela Zekman, "City building chief pledges a shake-up," *Chicago Sun-Times,* 12 January 1978, 7; Leon Pitt and Michael Flannery, "Probe asked to determine loss to state,"*Chicago Sun-Times,* 12 January 1978, 7; Editorial, "Next steps against graft," *Chicago Sun-Times,* 12 January 1978, 47; Pamela Zekman and Michael Flannery, "Reacts to our Mirage; Bilandic to tighten inspection practices," *Chicago Sun-Times,* 13 January 1978, 1; Pamela Zekman and Zay N. Smith, "Quick, the cash; 'I'm promoted,'"

*Chicago Sun-Times*, 13 January 1978, 1; Editorial, "Council still must act," *Chicago Sun-Times*, 13 January 1978, 49; Pamela Zekman and Michael Flannery, "Mirage triggers 3-way probe," *Chicago Sun-Times*, 14 January 1978, 1; Pamela Zekman and Zay N. Smith, "Tavern tax frauds cost state millions," *Chicago Sun-Times*, 15 January 1978, 1; Editorial, "State reforms needed," *Chicago Sun-Times*, 15 January 1978, Views 7; Pamela Zekman and Zay N. Smith, "State liquor inspectors; Take $50, give 'free' advice," *Chicago Sun-Times*, 16 January 1978, 1; Michael Flannery and Pamela Zekman, "Thompson backs curbs on tavern-tax cheats," *Chicago Sun-Times*, 17 January 1978, 1; Pamela Zekman and Zay N. Smith, "We pay $70 'extra' for sign," *Chicago Sun-Times*, 17 January 1978, 1; Pamela Zekman and Zay N. Smith, "What permits? City blind to own rules," *Chicago Sun-Times*, 17 January 1978, 6; Editorial, "Showdown in City Council," *Chicago Sun-Times*, 17 January 1978, 33; Michael Flannery and Pamela Zekman, "Council gets fraud probe motions," *Chicago Sun-Times*, 18 January 1978, 5; Pamela Zekman and Zay N. Smith, "'Premises clean'; 2 city health aides OK food amid filth," *Chicago Sun-Times*, 18 January 1978, 6; Michael Flannery and Pamela Zekman, "Suspend 2 who ignored health hazards," *Chicago Sun-Times*, 18 January 1978, 7; Michael Flannery and Pamela Zekman, "An honest cop is no match for clout," *Chicago Sun-Times*, 19 January 1978, 1; Pamela Zekman and Michael Flannery, "State panel investigating tax fraud," *Chicago Sun-Times*, 19 January 1978, 7; Editorial, "Council's spineless step," *Chicago Sun-Times*, 19 January 1978, 45; Pamela Zekman and Zay N. Smith, "Our liquor salesman; Illegal gifts, deals part of sales pitch," *Chicago Sun-Times*, 20 January 1978, 6; Michael Flannery, "State to audit 4 Mirage suppliers," *Chicago Sun-Times,* 21 January 1978, 5; Pamela Zekman and Zay N. Smith, "'Hot' trash taken − for cold cash," *Chicago Sun-Times*, 22 January 1978, 1; Pamela Zekman and Zay N. Smith, "He asks 'tip' for doing job," *Chicago Sun-Times*, 22 January 1978, 1; Editorial, "'Public service' ripoffs," *Chicago Sun-Times*, 22 January 1978, Views 7; Pamela Zekman and Zay N. Smith, "Vendors deal fraud, kickbacks," *Chicago Sun-Times*, 23 January 1978, 1; Pamela Zekman and Zay N. Smith, "Ex-cop in huge vending skim," *Chicago Sun-Times*, 24 January 1978, 1; Pamela Zekman and Zay N. Smith, "A vendor's pitch—Chicago style," *Chicago Sun-Times*, 24 January 1978, 7; Michael Flannery and Pamela Zekman, "78 unlicensed games seized," *Chicago Sun-Times*, 24 January 1978, 7; Michael Flannery and Pamela Zekman, "Mirage reaction; Thompson, legislators to push for tax probe," *Chicago Sun-Times*, 25 January 1978, 1; Pamela Zekman and Zay N. Smith, "Bartender's Tip: 'Your conscience is your guide,'" *Chicago Sun-Times*, 25 January 1978, 6; Pamela Zekman and Zay N. Smith, "On the rocks with Norty the bartender," *Chicago Sun-Times,* 25 January 1978, 7; Michael Flannery and Pamela Zekman, "Subpena liquor inspector records," *Chicago Sun-Times*, 26 January 1978, 5; Pamela Zekman and Zay N. Smith, "Hanging out with the Mirage menagerie," *Chicago Sun-Times*, 26 January 1978, 6; Editorial, "Solid steps toward action," *Chicago Sun-Times*, 26 January 1978, 61; Pamela Zekman and Zay N. Smith, "Pinball Wizard vs. Evel Knievel—tilt!" *Chicago Sun-Times*, 27 January 1978, 6; Michael Flannery and Pamela Zekman, "Bilandic office fails to back claim of earlier payoff action," *Chicago Sun-Times*, 27 January 1978, 7; Pamela Zekman and Zay N. Smith, "An inside look at a Wells St. brothel," *Chicago Sun-Times*, 29 January 1978, 4; Pamela Zekman and Zay N. Smith, "'Heavy mixing'—high-priced drinks, sex," *Chicago Sun-Times*, 30 January 1978, 8; Pamela Zekman and Zay N. Smith, "Roger's Angel dances for go-go dream," *Chicago Sun-Times*, 31 January 1978, 6; Flannery and Pamela Zekman, "Thompson: Probe more than revenue," *Chicago Sun-Times,* 31 January 1978, 7; Pamela Zekman and Zay N. Smith, "Mirage revolving door for life's misfits," *Chicago Sun-Times*, 1 February 1978, 6; Editorial, "Don't back off state probe," *Chicago Sun-Times*, 1 February 1978, 59; Pamela Zekman and Zay N. Smith, "Gunrunner boasts of arsenal for sale," *Chicago Sun-Times*, 2 February 1978, 6; Michael Flannery and Pamela Zekman, "'Mr. Fixit's' records subpenaed by U.S.," *Chicago Sun-Times*, 2 February 1978, 7; Pamela Zekman and Zay N. Smith, "Night at the fights—everybody's punchy," *Chicago Sun-Times*, 3 February 1978, 6; Pamela Zekman and Zay N. Smith, "On-duty firemen hustle tickets for boss' band," *Chicago Sun-Times*, 5 February 1978, 1; Pamela Zekman and Zay N. Smith, "Mission accomplished, the Mirage fades," *Chicago Sun-Times*, 5 February 1978, 7; Editorial, "Officials' job is clear: Get to work against corruption," *Chicago Sun-Times*, 5 February 1978, Views 7; Pamela Zekman and Zay N. Smith, "4 more suspensions in wake of Mirage," *Chicago Sun-Times*, 9 February 1978, 3; Editorial, "Bilandic's puny response," *Chicago Sun-Times*, 9 February 1978, 49.

23. T. R. Reid, "Government by Envelope: Chicago's System Exposed," *Washington Post,* 15 January 1978, A3.

24. Nathaniel Sheppard Jr., "Tavern Precipitates Latest Chicago Corruption Scandal," *New York Times,* 23 January 1978, A12.

25. Smith and Zekman, *Mirage,* 176. See also Mark Fitzgerald, "One Mirage That Proved All Too Real," *Editor & Publisher* 139.10 (October 2006): 8.

26. Michael Miner, "Undercover Journalism's Last Call," *Chicago Reader,* 2 October 2002, sec. 1.

27. John D. Moorhead, "Tales of Payoffs and Shakedowns Stir Up Chicago," *Christian Science Monitor,* 1 February 1978, 9.

28. Ibid.

29. Smith and Zekman, *Mirage,* 249–55.

30. Deirdre Carmody, "Exposure of Corruption Raises Questions About Reporters' Masquerade," *New York Times,* 23 February 1978, A16.

31. Ibid.

32. Ibid.

33. Ibid.

34. Ibid.

35. "Undercover Reporting Backed by Readers," *Editor & Publisher,* 23 August 1980, 13.

36. Moorhead, *Monitor,* 1 February 1978.

37. "Undercover Reporting." 13. See also Pamela Zekman and Gene Mustain, "The Accident Swindlers," *Chicago Sun-Times,* 10–15, 17–22, 24–27 February 1980. Follow-up articles: "The Accident Swindlers," 28–29 February 1980; 2, 11 March 1980; 3, 5, 6, 8, 10, 11 April 1980; 1, 12, 30, 31 June 1980; 1 July 1980. In Ralph Otwell's letter to the IRE Awards on December 24, 1980, he said that the project was six months in the making and "documented the fraudulent legal and medical practices which add one-third higher premiums to every driver's insurance bill. The series showed how unscrupulous lawyers and doctors conspire with their clients and patients to fake or exaggerate injuries to collect inflated insurance settlements—up to $3 billion annually," and that "the tort liability system of settling claims in Illinois enables the corrupt to fabricate a fraudulent claim that the insurance industry finds cheaper to pay, rather than contest in court." It also showed "how other states that

have adopted no-fault insurance laws have experienced fewer suits and lower premium costs."

38. "Undercover Reporting." The only method that met with a high disapproval rating was paying people for information. Forty-six percent of those interviewed opposed this while 45 percent said it was all right.

39. The Pulitzer Prize site, http://pulitzer.org, lists these twelve men as members of the 1979–1980 board: Elie Abel, dean, Graduate School of Journalism, Columbia University; Benjamin Bradlee, executive editor, *Washington* Post; Osborne Elliott, dean, Graduate School of Journalism, Columbia University; Howard H. Hays Jr., editor and publisher, *Riverside Press-Enterprise;* Lee Hills, president and executive editor, Knight Newspapers, Inc.; John Hughes, editor, *Christian Science Monitor;* Clayton Kirkpatrick, chief executive officer, *Chicago Tribune;* Richard H. Leonard, editor and vice president, *Milwaukee Journal;* William J. McGill, president, Columbia University; Warren H. Phillips, chairman and chief executive officer, Dow Jones & Co.; Joseph Pulitzer Jr. (III), editor and publisher, *St. Louis Post-Dispatch;* and James Reston, columnist, *New York Times.*

40. Myra MacPherson, "Donnybrook: The Rite of Spring and the Cries of Foul," *Washington Post,* 20 April 1979, B1, 8.

41. Ibid.

42. Ibid. She described the reform effort as "monumentally unsuccessful."

43. The board members that year included Elie Abel, then dean of the Graduate School of Journalism at Columbia University; Benjamin Bradlee, executive editor, *Washington Post;* Osborne Elliott, dean, Columbia; Howard H. Haye Jr., editor and publisher, *Riverside Press-Enterprise;* Lee Hills, president and executive editor, Knight Newspapers, Inc.; John Hughes, editor, *Christian Science Monitor;* Clayton Kirkpatrick, chief executive officer, *Chicago Tribune;* Richard H. Leonard, editor and vice president, *Milwaukee Journal;* William J. McGill, president, Columbia University; Warren H. Phillips, chairman and chief executive officer, Dow Jones & Co.; Joseph Pulitzer Jr., editor and publisher, *St. Louis Post-Dispatch;* and James Reston, columnist, *New York Times,* http://pulitzer.org.

44. MacPherson, "Donnybrook."

45. In 1979, the prize went to the *Pottsville Republican* for its series on

organized crime's role in the destruction of the Blue Coal Company. In 1971, the Pulitzer Prize for Local Investigative Specialized Reporting went to William Jones of the *Chicago Tribune* who took a job as an ambulance driver to uncover corrupt practices of local private ambulance companies. In 1973, it went to the *New York Daily News* for William Sherman's investigation into New York State Medicaid abuses (he posed as a Medicaid recipient). The *Tribune* won again in 1976 for exposing unsanitary conditions in local hospitals, an investigation for which William Gaines took a job at the hospital as a janitor.

46. MacPherson, "Donnybrook." Patterson would repeat the essence of his comments five months later in a published debate with another Pulitzer board member, Clayton Kirkpatrick, the editor of the *Chicago Tribune,* who understandably expressed a far more supportive view of the work of his hometown rival, as described in chapter 9. See Clayton Kirkpatrick and Gene Patterson, "Should Reporters Play Roles," *ASNE Bulletin,* September 1979, 12–13.

47. MacPherson, "Donnybrook." Re Bradlee's "no misrepresentation" edict, though the issue of what represents "misrepresentation" is arguable. Chapter 8 notes, for example, the pose of Joshua Solomon, a student at the University of Maryland, who reported his adventures in skin dyed black in 1994. See Joshua Solomon, "Skin Deep: Reliving 'Black Like Me': My Own Journey into the Heart of Race-Conscious America," *Washington Post,* 30 October 1994, C01.

48. MacPherson, "Donnybrook."

49. Ibid.

50. Ibid.

51. Ibid.

52. See, for example, Goldstein, *The News at Any Cost: How Journalists Compromise Their Ethics to Shape the News* (New York: Touchstone, 1985), 138; and Jack Fuller, *News Values: Ideas for an Information Age* (Chicago: University of Chicago Press, 1996), 48–49, 52–53. Bok's book was a 1979 finalist for the National Book Critics Circle Award and in 1980, in paperback, it was a National Book Awards finalist.

53. Richard Lingeman, "Books of the Times: *Lying: Moral Choice in Public and Private Life* by Sissela Bok," *New York Times,* 5 July 1978,

C16. Joan Beck, in "White Lies Shade into Darker Ones, Killing Trust," *Chicago Tribune,* 31 March 1978, B2, notes how journalists were tightening ethical standards.

54. Sissela Bok, *Lying* (New York: Vintage, 1989), 120–21. For instance, she takes particular exception to a passage in Bob Woodward and Carl Bernstein's *All the President's Men,* in which they describe the deceptive techniques they deployed in 1972 to report the Watergate scandal for the *Washington Post,* a Pulitzer Prize winner of 1973. While acknowledging her admiration for what the two young reporters accomplished, she also enumerated their moral offenses, including telling interviewees that information being requested was already available from other sources, when it was not; impersonating someone on the telephone; lying to get confirmation of a fact; and having the newspaper publish information for which evidence was too sparse to merit release. What seems to trouble Bok most is the absence of any reflection by the two reporters on the moral dilemmas their actions posed, however well justified by the end result. She also expresses concern over the bad example they set for younger reporters who might emulate their behavior "with lesser provocation" than a major national scandal in the making. "The results, therefore are severe," she wrote, "both in terms of risks to the personal professional standards of those directly involved, the public view of the profession, and to many within it or about to enter it."

55. Bok, *Lying,* quoted in Fuller, *News Values,* 48.

56. Steve Robinson, "Pulitzers: Was the Mirage a Deception?" *Columbia Journalism Review* 18.2 (July/August 1979): 14–15.

57. The following articles address the Mirage and the issue of entrapment: David Shaw, "Deception—Honest Tool of Reporting?" *Los Angeles Times,* 20 September 1979, B1; Carmody, "Exposure of Corruption," 23 February 1978, A16; Jonathan Steele, "The Pay-Off Parade at The Mirage Bar," *Guardian,* 10 January 1978, 11; MacPherson, "Donnybrook"; Editorial, "The Mirage Non-award," *Columbia Journalism Review* 18.3 (September/October 1979): 20; and Smith and Zekman, "The Mirage Takes Shape," *Columbia Journalism Review* 18.3 (September/October 1979): 51–57.

58. Robinson, "Pulitzers."

59. Edward W. Barrett [E. W. B.], "Publisher's Notes," *Columbia Jour-*

*nalism Review* 18.3 (September/October 1979): 20. For a good discussion of the ethics of the Mirage project, see also Edmund B. Lambeth, *Committed Journalism: An Ethic for the Profession* (Bloomington: Indiana University Press, 1986), 40–47. The *Sun-Times* also won the Sigma Delta Chi Distinguished Service Award from the Society of Professional Journalists for Mirage and was honored that same year for its "Abortion Profiteers" series. For the year's SPJ awards listing, see, Untitled, "Domestic News," Associated Press, 3 April 1979.

60. For an indication of the frequency, search terms *journalism* and *Sissela Bok.*

61. Fuller, *News Values,* 51–53.

62. Fuller, "Response to Daniel Kornstein," *Cordozo Studies in Law and Literature* 1.2 (October 1989): 157–60. Kornstein and Fuller debated Janet Malcolm's *New Yorker* piece of March 1989, "The Journalist and the Murderer."

63. Fuller, *News Values,* 51.

64. Ibid., 51–52.

65. Fuller, *Cordozo,* 157–60.

66. Ibid.

67. Fuller, *News Values,* 46–47, 50.

68. David H. Weaver and G. Cleveland Wilhoit, *The American Journalist in the 1990s* (Mahwah, N.J.: Lawrence Erlbaum Associates, 1996), 169; David H. Weaver et al., *The American Journalist in the 21st Century* (Mahwah, N.J.: Lawrence Erlbaum Associates, 2007), 178–79. See also Weaver, *The American Journalist: A Portrait of U.S. Newspeople and Their Work* (Bloomington: Indiana University Press, 1991).

69. The data comes from the three separate studies noted above, led by David H. Weaver, of the ethics, attitudes, and values of "U.S. newspeople" across all media, dated 1991, 1996, and 2007. Similar results were reported in a separate, less formal 1988 survey of journalists involved in investigative units for television, conducted by the Investigative Reporters and Editors, and showed similar results. See Charles Burke, "Survey on TV Reporting: How We Think About Surveillance Journalism," *IRE Journal* (Winter 1989): 22–23.

70. As seen elsewhere in this book, notably Ben Bradlee and Eugene Patterson in reaction to the Mirage controversy (chapters 9 and 14);

Howard Kurtz in response to the Food Lion and Turkmenistan controversies (chapters 10 and 15); and Jack Fuller in his book *News Values.*

71. Among those expressing continued support within specific parameters: ethics columnists Bob Steele of the Poynter Institute (chapter
15); Edward Wasserman of the *Miami Herald* (chapter 15); John Seigenthaler, now of the First Amendment Center (chapter 12); Tom Rosenstiel of
PEW's Project for Excellence in Journalism (chapter 15); and the many
editors noted throughout who have continued to assign such projects as
warranted.

72. William A. Henry III, "Journalism Under Fire," *Time,* 12 December 1983.

73. Carroll Doherty, "The Public Isn't Buying Press Credibility: The
Seeds of Public Distrust Were Sown Long Before the Recent Round of
Scandals," *Nieman Reports,* Summer 2005, 46–47.

74. Ibid.

75. A survey conducted by the *Sun-Times* showed that the Mirage's
undercover nature did not discount its validity, as 85 percent of respondents believed the investigation to be true, from "Tales of Payoffs and
Shakedowns Stir Up Chicago," *Christian Science Monitor,* 1 February 1978,
9. The release of the Pentagon Papers was supported by 58 percent of
respondents, from "Airing of Pentagon Data Backed in Poll," *New York
Times,* 5 July 1971, 2. An online poll by Bill Moyers about Ken Silverstein's Turkmenistan investigation showed that 85 percent of respondents
did not object to his methods. See http://www.pbs.org/moyers/journal/
blog/2007/06/poll_undercover_journalism.html, accessed 10 February
2011.

76. Fuller, *News Values,* 51.

77. I state in Kroeger, *Nellie Bly* (1994), 101: "In recent years, posing as
something other than a reporter in an effort to get better information has
fallen into disfavor among print journalists, although television reporters
still employ the device from time to time." On the basis of the research
conducted for this book, I would amend that statement to say "fallen into
disfavor among *some* print journalists."

78. John Seigenthaler, in a telephone interview on January 14, 2011,
could not recall if the Thompson reporting had been included in the
awards nomination submission. He checked with the *Tennessean,* but

the original correspondence could not be located. The Pulitzer archives housed at Columbia's Rare Book and Manuscript Library do not include finalist submissions. Members of the KKK task force that preceded Thompson's investigation included Susan Thomas, Kurt Loggins, and Nancy Warnecke Rhoda. The Pulitzer citation lists only the *Tennessean*'s "staff."

79. According to the Pulitzer Prize site, http://pulitzer.org, the 1981–1982 board included Osborn Elliott, dean, Graduate School of Journalism, Columbia University; Hanna H. Gray, president, University of Chicago; Howard H. Hays, Jr., editor and publisher, *Riverside Press-Enterprise;* Lee Hill, president and executive editor, Knight Newspapers, Inc.; John Hughes, editor, *Christian Science Monitor;* Clayton Kirkpatrick, chief executive officer, *Chicago Tribune;* Richard H. Leonard, editor and senior vice president, *Milwaukee Journal;* Warren H. Phillips, chairman and chief executive officer, Dow Jones & Co.; Joseph Pulitzer Jr. (III), editor and publisher, *St. Louis Post-Dispatch;* William J. Raspberry, columnist, *Washington Post;* Charlotte Saikowski, chief editorial writer, *Christian Science Monitor;* Michael I. Sovern, president, Columbia University; and Roger W. Wilkins, senior fellow, Joint Center for Political Studies. The category of Local Specialized or Investigative Reporting evolved before the 1985 judging, replaced by General News Reporting and Investigative Reporting and two new categories: Explanatory Reporting and Specialized Reporting. See *The Pulitzer Prizes: Winners, 1917 to the Present Including Nominated Finalists, 1980 to the Present* (New York: Pulitzer Prize Board at Columbia University, 2008), 21–22. By the 1980 round of judging, the same board, with the exception of the change in what was the then president of Columbia University, added the naming of finalists to the official record for the first time. By 1981, when the *Tennessean* and *Sun-Times* projects were named as finalists, both Bradlee and Patterson had rotated off the board.

80. Zekman and Gene Mustain, "The Accident Swindlers: They're Getting Away with $3 Billion a Year—and All You Drivers Pay," *Chicago Sun-Times,* 10 February 1980, 1, 6–7; "Legal Advice? Theirs Is Fraud: Five Who Traffic in Automobile-Accident Cases," 11 February 1980, 1, 6–7; "How Superswindling Pays: Just a Little Nets a Lot If Accident Case Is 'Perfect,'" 12 February 1980, 1, 6–7; "Lawyers' Swindling Side-

kicks," 13 February 1980, 1, 6–7; "Accidents Too Good to Leave to Lawyers," 14 February 1980, 1, 6–7; "Chasers Converge on Accident Scene," 15 February 1980, 6–7; "A Hospital for Greedy," 17 February 1980, 1, 6–7; "Our Own Phony Patient Is Hospitalized and Discovers the Hospital Is a Mirage," 18 February 1980, 6–7; "The Accident Mills—Clinics Processing Cheats by the Thousands," 19 February 1980, 6–7; "Probe Abuses at Hospital—State Legislator," 19 February 1980, 7; "These Chiropractors Are Master Hands . . . at Juggling the Facts on Injuries," 20 February 1980, 6–7; "Hospital Boss Vows to Probe Methods," 20 February 1980, 7; "Doctors' 'Treatments' Keep Fraud Alive," 21 February 1980, 6–7; "State Agency Probes Practices Uncovered in Swindler Series," 21 February 1980, 7; "The Hypocritical Oath—and Doctors Who Lie by It," 22 February 1980, 6–7; "Department Probes Moonlighting Cop Who Aids Fraudulent Claims," 22 February 1980, 7; "'Swindlers' Take Pains to Get Themselves Hospitalized," 24 February 1980, 6–7; "Accident Cheats Add to Hospital Image Problem," 25 February 1980, 6–7; "'Accident-Prone' Hospital Cures Itself," 26 February 1980, 6; "'No Fault'—an Answer to Accident Fraud," 27 February 1980, 9; "Agency Ignored Reports of Phony Patients," 28 February 1980, 9–10; "Federal Panel Probes Fake Car-Injury Claims," 29 February 1980, 3, 32; "Hospital Executive's Sideline Pads 'Take,'" 11 March 1980, 4; "State Board Orders Evanston Hospital to Hearing," 17 March 1980, 4; "Series Spawns a Wave of Hospital Shakeups," 3 April 1980, 6, 18; "Thompson Bills Hit Accident Fraud," 5 April 1980, 3, editorial, 15; "Smashup Cheats—How They Get YOU," 6 April 1980, 8, 35; "Hospital in Evanston Loses Accreditation," 8 April 1980, 2; "Panel Blasts Hospital Board," 10 April 1980, 7; "State Panel Asks Voiding of Chiropractor's License," 11 April 1980, 4; "Hospital Aide Ties to 2 Clinics Told," 12 May 1980, 6, 16; "State to Suspend License of Hospital in Evanston," 6 June 1980, 4; Maurice Possley and Zekman, "Year in Jail for Accident Swindler," 1 July 1980, 12; Zekman and Mustain, "Two Linked to Ripoffs Convicted," 30 May 1980, 3; Kay Rutherford, "Chiropractor to Aid Prosecutors," 31 May 1980, 18; Zekman and Mustain, "Hospital Under Fire in Probe Shuts Down," 3 June 1980, 3.

81. Zekman and Mustain, "Our Own Phony Patient Is Hospitalized and Discovers the Hospital Is a Mirage," *Chicago Sun-Times,* 18 February 1980, 6–7.

82. See http://www.duPontawards.org/year/1981. The series also won an Emmy. The letter of nomination to the Pulitzer jury from *Sun-Times* executive editor Ralph Otwell said that the project took six months during which reporters documented fraudulent legal and medical practices that were adding up to a third to driver's insurance premiums. It showed how "unscrupulous lawyers and doctors conspire with their clients and patients to fake or exaggerate injuries" so they can collect inflated settlements—up to $3 billion annually. And it showed how the tort liability system of settling claims in Illinois enables the corrupt to fabricate fraudulent claims that the insurance industry, in turn, finds cheaper to pay than to contest in court. The series also indicated states that have adopted no-fault insurance laws experienced fewer suits and lower premium costs.

83. Pulitzer 1984 finalist citation for George Getschow of the *Wall Street Journal:* for his series "Dirty Work," which disclosed the existence of temporary slave labor camps throughout the southwest United States. See also Goldstein, *News at Any Cost,* 132–33. Goldstein notes that by the early 1980s, "the message that the Pulitzer board looked on undercover reporting with disfavor had apparently spread." He quotes prize administrator Robert Christopher, saying that relatively few entries based on undercover reporting had been submitted between 1981 and 1983. (Christopher notes two finalists with undercover dimensions, but I count four with the *Sun-Times* accident swindlers, Wolin's sweatshops, the *Tennessean*'s KKK, and Getschow.) Still, even without the Pulitzer board's blessing, Goldstein confirms, "posing seems still be as entrenched among journalists as it has been for at least a century."

84. These included the *Atlanta Constitution,* the *Detroit News,* the *Los Angeles Times,* the *Rochester Democrat and Chronicle,* the *Buffalo Evening News,* the *Los Angeles Herald Examiner,* the *San Antonio Light,* the *Arizona Daily Star,* the *Wall Street Journal,* the *Miami Herald,* the *Albuquerque Tribune,* the *Washington Post,* the *New York Times,* the *Boston Globe,* the *Fort Wayne News Sentinel,* the *Travers City Record Eagle,* the *Muskegon Chronicle,* the *Indianapolis Star,* the *Lexington Herald-Leader,* the *Milwaukee Journal, Newsday,* the *Washington Times,* the *Hartford Courant,* and the *San Francisco Chronicle.* Please see the book's companion database, http://undercoverreporting.org, for full details.

85. Among the misfires are Gary Schuster, "Greasing a Moment in History," *Detroit News,* 27 March 1979. To expose lax security, Schuster, then *Detroit News'* Washington bureau chief, posed as a Michigan congressman to gain access to a bill-signing ceremony on the White House lawn. He was reproved by the Standing Committee of Correspondents to Congress. See also Michael Cordts, "Free Books Sold by Editors," *Rochester Democrat and Chronicle,* 5 August 1979. Cordts worked at Manhattan's Strand bookstore for two weeks to reveal that book reviewers were selling Strand their complimentary copies for a quick buck. And see Agnes Palazzetti, "Posing as Shoplifter Works Too Well," *Buffalo Evening News,* 10 July 1981. Palazzetti, in an effort to expose poor security at retail stores, attempted to shoplift but got caught. All cited in Goldstein, *News at Any Cost,* 139–40, 144.

86. Peter Johnson, "'Dateline' roots out predators; men seeking teens for sex via Internet," *USA Today,* 15 February 2006, B9. Story reports the program drew an average of 8.5 million viewers for its first two episodes.

87. In the aftermath of Mirage and Food Lion, too, television's highest honors have continued to go to dozens of projects that involved the use of hidden cameras and/or other undercover techniques, including these award-winning examples of broadcast pieces that used hidden cameras: "Missing the Beat," hosted by Caroline Lowe, WCCO-TV, 1 May 1994 (won 1995 Silver Baton duPont Award); "Rush to Read," *Primetime Live,* hosted by Diane Sawyer, ABC, 19 May 1994 (won Peabody Award in 1995); "The Unwanted Children of Russia," *20/20,* hosted by Diane Sawyer, ABC, 13 January 1999 (won duPont Silver Baton Award in 2000); "Caught off Guard," hosted by Jim Hoffer, WABC-TV, 24 October 2001 (won Silver Baton duPont Award in 2002); "Trafficked for the Military," hosted by Tom Merriman and Greg Easterly, WJW-TV, 25 September 2002 (IRE Award finalist in 2002); "The Sport of Sheikhs," *Real Sports with Bryant Gumbel,* HBO, 19 October 2004 (won duPont Silver Baton Award in 2006, as noted in chapter 4); "Seoul Train," *Independent Lens,* hosted by Lisa Seeth and Jim Butterworth, PBS (ITVS), 13 December 2005 (won duPont Silver Baton Award in 2007); "Pill Mills," *Carmel on the Case,* hosted by Carmel Cafiero, produced by Anthony Pineda, WSVN-TV, 18 June 2009 (won Silver Baton duPont Award in 2010).

Three local television stations won the prestigious duPont Award in 1988 alone for projects that featured the prominent use of hidden-camera techniques, all on themes of local corruption and wrongdoing, including WBRZ in Baton Rouge for exposing corruption to Louisiana government with the use of hidden cameras. State agents in a drinking club were filmed getting drunk in bars when they were supposed to be working ("I'll Drink to That," 23 October 1987); KMOV in St. Louis won for staking out bars in vans and witnessing police who were not enforcing drunk driving laws and were profiting from doing so ("Sauget: City of Shame," 1 January 1987); and WPLG in Miami for exposing the abuses of children and elderly using hidden cameras ("Florida: State of Neglect," 1 May 1987).

The same has been true of magazines. At a number of high-prestige publications, the techniques have been a mainstay in more recent years. Among them, *Harper's,* repeatedly, as well as the *New Yorker, Esquire, Vanity Fair, City Limits, New York, Rolling Stone,* and *Wired.* For example, Debra Seagal, "Tales from the Cutting-Room Floor: The Reality of 'Reality-Based' Television," *Harper's,* November 1993, 50–57; Barbara Ehrenreich, "Welcome to Cancerland: A Mammogram Leads to a Cult of Pink Kitsch," *Harper's,* November 2001, 43–53; Ehrenreich, "Nickel-and-Dimed: On (Not) Getting By in America" *Harper's,* January 1999, 37–52; Jake Silverstein, "What Is Poetry? And Does It Pay?" *Harper's,* August 2002, 55–64; Jeff Sharlet, "Jesus Plus Nothing: Undercover Among America's Secret Theocrats," *Harper's,* March 2003, 53–64; Morgan Meis, "Devil's Work: Secret Doings at the Queens Museum of Art," *Harper's,* April 2004, 65–71; Wells Tower, "Bird-Dogging the Bush Vote: Undercover with Florida's Republic Shock Troops," *Harper's,* March 2005, 45–57; Bill Wasik, "My Crowd: Or, Phase 5," *Harper's,* March 2006, 56–66; Kristoffer A. Garin, "A Foreign Affair: On the Great Ukrainian Bride Hunt," *Harper's,* June 2006, 69–77; Willem Marx, "Misinformation Intern: My Summer as a Military Propagandist in Iraq," *Harper's,* September 2006, 51–59; and Jeremy Miller, "Tyranny of the Test: One Year as a Kaplan Coach in the Public Schools," *Harper's,* September 2008, 35–46.

Also, in chronological order: Lawrence Otis Graham, "Invisible Man," *New York,* 17 August 1992, http://nymag.com/news/features/47949/; Helen Zia, "Made in the U.S.A.," *Ms.* 4 January 1996, 66–73; Kevin Held-

man, "7 1/2 Days," *City Limits,* 1 June 1998, http://www.citylimits.org/
news/articles/2454/7-1-2-days; Ted Conover, "A Reporter at Large:
Guarding Sing Sing," *New Yorker,* 3 April 2000, 54, http://www.tedconover
.com/2010/01/guarding-sing-sing/; Craig Unger, "American Rapture," *Vanity Fair,* December 2005, http://www.vanityfair.com/politics/
features/2005/12/rapture200512>; Evan Ratliff, "Vanish," *Wired,* 25 November 2009, http://www.wired.com/vanish/2009/11/ff_vanish2/; and
C. J. Chivers, "September," *Esquire,* September 2002, 144.

In long form, for books, the authorial conceit of going undercover
retains its narrative appeal. Ted Conover's *Newjack* received a National
Book Critics Circle Award in 2001, as well as a version published in
the *New Yorker.* See Ted Conover, "A Reporter at Large: Guarding Sing
Sing," *New Yorker,* 3 April 2000, 54, a separate piece published shortly
before the book. Jeff Sharlet's *The Family,* which grew out of his *Harper's*
piece, "Jesus Plus Nothing," is another more recent example. The list of
such projects which have received national attention since the mid-1800s
numbers into the dozens.

88. These include the *Chicago Sun-Times,* the *Nashville Tennessean,*
the *New York Times,* the *Seattle Post-Intelligencer,* the *New York Daily News,*
the *Spokane Review,* the *Los Angeles Times,* the *Washington Post,* and the
*Wichita Eagle.* Please see the companion undercover reporting database
at http://undercoverreporting.org for full details.

89. Recktenwald, telephone interview. He mentioned specifically the
*Tribune*'s "Miracle Merchants," a 1998 exposé for which a group of the
newspaper's reporters and editors sponsored twelve children through
four of the largest and best-known child sponsorship organizations for
two years. The journalists identified themselves by name but were not
asked nor did they disclose their *Tribune* affiliation· or the reason for their
commitment. They also traveled unannounced to the children's locations, finding that some had benefited from their largesse, some had not,
and that one had been dead for most of the time the reporter was sending money (see "About This Special Report Series: The Miracle Merchants. Special Report," *Chicago Tribune,* 15–22 March 1998, 2). He also
mentioned the *Tribune*'s team effort for its "Gateway to Gridlock" series
about the chaos of O'Hare International Airport, for which the news-

paper won the 2001 Pulitzer for explanatory journalism (see "Gateway to Gridlock," *Chicago Tribune,* 20–22 November 2000).

90. Michael Miner, "News Bites: Undercover Journalism's Last Call," *Chicago Reader,* 4, 11 October 2002.

91. Jennifer Tanaka, "Top 40 OMG Moments in Recent Chicago History," *Chicago,* November 2010, http://www.chicagomag.com/Chicago-Magazine/November-2010/Top-40-OMG-Most-Shocking-Moments-in-Recent-Chicago-History/.

92. Mark Fitzgerald, "One Mirage That Proved All Too Real," *Editor & Publisher,* October 2006, 8.

## CHAPTER FIFTEEN

1. Bill Wasik, ed., *Submersion Journalism: Reporting in the Radical First Person from Harper's Magazine* (New York: New Press, 2008), x.

2. Wells Tower, "Bird-Dogging the Bush Vote: Undercover with Florida's Republic Shock Troops," *Harper's,* March 2005, 45–57.

3. Ken Silverstein, telephone interview by author, 1 July 2007.

4. Ken Silverstein, *Turkmeniscam* (New York: Random House, 2008), xii.

5. Ibid.

6. Ibid., xii, xx-xxi.

7. Ibid., xii.

8. Ibid.

9. Silverstein, telephone interview.

10. Silverstein, "Their Men in Washington: Undercover with D.C.'s Lobbyists for Hire," *Harper's,* July 2007.

11. Silverstein, telephone interview.

12. Steve Benen, "Political Animal," *Washington Monthly,* 30 June 2007; Amy Alkon, "Oh, Boohoo, Somebody Was Sneaky," *Amy Alkon/Advice Goddess* (blog), 30 June 2007 (delivered by Newstex); Jack O'Dwyer, "Silverstein Raps Media," *Jack O'Dwyer's Newsletter* 3.40 (18 July 2007): 28; Doug Fisher, "Lobbying Flack—or Is that Flak?" *Common Sense Journalism,* 26 June 2007; "'Gotcha' Without a 'Get,'" "Public Eye," CBSnews.com,

26 June 2007; Joey Picador, "It's All Just ... A Mirage," *Justice for None,* 3 July 2007; Editorial, "A Flimsy Set of Laws," *Knight Ridder Tribune Business News,* 9 July 2007, 1; "Note: Journalism Not Stenography," *Stick with a Nose,* 30 June 2007; Ezra Klein, "Shed a Tear for the Lobbyists," 30 June 2007; "Going Undercover to Get a Story," *Carpetbagger,* 30 June 2007; Amy Goodman, "In New Exposé, Ken Silverstein of *Harper's Magazine* Goes Undercover to Find out What US Lobbyists Do for Dictators," *Democracy Now!* 28 June 2007; Leonard Lopate, "Lobbyists for Hire," WNYC, 27 June 2007; "Undercover with DC Lobbyists for Hire," *Daily Kos,* 24 June 2007; "Writer Sneaks a Look at Ways of Lobbyists," *Wall Street Journal,* 14 June 2007, B7; Kevin Roderick, "From Magazine to Screen," *LA Observed,* 27 July 2007; and Jon Friedman, "Why Aren't More People Buzzing About *Harper's,*" *MarketWatch,* 9 September 2008. Also noted in *The Next Hurrah* (blog), 16 June 2007, and in *Blog4Brains* (blog), 3 July 2007.

13. Howard Kurtz, "Stung by *Harper's* in a Web of Deceit," *Washington Post,* 25 June 2007, C1.

14. Silverstein, "Undercover Under Fire," *Los Angeles Times,* 30 June 2007, A29. See also Letters to the Editor, *Los Angeles Times,* 5 July 2007, A16.

15. Silverstein, "Undercover Under Fire."

16. Neal Conan, "Talk of the Nation: Lobbyists Offer Dictators a Door to D.C.," NPR, 19 June 2007; and Brooke Gladstone, "On the Media: Identity Crisis," WNYC, NPR, 29 June 2007. See also Neal Conan, "The Foreign Lobby: Turkmenistan of Bust," *Blog of the Nation,* 19 June 2007, http://npr.org/blogs/talk/2007/06/the_foreign_lobby_turmenistan_1.html.

17. "Bill Moyers Talks with Ken Silverstein: Transcript," *Bill Moyers Journal,* PBS, 22 June 2007, http://pbs.org/moyers/journal/06222007/transcript1.html.

18. "Bill Moyers Talks." See also APCO response to Silverstein, posted on Moyers' blog, "Do Lobby Firms Have Ethics?" http://moyerstalk.blogspot.com2007/05/do-lobby-firms-have-ethics.html.

19. Poll, *Bill Moyers Journal,* PBS, 22 June 2007, http://pbs.org/moyers/journal/blog/2007/06/poll_undercover_journalism.html. See also Letters to the Editor, *Los Angeles Times,* 5 July 2007.

20. Mark Lisheron, "Lying to Get the Truth," *American Journalism Review,* October–November 2007.

21. Lisheron, *American Journalism Review,* October–November 2007.

22. Edward Wasserman, "Can Trickery by Reporters Be Right?" *Miami Herald,* 9 July 2007, A17. See also http://edwardwasserman.com/2007/07/09/can-trickery-by-reporters-be-right/, 9 July 2007.

23. Wasserman, "Trickery by Reporters."

24. Ibid.

25. Wasserman, email exchange with author, 13–14 March 2011. See also Wasserman, "When Subterfuge Is an Acceptable Tool of Reporting," *Miami Herald,* 17 May 2006, 1; Wasserman, "Trickery by Reporters"; and Wasserman, "Journalistic Stings Go Mainstream," *Miami Herald,* 13 March 2011.

26. Wasserman, "Acceptable Tool of Reporting," 1.

27. Joe Strupp, "Spokane Probe: Other Editors Say They Forbid Undercover Operations," *Editor & Publisher,* 10 May 2005.

28. Wasserman, "Acceptable Tool of Reporting," 1. Wasserman was uncomfortable with the targeting of someone gay because, as a Republican legislative leader, the mayor routinely took antigay positions. And he was bothered that "the current allegations, involving males of legal age, were wrapped into the context of much-older allegations of far more serious and illegal misconduct with young boys, which seems unprovable." He also found the evidence of the mayor's abuse of office "thin" with the clearest instance being the unpaid internship the mayor had offered to the newspaper's plant. "That's an important weakness," Wasserman, wrote, "since it's the offer of job-based perks that turns the tale of a lonely man looking for companions into a story of official misconduct and makes his personal squalor legitimate news."

29. Bob Steele, "Lying in the Name of Truth: When Is it Justified for Journalists?" Poynteronline, 6 July 2007.

30. Wasserman, *Miami Herald,* 9 July 2007, A17.

31. Ian Murphy, "Koch Whore," *Beast,* 23 February 2011, http://www.buffalobeast.com/?p=5045. See also W. Paul Smith, "Prank Call to Governor Was Good Journalism," *Voyager,* 1 March 2011. See Murphy's reply to the editor of the student newspaper at West Florida University, chapter 13, n85.

32. See full citations for these episodes in chapter 13.

33. Silverstein, telephone interview.

34. For those not in the text, please consult the database at undercover reporting.org.

35. Matthieu Aikins, "The Master of Spin Boldak," *Harper's,* December 2009. See also Joshua Partlow, "Military Launches Afghanistan Intelligence-Gathering Mission," *Washington Post,* 20 February 2010, A12; and Laura Fraser, "Aikins Breaks New Journalistic Ground," *Chronicle-Herald* (Canada), 12 December 2010.

36. Silverstein, telephone interview.

37. Bill Kovach and Tom Rosenstiel, *The Elements of Journalism: What Newspeople Should Know and the Public Should Expect* (New York: Three Rivers Press, 2007), 97–98.

38. Kovach and Rosenstiel, *Elements of Journalism,* 83.

39. John Hersey, "The Legend on the License," *Yale Review,* Autumn 1980.

40. Philip Brian Harper, "Passing for What? Racial Masquerade and the Demands of Upward Mobility," *Callaloo* 21.2 (Spring 1998): 381–97.

# BIBLIOGRAPHY

"About This Special Report Series: The Miracle Merchants. Special Report." *Chicago Tribune,* 15–22 March 1998, 2.

Abramowitz, Michael, and Steve Vogel. "Army Secretary Ousted." *Washington Post,* 3 March 2007, A01.

Adler, Judith. "Youth on the Road: Reflections on the History of Tramping." *Annals of Tourism Research* 12.3 (1985): 335–54.

Aikins, Matthieu. "The Master of Spin Boldak." *Harper's,* December 2009.

"Airing of Pentagon Data Backed in Poll." *New York Times,* 5 July 1971, 2.

Alden, William L. "London Letter: Written for *The New York Times Sunday Review of Books* by William L. Alden." In *New York Times Sunday Review of Books,* 18 October 1902, BR6.

Alkon, Amy. "Oh, Boohoo, Somebody Was Sneaky." *Amy Alkon / Advice Goddess* (blog), 30 June 2007.

Allen, George N. *Undercover Teacher.* New York: Doubleday, 1960.

Alter, Jonathan. "'Candid Camera' Gone Berserk?" *Newsweek,* 30 August 1993, 36.

"Alumni Honor 5 in Journalism." *New York Times,* 7 May 1959, 34.

"Among the Poor." *Bookman* 25.736 (28 March 1896): 214.

———. *The Critic* 25.736 (28 March 1896): 214.

"Anas Is Journalist of the Year." Myjoyonline.com, 19 August 2010, http://news.myjoyonline.com/news/200708/7748.asp.

"Apologies to ABC, Producers." *IRE Journal* 22.6 (August 1999): 4.

Applegate, Jane. "Ex-Teacher Is Given 2 Years in Bombings." *Los Angeles Times,* 9 June 1987, 4.

———. "Mercenary Offers Tales of Secret U.S. Missions at Firebombing Trial." *Los Angeles Times,* 9.

———. "2 Mercenaries Convicted of Bombing Cars." *Los Angeles Times,* 14 April 1987, 1.

Aremeyaw, Anas. "Sex Ghetto Raided." *Crusading Guide* (Ghana), 28 January 2008.

"Arrest of the Fortune Tellers." *New York Daily Tribune,* 23 October 1858, 5.

Arthur, Anthony. *Upton Sinclair: Radical Innocent.* New York: Random House, 2006.

*Australian Dictionary of Biography.* Vol. 10. 1986 ed. S.v. "Melvin, Joseph Dalgarno (1852–1909)," by Peter Corris. Melbourne University Publishing, 2007 (Melbourne, Australia).

*Australian Dictionary of Biography.* Vol. 10. 1986 ed. S.v. "Morrison, George Ernest (Chinese) (1862–1920)," by J. S. Gregory. Melbourne University Publishing, 2007 (Melbourne, Australia).

Bagdikian, Ben H., and Leon Dash. "An Agenda for Reform of a Hell Behind Walls." *Washington Post,* 5 February 1972, A1.

———. "Bureaucratic Overload Turns Justice to Misery." *Washington Post,* 1 February 1972, A1.

———. "The Drive for Inmates Rights." *Washington Post,* 5 February 1972, A1.

———. "Female Homosexuality Prevalent." *Washington Post,* 2 February 1972, A1.

———. "A Human Wasteland in the Name of Justice." *Washington Post,* 30 January 1972, A1.

———. "Juvenile Prison: Society's Stigma." *Washington Post,* 3 February 1972, A1.

———. "No. 50061, Inside Maximum Security: Six Days in State Prison Through the Eyes of a 'Murderer,'" *Washington Post,* 31 January 1972, A1.

———. "Rehabilitation: A Frayed Hope." *Washington Post,* 4 February 1972, A1.

———. *The Shame of the Prisons.* New York: Pocketbooks, Simon and Schuster. 1972.

Baker, Ella, and Marvel Cooke. "The Slave Market." *Crisis* 42.11 (November 1935): 330.

Baker, Russ. "In Greensboro, Damning Undercover Tactics as 'Fraud.'" *Columbia Journalism Review* 35.6 (March/April 1997): 28.

Baker, Scott. "Does Raw Video of NPR Exposé Reveal Questionable Editing & Tactics?" *The Blaze,* 10 March 2011, http://theblaze

.com/stories/does-raw-video-of-npr-expose-reveal-questionable -editing-tactics.

Ball, John, Jr. "Southern Notes for Northern Circulation." *New York National Anti-Slavery Standard,* 9 December 1854.

Banda, Susan. "Working Undercover." *IRE Journal* 18.14 (January 1995): 14.

Banks, Elizabeth L. *The Autobiography of a "Newspaper Girl."* London: Methuen, 1902.

―――. "Banta Sentenced; Called a Traitor." *New York Times,* 1 December 1944, 16.

―――. *Campaigns & Curiosity: Journalistic Adventures of an American Girl in Late Victorian London.* London: Cassell, 1894.

Barrett, Edward W. "Publisher's Notes." *Columbia Journalism Review* 18.3 (September/October 1979): 20.

Battaile, Janet. "Supermarket Chain to Face Child-Labor Case." *New York Times,* 8 November 1992, A36.

Beck, Joan. "White Lies Shade Into Darker Ones, Killing Trust." *Chicago Tribune,* 31 March 1978, B2.

Beers, Clifford W. *A Mind That Found Itself.* New York: Longmans, Green, 1910.

Beggan, James K., and Scott T. Allison. "Tough Women in the Unlikeliest of Places: The Unexpected Toughness of the Playboy Bunny." *Journal of Popular Culture* 38.5 (August 2005): 812.

"Behind the Scenes!" *Chicago Daily Times,* 9 September 1937, 3.

Bell, Malcolm, Jr. *Major Butler's Legacy.* Athens: University of Georgia Press, 1987.

Benen, Steve. "Political Animal." *Washington Monthly,* 30 June 2007.

Benjamin, Mark. "Behind the Walls of Ward 54." *Salon,* 18 February 2005.

―――. "Insult to Injury." *Salon,* 27 January 2005.

Bent, Silas. *Newspaper Crusaders: A Neglected Story.* New York: Whittlesey House, 1939.

Bernstein, Adam. "George N. Allen: Undercover, He Exposed School's Disorder." *Washington Post,* 16 November 2007.

Berryman, John. *Stephen Crane: A Critical Biography.* New York: Cooper Square Press, 1950.

"Best Books of 1899." *New York Times,* 21 April 1900, BR13.

Beulin, Wolfgang. *A History of German Literature: From the Beginnings to Its Present Day.* London: Routledge, 1993.

Bicknell, Percy F. "The Life Story of an Odd-Job Man." *Dial* 49.581 (1 September 1910): 110–11.

Bienstock, Ric Esther. "Sex Slaves: Director's Notes." *Frontline,* PBS, 7 February 2006, http://www.pbs.org/wgbh/pages/frontline/slaves/making/.

"Bill Moyers Talks with Ken Silverstein." *Bill Moyers Journal,* PBS, 22 June 2007, http://pbs.org/moyers/journal/06222007/transcript1.html.

Biskupic, Joan, and Howard Kurtz. "'48 Hours' Wins 11th Hour Case to Show Undercover Videotape." *Washington Post,* 10 February 1994, A10.

Bixby, Lyn et al., "Some Real Estate Agents Discriminate Against Black Home Buyers." *Hartford Courant,* 21 May 1989, A1.

Bliss, George, and William Currie. "Kusper Asks Specifics: Vote Board Blocks G.O.P. Election Judges: LEAP." *Chicago Tribune,* 25 October 1972, 1.

———. "Vote Canvass Fails; Ghosts Haunt Rolls." *Chicago Tribune,* 30 October 1972, 2.

Bliss, George, and Jay Mullen. "20,000 Seek U.S. Marshals in Polls." *Chicago Tribune,* 13 September 1972, 6.

———. "Dem-Ruled Polls Kill 2-Party System." *Chicago Tribune,* 11 September 1972, 1.

———. "Kusper Office Vote Records Are Missing." *Chicago Tribune,* 10 October 1972, 1.

———. "Phony Election Judges on Kusper's Nov. 7 List." *Chicago Tribune,* 29 September 1972.

———. "Reveal Huge Vote Fraud." *Chicago Tribune,* 10, 1, 1972.

Bly, Nellie. "Among the Mad." *Godey's Lady's Book,* January 1889.

———. "The Girls Who Make Boxes." *New York World,* 27 November 1887, 10.

———. "In the Biggest New York Tenement." *New York World,* 5 August 1894, 21.

———. "The King of the Lobby." *New York World,* 1 April 1888, 19.

———. "Magdalen Home." *New York World,* 12 February 1888.

————. "Nellie Bly Again—She Interviews Emma Goldman and Other Anarchists." *New York World,* 17 September 1893, 1–5.

————. "Nellie Bly A Prisoner—She Has Herself Arrested to Gain Entrance to a Station-House." *New York World,* 24 February 1889, 9.

————. "Nellie Bly as a Mesmerist." *New York World,* 25 March 1888, 19.

————. "Nellie Bly in Pullman—She Visits Homes of Poverty in the 'Model Workingman's Town.'" *New York World,* 11 July 1894, 5.

————. "Nellie Bly on the Stage." *New York World,* 4 March 1888, 15.

————. "Nellie Bly's Doctors, Seven Well-Known Physicians Disagree About Her Case." *New York World.* October 27, 1889, 13.

————. "Shadowed by a Detective—Nellie Bly Makes a Test of the Private Spy Nuisance." *New York World,* 28 April 1889, 13.

————. *Ten Days in a Madhouse.* New York: Munro, 1887.

————. "Trying to Be a Servant." *New York World,* 30 October 1887, 9.

————. "U.S. Acts to Protect Vote." *Chicago Tribune,* 17 September 1972, 1.

————. "Visiting the Dispensaries." *New York World,* 2 December 1888, 9.

————. "Wanted—A Few Husbands." *New York World,* 4 December 1887, 25.

————. "What Becomes of Babies." *New York World,* 6 November 1887, 10.

Bok, Sissela. *Lying: Moral Choice in Public and Private Life.* New York: Vintage Random House, 1999.

Bonazzi, Robert. *Man in the Mirror: John Howard Griffin and the Story of "Black Like Me."* New York: Orbis, 1997.

"Book Exposes Destitution in Paris, London." *Washington Post,* 30 July 1933, S8.

"Books People Are Reading." *New York Tribune,* 2 November 1903, 8.

Borger, John P. "New Whines in Old Bottles: Taking Newsgathering Torts Off the Food Lion Shelf." *Tort and Law Insurance Journal* 34.61 (Fall 1998).

Bower, Fredson, ed. *Stephen Crane: Tales, Sketches, and Reports.* Charlottesville: University of Virginia Press, 1973.

Boynton, Robert, ed. *The New New Journalism.* New York: Vintage, 2005.

Bradley, Patricia. *Women and the Press: The Struggle for Equality.* Evanston: Northwestern University Press, 2005.

Branegan, Jay. "Hospital Tour Bares Apparent Violations." *Chicago Tribune,* 10 September 1975, 10.

"The Brig Was Bottom Up." *New York Daily Tribune,* 30 November 1891, 1.

Brommage, W. H. "The Blackbird Cruise: Further Details of the Slaver *Montserrat*'s Expedition to the Gilbert Islands." *San Francisco Examiner,* 16 October 1892, 1–2.

———. "A Sale of Souls." *San Francisco Examiner,* 15 October 1892, 1.

Broughton, Irv. *Producers on Producing.* Jefferson, N.C.: McFarland, 1986

Brown, Edwin A. *Broke, the Man Without the Dime.* Chicago: Browne and Howell, 1913.

Brown, Henry. "A Narrative of the Anti-Masonic Excitement in the Western Part of the State of New-York, During the Years 1827, 1828, and Part of 1829." *American Quarterly Review* 7.3 ( March 1830): 162.

Broyard, Anatole. "Fantasy of Freedom." *New York Times,* 13 December 1983, 17.

Bugher, Ellen. "At Massage Parlors Image Fits." *News-Sentinel,* 17 November 1984, 1A.

———. "City Policy Hinders Law Enforcement." *News-Sentinel,* 17 November 1984, 7A.

———. "Nothing Surprises Massage Manager." *News-Sentinel,* 17 November 1984, 7A.

———. "Stigma Irks Trained Massagists." *News-Sentinel,* 19 November 1984, 1B.

Bugher, Ellen, and Nancy Nall. "Studios offer varied 'conversation.'" *News-Sentinel,* 19 November 1984, 1B.

Burke, Charles. "Survey on TV Reporting: How We Think About Surveillance Journalism." *IRE Journal* (January 1989): 22–23.

Butler, Vincent, "*Chicago Tribune* Exposé wins a Pulitzer: Chicago Vote Fraud Disclosures Earn Top Local Reporting Award." *Chicago Tribune,* 8 May 1973, 1.

Calame, Byron. Telephone interview by author, 1, 2 June 2010.

Caldwell, Nat. "Fire Danger for Aged Ever Present." *Nashville Tennessean,* 2 April 1968, 1.

———. "'For 85 Years . . . And This Is All He Had to Show,'" *Nashville Tennessean,* 1 April 1968, 1.

———. "Nat Caldwell Reports: Public Shows Deep Concern for Nursing Home Patients." *Nashville Tennessean,* 12 April 1968, 4.

———. "Nursing Home's 'Pride' Pays Off." *Nashville Tennessean,* 4 April 1968, 1.

———. "'Old Man' Headed Team in 6-Week Investigation." *Nashville Tennessean,* 31 March 1968, 1.

———. "Reporter's Inside Story: Nursing Homes Crowded, Dirty." *Nashville Tennessean,* 31 March 1968, 1.

———. "Residents Are 'Guests': Belcourt Terrace Living's Good." *Nashville Tennessean,* 3 April 1968, 1.

———. "'Take Us Fishing,' Doctors Can't Cure Boredom." *Nashville Tennessean,* 9 April 1968, 4.

Campbell, Helen. "The City of the Simple." *Lippincott's* 24.144 (December 1879): 698–706.

———. "An Experience Meeting in Water Street." *Sunday Afternoon,* January 1879, 53–61.

———. "An Experiment and What Came of It." *Sunday Afternoon,* June 1879, 537–44.

———. "Max." *Sunday Afternoon,* July 1879, 624–30.

———. "Mrs. Herndon's Income." Pts. 1–27. *Christian Union,* 12 March 1885, 9–11; 19 March 1885, 9–11; 26 March 1885, 9–11; 2 April 1885, 9–11; 16 April 1885, 9–11; 23 April 1885, 9–11; 30 April 1885, 9–11; 7 May 1885, 9–11; 14 May 1885, 9–11; 21 May 1885, 10–11; 28 May 1885, 10–11; 4 June 1885, 9–11; 11 June 1885, 9–11; 18 June 1885, 9–11; 25 June 1885, 9–11; 2 July 1885, 9–11; 9 July 1885, 9–11; 16 July 1885, 9–11; 23 July 1885, 9–11; 30 July 1885, 9–11; 6 August 1885, 9–11; 13 August 1885, 9–11; 20 August 1885, 9–11; 27 August 1885, 9–11; 3 September 1885, 10–11; and 10 September 1885, 10–11.

———. *Mrs. Herndon's Income: A Novel.* Boston: Roberts, 1886.

———. "Prisoners of Poverty: Women Wage-Workers, Their Homes and Their Lives," Pts. 1–21. *New York Daily Tribune,* 24 October 1886, 13; 31 October 1886, 13; 7 November 1886, 13; 14 November 1886, 13; 21 November 1886, 13; 28 November 1886, 13; 5 December 1886, 13; 12 December 1886, 13; 19 December 1886, 13; 26 December 1886, 10; 2 January 1887, 10; 9 January 1887, 10; 16 January 1887, 10; 23 January 1887, 10; 30 January 1887, 10; 6 February 1887, 10; 13 February 1887, 9; 20 February 1887, 10; 27 February 1887, 10; 6 March 1887, 10; and 13 March 1887, 10.

——. *Prisoners of Poverty: Women Wage Workers, Their Trades, and Their Lives.* Boston: Little, 1900.

——. *Prisoners of Poverty Abroad.* Boston: Roberts, 1889.

——. *The Problem of the Poor: A Record of Quiet Work in Unquiet Places.* New York: Fords, 1882.

——. "Six Stories in One." *Sunday Afternoon,* May 1879, 393–98.

——. "Sunday in Water Street, II." *Sunday Afternoon,* February 1879, 167–74.

——. "Studies in the Slums." Pts. 1–6. *Lippincott's,* May 1880, 568–73; June 1880, 740–45; July 1880, 103–9; August 1880, 213–17; September 1880, 362–67; and October 1880, 498–502.

——. "The Tenement House Question." *Sunday Afternoon,* April 1879, 317–23.

Caputo, Phil. "Crippled and Elderly Patients Abused in North Side Home." *Chicago Tribune,* 3 March 1971, 2.

——. "2 Aides Arrested for Striking Elderly Nursing Home Patients." *Chicago Tribune,* 29 May 1971, 6.

Caputo, Phil, and William Currie. "Halt Nursing Home Funds: State Welfare Is Withheld, Probe Begins." *Chicago Tribune,* 2 March 1971, 1.

Carlson, John Roy. *Cairo to Damascus.* New York: A. A. Knopf, 1951.

——. *Undercover.* Philadelphia: Blakiston, 1943.

Carmody, Deirdre. "Exposure of Corruption Raises Questions About Reporters' Masquerade." *New York Times,* 23 February 1978, A16.

Castle, Robert. Comment on Bill Moyers, "Polls: Undercover Journalism," June 21, 2007, http://www.pbs.org/moyers/journal/blog/2007/06/poll_undercover_journalism.html.

Catapano, Peter. "Opinionator: Masters of Deception." *New York Times* (blog), 11 March 2011, http://opinionator.blogs.nytimes.com/2011/03/11/masters-of-deception/.

"Caught off Guard." Hosted by Jim Hoffer. WABC-TV, 24 October 2001.

"Chicago Letter." *Literary World,* 1 May 1903, 127.

Chivers, C. J. "September." *Esquire,* September 2002, 144.

"The City's Medicaid System: Still Sick, Sick, Sick." *New York Daily News,* 23 January 1973, 7.

Clifton, Doug. "How the Herald Covered the Pope's Visit to Cuba." *Miami Herald,* 1 February 1998, 1L.

Clinton, Catherine, ed. *Fanny Kemble's Journals.* Cambridge: Harvard University Press, 2000.

Clouse, Thomas. "ATF, FBI Agents Pose as Journalists: Sheriff Pulls Media Credentials After Learning of Undercover Operation at Aryan Nations Trial." *Spokane Spokesman-Review,* 31 August 2000, A1.

Colbron, Grace Isabel. "Five Books of the Moment." Review of John Van Vorst and Bessie Van Vorst, *The Woman Who Toils. Bookman* 17.2 (April 1903): 187.

Collins, Scott. "CBS Blog Takes Some Swipes at NBC's *Dateline.*" *Los Angeles Times,* 31 March 2006, E27.

Conan, Neal. "The Foreign Lobby: Turkmenistan of Bust." *Blog of the Nation,* 19 June 2007, http://npr.org/blogs/talk/2007/06/the_foreign_lobby_turmenistan_1.html.

Conover, Ted. "Contemporary Literature." Review of Helen Campbell, *Prisoners of Poverty. Church Review,* June 1887, 688.

———. *Coyotes: A Journey Through the Secret World of America's Illegal Aliens.* New York: Vintage Books, 1987.

———. Email interview by author, 18 January, 1 April, 7 July, 2010.

———. "A Morning with Pops." *Amherst,* Winter 1981, 14–17, 26.

———. *Newjack: Guarding Sing Sing.* New York: Vintage, 2001.

———. *Rolling Nowhere: Riding the Rails with America's Hoboes.* New York: Random House Vintage Departures, 2001.

Cooke, Marvel. "I Was a Part of the Bronx Slave Market." *Daily Compass* (*Sunday Compass*), 8 January 1950, 1, 15.

———. "Modern Slaves: Domestic Jobs Are Miserable in Hours, Pay. Union Is Seeking to Relieve Their Bad Situation." *Amsterdam News,* 16 October 1937, 13.

———. "'Mrs. Legree' Hires Only on the Street, Always 'Nice Girls.'" *Daily Compass,* 11 January 1950, 4, 21.

———. "'Paper Bag Brigade' Learns How to Deal with Gypping Employers." *Daily Compass,* 10 January 1950, 4, 21.

———. "Some Ways to Kill the Slave Market." *Daily Compass,* 12 January 1950, 6.

———. "Where Men Prowl and Women Prey on Needy Job-Seekers." *Daily Compass,* 9 January 1950, 4, 7.

Cooper, Gloria. "Darts and Laurels." *Columbia Journalism Review* 28.4 (November/December 1989): 22.

Cordts, Michael. "Title Free Books Sold by Editors: Scandal Embarrasses Newspapers." *Rochester Democrat and Chronicle,* 5 August 1979, 18.

"Crackdown on Quackery." *Life,* 1 November 1963, 72.

Crowe, Cameron. *Fast Times at Ridgemont High.* New York: Simon and Schuster, 1981.

"Current Literature." Review of *Prisoners of Poverty,* by Helen Campbell. *Washington Post,* 17 April 1887, 4.

Currie, William. "Reporter 'Directs' Home." *Chicago Tribune,* 6 March 1971, 1.

David, Deirdre. *Fanny Kemble: A Performed Life.* Philadelphia: University of Pennsylvania Press, 2007.

Davidson, John. "The Long Road North." *Texas Monthly,* October 1977.

———. Telephone interview by author, 8 April 2010.

Davidson, Sandra. "Food Lyin' and Other Buttafucos." *IRE Journal* 2.6 (November/December 1998): 6.

Davies, John. "Aged Homes Shut, Patients Moved." *Chicago Tribune,* 21 March 1971, 4.

Dean. "Pierce Butler's Slave Sale." *Independent* 11.537 (17 March 1859): 1.

del Olmo, Frank. "The Borderline Case of America's Illegal Aliens." *Los Angeles Times,* 24 December 1978, L3.

Department of State. *Trafficking in Persons Report.* Washington, D.C.: n.p., June 2008, http://www.state.gov/documents/organization/105655.pdf.

Depastino, Todd. *Citizen Hobo: How a Century of Homelessness Shaped America.* Chicago: University of Chicago Press, 2003.

Deutsch, Albert. "Dorothea Lynde Dix: Apostle of the Insane." *The American Journal of Nursing* 36.10 (October 1936): 987–997.

———. "The Exposé as a Progressive Tool." *Mental Hygiene* 341.1 (1950): 80–89.

Dicken-Garcia, Hazel. *Journalistic Standards in Nineteenth-Century America.* Madison: University of Wisconsin Press, 1989.

Dickstein, Morris. Introduction to *The Jungle,* by Upton Sinclair. New York: Bantam Books, 1981.

*Dictionary of American Biography.* New York: Charles Scribner's Sons, 1935–36, vol. 9, 487–88. S.v. "Mortimer Thomson," by Franklin J. Meine.

*Dictionary of Literary Biography.* 2005–2006 ed. S.v. "Mortimer Thomson," by David E. Sloane.

Dienes, C. Thomas. "Symposium: The Media's Intrusion on Privacy: Panel, Protecting Investigative Journalism." *George Washington Law Review,* June/August 1999.

Dimand, Robert W. "Nineteenth-Century American Feminist Economics: From Caroline Dall to Charlotte Perkins Gilman." *American Economic Review,* May 2000, 480–84.

Doherty, Carroll. "The Public Isn't Buying Press Credibility: The Seeds of Public Distrust Were Sown Long Before the Recent Round of Scandals." *Nieman Reports,* Summer 2005, 46–47.

Dorr, Rheta Childe. *A Woman of Fifty.* New York: Funk, 1924.

Douglas, Linda Brown, and Tim Gray. "Food Lion to Close 88 Stores." *News & Observer,* 8 January 1994.

Downie, Jill. *A Passionate Pen: The Life and Times of Faith Fenton.* Toronto: HarperCollins, 1996.

Downie, Len, Jr. Len Downie Jr. to the Pulitzer Prize Committee. 25 January 2008, New York. Category 1, Public Service. Letter of Introduction, dated 25 January 2008. Courtesy of the Pulitzer Prize Committee.

Doyle, Jennifer. *Sex Objects: Art and the Dialectics of Desire.* Minneapolis: University of Minnesota Press, 2006.

"Dr. Levering Tyson Dies at 77; Muhlenberg's Former President." *New York Times,* 11 June 1966.

Dubner, Stephen J., and Steven D. Levitt. "Hoodwinked?" *New York Times Magazine,* 8 January 2006, 26.

duCille, Michel. "The Invisibly Wounded." *Washington Post,* 14 October 2007, A1.

Dufresne, Marcel. "Judgment Call: To Sting or Not to Sting?" *Columbia Journalism Review* 30.1 (May/June 1991): 49.

Dygert, James H. *The Investigative Journalist: Heroes for a New Era.* New York: Prentice-Hall, 1976.

Eby, Cecil D., Jr. "Whittier's 'Brown of Ossawatomie.'" *New England Quarterly* 33.4 (1960): 452–61.

Editorial. *Age* (Melbourne), 10 May 1883, 4.

"Education: Undercover Teacher." *Time,* 24 November 1958.

"Education: Undercover Uproar." *Time,* 8 December 1958.

Ehrenreich, Barbara. *Nickel and Dimed: On (Not) Getting By in America.* New York: Metropolitan, 2001.

———. "Welcome to Cancerland: A Mammogram Leads to a Cult of Pink Kitsch." *Harper's,* November 2001, 43–53.

"Eldorado Principal Speaks About 'Undercover Student.'" *Albuquerque Tribune,* 17 March 1983, A5B.

Ellis, Kristi Lamonth. "Writer-Adventurer Backs Venture." *Birmingham News,* 29 July 2001.

Elmer, John. "House Panel O.K.'s Rest Home Probe." *Chicago Tribune,* 11 March 1971, 5.

———. "3 Call for Tightening of Nursing Home Laws." *Chicago Tribune,* 9 March 1971, 3.

Emerson, Ralph Waldo. *Essays: Second Series.* Boston: James Munroe, 1844.

"Ethics of NBC's Sting Show 'To Catch a Predator.'" Hosted by Neil Conan. *Talk of the Nation,* NPR, 16 January 2007.

Everhart, Karen. "NPR Loses CEO, Its Third Exec Swept Away by Political Tornado." Current.org, 9 March 2011.

"Every Human Has Rights Media Awards." *Internews Europe,* n.d., http://www.internews.eu/projects/every-human-has-rights-media-awards, accessed 8 February 2011.

"The Execution of John Brown. He Makes No Speech." *New York Daily Tribune, 3* December 1859, 7.

"Facts of Slavery." *New York Daily Tribune,* 18 August 1854, 2.

Fallows, James. "Working Classes: An Exchange with Barbara Ehrenreich, the Author of *Nickel and Dimed: On (Not) Getting By in America.*" *Atlantic Unbound,* 2, 4, and 11 May 2001, http://www.theatlantic .com/past/docs/unbound/fallows/jf2001-05-02/.

Farhi, Paul. "*Dateline* Pedophile Sting: One More Point; NBC Collaboration Raises Eyebrows as Well as Awareness." *Washington Post,* 9 April 2006, D01.

Faue, Elizabeth. *Writing the Wrongs: Eva Valesh and the Rise of Labor Journalism.* Ithaca: Cornell University Press, 2002.

"Ferguson's Story." *San Francisco Examiner,* 16 October 1892, 2.

Findley, Tim. "Behind Prison Bars." *San Francisco Chronicle,* 4 March 1971, A8.

———. "Con's Main Street." *San Francisco Chronicle,* 23 February 1971, A1.

———. "Folsom—Where the 'Elite' Meet." *San Francisco Chronicle,* 2 March 1971, A16.

———. "I Was a UC Prisoner." *San Francisco Chronicle,* 24 May 1969, A1.

———. "The Men Who Can Set a Con Free." *San Francisco Chronicle,* 11 March 1971, A8.

———. "The Men Who Dictate Prison Terms." *San Francisco Chronicle,* 10 March 1971, A18.

———. "The Men Without Hope." *San Francisco Chronicle,* 3 March 1971, A1.

———. "Reporter's Story—'I'm in Soledad.'" *San Francisco Chronicle,* 22 February 1971, A1.

———. "The Soledad 'Games.'" *San Francisco Chronicle,* 25 February 1971, A1.

———. "Soledad's 'Hole'—A Setting for Death, Revenge." *San Francisco Chronicle,* 24 February 1971, A1.

———. Telephone interview by author, 26 July 2010.

Findley, Tim, and Charles Howe. "Behind Prison Bars: Sex Fears Among the Cons." *San Francisco Chronicle,* 1 March 1971, A1.

Fischer, John. "Edgar May." *Harper's,* July 1971, 4.

Fisher, Doug. "Lobbying Flack—or Is That Flak?" *Common Sense Journalism,* 26 June 2007.

Fitzgerald, Mark. "One Mirage That Proved All Too Real." *Editor & Publisher* 139:10 (October 2006): 8.

"A Flimsy Set of Laws." *Knight Ridder Tribune Business News,* 9 July 2007, 1.

"Florida: State of Neglect." WPLG, 1 May 1987.

Flynt, Josiah. "The American Tramp." *Contemporary Review* 60 (August 1891): 253–61.

———. "Club Life Among Outcasts." *Harper's,* April 1895, 712.

———. "How Men Become Tramps: Conclusions from Personal Experience as an Amateur Tramp." *Century* 50.119 (October 1895): 941–45.

———. "Jamie the Kid." *Harper's,* October 1895, 776–83.

———. *Tramping with the Tramps.* New York: Century, 1899.

———. "Two Tramps in England." *Century* 50.2 (June 1895): 289.

"Food Lion to Scale Back Expansion Plans for 1993." *Washington Post,* 25 December 1992, C9.

"Food Lion Slows Expansion in Wake of TV Report." *New York Times,* 25 December 1992, D3.

"Food Lion Stock Falls After Report." *New York Times,* 7 November 1992, A37.

"For 'Babies Who've Died'—His Mission." *Chicago Sun-Times,* 28 November 1978, 7.

Fowler, Glenn. "Arthur Derounian, 82, an Author of Books on Fascists and Bigots." *New York Times,* 25 April 1991, B14.

Franceschina, Peter, and Jon Burstein. "TV Sting Prompts Ethics Debate: Prosecutor's Arrest Spurs Discussion of Journalists' Roles, Authorities Disclose Details of Investigation." *South Florida Sun-Sentinel,* January 23 2003, 1B.

Frankel, Alex. *Punching In: The Unauthorized Adventure of a Front-Line Employee.* New York: Collins, 2007.

Fraser, Laura. "Aikins Breaks New Journalistic Ground." *Chronicle-Herald* (Canada), 12 December 2010.

Freedman, Alix. "Peddling Dreams: A Marketing Giant Uses Its Sales Prowess to Profit on Poverty—Thorn EMI's Rental Centers Push Sofas, Rings, VCRs to the Poor at High Rates—Repos and 'Couch Payments.'" *Wall Street Journal,* 22 September 1993, A1.

Freeman, Barbara M. *Kit's Kingdom: The Journalism of Kathleen Blake Coleman.* Carleton: Ottawa University Press, 1989.

Friendly, Jonathan. "Investigative Journalism Is Found Shifting Goals." *New York Times,* 23 August 1983, A16.

Friedman, Jon. "Why Aren't More People Buzzing About *Harper's?*" *MarketWatch,* 9 September 2008.

"From Charlestown. A Pro-Slavery Clergyman." *New York Daily Tribune,* 1 December 1859, 5.

"From Charlestown. A Visit to the Prisoners." *New York Daily Tribune,* 30 November 1859, 5.

"From Charlestown. The Visits of Clergymen." *New York Daily Tribune,* 2 December 1859, 5.

"From Home Economics to Human Ecology: A One Hundred-Year History at the University of Wisconsin-Madison—Campbell, Helen Stuart (1839–1918)." *University of Wisconsin-Madison's School of Human Ecology,* n.d., http://www.sohe.wisc.edu/depts/history/bios/campbell.htm, accessed 8 February 2011.

"From Virginia." *New York Daily Tribune,* 12 March 1856, 6.

Fuller, Jack. *News Values: Ideas for an Information Age.* Chicago: University of Chicago Press, 1996.

"Further from Charlestown. Additional Troops Expected." *New York Daily Tribune,* 29 November 1859, 5.

Gaines, William. "By von Solbrig Physician: Surgery Done on Assembly Line." *Chicago Tribune,* 8 September 1975, 1.

———. "Janitor Helps with Patients: Lives Are Held in Grimy Hands." *Chicago Tribune,* 7 September 1975, 10.

———. "Von Solbrig Hospital Sued for Violations." *Chicago Tribune,* 16 October 1975, 2

Gaines, William, and Jay Branegan. "Federal Probe of Two Hospitals Set Here." *Chicago Tribune,* 14 November 1975, A1.

———. "Hospital Tour Bears Apparent Violations." *Chicago Tribune,* 10 September 1975, 10.

———. "Probe Started at von Solbrig." *Chicago Tribune,* 9 September 1975, 1.

———. "Von Solbrig Hospital Shuts in Wake of Probe." *Chicago Tribune,* 13 November 1975, 1.

Garin, Kristoffer A. "A Foreign Affair: On the Great Ukrainian Bride Hunt." *Harper's,* June 2006, 69–77.

Garrett, Charles H. "Lived Three Months on Five Cents a Day." *New York Evening World,* 18 July 1898, 1.

"Gateway to Gridlock." *Chicago Tribune,* 20–22 November 2000.

Gatti, Fabrizio. "I Was a Slave in Puglia." Translated by Wolfgang Achtner, *L'Espresso,* 4 September 2006.

Gilliam, Dorothy. "A White Woman in 'Black' Skin." *Washington Post,* 4 November 1959, B4.

Ginsberg, Elaine K. *Passing and the Fictions of Identity.* Durham, N.C.: Duke University Press, 1996.

"Girls for Sale." Narrated by Cynthia McFadden, Diane Sawyer, and Charles Gibson. *20/20,* ABC, 2 June 1999.

Glazer, Nathan. "Letter from East Harlem." *City,* Autumn 1991.

Goffman, Erving. *Asylums: Essays on the Social Situation of Mental Patients and Other Inmates.* New York: Anchor Books, 1961.

"Going Undercover to Get a Story." *Carpetbagger,* 30 June 2007.

Goldman, John J. "Times' Bernheimer Wins Pulitzer for Music Criticism." *Los Angeles Times,* 13 April 1982, B1.

Goldstein, Tom. *The News at Any Cost: How Journalists Compromise Their Ethics to Shape the News.* New York: Touchstone, 1985.

Goodman, Amy. "In New Exposé, Ken Silverstein of *Harper's Magazine* Goes Undercover to Find Out What US Lobbyists Do for Dictators." *Democracy Now!* 28 June 2007.

Goodman, Mike. "Juvenile Hall: Powder Keg of Rage, Racism: Youths Subjected to Sexual Degradation, Beatings and Rat-Pack Struggle to Survive." *Los Angeles Times,* 17 May 1974, A3.

———. "Workers Complain of Boredom, 'Rip-Off.'" *Los Angeles Times,* 18 November 1975, A2.

———. "Youngsters of All Ages Free to Browse Among Hashish Pipes, Obscene Comic Books and Posters." *Los Angeles Times,* 9 April 1972, C1.

Goolrick, Chester. Telephone interview by author, 15 November 2009.

Gorman, Herbert. "On Paris and London Pavements." *New York Times,* 6 August 1933, BR4.

"'Gotcha' Without a 'Get.'" CBSnews.com, 26 June 2007.

Gottesman, Ronald. Introduction to *The Jungle,* by Upton Sinclair. New York: Penguin Classics, 1985.

Graham, Lawrence Otis. "Invisible Man." *New York,* 17 August 1992, http://nymag.com/news/features/47949/.

―――. "Invisible Man: Why Did This $105,000-a-Year Lawyer from Harvard Go to Work as a $7-an-Hour Busboy at the Greenwich Country Club?" *New York,* 17 August 1992.

―――. *Members of the Club.* New York: HarperCollins, October 1996.

"A Great Slave Sale at Savannah: Chattels at Public Auction." *Independent* 11.536 (10 March 1859): 1.

Greeley, Horace. *Aunt Sally, Come Up! Or, the Nigger Sale.* London: Ward and Lock, 1859.

"Great Auction-Sale of Slaves, at Savannah, Georgia." *Atlantic Monthly* 4.23 (September 1859): 386.

Griffin, John Howard. "Journey into Shame." Pts. 1–5. *Sepia,* April 1960, 12–18; May 1960, 44–52; June 1960, 32–37; July 1960, 30–35; August 1960, 28–34; and September 1960, 28–34.

―――. "White Man Turned Negro Is Praised and Damned." *Sepia,* October 1960, 11–18.

Greenwood, James. "A Night in a Workhouse." In *Into Unknown England, 1866–1913: Selections from the Social Explorers.* Manchester, UK: Manchester University Press, 1976.

Grob, Gerald N. *The Mad Among Us: A History of the Care of American's Mentally Ill.* New York: Free Press, 1994.

Gross, Dan. "VA Pokes CBS 3 in the Eye." *Philadelphia Daily News,* 2 April 2007, 41.

Gumprecht, Blake. *The Los Angeles River: Its Life, Death, and Possible Rebirth.* Baltimore: Johns Hopkins University Press, 1999.

Hackett, Alice Payne, and James Henry Burke. *80 Years of Best Sellers: 1895–1975.* New York: R. R. Bowker, 1977.

Haddon, Michael. "I Have Chosen to Belong to the Remedy." Journalism .co.uk, 25 November 2008, http://www.journalism.co.uk/news -features/-i-have-chosen-to-belong-to-the-remedy—ghana-s -anas-aremayew-anas-on-undercover-journalism/s5/a532917/.

Hale, John. "Mental Health Deserves Top Assembly Priority." *Nashville Tennessean,* 31 January 1974, 14.

————. "Mental Health Fund Needed." *Nashville Tennessean,* 31 January 1974, 1.

Hall, Doug. "Tragle Raps Hospital Critics." *Nashville Tennessean,* 24 February 1974, 4.

Halsell, Grace. *Bessie Yellowhair.* New York: William Morrow, 1973.

————. *The Illegals.* New York: A John L. Hochmann Books, 1978.

————. *Soul Sister.* New York: World, 1969.

————. "When You've Walked a Mile in Their Shoes." *New York Times,* 10 November 1973, 31.

Hamper, Ben. *Rivethead: Tales from the Assembly Line.* New York: Warner Books, 1992.

Harper, Douglas. *Good Company: A Tramp Life.* Chicago: University of Chicago Press, 1982.

Harper, Philip Brian. *Are We Not Men? Masculine Anxiety and the Problem of African-American Identity.* New York: Oxford University Press, 1996.

————. "Harvest of Shame." Narrated by Edward R. Murrow. *CBS Reports,* CBS, 24 November 1960.

————. "Passing for What? Racial Masquerade and the Demands of Upward Mobility." *Callaloo* 21 (Spring 1998): 381–97.

Harris, Leon. *Upton Sinclair: An American Rebel.* New York: Thomas Y. Crowell, 1975.

Hart, William. "L.A.'s Giant Jail Is a Giant Headache." *Corrections,* December 1980, 32–37.

————. Telephone interview by author, 21 July 2010.

————. "What Welfare Means to You." *Buffalo Evening News,* 7 June 1960, 1.

Hattenstone, Simon. "Undercover and Overexposed." *Guardian,* 5 December 2007.

Hays, Tom. "New York Federal Appeals Court Rules Against ACORN." Associated Press, 13 August 2010.

Hedrick, Joan D. *Harriet Beecher Stowe: A Life.* New York: Oxford University Press, 1994.

Heilbrun, Carolyn G. *The Education of a Woman: The Life of Gloria Steinem.* New York: Ballantine Books, 1996.

Heldman, Kevin. "7 ½ Days." *City Limits,* June–July 1998, http://journalismworksproject.org/psych_hosp01.html.

Henry, Neil. "All-Night Café: A Classroom on How to Survive." *Washington Post,* 2 May 1980, A01.

———. *American Carnival: Journalism Under Siege in an Age of New Media.* Berkeley: University of California Press, 2007.

———. "Exploring the World of the Urban Derelict: Inside the Crumbling Walls of Baltimore's Helping-Up Mission, Where Men Recount the Legend of Old Louie, Eat Macaroni, and Mumble in Their Sleep." *Washington Post,* 27 April 1980, A01.

———. "Half a Day Nets $1.50 and 'Supper.'" *Washington Post,* 11 October 1983, A01.

———. "'Holy Roller' Resounds with Joy, Wrath." *Washington Post,* 30 April 1980, C01.

———. "Homeward Bound." *Washington Post,* 13 October 1983, A01.

———. "In D.C., Raw and Threatening Things." *Washington Post,* 4 May 1980, A01.

———. "Learning the Tricks of Walking a Md. Throwaway Paper Route." *Washington Post,* 30 April 1980, A01.

———. "The Long, Hot Wait for Pickin' Work." *Washington Post,* 9 October 1983, A01.

———. "Looking for Answers About Workers and Wages." *Washington Post,* 14 October 1983, A01.

———. "Money Brings a Taste of 'Real Living.'" *Washington Post,* 1 May 1980, A01.

———. "Mozart-Playing New Yorker Learns a Secret, and Laughs." *Washington Post,* 8 May 1980, A01.

———. "Slim Pickin': Taken for a Ride, Sold 'Like Cattle.'" *Washington Post,* 10 October 1983, A01.

———. "Snug Haven But No Sleep at Crisis Center." *Washington Post,* 3 May 1980, A01.

———. "Street People Share Secrets of Survival." *Washington Post,* 28 April 1980, A01.

———. "Tapping 'The Bank.'" *Washington Post,* 6 May 1980, A01.

———. "A Washington Winter's Tale: Fear, Hunger, Loathing, Abuse." *Washington Post,* 5 May 1980, A01.

———. "'What's in It For Me?' in Washington." *Washington Post,* 7 May 1980, A01.

————. "'Work!' Brings Cheers at Local 194's Hiring Hall." *Washington Post,* 29 April 1980, A01.

————. "A Wretched Reality of Life in the Fields." *Washington Post,* 12 October 1983, A01.

Henry, Susan. "Reporting 'Deeply and at First Hand' in the Nineteenth-Century Slums." *Journalism History* 11.1–2 (Spring/Summer 1984): 18–25.

Henry, William A. "Journalism Under Fire." *Time,* 12 December 1983, http://www.time.com/time/magazine/article/0,9171,921424,00.html.

Hersey, John. "The Legend on the License." *Yale Review,* Autumn 1980.

Higbie, Toby. "Crossing Class Boundaries: Tramp Ethnographers and Narratives of Class in Progressive Era America." *Social Science History* 21.4 (Winter 1997): 559–92.

Hochberg, Adam. "Planned Parenthood Videos, Undercover Recordings Have Roots in Journalism They Challenge." Poynteronline, 23 February 2011, http://www.poynter.org/latest-news/making-sense-of-news/120446/planned-parenthood-videos-undercover-recordings-have-roots-in-journalism-they-challenge/.

Hoffman, Abbie. "Undercover in the New Germany: The Many Cloaks and Daggers of Günter Wallraff." *Mother Jones,* February/March 1979, 44–54.

"Home Summary." *Evangelist* 30.10 (10 March 1859): 5.

Hopper. "A Northerner in New-Orleans." *New York Daily Tribune,* 16 February 1855, 6.

————. "Scenes at a Slave Auction." *New York Daily Tribune,* 24 March 1855, 6.

Horwitz, Tony. "*The Jungle* Revisited." *Wall Street Journal,* 1 December 1994, A8.

————. "9 to Nowhere: These Six Growth Jobs are Dull, Dead-End, Sometimes Dangerous." *Wall Street Journal,* 1 December 1994, A1.

————. Telephone interview by author, 21 January 2010.

Horwitz, Tony, and Ellen Bugher, "About the Visits." *News-Sentinel,* 17 November 1984, 7A.

Hosmer, Lucy. "Factory Girls in a Big City." *St. Louis Post-Dispatch,* 26 November 1896, 1.

"Hospital Under Fire in Probe Shuts Down." *Chicago Sun-Times,* 3 June 1980.

Houston, Brant. "Solid Reporting Defies Last Year's Worst." *IRE Journal* 22.1 (January/February 1999): 2.

"How He Read Prison Story." *Chicago Tribune,* 1 November 1978, 16.

Howe, Charles. "California Penal System—World's 3rd Biggest." *San Francisco Chronicle,* 22 February 1971, A1.

———. "Cons Get It Together." *San Francisco Chronicle,* 2 March 1971, A1.

———. "The Day We Shook the Yard Down." *San Francisco Chronicle,* 9 March 1971, A14.

———. "How Experts Want to Change Prisons." *San Francisco Chronicle,* 15 March 1971, A1.

———. "I Was a Guard at San Quentin." *San Francisco Chronicle,* 8 March 1971, A1.

———. "Loneliness, Unemployment: Problems of Parolees." *San Francisco Chronicle,* 12 March 1971, A8.

———. "The Prison Clientele Is Tougher." *San Francisco Chronicle,* 1 March 1971, A13.

———. "San Quentin's Elite Force in Action." *San Francisco Chronicle,* 10 March 1971, A1.

———. "Vacaville, the First Stop." *San Francisco Chronicle,* 8 March 1971, A10.

———. "Why Prisoners Keep Coming Back." *San Francisco Chronicle,* 9 March 1971, A14.

Howe, Daniel Walker. *What Hath God Wrought.* Oxford: Oxford University Press, 2007.

Howell, Deborah. "A Powerful Story at Walter Reed." *Washington Post,* 4 March 2007, B6.

Howells, William Dean. "Editor's Study." *Harper's,* August 1889, 479.

"HSUS Exposes Inhumane Treatment of Pigs at Smithfield." Humane Society of the United States, 15 December 2010, http://www

.humanesociety.org/news/press_releases/2010/12/smithfield_pigs_
121510.html.

Hui-min, Lo, ed. *The Correspondence of G. E. Morrison.* Vol. 2. Cambridge:
Cambridge University Press, 1976.

Hull, Anne, and Dana Priest. "Army Fixing Patients' Housing." *Washington Post,* 20 February 2007, A01.

———. "Anne Hull and Dana Priest on their Walter Reed Stories."
*Nieman Reports,* 4 July 2008, http://niemanwatchdog.org/index
.cfm?fuseaction=showcase.view&showcaseid=85.

———. "The Hotel Aftermath." *Washington Post,* 19 February 2007, A01.

———. "Humane Society Claims Pigs Abused at Va. Farm." *Washington
Post* via Associated Press, 15 December 2010.

———. "Identity Crisis." Hosted by Brooke Gladstone. *On the Media,*
WNYC, 29 June 2007.

———. "'It Is Just Not Walter Reed.'" *Washington Post,* 5 March
2007, A01.

———. "Little Relief on Ward 53." *Washington Post,* 18 June 2007, A01.

———. "A Wife's Battle." *Washington Post,* 14 October 2007, A01.

"I'll Drink to That." KMOV, 23 October 1987.

Inkersley, Arthur. "A Trip to the Kingsmill Islands on a Labor-Vessel."
*Travel* 1.6, January 1896, 443–446.

Inkersley, Arthur, and W.H. Brommage. "Experiences of a Blackbirder
Among the Gilbert Islanders." *Overland Monthly* 23.138 (June 1894):
565–575.

Irvine, John. "Hospitals: Army Pledges Fixes at Walter Reed." *Health Care*
(blog), 21 February 2007.

"Is It a Cargo of Slaves?" *New York Daily Tribune,* 8 September 1891, 1.

Iverson, Jeremy. *High School Confidential: Secrets of an Undercover Student.*
New York: Atria Books, 2007.

"Jack London's *People of the Abyss.*" *Current Literature* 36.4 (April 1904):
413–16.

Jacobs, Jane. Introduction to *The Jungle,* by Upton Sinclair. New York:
Modern Library, 2006.

Jenks, Edward N. "Fifth Column—with American Labels." *New York
Times,* 18 July 1943, BR8.

"John Brown's Invasion." *New York Daily Tribune,* 28 November 1859, 6.

"John Brown's Invasion." *New York Daily Tribune,* 30 November 1859, 6.

"John Brown's Invasion." *New York Daily Tribune,* 1 December 1859, 6.

"John Brown's Invasion." *New York Daily Tribune,* 5 December 1859, 5.

"John Brown's Invasion. The Fugitives—Cooke and Virginia in Kansas." *New York Daily Tribune,* 7 December 1859, 3.

"John Brown's Invasion. Further Interesting Incidents of the Execution." *New York Daily Tribune,* 6 December 1859, 6.

"John Brown's Invasion. The Martial Law Illegal—Reaction against Wise." *New York Daily Tribune,* 8 December 1859, 6.

Johnson, Peter. "'Dateline' Roots out Predators; Men Seeking Teens for Sex via Internet." *USA Today,* 15 February 2006, B9.

Jones, William. "Ambulance Firm's President Fined $100 in Municipal Court." *Chicago Tribune,* 24 November 1970, A11.

———. "Ambulance Hearing Is Told of Violations." *Chicago Tribune,* 28 August 1970, 6.

———. "Ambulance Jury Cites 16." *Chicago Tribune,* 20 November 1970, 1–2.

———. "Ambulance Probe Firm Folds Here." *Chicago Tribune,* 10 December 1970, C21.

———. "Ambulance Quiz in Senate Urged." *Chicago Tribune,* 13 June 1970, 1.

———. "Ambulance Quiz Ordered." *Chicago Tribune,* 10 June 1970, 1–2.

———. "Ambulances' Crews Pilfer Hospital Goods for Their Supplies." *Chicago Tribune,* 12 June 1970, 1–2.

———. "As 'Patients,' Probers Learn Ordeal of Nursing Home Life." *Chicago Tribune,* 4 March 1971, 2.

———. "Calls for City Ambulances Set a Record: Follows Addition of 11 Vehicles to Fleet." *Chicago Tribune,* 14 August 1970, 18.

———. "City Ambulance Firms Linked to Mob Loans." *Chicago Tribune,* 21 June 1970, 3.

———. "City Ambulance Reform: Daley Vows More Units, Better Care." *Chicago Tribune,* 18 June 1970, 1–2.

———. "City Controls on Ambulance Services Proposed." *Chicago Tribune,* 24 June 1970, A4.

———. "City Council Passes Tough, New Controls on Ambulance Firms." *Chicago Tribune,* 11 August 1970, 5.

————. "Delay Predicts City to File Suit Against More Nursing Homes." *Chicago Tribune,* 26 March 1971, 1.

————. "5 Ambulance Reforms Told: Association Acts to End Mistreatment." *Chicago Tribune,* 22 July 1970, 1–2.

————. "4 More Cops Face Possibility of Being Fired." *Chicago Tribune,* 21 November 1970, 2.

————. "Hearings End in Ambulance Abuse Cases: Licenses of 3 Firms Are in Jeopardy." *Chicago Tribune,* 22 September 1970, A8.

————. "Heart Victim Is Left in Flat; Had Only $2." *Chicago Tribune,* 9 June 1970, 1–2.

————. "Investigators Find Three Linked to Mob Control Ambulance Firm." *Chicago Tribune,* 25 June 1970, 2.

————. "Landlady Almost Ruins Probe." *Chicago Tribune,* 9 June 1970, 2.

————. "Left by Ambulance, Prober Says at Quiz." *Chicago Tribune,* 19 September 1970, N19.

————. "Men of Mercy Profit in Pain." *Chicago Tribune,* 7 June 1970, 1.

————. "New Ambulance Service to Begin." *Chicago Tribune,* 12 November 1970, C16.

————. "'Nobody Works Too Hard Here,'" *Chicago Tribune,* 2 March 1971, 2.

————. "Ordinance Seeks Ban on Ambulance Sirens." *Chicago Tribune,* 25 July 1970, 1, 6.

————. "Percy Predicts Wide Rest Home Reforms." *Chicago Tribune,* 22 March 1971, 1.

————. "Plea for Aid Spurs Probe, Jury Action." *Chicago Tribune,* 20 November 1970, 2.

————. "Police Probed in Ambulance Payoff Plot." *Chicago Tribune,* 8 August 1970, 12.

————. "Police Sell Ambulance Cases; $10 Is Common Fee." *Chicago Tribune,* 10 June 1970, 1–2.

————. "Probe Finds More Ambulance Abuses." *Chicago Tribune,* 20 October 1970, A10.

————. "Report Urges Control Over Ambulances." *Chicago Tribune,* 14 June 1970, 27.

————. "Sadism Rides an Ambulance." *Chicago Tribune,* 8 June 1970, 1.

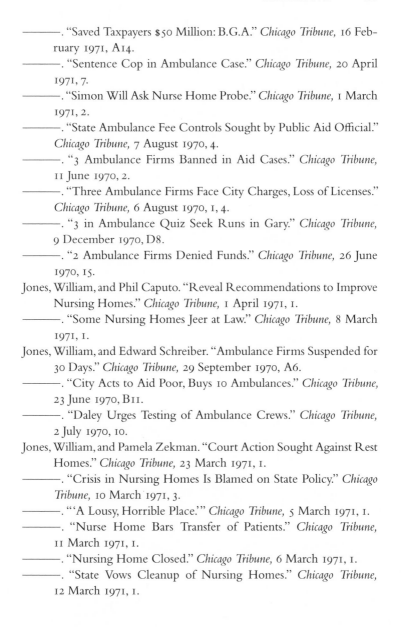

————. "Saved Taxpayers $50 Million: B.G.A." *Chicago Tribune,* 16 February 1971, A14.

————. "Sentence Cop in Ambulance Case." *Chicago Tribune,* 20 April 1971, 7.

————. "Simon Will Ask Nurse Home Probe." *Chicago Tribune,* 1 March 1971, 2.

————. "State Ambulance Fee Controls Sought by Public Aid Official." *Chicago Tribune,* 7 August 1970, 4.

————. "3 Ambulance Firms Banned in Aid Cases." *Chicago Tribune,* 11 June 1970, 2.

————. "Three Ambulance Firms Face City Charges, Loss of Licenses." *Chicago Tribune,* 6 August 1970, 1, 4.

————. "3 in Ambulance Quiz Seek Runs in Gary." *Chicago Tribune,* 9 December 1970, D8.

————. "2 Ambulance Firms Denied Funds." *Chicago Tribune,* 26 June 1970, 15.

Jones, William, and Phil Caputo. "Reveal Recommendations to Improve Nursing Homes." *Chicago Tribune,* 1 April 1971, 1.

————. "Some Nursing Homes Jeer at Law." *Chicago Tribune,* 8 March 1971, 1.

Jones, William, and Edward Schreiber. "Ambulance Firms Suspended for 30 Days." *Chicago Tribune,* 29 September 1970, A6.

————. "City Acts to Aid Poor, Buys 10 Ambulances." *Chicago Tribune,* 23 June 1970, B11.

————. "Daley Urges Testing of Ambulance Crews." *Chicago Tribune,* 2 July 1970, 10.

Jones, William, and Pamela Zekman. "Court Action Sought Against Rest Homes." *Chicago Tribune,* 23 March 1971, 1.

————. "Crisis in Nursing Homes Is Blamed on State Policy." *Chicago Tribune,* 10 March 1971, 3.

————. "'A Lousy, Horrible Place.'" *Chicago Tribune,* 5 March 1971, 1.

————. "Nurse Home Bars Transfer of Patients." *Chicago Tribune,* 11 March 1971, 1.

————. "Nursing Home Closed." *Chicago Tribune,* 6 March 1971, 1.

————. "State Vows Cleanup of Nursing Homes." *Chicago Tribune,* 12 March 1971, 1.

Jordan, Pete. *Dishwasher: One Man's Quest to Wash Dishes in All Fifty States.* New York: Harper Perennial, 2007.

Josiah, Ryan. "Planned Parenthood Agreed to Accept Race-Motivated Donations." CNS News, 7 July 2008.

"Josiah Flynt's Own Life Story." *New York Times,* 24 October 1908, BR 619.

"Judge for Yourself." TheProjectVeritas.com, 8 March 2011, http://theprojectveritas.com/nprjudge.

"Judge to Rule Friday on Suit to End Lockup." *Chicago Tribune,* 1 November 1978, 16.

"Just as We Said." *Chicago Tribune,* 28 September 1972, 20.

Justice, Keith L. *Bestseller Index: All Books, "Publishers Weekly" and the "New York Times" Through 1990.* Jefferson, N.C.: McFarland, 1998.

"The Kanaka Labour Traffic: A Full Ship. The Nineteenth 'Boy' Obtained." *Argus,* 19 December 1892, 5–6.

Kemble, Fanny. *Journal of a Residence on a Georgia Plantation in 1838–1839.* Athens: University of Georgia Press, 1984.

Kennedy, Stetson. *I Rode with the Ku Klux Klan.* London: Arco, 1954.

———. *The Klan Unmasked.* Boca Raton: Florida Atlantic University Press, 1990.

Kentuckian. "Facts of Slavery in Kentucky." *New York Daily Tribune,* 1 May 1855, 5.

Kershaw, Alex. *Jack London: A Life.* New York: Thomas Dunne Books, 1997.

Kilian, Michael. "Rangel on Probe." *Chicago Tribune,* 3 March 1971, 1.

King, Catherine. "Girl Toilers of the City." *New York Evening World,* 26 July 1898, 7.

"Kings Jury Praises Series on Schools." *New York Times,* 20 February 1959, 9.

Kirkpatrick, Clayton, and Gene Patterson. "Should Reporters Play Roles?" *ASNE Bulletin,* September 1979, 12–13.

Kirtley, Jane. "Don't Pop That Cork" *American Journalism Review* 22.1 (January/February 2000): 84.

Klein, Ezra. "Shed a Tear for the Lobbyists." *Ezra Klein* (blog), 30 June 2007.

Klein, Woody. "At the End of the Road—Welfare." *New York World-Telegram & Sun,* 29 June 1959, 1.

———. "'At Home' in a Filthy Cage, Family Is Trapped in West Side's Jungle." *New York World-Telegram & Sun,* 23 June 1959, 1.

———. "Boy on the Brink: Miguel Is Trapped in Slum Jungle." *New York World-Telegram & Sun,* 6 July 1959, 1.

———. "Bugs Reign in Squalor." *New York World-Telegram & Sun,* 24 June 1959, 1.

———. "City Aids Admit Blight Is Gaining." *New York World-Telegram & Sun,* 2 July 1959, 1.

———. Email interview by author, 7, 8, 9 July 2008 and 18 September 2010.

———. "Klein, "I'm Frightened When I Rob; I'm Sick . . . Got to Get Money." *New York World-Telegram & Sun,* 18 June 1963, 6.

———. "Lack of Inspection Brings Squalor." *New York World-Telegram & Sun,* 1 July 1959, 1.

———. *Let in the Sun.* New York: Macmillan, 1964.

———. "Out of the Rubble and Filth, An Addict's Cry of Despair." *New York World-Telegram & Sun,* 17 June 1963, 1.

———. "Tenant Rights Lost in Ignorance." *New York World-Telegram & Sun,* 30 June 1959, 1.

———. "Tenants Battle to Survive in Lower East Side's 'Korea.'" *New York World-Telegram & Sun,* 25 June 1959, 1.

———. "'We Ain't Alive, Just Hangin' On.'" *New York World-Telegram & Sun,* 26 June 1959, 1.

Knight, Athelia. "Drug Smuggling and Hot Goods: A Ride on Prison Visitors' Buses." *Washington Post,* 4 March 1984, A1.

———. "Officials Differ on Depth of Prison Drug Problem." *Washington Post,* 7 March 1984, A1.

———. "Threat of Violence Haunts Drivers." *Washington Post,* 6 March 1984, A1.

———. "Visitors Make Drug Deliveries to Inmates." *Washington Post,* 5 March 1984, A1.

Koshner, Karen. "State Inspects Abortion Clinics." *Chicago Sun-Times,* 15 November 1978, 5.

Koshner, Karen, and Dolores McCahill. "Court Revokes Dr. Hah's License." *Chicago Sun-Times,* 21 November 1978, 3.

Koshner, Karen, and Pamela Zekman. "Closed Clinic Oks Appointments." *Chicago Sun-Times,* 23 November 1978, 3.

———. "Other Officials' Reactions—Jury Subpoenas Records of Abortion Clinic." *Chicago Sun-Times,* 12 November 1978, 5.

Kovach, Bill, and Tom Rosenstiel. *The Elements of Journalism: What Newspeople Should Know and the Public Should Expect.* New York: Crown, 2001, 2007.

Kovar, Claudia. "Court Judgment Provides Food for Thought." *Tulsa World,* 19 March 1997, 2.

Koven, Seth. *Slumming: Sexual and Social Politics in Victorian London.* Princeton: Princeton University Press, 2004.

Kroeger, Brooke. "Journalism with a Scholar's Intent." *Zoned for Debate,* 16 October 2002, NYU Arthur L. Carter Journalism Institute Faculty Web Forum, http://journalism.nyu.edu/publishing/archives/debate/forum.1.essay.kroger.html.

———. *Nellie Bly: Daredevil, Reporter, Feminist.* New York: Times Books, 1994.

Kurtz, Howard. "The Army's Preemptive News Briefing." *Washington Post,* 24 February 2007.

———. "Hidden Network Cameras: A Troubling Trend? Critics Complain of Deception as Dramatic Footage Yields High Ratings." *Washington Post,* 30 November 1992, A1.

———. "Stung by *Harper's* in a Web of Deceit." *Washington Post,* 25 June 2007, C1.

Kusmer, Kenneth L. *Down and Out, On the Road: The Homeless in American History.* New York: Oxford University Press, 2002.

Labor, Earle et al., eds. *The Letters of Jack London.* Stanford: Stanford University Press, 1988.

Lambeth, Edmund B. *Committed Journalism: An Ethic for the Profession.* Indiana: Indiana University Press, 1986.

Larsen, Nella. *Passing.* New York: Arno, 1969.

Laurie, Annie. "A City's Disgrace: Sample of Civilization of the Nineteenth Century; Brutality of Public Servants; The 'Examiner's' Annie Laurie in the Receiving Hospital; An Emetic Given for Hysterics." *San Francisco Chronicle,* 19 January 1890, 11.

"The Lavinia Outrages." *Brisbane Courier,* 9 February 1884, 5.

LeDuff, Charlie. "The Crossing: A Perilous 4,000 Mile Passage to Work." *New York Times,* 29 May 2001.

————. "Who Kills, Who Cuts, Who Bosses Can Depend on Race." *New York Times,* 16 June 2000, A1.

Lelyveld, Joseph., ed., *How Race Is Lived in America.* New York: Times Books, 2001.

Letter to the Editor. *Age.* 10 May 1883, 7.

Letter to the Editor. *Age.* 14 May 1883, 1.

Lewis, Jon E., ed. *The Mammoth Book of Journalism.* New York: Carroll, 2003.

"A Libel Suit for $50,000." *Dunkirk Observer-Journal,* 1 August 1888, 1.

Lieberman, Paul. Email and telephone interview by author, 10 February, 15 and 17 March 2010.

Lieberman, Paul, and Chester Goolrick. "Endless Debt Haunts Turpentiners." *Atlanta Constitution,* 2 December 1979, 1A.

————. "For Many Americans, Work Pays off in Poverty." *Atlanta Constitution,* 1 December 1979, A1.

————. "Jim Palmer: He Recalls Bad Days in the Woods." *Atlanta Constitution,* 1 December 1979, 4A.

————. "'Junior' Sears: A Man Born to Turpentine." *Atlanta Constitution,* 1 December 1979, 4A.

————. "Naval Stores Ages-Old, But Few Like Living in Past." *Atlanta Constitution,* 2 December 1979, 32A.

————. "Part I: The Turpentine Men: Hard Woods Toil for Little Pay." *Atlanta Constitution,* 1 December 1979, 1A.

————. "Part III: No Golden Eggs in Georgia's Chicken Sheds, Whole Families Labor on Poultry Farms to Earn Paycheck of a Single Worker." *Atlanta Constitution,* 3 December 1979, A1.

————. "Part IV: Motels, Gas Stations, Motel Maid's Wages Fall into Crevice in the Law." *Atlanta Constitution,* 4 December 1979, 1A.

————. "Part V: Ice Toters, Ministore Clerks: Over 40 Years, a Corporation's Pattern of Underpaying Workers." *Atlanta Constitution,* 5 December 1979, A1.

————. "Part VI: Works Ethic Amidst Poverty: They'd Rather Collect Weeds Than Welfare." *Atlanta Constitution,* 6 December 1979, A1.

————. "Pulse of the Public: 'Underpaid . . .' Series 'Excellent Work.'" *Atlanta Constitution,* 7 December 1979, 5A.

————. "Some 'Surprised I Pay $2.50.'" *Atlanta Constitution,* 4 December 1979, 10A.

————. "Unique Deductions Push Pay Below U.S. Minimum." *Atlanta Constitution,* 4 December 1979, A1.

————. "Wage Law Enforcers Overwhelmed by Complaints." *Atlanta Constitution,* 6 December 1979, A1.

Lii, Jane H. "65 Cents an Hour—A Special Report. Week in Sweatshop Reveals Grim Conspiracy of the Poor." *New York Times,* 12 March 1995, 1.

Lingeman, Richard. "Books of the Times: *Lying: Moral Choice in Public and Private Life* by Sissela Bok." *New York Times,* 5 July 1978, C16.

Linthicum, Leslie. "High School Revisited: Reporter Gets an Education in Paperwork." *Albuquerque Tribune,* 7 March 1983, 1.

————. "Undercover Student." *Albuquerque Tribune,* 7–14 March 1983.

————. "When to Go Undercover? As Last Resort to Get a Story." National Ethics Committee. Society of Professional Journalists. Sigma Delta Chi, 1983. Journalism Ethics Report, 20.

Lisheron, Mark. "Lying to Get the Truth." *American Journalism Review* 29.5 (October/November 2007): 29.

"Lobbyists Offer Dictators a Door to D.C." Hosted by Neal Conan. *Talk of the Nation,* NPR, 19 June 2007.

Locin, Mitchell. "Pontiac Disclosures No Shock—Thompson." *Chicago Tribune,* 31 October 1978, 10.

Lockard, Joe. *Watching Slavery: Witness Texts and Travel Reports.* New York: Peter Lang, 2008.

London, Jack. *People of the Abyss.* Cornwall: Diggery Press, 2008.

Long, John S. "Holding Down the Fort." *Arizona Daily Star,* 8 August 1982, 36.

Lopate, Leonard. "Lobbyists for Hire." WNYC, 27 June 2007.

"Los Angeles Journal; Los Angeles by Kayak: Vistas of Concrete Banks." *New York Times,* 8 December 2003.

*Lotos Leaves: Original Stories, Essays, and Poems.* Boston: Gill, 1875, 233–49.

Lyons, Leonard. "Broadway Bulletins." *Washington Post,* 14 February 1944, 11.

Maisel, Albert Q. "Bedlam." *Life,* May 1946.

Marsh, Edward Clark. "Jack London's People of the Abyss." *Bookman* 18.6 (February 1904): 647–48.

Martinez, Ruben. "Promised Land: *Enrique's Journey: The Story of a Boy's Dangerous Odyssey to Reunite with His Mother." Los Angeles Times,* 9 February 2006, R2.

"Marvel Jackson Cooke, 99, Pioneering Black Newspaper Reporter." *New York Times,* 10 December 2000.

Marx, Willem. "Misinformation Intern: My Summer as a Military Propagandist in Iraq." *Harper's,* September 2006, 51–59.

Massey, Daniel. "ACORN Files for Bankruptcy." *Crain's New York Business,* 3 November 2010.

May, Edgar. *The Wasted Americans.* New York: Signet, 1965.

May, Lee. Telephone interview by author, 17 March 2010.

———. "Way out of the Welfare Mess." *Harper's,* October 1961, 37–42.

McCarthy, Coleman. "Getting Truth Untruthfully." 22 December 1992, D21.

McCollam, Douglas. "The Shame Game." *Columbia Journalism Review* 45.5 (January/February 2007): 28–33.

McCreery, David, and Doug Munro. "The Cargo of the *Montserrat*: Gilbertese Labor in Guatemalan Coffee, 1890–1906." *The Americas* 49:3 (January 1993): 271–95.

McGray, Mary. Letter to the editor. *Chicago Daily Times,* 27 August 1888, 1.

McKivigan, John R. *Forgotten Firebrands: James Redpath and the Making of Nineteenth-Century America.* Ithaca: Cornell University Press, 2008.

McMahon, John. "'Our Costly Dilemma' and Welfare Revisited, 50 Years Later." *Buffalo News,* 13 June 2010.

McNulty, Henry. "Real-Estate Probe Built on Deception." *Hartford Courant,* 8 June 1989.

———. "White Lies: Bending the Truth to Expose Injustice." *FineLine: The Newsletter on Journalism Ethics* 1.4 (August 1989): 6–7.

Meares, Joel. "Stingers from our Past: James O'Keefe's Ethics, Their Stings, and Their Ethics." *Columbia Journalism Review,* 10 March 2011.

Meek, George. *Bath Chair-Man.* New York: E. P. Dutton, 1910.

Meis, Morgan. "Devil's Work: Secret Doings at the Queens Museum of Art." *Harper's,* April 2004, 65–71.

Melvin, J. D., and Peter Corris, eds. *The Cruise of the Helena: A Labour-Recruiting Voyage to the Solomon Islands.* Melbourne, Australia: Hawthorn Press, 1977.

Merriner, James L. *Grafters and Goo Goos: Corruption and Reform in Chicago.* Carbondale, Ill.: Southern Illinois University Press, 2004.

Metcalfe, James J. "Chicago Police 'with Us,' Ex G-Man Hears Nazi Boast." *Chicago Daily Times,* 23 September 1937, 14.

———. "Ex G-Man Finds Friction in Nazi Ranks." *Chicago Daily Times,* 22 September 1937, 20.

———. "Ex G-Man Hears Bund Edict on Kenosha March." *Chicago Daily Times,* 20 September 1937, 14.

———. "Ex G-Man in U.S. Alien Nazi Army!" *Chicago Daily Times,* 15 September 1937, 3; 16 September 1937, 15; and 19 September 1937, 19.

———. "Ex G-Man Learns Nazi Drill Plans." *Chicago Daily Times,* 17 September 1937, 21.

———. "German Citizens Join U.S. Bund, Ex G-Man Learns." *Chicago Daily Times,* 21 September 1937, 19.

———. "Nazis Spy on 'Reds' Here, Ex G-Man Told." *Chicago Daily Times,* 24 September 1937, 20.

Metcalfe, John C. "Boasts Rabbis Aid U.S. Nazis." *Chicago Daily Times,* 22 September 1937, 21.

———. "Fuehrer Kuhn Travels Secretly on His Tours." *Chicago Daily Times,* 23 September 1937, 14.

———. "I Am a Nazi Storm Trooper in the U.S." *Chicago Daily Times,* 15 September 1937, 14.

———. "I Am a Storm Trooper in U.S. Nazi Army." *Chicago Daily Times,* 19 September 1937, 22; and 20 September 1937, 14.

———. "I Am a U.S. Nazi Army Storm Trooper." *Chicago Daily Times,* 16 September 1937, 15.

———. "I Am a U.S. Nazi Storm Trooper." *Chicago Daily Times,* 9 September 1937, 3; 10 September 1937, 3; 12 September 1937, 3; 13 September 1937, 3; and 14 September 1937, 3.

———. "Mercenary Tales of Espionage / This Vietnam Veteran Sells Computers and Writes Books. But His Former Life Was Tied Up with Intrigue and Secret Work for the FBI." *Chatanooga Free Press,* 12 August 1995.

————. "Storm Trooper Learns of Black Shirts' Plans." *Chicago Daily Times,* 17 September 1937, 22.

————. "Texas Nazi Bund Claims Own Rule." *Chicago Daily Times,* 21 September 1937, 10.

Meyers, Jeffrey. *Orwell: Wintry Conscience of a Generation.* New York: W. W. Norton, 2000.

Miller, Annetta, Verne E. Smith, and Marcus Mabry. "Shooting the Messenger." *Newsweek,* 23 November 1992, 51.

Miller, David C. *A Narrative of the Facts and Circumstances Relating to the Kidnapping and Murder of William Morgan and of the Attempt to Carry off David. C. Miller and to Burn and Destroy the Printing-Office of the Latter for the Purpose of Preventing the Printing and Publishing of a Book, Entitled "Illustrations of Masonry" Prepared Under the Direction of the Several Committees Appointed at Meetings of the Citizens of the Counties of Genessee, Livingston, Ontario, Monroe and Niagara in the State of New York.* Chicago: Ezra Cook, 1827.

Miller, Jeremy. "Tyranny of the Test: One Year as a Kaplan Coach in the Public Schools." *Harper's,* September 2008, 35–46.

Miner, Michael. "News Bites: Undercover Journalism's Last Call." *Chicago Reader,* 11 October 2002, 4.

————. "Undercover Journalism's Last Call." *Chicago Reader,* 2 October 2002, 1.

————. "When Undercover Was King: More Bleeding at the Sun-Times." *Chicago Reader,* 9 August 2001.

"The Mirage Nonaward." *Columbia Journalism Review* 18.3 (September/October 1979): 20.

Miraldi, Robert G. *Muckraking and Objectivity: Journalism's Colliding Traditions.* New York: Greenwood Press, 1990.

"Missing the Beat." Hosted by Caroline Lowe. WCCO-TV, 1 May 1994.

Mok, Michael. "Crowd Turns Visiting Hours into Bedlam." *New York World-Telegram & Sun,* 18 March 1961, 1.

————. "Entering Hospital Easier Than Exit." *New York World-Telegram & Sun,* 22 March 1961, 1.

————. "Inmates Sleep on the Floor, Mutter, Stare into Corner." *New York World-Telegram & Sun,* 16 March 1961, 1.

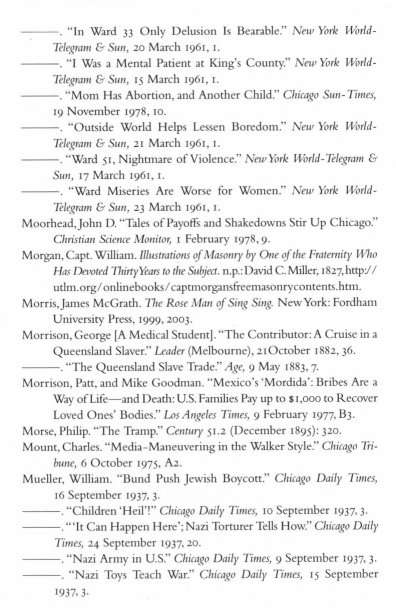

———. "In Ward 33 Only Delusion Is Bearable." *New York World-Telegram & Sun,* 20 March 1961, 1.

———. "I Was a Mental Patient at King's County." *New York World-Telegram & Sun,* 15 March 1961, 1.

———. "Mom Has Abortion, and Another Child." *Chicago Sun-Times,* 19 November 1978, 10.

———. "Outside World Helps Lessen Boredom." *New York World-Telegram & Sun,* 21 March 1961, 1.

———. "Ward 51, Nightmare of Violence." *New York World-Telegram & Sun,* 17 March 1961, 1.

———. "Ward Miseries Are Worse for Women." *New York World-Telegram & Sun,* 23 March 1961, 1.

Moorhead, John D. "Tales of Payoffs and Shakedowns Stir Up Chicago." *Christian Science Monitor,* 1 February 1978, 9.

Morgan, Capt. William. *Illustrations of Masonry by One of the Fraternity Who Has Devoted Thirty Years to the Subject.* n.p.: David C. Miller, 1827, http://utlm.org/onlinebooks/captmorgansfreemasonrycontents.htm.

Morris, James McGrath. *The Rose Man of Sing Sing.* New York: Fordham University Press, 1999, 2003.

Morrison, George [A Medical Student]. "The Contributor: A Cruise in a Queensland Slaver." *Leader* (Melbourne), 21 October 1882, 36.

———. "The Queensland Slave Trade." *Age,* 9 May 1883, 7.

Morrison, Patt, and Mike Goodman. "Mexico's 'Mordida': Bribes Are a Way of Life—and Death: U.S. Families Pay up to $1,000 to Recover Loved Ones' Bodies." *Los Angeles Times,* 9 February 1977, B3.

Morse, Philip. "The Tramp." *Century* 51.2 (December 1895): 320.

Mount, Charles. "Media-Maneuvering in the Walker Style." *Chicago Tribune,* 6 October 1975, A2.

Mueller, William. "Bund Push Jewish Boycott." *Chicago Daily Times,* 16 September 1937, 3.

———. "Children 'Heil'!" *Chicago Daily Times,* 10 September 1937, 3.

———. "'It Can Happen Here'; Nazi Torturer Tells How." *Chicago Daily Times,* 24 September 1937, 20.

———. "Nazi Army in U.S." *Chicago Daily Times,* 9 September 1937, 3.

———. "Nazi Toys Teach War." *Chicago Daily Times,* 15 September 1937, 3.

————. "Nazis—and Church." *Chicago Daily Times,* 14 September 1937, 3.

————. "Nazis in U.S. Boast German Consul Control." *Chicago Daily Times,* 19 September 1937, 3.

————. "Nazis' Merger Scheme." *Chicago Daily Times,* 12 September 1937, 3.

————. "Storm Troopers Develop Skill on Rifle Range." *Chicago Daily Times,* 17 September 1937, 3.

————. "Swastika in Flames." *Chicago Daily Times,* 13 September 1937, 3.

Mullen, George, and Pamela Zekman. "14668 on North Side Vote Lists Are Called Ineligible." *Chicago Tribune,* 12 October 1972, 1, 14.

————. "Mass Vote Fraud Arrests: 40 Reported Cited by U.S. Grand Jury." *Chicago Tribune,* 16 September 1972.

Mullen, Jay. "Election Board Infiltrated by *Chicago Tribune*'s Reporter." *Chicago Tribune,* 10 September 1972, 1.

————. "Loose Controls Permit Vote Judges to Switch Parties." *Chicago Tribune,* 13 September 1972, 2.

Mullen, Jay, and George Bliss. "Kusper Crony Draws Big Fee from Vote Board." *Chicago Tribune,* 9 October 1972, 1.

————. "Poll Judge Violations Condoned in Election." *Chicago Tribune,* 12 September 1972, 2.

Mullen, William. "BGA: A Civic Watchdog Under Fire." *Chicago Tribune,* 3 May 1981, A1.

Mulpetre, Owen. W. T. Stead Resource Site. n.d., http://attackingthedevil .co.uk, accessed 7 February 2011.

Munro, Doug. "The Origins of Labourers in the South Pacific: Commentary and Statistics." In Moore, Clive, Jacqueline Leckie, and Dough Munro, eds. *Labour in the South Pacific.* Townsville: James Cook University, 1992.

Murphy, Ian. "Koch Whore: Wisconsin Governor Scott Walker Answers His Master's Call." BuffaloBeast.com, 23 February 2011, http:// www.buffalobeast.com/?p=5045.

"N.A.A.W.P." Narrated by Sam Donaldson and Diane Sawyer. *Primetime Live,* ABC, 14 May 1997.

Namako, Tom. "I Was a Clinton Volunteer." *Philadelphia City Paper,* 16 April 2008.

Nathan, Rebekah. *My Freshman Year: What a Professor Learned by Becoming a Student*. New York: Penguin Books, 2006.

"The Natural History of the Vagabond." *New York Times,* 31 March 1900, BR19.

Nazario, Sonia. "Enrique's Journey." *Los Angeles Times,* 29 September 2002, A1; 30 September 2002, A1; 2 October 2002, A1; 4 October 2002, A1; 6 October 2002, A1; and 7 October 2002, A1.

Nelson, Nell. "City Slave Girls." *Chicago Daily Times,* 30 July 1888–11 August 1888, 1–2; 13 August 1888–18 August 1888, 1–2; 5 August 1888, 17; and 12 August 1888, 17.

———. "White Slave Girls." *New York World,* 23 September 1888, 17; 14 November 1888, 9; 25 November 1888, 21; 21 October 1888, 17; 11 November 1888, 12; 2 December 1888, 20; 16 December 1888, 22.

———. *The White Slave Girls of Chicago.* Chicago: Barkley, 1888.

Newall, Mike. "I Was an Obama Volunteer." *Philadelphia City Paper,* 16 April 2008.

Newman, Jerry. *My Secret Life on the McJob: Lessons from Behind the Counter Guaranteed to Supersize Any Management Style.* New York: McGraw-Hill, 2007.

"A New Volume of Tenement Sketches." *Bookman* 2. 5 (January 1896): 425–25.

"N.Y. Daily Gets First Negro Woman." *Chicago Defender,* 28 January 1950, 10.

"The News This Morning." *New York Daily Tribune,* 8 September 1891, 6.

"1992 IRE Awards." Investigative Reporters and Editors. n.d., http://ire.org/resourcecenter/contest/past/1992.html, accessed 18 February 2011.

Nissen, Beth. "An Inside View." *Wall Street Journal,* 28 July 1978, 1.

Nix, Shann. "Why *Chronicle* Reporter Posed as a Student." *San Francisco Chronicle,* 16 November 1992, A7.

Noble, Brett. "Ethics Apply to Indie Media, Too." *Daily Bruin,* 10 March 2008.

Northrop. "Slave Dealing in New Orleans—An Auction." *New York Daily Tribune,* 11 February 1846, 1.

"Notice." *New York Daily Tribune,* 11 March 1859.

Nowell, Paul. "Food Lion Stock Falls After ABC Broadcast." Associated Press (*Times-Picayune*), 7 November 1992, C2.

"Occasional Notes." *West Australian* (Perth), 11 March 1884, 3.

Oder, Norman. "In the Belly of the Beast." *Publishers Weekly,* 8 May 2000, 200–201.

O'Dwyer, Jack. "Silverstein Raps Media." *Jack O'Dwyer's Newsletter* 3.40 (18 July 2007): 28.

Olasky, Marvin. *The Press and Abortion, 1838–1988.* Hillsdale, N.J.: Lawrence Erlbaum Associates, 1988.

Olcott, Henry S. "How We Hung John Brown." In *Lotos Leaves: Original Stories, Essays, and Poems,* 233–49. Boston: Gill, 1875.

Oppel, Richard A. "Government Relations, Past and Present." *American Society of Newspaper Editors,* 27 July 2000, http://asne.org/kiosk/editor/00.nov-dec/oppel1.htm.

Orwell, George. *The Road to Wigan Pier.* New York: Harcourt, 1958.

Orwell, Sonia. *The Collected Essays, Journalism and Letters of George Orwell.* Jaffrey, N.H.: David R. Godine, 1968.

Orwell, Sonia, and Ian Angus, eds. *The Collected Essays, Journalism, and Letters of George Orwell.* Vol. I, *An Age Like This, 1920–1940.* New York: Harvest, 1968.

Owen, David. "Shouts and Murmers: Passing." *New Yorker,* 2 April 2007, x–xi.

"The Pacific Labor Trade—Report of the Western Pacific Commission." *Age,* 10 March 1884, 5.

Packard, Elizabeth Parsons Ware. *Modern Persecution.* Hartford, Conn.: n.p., 1887.

———. *Mrs. Packard's Prison Life.* n.p.: Chicago, 1867.

Page, Clarence. "RIP: Undercover Journalism." *Chicago Tribune,* 29 January 1997, 17.

Palazzetti, Agnes. "Posing as Shoplifter Works Too Well." *Buffalo Evening News,* 10 July 1981.

Parker, Cornelia Stratton. *Working with the Working Woman.* New York: Harper, 1922.

Parker, Elliott. "Undercover Reporting, Hidden Cameras and the Ethical Decision-Making Process: A Refinement." AEJMC Conference Paper, 11 October 1997, 2.

Partlow, Joshua. "Military Launches Afghanistan Intelligence-Gathering Mission." *Washington Post,* 20 February 2010, A12.

Paterno, Susan. "The Lying Game." *American Journalism Review* 19.4 (May 1997): 40.

Patton, Charles. "Investigation of Stephen J. Dubner & Seven D. Leavitt Article." *Florida Times-Union,* 29 January 2006.

Paulson, Rose E. "Helen Stuart Campbell." *Notable American Women, 1607–1950.* Cambridge: Belknap, 1974.

Pendennis, Emmeline. "Where Can a Girl Alone in New York Find Assistance?" *New York Evening World,* 4 February 1905, 8; 6 February 1905, 3; 7 February 1905, 3; 8 February 1905, 3; 9 February 1905, 14; and 10 February 1905, 8.

Peterson, Merrill D. *John Brown: The Legend Revisited.* Charlottesville: University of Virginia Press, 2004.

Pettengill, Lillian. "Toilers of the Home: A College Woman's Experiences as a Domestic Servant." *Everybody's* 8.3 (March 1903): 273–79; 8.4 (April 1903): 375–84; 8.5 (May 1903): 471–79; 8.6 (June 1903): 561–68.

———. *Toilers of the Home: The Record of a College Woman's Experience as a Domestic Servant.* New York: Doubleday, 1903.

Picador, Joey. "It's All Just . . . A Mirage . . ." *Justice for None,* 3 July 2007.

Pilger, John, ed. *Tell Me No Lies: Investigative Journalism That Changed the World.* New York: Thunder's Mouth Press, 2005.

"Pill Mills." Hosted by Carmel Cafiero. *Carmel on the Case,* WSVN-TV, 18 June 2009.

"'Pimp' in ACORN Video Shares Story." *Washington Post,* 9 September 2009.

Pittenger, Mark. "A World of Difference: Constructing the 'Underclass' in Progressive America." *American Quarterly* 49.1 (March 1997): 26–65.

"The Plain Facts." *Minneapolis Tribune,* 13 May 1888.

Poole, Ernest. *The Bridge: My Own Story.* New York: MacMillan, 1940.

Possley, Maurice, and Pamela Zekman. "Year in Jail for Accident Swindler." *Chicago Sun-Times,* 1 July 1980, 12.

Potter, Deborah. "Over the Line: The Questionable Tactics of 'To Catch a Predator.'" *American Journalism Review* 29.4 (August/September 2007): 54.

Prall, Robert H. "I Lived in a Slum: Sickening Story Unfolds in City's Blighted Areas." *New York World-Telegram & Sun,* 22 June 1959, 1.

"The Press: Chicago Thorn." *Time,* 20 September 1937.

Priest, Dana, and Anne Hull. "Almost Home, But Facing More Delays at Walter Reed." *Washington Post,* 15 September 2007, A01.

———. "Hospital Investigates Former Aid Chief." *Washington Post,* 20 February 2007, A01.

———. "A Patient Prosecuted." *Washington Post,* 2 December 2007, A01.

———. "Recovering at Walter Reed." *Washington Post,* 20 February 2007, http://www.washingtonpost.com/wp-dyn/content/discussion/2007/02/23/DI2007022302220.html.

———. "Soldier Finds Comfort at Dark Journey's End." *Washington Post,* 17 June 2007, A13.

———. "Soldiers Face Neglect, Frustration at Army's Top Medical Facility." *Washington Post,* 18 February 2007, A01.

———. "The War Inside." *Washington Post,* 17 June 2007, A01.

*Primetimelive.* [Food Lion segment] Hosted by Diane Sawyer, ABC, 5 November 1992.

Prince, Richard. "Dale R. Wright, 86, Integrated a New York Newsroom." *Richard Prince's Journal-isms,* Maynard Institute, 16 December 2009, http://www.mije.org/richardprince/afro-picks-apology-not-unanimous.

"Prison Boss Says Findings 'Inexcusable.'" *Chicago Tribune,* 29 October 1978, 22.

"Prisoners Get Exercise: Pontiac Deadlock Ending." *Chicago Tribune,* 2 November 1978, C14.

"Probe Michigan Av. Abortion Clinic Death," *Chicago Sun-Times,* 17 November 1978, 1.

"The Publishers." *New York Times,* 28 March 1903, BR14.

*The Pulitzer Prizes: Winners, 1917 to the Present Including Nominated Finalists, 1980 to the Present.* New York: Pulitzer Prize Board at Columbia University, 2008.

Rainey, James. "On the Media: NPR Video Stings Ethics Too." *Los Angeles Times,* 11 March 2011.

Ratliff, Evan. "Vanish." *Wired,* 25 November 2009.

"The Real Annie Laurie: A Personal Introduction to a Famous and Talented Lady." *San Francisco Examiner,* 18 December 1892, 13.

Reavis, Dick J. *Without Documents.* New York: Condor, 1978.

———. Telephone and email interview by author, 2 April 2010.

Recktenwald, William. "How *Tribune* Investigator Was Hired." *Chicago Tribune,* 29 October 1978, 22.

———. "'I Was a Guard in Pontiac Prison,'" *Chicago Tribune,* 29 October 1978, 1.

———. "'Just Keep 'Em Locked Up, That's All.'" *Chicago Tribune,* 31 October 1978, 1.

———. "New Pontiac Warden Moves to End Deadlock." *Chicago Tribune,* 1 November 1978, 1.

———. "One Visitor's Return." *Chicago Tribune,* 22 July 1979, A1.

———. Telephone interview by author, 23 December 2010.

———. "Working the Cells Where Three Died." *Chicago Tribune,* 30 October 1978, 1.

Reeves, Jay. "Ex-Mercenary Frank Camper Trades Guns for Computers." *Birmingham News,* 12 June 1995, 1B.

Reid, T. R. "Government by Envelope: Chicago's System Exposed." *Washington Post,* 15 January 1978, A3.

Reitman, Dr. Ben. "Good Samaritans Few in Chicago." *Chicago Daily Tribune,* 12 May 1907, 1.

Remnick, David. "Big Think Interview." BigThink, 20 April 2010, http:// bigthink.com/davidremnick.

"Reporters Who Broke Story on Conditions at Walter Reed." Narrated by Neal Conan. *Talk of the Nation,* NPR, 6 March 2007.

"A Representative on a Recruiting Schooner, the Kanaka Labour Traffic: Special Investigation by *The Argus.*" *Argus* (Melbourne), 3 December 1892, 9.

"Rescued from Sex Slavery: *48 Hours* Goes Undercover into the International Sex Slave Trade." Narrated by Rebecca Leung. *48 Hours,* CBS, 23 February 2005.

"Reviews and Literary Notices." *Atlantic Monthly* 4.23 (September 1859).

Reviews of *Mrs. Herndon's Income,* by Helen Campbell: *New York Times,* 22 November 1885, 5; and *New York Tribune,* 22 November 1885, 8.

Reviews of *Prisoners of Poverty,* by Helen Campbell: *Chautauquan,* June 1887, 573; *Critic: A Weekly Review of Literature and the Arts,* 11 June 1887, 294; *Independent,* 28 April 1887, 12; *Literary World,* 28 May 1887, 169; *New York Tribune,* 14 April 1887, 6; and *Overland Monthly and Out West Magazine,* March 1889, 327.

Reviews of *The Woman Who Toils,* by Mrs. John Van Vorst and Marie Van Vorst: *Christian Advocate,* 23 April 1903, 677; *Literary World: A Monthly Review of Current Literature,* April 1903, 78; *Overland Monthly and Out West Magazine,* May 1903, 397; and *San Francisco Chronicle,* 22 March 1903, 18.

"Revolution and Early Republic." *Journal of the Early Republic* 23.2 (2003): 151–72.

Reynolds, Quentin. "Danger at Every Step." *New York Times,* 14 October 1951, 213.

Richardson, Albert D. *The Secret Service: The Field, the Dungeon and the Escape.* Hartford: American, 1865.

Ring, Ray. Telephone interview by author, 1 July 2010.

———. "'This Ain't That Kind of Prison.'" *Arizona Daily Star,* 8 August 1982, 23.

Robertson, Lori. "Uncovering Misery at Walter Reed." *American Journalism Review* 29.2 (April/May 2007): 10.

Robertson, Michael. *Stephen Crane, Journalism, and the Making of Modern American Literature.* New York: Columbia University Press, 1997.

Robinson, Steve. "Pulitzers: Was the Mirage a Deception?" *Columbia Journalism Review* 18.2 (July/August 1979): 14–15.

Roderick, Kevin. "From Magazine to Screen." *LA Observed,* 27 July 2007.

Rohter, Larry. "With Pope Due, the Cubans Wrest Dollars from Heaven." *New York Times,* 20 January 1998, A1.

Rolfes, Louis. "FBI Agents Pose as Photographers During Aryan Nation Trial." *News Media and the Law* 24.4 (Fall 2000): 11–12.

Roose, Kevin. *The Unlikely Disciple: A Sinner's Semester at American's Holiest University.* New York: Grand Central, 2009.

Rosen, Jay. "They Brought a Tote Bag to a Knife Fight." Pressthink.org, 10 March 2011, http://pressthing.org/2011/03/they-brought-a-tote-bag-to-a-knife-fight-the-resignation-of-vivian-schiller/.

"Rush to Read." Hosted by Diane Sawyer. *PrimeTime Live,* ABC, 19 May 1994.

Russell, Edward. "The Greatest Trust in the World." *Everybody's,* August 1905.

"Russia's Unwanted Children; Update on Russia's Orphans Living in Institutions." Hosted by Charles Gibson and Diane Sawyer. *20/20,* ABC, 26 April 2000.

Rutherford, Kay. "Chiropractor to Aid Prosecutors." *Chicago Sun-Times,* 31 May 1980, 18.

Sachar, Emily. *Shut Up and Let the Lady Teach.* New York: Poseidon Press, 1996.

"The Sale of the Butler Slaves." *New York Daily Tribune,* 30 April 1859, 5.

Salinger, Pierre. "Alameda Jail—'Best in Nation'—County Prisoners Work, Go to School, Eat Well." *San Francisco Chronicle,* 4 February 1953, 1.

———. "A Beating in Jail: In the Pre-Dawn, a Man Is Marked Up for Life." *San Francisco Chronicle,* 3 February 1953, 1.

———. "County Jail Reform Urged: Warren, Brown Tell How Conditions Can Be Improved." *San Francisco Chronicle,* 8 February 1953, 1.

———. "Exclusive! Brutal, Filthy Jails Exposed: *Chronicle* Reporter Does Time, Tells Inside Story of Cruel, Crowded Cells." *San Francisco Chronicle,* 26 January 1953, 1.

———. "A Fight for Reform: Modesto Aroused by Its Rotten Jail." *San Francisco Chronicle,* 10 February 1953, 1.

———. "Honor Rancho Has Its Faults: One of the Best—But: No Medical Care, Not Enough Rehabilitation." *San Francisco Chronicle,* 1 February 1953, 1.

———. "Honor Rancho in L.A. Better Than Others." *San Francisco Chronicle,* 31 January 1953, 1.

———. "Inside Story of Kern Jail: Reporter's Hitch at Bakersfield Reveals Bad Food, Crowding." *San Francisco Chronicle,* 2 February 1953, 1.

———. "Men in S.F. Jails Get Helping Hand." *San Francisco Chronicle,* 7 February 1953, 1.

———. *P.S.: A Memoir.* New York: St. Martin's Press, 1995.

———. "S.F. County Jail Is Too Much Like a Penitentiary." *San Francisco Chronicle,* 6 February 1953, 1.

———. "Sex Perverts, Extortionists Run the Cells." *San Francisco Chronicle,* 30 January 1953, 1.

———. "Shame of County: Degradation in Stinking Cells." *San Francisco Chronicle,* 5 February 1953, 1.

———. "The Slip at 18 ... Al's in a Cell: He Met Thieves, Cons, in S.F. Jail ... 'Dismal' System, Says Expert." *San Francisco Chronicle,* 29 January 1953, 1.

———. "Ugly Violence Behind Bars: Reporter Tells How Cellmate Blew His Top." *San Francisco Chronicle,* 28 January 1953, 1.

———. "Worst Institutions: Poor Jails Cause Crowding in Prison." *San Francisco Chronicle,* 9 February 1953, 1.

———. "Youths Cooped Up with Older, Hardened Crooks." *San Francisco Chronicle,* 27 January 1953, 1.

Sanborn, Alvan Francis. *Moody's Lodging House and Other Tenement Sketches.* Boston: Copeland and Day, 1896.

Sanchez, Mary. "The Ethical Bankruptcy of 'Gotcha!'" *Bellingham Herald,* 11 March 2011, http://www.bellinghamherald.com/2011/03/11/1910885/the-ethical-bankruptcy-of-gotcha.html#ixzz1GNnGgxPF.

Sareyan, Alex. *The Turning Point: How Men of Conscience Brought About Major Change in the Care of America's Mentally Ill.* Washington, D.C.: American Psyciatric Press, 1994.

"Sauget: City of Shame." WPLG, 1 January 1987.

Saviano, Roberto. *Gomorrah.* New York: Picador, 2006.

Savini, Dave. "Rotting Meat, Security Documents, and Corporal Punishment." *Nieman Reports,* Summer 2009, http://www.nieman.harvard.edu/reports/article/101556/Rotting-Meat-Security-Documents-and-Corporal-Punishment.aspx.

"A Scene in St. Louis—Slave Auction." *New York Daily Tribune,* 15 January 1850, 4.

Schiem, Charles C. "Trash Tort or Trash TV? *Food Lion, Inc., v. ABC, Inc.,* and Tort Liability of the Media for Newsgathering." *St. John's Law Review* 7.1 (Winter 1998): 185.

Schmidle, Nicholas. "Smuggler, Forger, Writer, Spy." *Atlantic,* 16 October 2010.

Schuster, Gary C. "Crashing a Moment in History." *Detroit News,* 27 March 1979, 1A.

Scott, Katherine Leigh. *The Bunny Years.* Los Angeles: Pomegranate Press, 1999.

Seagal, Debra. "Tales from the Cutting-Room Floor: The Reality of 'Reality-Based' Television." *Harper's,* November 1993, 50–57.

Seigenthaler, John. Telephone interview by author, 14 January 2011.

"Seoul Train." Hosted by Lisa Seeth and Jim Butterworth. *Independent Lens,* PBS, 13 December 2005.

Shafer, Jack. "The NPR Body Count." *Slate,* 10 March 2011.

———. "The Same River Twice." *Slate,* 16 December 2003, http://slate .com/toolbar.aspx?action=print&id=2092708.

Shalev, Eran. "Ancient Masks, American Fathers: Classical Pseudonyms During the American Revolution and Early Republic." *Journal of the Early Republic* 23.2 (2003): 151–72.

Shapiro, Paul. Telephone interview by author, 14 March 2011.

Sharlet, Jeff. "Jesus Plus Nothing: Undercover Among America's Secret Theocrats." *Harper's,* March 2003, 53–64.

———. "Through a Glass, Darkly: How the Christian Right Is Reimagining U.S. History." *Harper's,* December 2006, 33–34.

Shaw, David. "Deception—Honest Tool of Reporting?" *Los Angeles Times,* 20 September 1979, B1.

———. "Masquerades: Deception—Honest Tool of Reporting?" *Los Angeles Times,* 20 September 1979, B1.

Shenon, Philip. "Welfare Hotel Families: Life on the Edge." *New York Times,* 31 August 1983, B1.

Shepard, Adam. *Scratch Beginnings: Me, $25, and the Search for the American Dream.* Chapel Hill, N.C.: SB Press, 2008.

Sheppard Jr., Nathaniel. "Tavern Precipitates Latest Chicago Corruption Scandal." *New York Times,* 23 January 1978, A12.

Sherman, William. "Bureaucracy Choking in Attempts at Control." *New York Daily News,* 11 February 1973, 5.

"City Gives Dr. Hi Billmore Shot of Comedownance." *New York Daily News,* 8 February 1973, 5.

———. "Drawing a Map of Land of Nod." *New York Daily News,* 10 February 1973, 3.

———. "Foot Docs Wearing a 35M Golden Slipper." *New York Daily News,* 31 January 1973, 5.

———. "How a Physician Can Prescribe Pure Dollars." *New York Daily News,* 30 January 1973, 5.

———. "How Medicaid Dentist Pulled City's 800G." *New York Daily News,* 6 February 1973, 5.

———. "How Medicaid Paid $757,000 for Sesame Oil." *New York Daily News,* 25 January 1973, 2.

———. "In Race for Medibucks, the City's Poor Lose." *New York Daily News,* 5 February 1973, 5.

———. "Medicaid Loses as Docs Play Beat the Clock." *New York Daily News,* 2 February 1973, 3.

———. "Medicaid Probe—A Cold? Take 3 Doctors Every Hour." *New York Daily News,* 23 January 1973, 7.

———. "Medicaid's Deaf Ear to Hearing Aid Dealers." *New York Daily News,* 7 February 1973, 7.

———. "Our 'Patient' Gets More Tests on 2nd Visit." *New York Daily News,* 24 January 1973, 2.

———. "Pair of Medicaid Kings with a Midas Touch." *New York Daily News,* 1 February 1973, 3.

———. "You Don't Need Glasses to See Thru This." *New York Daily News,* 29 January 1973, 5.

Siddon, Arthur. "Two *Tribune* Reporters Tell Hospital Abuses; Senate Unit 'Shocked.'" *Chicago Tribune,* 27 September 1975, N1.

Sigma. "Valor for the Church." *Independent* 11.540 (7 April 1859): 2.

Silverstein, Jake. "What Is Poetry? And Does It Pay?" *Harper's,* August 2002, 55–64.

Silverstein, Ken. "Their Men in Washington: Undercover with D.C.'s Lobbyists for Hire." *Harper's,* July 2007.

———. Telephone interview by author, 1 July 2007, 5 December 2010.

———. *Turkmeniscam.* New York: Random House, 2008.

———. "Undercover Under Fire." *Los Angeles Times,* 30 June 2007, A29.

Sims, Patsy. *The Klan.* Lexington: University Press of Kentucky, 1996.

Sinclair, Upton. *American Outpost: A Book of Reminiscences.* New York: Farrar and Rinehart, 1932.

———. *The Autobiography of Upton Sinclair.* New York: Harcourt, Brace and World, 1962.

———. "Is *The Jungle* True?" *Independent* 60.2998 (17 May 1906): 1129–33.

————. *Love's Pilgrimage.* New York: Mitchell Kennerley, 1911.

————. *My Lifetime in Letters.* Columbia: University of Missouri Press, 1960.

————. "What Life Means to Me." *Cosmopolitan,* October 1906, 594.

Slater, Daniel Fletcher. "The Life and Letters of Mortimer Thomson." M.A. diss., Northwestern University, August 1931.

"A Slave Auction in Virgenia [*sic*]." *New York Daily Tribune,* 15 January 1850, 6.

"A Slave Auction in Virginia." *New York Daily Tribune,* 10 March 1853, 6.

"Slavery by Another Name." *Sioux Valley News,* 6 October 1892, 1.

Smallman, David B. "The Long-Awaited Food Lion Ruling." *IRE Journal* 22.8 (October/November 1999): 5.

Smith, Emily Esfahani. "Ends Vs. Means: The Ethics of Undercover Journalism." *The Blaze,* 9 March 2011, http://theblaze.com/stories/ednds-vs-means-the-ethics-of-undercover-journalism.

Smith, Frank. "Attempted Suicide at Kankakee Hospital." *Chicago Times,* 24 July 1935, 3.

————. "Crazy Rhythm! Dance at Kankakee." *Chicago Times,* 23 July 1935, 3.

————. "'Death Cup' Perils Kankakee Inmates." *Chicago Times,* 18 July 1935, 3.

————. "Freedom! Reporter Leaves Kankakee." *Chicago Times,* 26 July 1935, 3.

————. "Haunted by Kankakee Fire Hazards." 22 July 1935.

————. "'Railroaded to Kankakee as Insane.'" *Chicago Times,* 19 July 1935, 3.

————. "Reporter's Night of Terror at Kankakee." *Chicago Times,* 17 July 1935, 3.

————. "Reporter Takes Kankakee 'Water Cure.'" *Chicago Times,* 16 July 1935, 3.

————. "Seven Days in the Madhouse: Reporter's Experience at Kankakee." *Chicago Daily Times,* 15 July 1935, 1, 3.

————. "Water Perils Inmates at Kankakee." *Chicago Times,* 25 July 1935, 3.

Smith, Ron F. *Groping for Ethics.* Iowa: Iowa State Press, 2003.

Smith, Timothy K. "War Games: In Alabama's Woods, Frank Camper Trains Men to Repel Invaders—Prep School for Mercenaries Has Notorious Graduates, Seminar in Throat Cutting—A Paramilitary Fantasy Land." *Wall Street Journal,* 19 August 1985, 1.

Smith, W. Paul. "Prank Call to Governor Was Good Journalism." *Voyager,* 1 March 2011.

Smith, Zay N., and Pamela Zekman. *The Mirage.* New York: Random House, 1979.

———. "The Mirage Takes Shape." *Columbia Journalism Review* 18.3 (September/October 1979): 51–57.

———. "Smithfield Defends Handling of Pigs." *Virginian-Pilot,* 23 December 2010, B2.

———. "Smithfield Foods Fires Three After Complaint of Pig Abuse." *Virginian-Pilot,* 22 December 2010, B3.

———. "Smithfield's Treatment of Pigs Under Scrutiny." *Virginian-Pilot,* 16 December 2010; B1.

"Social Crime in London." *Independent,* 16 July 1885, 1911.

Solomon, Joshua. "Skin Deep: Reliving 'Black Like Me': My Own Journey into the Heart of Race-Conscious America." *Washington Post,* 30 October 1994, C01.

"SPJ, RTNDA Protest FBI Agents' Posing as Journalists." Associated Press and Freedom Forum Online, 5 September 2000, http://www.freedomforum.org/templates/document.asp?documentID=3695.

"SPJ Demands FBI Discipline Agents for Posing as Journalists." Society of Professional Journalists, 1 September 2000, http://www.spj.org/news.asp?ref=97.

Sprigle, Ray. "Broken Negro Women Tells Sprigle How White Folks Murdered Husband in Jail." *Pittsburgh Post-Gazette,* 13 August 1948, 1.

———. "I Was a Negro in the South for 30 Days." *Pittsburgh Post-Gazette,* 9–31 August 1948, 1.

———. "Sprigle, Mildly Sun-Tanned, Encounters Many Negros with Lighter Skin Than His." *Pittsburgh Post-Gazette,* 10 August 1948, 1.

————. "Sprigle Finds Negro Parents Face Problem in Teaching Racial Facts to Children." *Pittsburgh Post-Gazette,* 12 August 1948, 1.

————. "Sprigle Found Life as Negro Was Not Quite Slavery—Not Quite Freedom, Either." *Pittsburgh Post-Gazette,* 11 August 1948, 1.

————. "10,000 Homestead Projects Needed to Dent South's Evil System of Share-Cropping." *Pittsburgh Post-Gazette,* 14 August 1948, 1.

St. Clair, Augustus. "The Evil of the Age." *New York Times,* 23 August 1871, 6; 27 August 1971, 1; 28 August 1871, 8; 29 August 1871, 8; 30 August 1871, 4, 8; 2 September 1871, 8; 6 September 1871, 8; 3 September 1871, 8.

St. Johns, Adela Rogers. *Honeycomb.* New York: Doubleday, 1969.

"Statement of Concern: Committee of Concerned Journalists." *IRE Journal* 21.1 (January/February 1998): 2.

"State's Mentally Ill Deserve Better Care." *Nashville Tennessean,* 22 January 1974, 6.

Stead, W. T. "The Maiden Tribute of Modern Babylon." Pts. 1–4. *Pall Mall Gazette,* 6 July 1885, 1–6; 7 July 1885, 1–6; 8 July 1885, 1–5; and 10 July 1885, 1–6.

Steele, Bob. "Lying in the Name of Truth: When Is It Justified for Journalists?" Poynteronline, 5 July 2007. http://www.poynter.org/latest-news/everyday-ethics/83268/lying-in-the-name-of-truth when-is-it-justified-for-journalists.

Steele, Jonathan. "The Pay-Off Parade at the Mirage Bar." *Guardian,* 10 January 1978, 11.

Stegman, Michael A. "Slumlords and Public Policy." *Appraisal Journal,* April 1968, 204–6.

Steiger, Paul. To the Pulitzer Committee Judges, 23 January 1995, New York. Pulitzer Prize Archives. Courtesy of the Columbia University Rare Books and Manuscript Library.

————. Telephone interview by author, 19 May 2010.

Steinem, Gloria. "I Was a Playboy Bunny." *Show,* May and June 1963.

————. *Outrageous Acts and Everyday Rebellions.* New York: Henry Holt, 1995.

Stephen, Andrew. "Iraq: The Hidden Cost of War." *New Statesman,*

12 March 2007, http://www.newstatesman.com/world-affairs/2007/03/iraq-war-wounded-bilmes-cost.

Stern, Willy. "Grading the Daily Part I—The Way Things Were." *Nashville Scene,* 26 April 2001.

Stewart, Richard H. "The Cell Block: Life in a Barren 5-by-8 Space; Second of a Five-Part Series." *Boston Globe,* 28 December 1983, Living 1.

———. "The Final Days in Jail; Last of a Five-Part Series." *Boston Globe,* 31 December 1983, Living 1.

———. "The First Day; Dignity Leaves and Fear Arrives." *Boston Globe,* 27 December 1983, Living 1.

———. "Jail Boredom Biggest Hassle; Fourth of a Five-Part Series." *Boston Globe,* 30 December 1983, Living 1.

———. "Rules to Learn; Cigarettes are Money, Bells Control Life; Salem—Locked in My Cell for the First Time I Began to Sense the Isolation; And the First Pangs of Frustration from the Loss of Freedom." *Boston Globe,* 29 December 1983, Living 1.

———. "Stockholder Sues Food Lion." *Herald,* 14 November 1992, 7B.

Stowe, Harriet Beecher. *A Key to Uncle Tom's Cabin: Presenting the Original Facts and Documents upon Which the Story Is Founded. Together with Corroborative Statements Verifying the Truth of the Work.* Boston: Jewett, 1853.

Striffler, Steve. *Chicken.* New Haven: Yale University Press, 2005.

Strupp, Joe. "Spokane Probe: Other Editors Say They Forbid Undercover Operations." *Editor & Publisher,* 10 May 2005.

Styron, William. *Darkness Visible: A Memoir of Madness.* New York: Modern Library, 2007.

"Summary of News." *Friends' Review: a Religious, Literary and Miscellaneous Journal* 12.28 (19 March 1859): 448.

"Survey: 2 Abortion Clinics Found 'Pregnancy' in Men." *New York Post,* 16 December 1976, 9.

Sutherland, Frank. "Aides, Many Untrained, Run Central State." *Nashville Tennessean,* 22 January 1974, 1.

———. "Central State Needs Action Right Now!" *Nashville Tennessean,* 3 March, 1974, 1B.

————. "Central State Woes Reflected at East State Hospital." *Nashville Tennessean,* 10 February 1974, 10.

————. "Change in Central State Role, Scope Advised." *Nashville Tennessean,* 21 February 1974, 1.

————. "Christmas Means Joyless Tension in Locked Ward." *Nashville Tennessean,* 23 January 1974, 1.

————. "Hospital Complex Old, Battered, But in Use." *Nashville Tennessean,* 26 January 1974, 1.

————. "Officials Agree Central State Needs Reform." *Nashville Tennessean,* 28 January 1974, 1.

————. "Personal Experience: Central State Conditions Found Poor." *Nashville Tennessean,* 20 January 1974, 1.

————. "Report Urges Central State Improvements." *Nashville Tennessean,* 19 February 1974, 1.

————. "Reporter Finds Hospital Stay Demoralizing." *Nashville Tennessean,* 21 January 1974, 1.

————. "Skimpy, Unprofessional Patient File Reveals Inadequate Treatment." *Nashville Tennessean,* 24 January 1974, 1.

————. "State Help Dire Need at Hospital." *Nashville Tennessean,* 27 January 1974, 1.

————. "State Mental Hospitals 'Could Lose Millions,'" *Nashville Tennessean,* 29 January 1974, 1.

————. "Undercover Reporting Discouraged: The Practice Usually Is Not Necessary to Get a Story." *Editorially Speaking* 53.4 (July/August 1999).

————. "'Ward Meeting' Breaks Silence." *Nashville Tennessean,* 25 January 1974, 1.

Sweet, Lynn. "Indiana Abortion Clinic Is Thriving." *Chicago Sun-Times,* 1 December 1978, 3.

Swoboda, Frank. "Food Lion Faces Huge U.S. Complaint: Labor Dept. to Allege Thousands of Child Labor, Overtime Violations." *Washington Post,* 7 November 1992, A1.

Symons, Arthur. Introduction to *My Life,* by Josiah Flynt. New York: Outing, 1908.

"The *Tahiti* Carried No Slaves." *New York Daily Tribune,* 1 December 1891, 5.

"*Tahiti* Disaster: Another Chapter in the Mishaps That Befell the Slave Trading Vessel." *Hamilton Daily Democrat,* 21 July 1892, 1.

"The *Tahiti*'s Passengers Not Slaves." *New York Daily Tribune,* 9 September 1891, 7.

Taibbi, Matt. *The Great Derangement: A Terrifying True Story of War, Politics, & Religion at the Twilight of the American Empire.* New York: Spiegel and Grau, 2008.

———. "Jesus Made Me Puke and Other Tales from the Evangelical Front Lines." *Rolling Stone,* 1 May 2008, 69+.

"Tales of Payoffs and Shakedowns Stir Up Chicago." *Christian Science Monitor,* 1 February 1978, 9.

Tanaka, Jennifer. "Top 40 OMG Moments in Recent Chicago History." *Chicago,* November 2010.

Tarbell, Ida. "Women in Journalism." *Chautauquan,* April 1887, 395.

"Task Force Report." *Chicago Tribune,* 10 September 1972, 1.

"Task Force Report." *Chicago Tribune,* 14 September 1972, 2.

Taylor, Steven J. *Acts of Conscience: World War II, Mental Institutions, and Religious Objectors.* Syracuse: Syracuse University Press, 2009.

"Thanks 'The Times.'" *Chicago Daily Times,* 21 August 1888, 1.

Thompson, Ginger, and Sandra Ochoa. "By a Back Door to the U.S.: A Migrant's Grim Sea Voyage; Dangerous Passage: From Ecuador by Sea." *New York Times,* 13 June 2004, 1.

Thomson, Mortimer [Doesticks, P. B., Q. K. Philander]. "American Civilization Illustrated." *New York Daily Tribune,* 9 March 1859, 5.

———. "The Witches of New-York." Nos. 1–16. *New York Daily Tribune,* 22 January 1857, 6; 23 January 1857, 6; 24 January 1857, 3; 27 January 1857, 5; 28 January 1857, 7; 31 January 1857, 5; 6 February 1857, 5; 13 February 1857, 6; 14 February 1857, 5; 24 February 1857, 7; 25 February 1857, 7; 2 April 1857, 6; 4 April 1857, 10; 25 April 1857, 9; 9 May 1857, 10; and 20 May 1857, 7.

———. *What Became of the Slaves on a Georgia Plantation? Great Auction Sale of Slaves, at Savannah, Georgia, March 2d and 3d, 1859. A Sequel to Mrs. Kemble's Journal.* American Anti-Slavery Society, 1863.

———. *The Witches of New York.* Philadelphia: T. B. Peterson and Bros., 1858.

Timnick, Lois. "Despair for the Mentally Ill: Metro Hospital—Place of Little Hope." *Los Angeles Times,* 23 August 1979, A1.

Tisdale, Sallie. "We Do Abortions Here." *Harper's,* October 1987, 66–70.

Tompkins, Al. "Anatomy of a Pulitzer: Q&A with Hull and Priest." Poynteronline, 8 April 2008, http://www.poynter.org/latest-news/top-stories/88125/anatomy-of-a-pulitzer-qa-with-hull-and-priest/>.

Tower, Wells. "Bird-Dogging the Bush Vote: Undercover with Florida's Republic Shock Troops." *Harper's,* March 2005, 45–57.

Toy, Vivian S. Telephone interview by author, 18 July 2008.

"Trafficked for the Military." Hosted by Tom Merriman and Greg Easterly. WJW-TV, 25 September 2002.

"Tramp King Plans Union." *Washington Post,* 15 December 1907, M16.

"Tramps with the Genius of London." *Toronto Daily Mail,* 12 March–16 April 1892, 5.

Traveler. "Facts of Slavery." *New York Daily Tribune,* 17 January 1854, 3.

Tremlett, Giles. "Carlos the Jackal Was My Friend." *Guardian,* 10 October 2010.

"Tribune Employees Win 1978 Beck Awards." *Chicago Tribune,* 9 December 1978, N4.

Tschirch, Victoria. *The Sphere of Rigour Reporting: An Essay on Investigative Journalism and Its Importance: In General and In Some Respects to New Zealand.* Germany: Grin Verlag, 2008.

Tucker, Eric. "Ivy Leaguer 'Infiltrates' Falwell's University." Associated Press via Yahoo! News, 22 April 2009.

"Twenty-Five Years of Pure Food Law." *New York Times,* 13 July 1931, 9.

"Two Linked to Ripoffs Convicted." *Chicago Sun-Times,* 30 May 1980.

"2006 Silver Baton: HBO, 'Real Sports with Bryant Gumbel: The Sport of Sheikhs.'" Alfred I. duPont Columbia University Awards in Broadcast News. n.d., http://www.dupontawards.org/year/2006#2009_goldbaton, accessed 8 February 2011.

"Two Tribune Writers Cited." *Chicago Tribune,* 9 May 1979, 5.

"Undercover Reporting Backed by Readers." *Editor & Publisher,* 23 August 1980, 13.

"Undercover with DC Lobbyists for Hire." *Daily Kos,* 24 June 2007.

Unger, Craig. "American Rapture." *Vanity Fair,* December 2005.

———. *The Fall of the House of Bush.* New York: Scribner, 2007.

————. "The Fool on the Hill." Huffingtonpost.com, 13 December 2007.

————. Telephone interview by author, 15 October 2010.

V. "A Virginia Slave Auction." *New York Daily Tribune,* 28 March 1856.

Van Vorst, Bessie. "The Woman That Toils: Experiences of a Literary Woman as a Working Girl." *Everybody's* 7.5 (November 1902): 413–25.

————. "The Woman That Toils: Experiences of a Literary Woman as a Working Girl." *Everybody's* 8.1 (January 1903): 3–17.

————. "The Woman That Toils: Experiences of a Working Girl." *Everybody's Magazine* 7.3 (September 1902): 211–25.

Van Vorst, Marie. "The Woman That Toils: Experiences of a Literary Woman as a Working Girl." *Everybody's* 7.4 (October 1902): 361–77.

————. "The Woman That Toils: Experiences of a Literary Woman as a Working Girl." *Everybody's* 7.5 (December 1902): 540–52.

Van Vorst, Mrs. John. "The Woman of the People." *Harper's,* May 1903, 871–75.

Van Vorst, Mrs. John, and Marie Van Vorst. *The Woman Who Toils: Being the Experiences of Two Ladies as Factory Girls.* New York: Doubleday, 1903.

*Very Young Girls.* Directed by David Schisgall, Nina Alvarez, and Priya Swaminathan. Showtime Independent Films, 2007.

Vincent, Norah. *Self-Made Man: One Woman's Journey into Manhood and Back Again.* New York: Viking Adult, 2006.

————. *Voluntary Madness: My Year Lost and Found in the Loony Bin.* New York: Viking, 2008.

Vitiello, Greg. "Where Are the Documentaries of Yesteryear?" *Television Quarterly* 36.3–4 (Spring/Summer 2006): 7–8.

Vogel, Steve, and William Branigin. "Army Fires Commander of Walter Reed." *Washington Post,* 2 March 2007, A01.

W. "Visit to a Slave Auction." *New York Daily Tribune,* 30 January 1855, 3.

Wallraff, Günter. *The Lowest of the Low.* London: Methuen, 1985.

————. *The Undesirable Journalist.* Woodstock: Overlook Press, 1979.

Walzer, Philip. "Humane Society Claims Abuse at Smithfield Foods Farm." *Virginian-Pilot,* 15 December 2010.

"The Wanderer and the Slave Sale." *Independent* 11.537 (17 March 1859): 1.

Warden, Philip. "Senate Sets Hearings on Nurse Homes." *Chicago Tribune,* 10 March 1971, 1.

Warren, Ellen. "The Politics of Abortion—A Big Business." *Chicago Sun-Times,* 27 November 1978, 6.

———. "Probe Abortions, House Asked." *Chicago Sun-Times,* 2 December 1978, 4.

———. "State Aid Chief Raps HEW on Abortion Issue." *Chicago Sun-Times,* 1 December 1978, 6.

Wasik, Bill. "My Crowd: Or, Phase 5." *Harper's,* March 2006, 56–66.

———, ed. *Submersion Journalism: Reporting in the Radical First Person from Harper's Magazine.* New York: New Press, 2008.

Wasserman, Edward. "Can Trickery by Reporters Be Right?" *Miami Herald,* 9 July 2007, A17.

———. Email interview by author, 13, 14 March 2011.

———. "Journalist Stings Go Mainstream." *Miami Herald,* 13 March 2011.

———. "When Subterfuge Is an Acceptable Tool of Reporting." *Miami Herald,* 17 May 2006, 1.

Watts, Douglas. "The Thing Which Is Not." *Talking Points Memo Reader* (blog), 26 February 2007, http://www.talkingpointsmemo.com/talk/blogs/douglas_watts/2007/02/the-thing-which-is-not.php.

Weaver, David H. *The American Journalist in the Twenty-First Century.* Mahwah, N.J.: Lawrence Erlbaum Associates, 2007.

Wegman, Jesse. "Dateline: To Kill a Predator." *Huffington Post,* 23 February 2007.

Weinberg, Steve. "Interview with William Gaines." *IRE Journal* 20.6 (November/December 1997), 3, 10.

———. *Taking on the Trust: The Epic Battle of Ida Tarbell and John D. Rockefeller.* New York: Norton, 2008.

———. Telephone and email interview by author, 27 November 2007, 27 August 2009, and 8–10 June 2010.

Wemyss, Courtney T., and Alexej Ugrinsky, eds. *George Orwell.* New York: Greenwood Press, 1987.

Westlake, Neda M. Preface to *An Amateur Laborer,* by Theodore Dreiser. Philadelphia: University of Pennsylvania Press, 1983.

"What the Press Tour Saw Oct. 9; What Our Reporter Saw Oct. 17." *Chicago Tribune,* 29 October 1978, 22.

Wheeler III, Charles N., and G. Robert Hilman. "Medic Blames State for Abortion Clinic Abuses." *Chicago Sun-Times,* 29 November 1978, 7.

White, Josh. "Surgeon General of the Army Steps Down." *Washington Post,* 13 March 2007, A01.

White, Walter F. "The Burning of Jim McIlherron: An N.A.A.C.P. Investigation." *Crisis* 16.1 (May 1918): 16–20.

———. "I Investigate Lynchings." *American Mercury* 16 (January 1929): 81.

Wiedrich, Bob. "Asked $500,000 for Prosecuting Prison Rioters." *Chicago Tribune,* 26 November 1978, B7.

———. "Charles Rowe's Sudden Discovery." *Chicago Tribune,* 1 November, 1978, B4.

———. "One Visitor's Return." *Chicago Tribune,* 22 July 1979, A1.

———. "Special Committee: Assembly Leaders Act to Probe Prisons." *Chicago Tribune,* 5 November 1978, 5.

Willard, Frances E., and Mary A. Livermore, eds. *A Woman of the Century: Fourteen Hundred-Seventy Biographical Sketches Accompanied by Portraits of Leading American Women in All Walks of Life.* Buffalo: Moulton, 1893.

Williams, Whiting. *What's on the Worker's Mind: By One Who Put on Overalls to Find Out.* New York: Charles Scribner's Sons, 1920.

Winerip, Michael. Telephone interview by author, 1 June 2010.

"Winners of the 2008 Kurt Schork Awards in International Journalism." Institute for War and Peace Reporting, n.d., http://iwpr.net/special/winners-2008-kurt-schork-awards>, accessed 8 February 2011.

Wolin, Merle Linda. "Bradley: 'I Wouldn't Want to Speculate . . .'" *Los Angeles Herald-Examiner,* 29 January 1981, A12.

———. "Brown: 'It's Wrong for Civilized Society . . .'" *Los Angeles Herald-Examiner,* 30 January 1981, A1.

———. "Employer Meets Employer—Merlina, Melton, Mendoza." *Los Angeles Herald-Examiner,* 25 January 1981, A1, A12.

———. "The Fading of Felix Mendoza's Dream." *Los Angeles Herald-Examiner,* 23 January 1981, A1, A8.

———. "Five Days' Work for Felix Mendoza, $38.74." *Los Angeles Herald-Examiner,* 15 January 1981, A1, A10.

———. "Homework: The Alien's Secret Support System." *Los Angeles Herald-Examiner,* 18 January 1981, A1, A12.

———. "'I'm Not Joan of Arc. I'm a Garment Manufacturer.'" *Los Angeles Herald-Examiner,* 21 January 1981, A10.

———. "'It's Another Mike Wallace Trick!'" *Los Angeles Herald-Examiner,* 26 January 1981, A8.

———. "Merlina Faces the Labor Commissioner—And Wins." *Los Angeles Herald-Examiner,* 20 January 1981, A1, A10.

———. "The Retailers' Side of the Story." *Los Angeles Herald-Examiner,* 27 January 1981, A10.

———. "Seven Hours in a Union Shop for $2.50." *Los Angeles Herald-Examiner,* 19 January 1981, A1, A8.

———. "Sweatshop: Merlina's Job in Oscar Herrera's Factory." *Los Angeles Herald-Examiner,* 14 January 1981, A1, A10.

———. Telephone interview by author, 18 March 2010.

———. "'This Is the Filthiest of All Industries.'" *Los Angeles Herald-Examiner,* 16 January 1981, A1, A10.

———. "What It Will Take to 'Outlaw Slavery.'" *Los Angeles Herald-Examiner,* 1 February 1981, A12

———. "What to Do About 'Sweatshop.'" 8 February 1981, F2.

———. "Who Are the Players? What Are the Problems?" *Los Angeles Herald-Examiner,* 28 January 1981, A8.

———. "Working Women, 1800–1930." Harvard Open Collection Program, n.d., http://ocp.hul.harvard.edu/ww/people_campbell .html, accessed 8 February 2011.

———. "The Work Is 'Killing' Martha and Oscar." *Los Angeles Herald-Examiner,* 22 January 1981, A10.

Wright, Dale. "Drudgery and Despair." *Newsweek,* 23 October 1961.

———. "Farm Camp Slum Exposed 8 Years Ago, Is Still Hell." *New York World-Telegram & Sun,* 18 October 1961, 33.

———. "The Forgotten People: I Saw Human Shame as a Migrant Worker." *New York World-Telegram & Sun,* 10 October 1961, 1.

———. "Migrant Accepts Gyp as Part of Life." *New York World-Telegram & Sun,* 19 October 1961, 13.

———. "Migrant Labor Exploited by Delay Trick." *New York World-Telegram & Sun,* 13 October 1961, 1.

———. "Migrant Pay $4.32 a Day in Florida Tomato Field." *New York World-Telegram & Sun,* 11 October 1961, 1.

———. "Migrant Workers Need U.S. Protection." *New York World-Telegram & Sun,* 17 October 1961, 25.

———. "Migrants Exist in Duck Shed." *New York World-Telegram & Sun,* 20 October 1961, 27.

———. "Migrants Live Horror Story in Job Travel." *New York World-Telegram & Sun,* 12 October 1961, 1.

———. "Speed-Up Forces Migrants to Quit Job Before Pay Day." *New York World-Telegram & Sun,* 16 October 1961, 1.

———. "State Could Remedy Conditions for Migrant Labor." *New York World-Telegram & Sun,* 23 October 1961, 3.

———. *They Harvest Despair: The Migrant Farm Worker.* Boston: Beacon Press, 1965.

Wright, Louise E. "Talk about Real Men: London's Correspondence with Maurice Magnus." *Journal of Popular Culture* 40.2 (April 2007): 366.

"Writer Sneaks a Look at Ways of Lobbyists." *Wall Street Journal,* 14 June 2007, B7.

Wyckoff, Walter. *The Workers.* New York: Charles Scriber's Sons, 1898.

"The Year in Hate, 1998: Hate Group Count Tops 500, Internet Sites Soar." *Intelligence Report* 93 (Winter 1999).

Zekman, Pamela. "Chicago Board of Health Calls Nurse Home Staffs to Account." *Chicago Tribune,* 13 March 1971, 5.

———. "City's Health Chief Closes 3 Nursing Homes for Abuses." *Chicago Tribune,* 9 March 1971, 1.

———. "Cries for Help from Aged Answered with Brutality." *Chicago Tribune,* 1 March 1971, 1.

———. "Hospital on Probation: von Solbrig Hearing Set." *Chicago Tribune,* 7 October 1975, A1.

Zekman, Pamela, and Jay Branegan. "Daley Will Back Probe of Hospitals." *Chicago Tribune,* 2 September 1975, 2.

———. "Half a Job Well Done." *Chicago Tribune,* 13 October 1975, A2.

———. "Powers Sought by Health Board." *Chicago Tribune,* 11 October 1975, S7.

Zekman, Pamela, and Phil Caputo. "Abuses in Nursing Homes: Some Elderly Prefer Death, Reporters Find." *Chicago Tribune,* 28 February 1971, 1.

————. "Delay Asks Nurse Home Change." *Chicago Tribune,* 11 March 1971, 4.

————. "Filth and Neglect Bared at von Solbrig Hospital." *Chicago Tribune,* 7 September 1975, 1.

————. "Flay Nursing Home Chiefs: Legislators Charge Lack of Standards." *Chicago Tribune,* 16 March 1971, 1.

————. "Man's Inhumanity." *Chicago Tribune,* 2 March 1971, 14.

————. "Nursing Home Investigators Cite Examples of Good Care." *Chicago Tribune,* 5 March 1971, 2.

————. "Nursing Home Unit Backs State's Probe." *Chicago Tribune,* 4 March 1971, 3.

————. "Nursing Home's Shaving Time Becomes Torture for Patient." *Chicago Tribune,* 2 March 1971, 1.

————. "Regulations Fail to Aid 'Living Dead,'" *Chicago Tribune,* 3 March 1971, 2.

————. "State Attacked on Nursing Home Licenses." *Chicago Tribune,* 7 March 1971, 5.

————. "Subpoena Homes for Elderly." *Chicago Tribune,* 4 March 1971, 1.

————. "Tribune Task Force Reports from Inside." *Chicago Tribune,* 28 February 1971, 2.

————. "Two Hospitals Take the Cure." *Chicago Tribune,* 12 September 1975, A2.

————. "Warehouses for Neglected: Nurse Homes Defy Health, Fire Codes." *Chicago Tribune,* 1 March 1971, 1.

Zekman, Pamela, and William Crawford Jr. "Health Violations Found at Northeast Hospital." *Chicago Tribune,* 31 October 1975, B16.

————. "Senate to Hold Hearings on Aid Fraud at Hospitals." *Chicago Tribune,* 14 September 1975, 3.

————. "Second Facility to Stay Shut: Rush Medical Center to Operate Northeast." *Chicago Tribune,* 22 November 1975, S2.

————. "Second Hospital in Probe Closes." *Chicago Tribune,* 20 November 1975, 1.

————. "3 Northeast Hospital Probes Begin." *Chicago Tribune,* 11 September 1975, 1.

Zekman, Pamela, and William Gaines. "City Is Asked to Close von Solbrig Hospital." *Chicago Tribune,* 10 October 1975, 1.

———. "3 Northeast Hospital Probes Begin." *Chicago Tribune,* 11 September 1975, 1.

———. "Von Solbrig Hospital Placed on Probation." *Chicago Tribune,* 10 September 1975, 1.

Zekman, Pamela, and William Jones. "Daley Orders New Laws, Nurse Home Inspections." *Chicago Tribune,* 3 March 1971, 1.

Zekman, Pamela, and Karen Koshner. "Doctor Loses out in 2 Court Battles." *Chicago Sun-Times,* 16 November 1978, 5.

———. "Health Chief Defends His Clinic Curbs." *Chicago Sun-Times,* 5 December 1978, 4.

———. "Report of Record Changing at Abortion Clinic Probed." *Chicago Sun-Times,* 30 November 1978, 8.

———. "State to Act on Abortion Clinics." *Chicago Sun-Times,* 13 November 1978, 3.

———. "Thompson Orders Clinic Check Step-Up." *Chicago Sun-Times,* 14 November 1978, 3.

———. "2 Abortion Referral Firms are Subpoenaed." *Chicago Sun-Times,* 17 November 1978, 5.

Zekman, Pamela, and Gene Mustain. "Accident Cheats Add to Hospital Image Problem." *Chicago Sun-Times,* 25 February 1980, 6–7.

———. "The Accident Mills—Clinics Processing Cheats by the Thousands." *Chicago Sun-Times,* 19 February 1980, 6–7.

———. "'Accident-Prone' Hospital Cures Itself." *Chicago Sun-Times,* 26 February 1980, 6.

———. "The Accident Swindlers: They're Getting Away with $3 Billion a Year—And All You Drivers Pay." *Chicago Sun-Times,* 10 February 1980, 1.

———. "Accidents Too Good to Leave to Lawyers." *Chicago Sun-Times,* 14 February 1980, 1, 6–7.

———. "Agency Ignored Reports of Phony Patients." *Chicago Sun-Times,* 28 February 1980, 9–10.

———. "Chasers Converge on Accident Scene . . ." *Chicago Sun-Times,* 15 February 1980, 6–7.

————. "Department Probes Moonlighting Cop Who Aids Fraudulent Claims." *Chicago Sun-Times,* 22 February 1980, 7.

————. "Doctors' 'Treatments' Keep Fraud Alive." *Chicago Sun-Times,* 21 February 1980, 6–7.

————. "Federal Panel Probes Fake Car-Injury Claims." *Chicago Sun-Times,* 29 February 1980, 3, 32.

————. "Hospital Aide Ties to 2 Clinics Told." *Chicago Sun-Times,* 12 May 1980, 6, 16.

————. "Hospital Boss Vows to Probe Methods." *Chicago Sun-Times,* 20 February 1980, 7.

————. "Hospital Executive's Sideline Pads 'Take,'" *Chicago Sun-Times,* 11 March 1980, 4.

————. "A Hospital for Greedy." *Chicago Sun-Times,* 17 February 1980, 1, 6–7.

————. "Hospital in Evanston Loses Accreditation." *Chicago Sun-Times,* 8 April 1980, 2.

————. "How Superswindling Pays: Just a Little Nets a Lot If Accident Case Is 'Perfect.'" *Chicago Sun-Times,* 12 February 1980, 1, 6–7.

————. "The Hypocritical Oath—And Doctors Who Lie by It." *Chicago Sun-Times,* 22 February 1980, 6–7.

————. "Lawyers' Swindling Sidekicks." *Chicago Sun-Times,* 13 February 1980, 1, 6–7.

————. "Legal Advice? Theirs Is Fraud: Five Who Traffic in Automobile-Accident Cases." Chicago *Sun-Times,* 11 February 1980, 1, 6–7.

————. "'No Fault'—An Answer to Accident Fraud." *Chicago Sun-Times,* 27 February 1980, 9.

————. "Our Own Phony Patient Is Hospitalized and Discovers the Hospital Is a Mirage." *Chicago Sun-Times,* 18 February 1980, 6–7.

————. "Panel Blasts Hospital Board." *Chicago Sun-Times,* 10 April 1980, 7.

————. "Probe Abuses at Hospital—State Legislator." *Chicago Sun-Times,* 19 February 1980, 7.

————. "Series Spawns a Wave of Hospital Shakeups." *Chicago Sun-Times,* 3 April 1980, 6, 18.

————. "Smashup Cheats—How They Get YOU." *Chicago Sun-Times,* 6 April 1980, 8, 35.

————. "State Agency Probes Practices Uncovered in Swindler Series." *Chicago Sun-Times,* 21 February 1980, 7.

————. "State Board Orders Evanston Hospital to Hearing." *Chicago Sun-Times,* 17 March 1980, 4.

————. "State Panel Asks Voiding of Chiropractor's License." *Chicago Sun-Times,* 11 April 1980, 4.

————. "State to Suspend License of Hospital in Evanston." *Chicago Sun-Times,* 6 June 1980, 4.

————. "'Swindlers' Take Pains to Get Themselves Hospitalized." *Chicago Sun-Times,* 24 February 1980, 6–7.

————. "These Chiropractors Are Master Hands . . . at Juggling the Facts on Injuries." *Chicago Sun-Times,* 20 February 1980, 6–7.

————. "Thompson Bills Hit Accident Fraud." *Chicago Sun-Times,* 5 April 1980, 3; Editorial, 15.

Zekman, Pamela, and Pamela Warrick. "The Abortion Lottery: Women Take Chances with 'Tryout' Doctors." *Chicago Sun-Times,* 14 November 1978, 1.

————. "Abortion Peril Greater Before Legalization." *Chicago Sun-Times,* 12 November 1978, 6.

————. "The Abortion Profiteers—Making a Killing in Michigan Av. Clinics." *Chicago Sun-Times,* 12 November 1978, 1.

————. "Big Kickbacks to Abortion Mills." *Chicago Sun-Times,* 20 November 1978, 1.

————. "Counseling the Patient: Buy This Abortion." *Chicago Sun-Times,* 24 November 1978, 5.

————. "Dr. Ming Kow Hah: Physician of Pain." *Chicago Sun-Times,* 15 November 1978, 1.

————. "Hospital Abortion Issue 'Hot.'" *Chicago Sun-Times,* 2 December 1978, 4.

————. "Hot Line Deceptions Sell Most Abortions." *Chicago Sun-Times,* 25 November 1978, 4.

————. "Infamous Doctor Is Detroit Connection." *Chicago Sun-Times,* 21 November 1978, 8.

———. "Inside Story of City's Pro-life Movement." *Chicago Sun-Times,* 28 November 1978, 6.

———. "Meet the Profiteers: Men Who Profit From Women's Pain." *Chicago Sun-Times,* 13 November 1978, 1.

———. "Nurse to Aide:'Fake That Pulse!'" *Chicago Sun-Times,* 16 November 1978, 1.

———. "Pregnant or Not, Women Given Abortions." *Chicago Sun-Times,* 22 November 1978, 8.

———. "Profiteering Shocks These Abortion Pioneers." *Chicago Sun-Times,* 3 December 1978, 10.

———. "Soft Voices, Hard Sells—Twin Swindles." *Chicago Sun-Times,* 17 November 1978, 4.

———. "12 Dead After Abortions in State's Walk-In Clinics." *Chicago Sun-Times,* 19 November 1978, 1.

Zia, Helen. "Made in the U.S.A." *Ms.,* January 1996, 66–73.

# INDEX

Brooke Kroeger, a professor of journalism at New York University's Arthur L. Carter Journalism Institute, is also the author of *Nellie Bly: Daredevil, Reporter, Feminist*; *Fannie: The Talent for Success of Writer Fannie Hurst*; and *Passing: When People Can't Be Who They Are.*

Pete Hamill is a journalist, novelist, and essayist. The author of more than twenty books, he is the winner of the Ernie Pyle Lifetime Achievement Award from the National Society of Newspaper Columnists and the Louis Auchincloss Prize from the Museum of the City of New York. He is currently a Distinguished Writer in Residence at the Arthur L. Carter Journalism Institute at New York University.